THIS BOOK BELONGS TO

MEMBER OF

---.....Troop

MY SCOUT RECORD

Registration Date and Place...

Passed Tenderfoot Test...

Passed Second Class Test...

Passed ....

SCOUTING *for* GIRLS

MAGDELAINE DE VERCHÈRES
The First Girl Scout in the New World. From Statue erected
by Lord Grey, near the site of Fort Verchères on the St. Lawrence.

SCOUTING *for* GIRLS

OFFICIAL HANDBOOK

OF THE

GIRL SCOUTS

FIRST EDITION

PUBLISHED BY THE GIRL SCOUTS, Inc.

National Headquarters

189 LEXINGTON AVENUE, NEW YORK, N.Y.

Editor's Note © 2005 by Barnes & Noble, Inc.

Originally published in 1920

This 2005 edition published by Barnes & Noble, Inc.

Cover design is a replication by Jo Obarowski
of the original 1920 edition

ISBN-13: 978-0-7607-7988-0
ISBN-10: 0-7607-7988-0

Printed and bound in the United States of America

3 5 7 9 10 8 6 4 2

EDITOR'S NOTE

In 1919 Josephine Daskam Bacon, Chairman of Publications for Girls Scouts, Inc., began constructing this guidebook on scouting. She enlisted the aid of a number of experts in child development to help her with the project, which resulted in 1920 with the publication of the first edition of the book, titled *Scouting for Girls*. This Barnes & Noble edition is a replica of that book.

FOREWORD
How Scouting Began

"How did Scouting come to be used by girls?" That is what I have been asked. Well, it was this way. In the beginning I had used Scouting—that is, Woodcraft, handiness, and cheery helpfulness—as a means for training young soldiers when they first joined the army, to help them become handy, capable men and able to hold their own with anyone instead of being mere drilled machines.

You have read about the wars in your country against the Red Indians, of the gallantry of your soldiers against the cunning of the Red Man, and what is more, of the pluck of your women on those dangerous frontiers

Well, we have had much the same sort of thing in South Africa. Over and over again I have seen there the wonderful bravery and resourcefulness of the women when the tribes of Zulu or Matabels have been out on the war path against the white settlers.

In the Boer war a number of women volunteered to help my forces as nurses or otherwise; they were full of pluck and energy, but unfortunately they had never been trained to do anything, and so with all the good-will in the world they were of no use. I could not help feeling how splendid it would be if one could only train them in peace time in the same way one trained the young soldiers—that is, through Scoutcraft.

I afterwards took to training boys in that way, but I had not been long at it before the girls came along, and offered to do the very thing I had hoped for, they wanted to take up Scouting also.

They did not merely want to be the imitators of the boys; they wanted a line of their own.

So I gave them a smart blue uniform and the names of "Guides" and my sister wrote an outline of the scheme. The name Guide appealed to the British girls because the pick of our frontier force in India is the Corps of Guides. The term cavalry or infantry hardly describes it since it is composed of all-round handy men ready to take on any job in the campaigning line and do it well.

Then too, a woman who can be a good and helpful comrade to her brother or husband or son along the path of life is really a guide to him.

The name Guide therefore just describes the members of our sisterhood who besides being handy and ready for any kind of duty are also a jolly happy family and likely to be good, cheery comrades to their mankind.

The coming of the Great War gave the Girl Guides their opportunity, and they quickly showed the value of their training by undertaking a variety of duties which made them valuable to their country in her time of need.

My wife, Lady Baden-Powell, was elected by the members to be the Chief Guide, and under her the movement has gone ahead at an amazing pace, spreading to most foreign countries.

It is thanks to Mrs. Juliette Low, of Savannah, that the movement was successfully started in America, and though the name Girl Scouts has there been used it is all part of the same sisterhood, working to the same ends and living up to the same Laws and Promise.

If all the branches continue to work together and become better acquainted with each other as they continue to become bigger it will mean not only a grand step for the sisterhood, but what is more important it will be a real help toward making the new League of Nations a living force.

How can that be? In this way:

If the women of the different nations are to a large extent members of the same society and therefore in close touch and sympathy with each other, although belonging to different countries, they will make the League a real bond not merely between the Governments, but between the Peoples themselves and they will see to it that it means Peace and that we have no more of War.

Robert Baden Powell.

PREFACE

The present edition of "Scouting For Girls" is the result of collaboration on the part of practical workers in the organization from every part of the country. The endeavor on the part of its compilers has been to combine the minimum of standardization necessary for dignified and efficient procedure, with the maximum of freedom for every local branch in its interpretation and practice of the Girl Scout aims and principles.

Grateful acknowledgments are due to the following:

Miss Sarah Louise Arnold, Dean, and Miss Ula M. Dow, A.M., and Dr. Alice Blood, of Simmons College for the Part of Section XI entitled "Home Economics"; Sir Robert Baden-Powell for frequent references and excerpts from "Girl Guiding"; Dr. Samuel Lambert for the Part on First Aid Section XI, and Dr. W. H. Rockwell for reading and criticizing this; Miss Marie Johnson with the assistance of Miss Isabel Stewart of Teachers College, for the Part entitled "Home Nursing" in Section XI; Dr. Herman M. Biggs for reading and criticizing the Parts dealing with Public Health and Child Care; Mr. Ernest Seton Thompson and The Woodcraft League, and Doubleday and Page for Section XIII and plates on "Woodcraft"; Mr. Joseph Parsons, Mr. James Wilder, Mrs. Eloise Roorbach, and Mr. Horace Kephart and the MacMillan Company for the material in Section XIV "Camping for Girl Scouts"; Mr. George H. Sherwood, Curator, and Dr. G. Clyde Fisher, Associate Curator of the Department of Public Education of the American Museum of Natural History for the specially prepared Section XV and illustrations on "Nature Study," and for all proficiency tests in this subject; Mr. David Hunter for Section XVI "The Girl Scout's Own Garden," and

Miss Ellen Shipman for the part on a perennial border with the specially prepared drawing, in the Section on the Garden; Mr. Sereno Stetson for material in Section XVII "Measurements, Map Making and Knots"; Mr. Austin Strong for pictures of knots; Mrs. Raymond Brown for the test for Citizen; Miss Edith L. Nichols, Supervisor of Drawing in the New York Public Schools, for the test on Craftsman; Mr. John Grolle of the Settlement Music School, Philadelphia, for assistance in the Music test; Miss Eckhart for help in the Farmer test; The Camera Club and the Eastman Kodak Company for the test for Photographer; Mrs. Frances Hunter Elwyn of the New York School of Fine and Applied Arts, for devising and drawing certain of the designs for Proficiency Badges and the plates for Signalling; Miss L. S. Power, Miss Mary Davis and Miss Mabel Williams of the New York Public Library, for assistance in the preparation of reference reading for Proficiency Tests, and general reading for Girl Scouts.

It is evident that only a profound conviction of the high aims of the Girl Scout movement and the practical capacity of the organization for realizing them could have induced so many distinguished persons to give so generously of their time and talent to this Handbook.

The National Executive Board, under whose auspices it has been compiled, appreciate this and the kindred courtesy of the various organizations of similar interests most deeply. We feel that such hearty and friendly co-operation on the part of the community at large is the greatest proof of the vitality and real worth of this and allied movements based on intelligent study of the young people of our country.

JOSEPHINE DASKAM BACON,
Chairman of Publications.

CONTENTS

Foreword by Sir Robert Baden-Powell.
Preface by Josephine Daskam Bacon, *Editor*.

SECTIONS:

I.	HISTORY OF THE GIRL SCOUTS	1
II.	PRINCIPLES OF THE GIRL SCOUTS	3
III.	ORGANIZATION OF THE GIRL SCOUTS	13
IV.	WHO ARE THE SCOUTS?	17
V.	THE OUT OF DOOR SCOUT	35
VI.	FORMS FOR GIRL SCOUT CEREMONIES	44
VII.	GIRL SCOUT CLASS REQUIREMENTS	60
VIII.	WHAT A GIRL SCOUT SHOULD KNOW ABOUT THE FLAG	67
IX.	GIRL SCOUT DRILL	84
X.	SIGNALLING FOR GIRL SCOUTS	97
XI.	THE SCOUT AIDE	105
	Part 1. The Home Maker	106
	Part 2. The Child Nurse	157
	Part 3. The First Aide	164
	Part 4. The Home Nurse	217
	Part 5. The Health Guardian	254
	Part 6. The Health Winner	257
XII.	SETTING-UP EXERCISES	273
XIII.	WOODCRAFT	280
XIV.	CAMPING FOR GIRL SCOUTS	313
XV.	NATURE STUDY FOR GIRL SCOUTS	373
XVI.	THE GIRL SCOUT'S OWN GARDEN	456
XVII.	MEASUREMENTS, MAP-MAKING AND KNOTS	466
XVIII.	PROFICIENCY TESTS AND SPECIAL MEDALS	497
XIX.	REFERENCE READING FOR GIRL SCOUTS	540
	INDEX	548

SECTION I

HISTORY OF THE AMERICAN GIRL SCOUTS

When Sir Robert Baden-Powell founded the Boy Scout movement in England, it proved too attractive and too well adapted to youth to make it possible to limit its great opportunities to boys alone. The sister organization, known in England as the Girl Guides, quickly followed and won an equal success.

Mrs. Juliette Low, an American visitor in England, and a personal friend of the Father of Scouting, realized the tremendous future of the movement for her own country, and with the active and friendly co-operation of the Baden-Powells, she founded the Girl Guides in America, enrolling the first patrols in Savannah, Georgia, in March, 1912. In 1915 National Headquarters were established in Washington, D. C., and the name was changed to Girl Scouts.

In 1916 National Headquarters were moved to New York and the methods and standards of what was plainly to be a nation-wide organization became established on a broad, practical basis.

The first National Convention was held in 1915, and each succeeding year has shown a larger and more enthusiastic body of delegates and a public more and more interested in this steadily growing army of girls and young women who are learning in the happiest way how to combine patriotism, outdoor activities of every kind, skill in every branch of domestic science and high standards of community service.

Every side of the girl's nature is brought out and developed by enthusiastic Captains, who direct their games and various forms of training, and encourage team-work

1

and fair play. For the instruction of the Captains national camps and training schools are being established all over the country; and schools and churches everywhere are co-operating eagerly with this great recreational movement, which, they realize, adds something to the life of the growing girl that they have not been able to supply.

Colleges are offering fellowships in scouting as a serious course for would-be Captains, and prominent citizens in every part of the country are identifying themselves with the Local Councils, in an advisory and helpful capacity.

At the present writing nearly 82,000 girls and more than 3,600 Captains represent the original little troop in Savannah—surely a satisfying sight for our Founder and First President, when she realizes what a healthy sprig she has transplanted from the Mother Country!

SECTION II

PRINCIPLES OF THE GIRL SCOUTS
The Motto:
Be Prepared

A Girl Scout learns to swim, not only as an athletic accomplishment, but so that she can save life. She passes her simple tests in child care and home nursing and household efficiency in order to be ready for the big duties when they come. She learns the important facts about her body, so as to keep it the fine machine it was meant to be. And she makes a special point of woodcraft and camp lore, not only for the fun and satisfaction they bring in themselves, but because they are the best emergency course we have today. A Girl Scout who has passed her First Class test is as ready to help herself, her home and her Country as any girl of her age should be expected to prove.

The Slogan:
"Do a Good Turn Daily"

This simple recipe for making a very little girl perform every day some slight act of kindness for somebody else is the *seed* from which grows the larger *plant* of helping the world along—the steady attitude of the older Scout. And this grows later into the great tree of organized, practical community service for the grown Scout— the ideal of every American woman today.

The Pledge:
"I pledge allegiance to my flag, and to the Republic for which it stands; one nation indivisible, with liberty and justice for all."

This pledge, though not original with the Girl Scouts, expresses in every phrase their principles and practice. Practical patriotism, in war and peace, is the cornerstone of the organization. A Girl Scout not only knows how to make her flag, and how to fly it; she knows how to respect it and is taught how to spread its great lesson of democracy. Many races, many religions, many classes' of society have tested the Girl Scout plan and found that it has something fascinating and helpful in it for every type of young girl.

This broad democracy is American in every sense of the word; and the Patrol System, which is the keynote of the organization, by which eight girls of about the same age, and interests elect their Patrol Leader and practice local self-government in every meeting, carries out American ideals in practical detail.

The Promise:
On My Honor I Will Try
To be true to God and my country.
To help others at all times.
To obey the Scout Laws.

This binds the Scouts together as nothing else could do. It is a promise each girl *voluntarily* makes; it is not a rule of her house nor a command from her school nor a custom of her church. She is not forced to make it— she deliberately chooses to do so. And like all such promises, it means a great deal to her. Experience has shown that she hesitates to break it.

THE LAWS OF THE GIRL SCOUTS

I. A Girl Scout's Honor Is to Be Trusted

This means that a Girl Scout's standards of honor are so high and sure that no one would dream of doubting her simple statement of a fact when she says: "This is so, on my honor as a Girl Scout."

She is not satisfied, either, with keeping the letter of

the law, when she really breaks it in spirit. When she answers you, *she* means what *you* mean.

Nor does she take pains to do all this only when she is watched, or when somebody stands ready to report on her conduct. This may do for some people, but not for the Scouts. You can go away and leave her by herself at any time; she does not require any guard but her own sense of honor, which is always to be trusted.

II. A Girl Scout Is Loyal

This means that she is true to her Country, to the city or village where she is a citizen, to her family, her church, her school, and to those for whom she may work, or who may work for her. She is bound to believe the best of them and to defend them if they are slandered or threatened. Her belief in them may be the very thing they need most, and they must feel that whoever may fail them, a Girl Scout never will.

This does not mean that she thinks her friends and family and school are perfect; far from it. But there is a way of standing up for what is dear to you, even though you admit that it has its faults. And if you insist on what is best in people, behind their backs, they will be more likely to take your criticism kindly, when you make it to their faces.

III. A Girl Scout's Duty Is to Be Useful and to Help Others

This means that if it is a question of being a help to the rest of the world, or a burden on it, a Girl Scout is always to be found among the helpers. The simplest way of saying this, for very young Scouts, is to tell them to do a GOOD TURN to someone every day they live; that is, to be a *giver* and not a *taker*. Some beginners in Scouting, and many strangers, seem to think that any

simple act of courtesy, such as we all owe to one another, counts as a good turn, or that one's mere duty to
one's parents is worthy of Scout notice. But a good
Scout laughs at this idea, for she knows that these things
are expected of all decent people. She wants to give
the world every day, for good measure, something over
and above what it asks of her. And the more she does,
the more she sees to do.

This is the spirit that makes the older Scout into a
fine, useful, dependable woman, who does so much good
in her community that she becomes naturally one of its
leading citizens, on whom everyone relies, and of whom
everyone is proud. It may end in the saving of a life, or
in some great heroic deed for one's Country. *But these
things are only bigger expressions of the same feeling
that makes the smallest Tenderfoot try to do at least one
good turn a day.*

IV. A Girl Scout Is a Friend to All, and a Sister to Every Other Girl Scout

This means that she has a feeling of good will to all
the world, and is never offish and suspicious nor inclined
to distrust other people's motives. A Girl Scout should
never bear a grudge, nor keep up a quarrel from pride,
but look for the best in everybody, in which case she
will undoubtedly find it. Women are said to be inclined
to cliques and snobbishness, and the world looks to great
organizations like the Girl Scouts to break down their
petty barriers of race and class and make our sex a great
power for democracy in the days to come.

The Girl Scout finds a special comrade in every other
Girl Scout, it goes without saying, and knows how to
make her feel that she need never be without a friend
or a meal or a helping hand as long as there is another
Girl Scout in the world.

She feels, too, a special responsibility toward the very old, who represent what she may be, some day; toward the little children, who remind her of what she used to be; toward the very poor and the unfortunate, either of which she may be any day. The sick and helpless she has been, as a Scout, especially trained to help, and she is proud of her handiness and knowledge in this way.

V. A Girl Scout Is Courteous

This means that it is not enough for women to be helpful in this world; they must do it pleasantly. The greatest service is received more gratefully if it is rendered graciously. The reason for this is that true courtesy is not an affected mannerism, but a sign of real consideration for the rights of others, a very simple proof that you are anxious to "do as you would be done by." It is society's way of playing fair and giving everybody a chance. In the same way, a gentle voice and manner are very fair proofs of a gentle nature; the quiet, self-controlled person is not only mistress of herself, but in the end, of all the others who cannot control themselves.

And just as our great statesman, Benjamin Franklin, proved that "honesty is the best policy," so many a successful woman has proved that a pleasant, tactful manner is one of the most valuable assets a girl can possess, and should be practised steadily. At home, at school, in the office and in the world in general, the girl with the courteous manner and pleasant voice rises quickly in popularity and power above other girls of equal talent but less politeness. Girl Scouts lay great stress on this, because, though no girl can make herself beautiful, and no girl can learn to be clever, *any girl can learn to be polite.*

VI. A Girl Scout Is a Friend to Animals

All Girl Scouts take particular care of our dumb friends, the animals, and are always eager to protect them from stupid neglect or hard usage. This often leads to a special interest in their ways and habits, so that a Girl Scout is more likely to know about these little brothers of the human race than an ordinary girl.

VII. A Girl Scout Obeys Orders

This means that you should obey those to whom obedience is due, through thick and thin. If this were not an unbreakable rule, no army could endure for a day. It makes no difference whether you are cleverer, or older, or larger, or richer than the person who may be elected or appointed for the moment to give you orders; once they are given, it is your duty to obey them. And the curious thing about it is that the quicker and better you obey these orders, the more quickly and certainly you will show yourself fitted to give them when your time comes. The girl or woman who cannot obey can never govern. The reason you obey the orders of your Patrol Leader, for instance, in Scout Drill, is not that she is better than you, but because she happens to be your Patrol Leader, and gives her orders as she would obey yours were you in her place.

A small, well trained army can always conquer and rule a big, undisciplined mob, and the reason for this is simply because the army has been taught to obey and to act in units, while the mob is only a crowd of separate persons, each doing as he thinks best. The soldier obeys by instinct, in a great crisis, only because he has had long practice in obeying when it was a question of unimportant matters. So the army makes a great point of having everything ordered in military drill, carried out with snap and accuracy; and the habit of this, once fixed, may save thousands of lives when the great crisis comes, and turn defeat into victory.

A good Scout must obey instantly, just as a good soldier must obey his officer, or a good citizen must obey the laws, with no question and no grumbling. If she considers any order unjust or unreasonable, let her make complaint through the proper channels, and she may be sure that if she goes about it properly she will receive attention. *But she must remember to obey first and complain afterward.*

VIII. A Girl Scout Is Cheerful

This means that no matter how courteous or obedient or helpful you try to be, if you are sad or depressed about it nobody will thank you very much for your efforts. A laughing face is usually a loved face, and nobody likes to work with a gloomy person. Cheerful music, cheerful plays and cheerful books have always been the world's favorites; and a jolly, good-natured girl will find more friends and more openings in the world than a sulky beauty or a gloomy genius.

It has been scientifically proved that if you deliberately *make* your voice and face cheerful and bright you immediately begin to feel that way; and as cheerfulness is one of the most certain signs of good health, a Scout who appears cheerful is far more likely to keep well than one who lets herself get "down in the mouth." There is so much real, unavoidable suffering and sorrow in the world that nobody has any right to add to them unnecessarily, and "as cheerful as a Girl Scout" ought to become a proverb.

IX. A Girl Scout Is Thrifty

This means that a Girl Scout is a girl who is wise enough to know the value of things and to put them to the best use. The most valuable thing we have in this life is time, and girls are apt to be stupid about getting the most out of it. A Girl Scout may be known by the fact that she is either working, playing or resting. All are necessary and one is just as important as the other.

Health is probably a woman's greatest capital, and a Girl Scout looks after it and saves it, and doesn't waste it in poor diet and lack of exercise and fresh air, so that she goes bankrupt before she is thirty.

Money is a very useful thing to have, and the Girl Scout decides how much she can afford to save and does it, so as to have it in an emergency. A girl who saves more than she spends may be niggardly; a girl who spends more than she saves may go in debt. A Girl Scout saves, as she spends, on some system.

Did you ever stop to think that no matter how much money a man may earn, the women of the family generally have the spending of most of it? And if they have not learned to manage their own money sensibly, how can they expect to manage other people's? If every Girl Scout in America realized that she might make all the difference, some day, between a bankrupt family and a family with a comfortable margin laid aside for a rainy day, she would give a great deal of attention to this Scout law.

In every great war all nations have been accustomed to pay the costs of the war from loans; that is, money raised by the savings of the people. Vast sums were raised in our own country during the great war by such small units as Thrift Stamps. If the Girl Scouts could save such wonderful sums as we know they did in war, why can they not keep this up in peace? For one is as much to their Country's credit as the other.

X. A Girl Scout Is Clean in Thought, Word and Deed

This means that just as she stands for a clean, healthy community and a clean, healthy home, so every Girl Scout knows the deep and vital need for clean and healthy bodies in the mothers of the next generation. This not only means keeping her skin fresh and sweet and her system free from every impurity, but it goes far deeper than this, and requires every Girl Scout to respect her body and mind so much that she forces everyone else to respect them and keep them free from the slightest familiarity or doubtful stain.

A good housekeeper cannot endure dust and dirt; a well cared for body cannot endure grime or soil; a pure mind cannot endure doubtful thoughts that cannot be freely aired and ventilated. It is a pretty safe rule for

SALUTING THE FLAG IN A GIRL SCOUT CAMP

a Girl Scout not to read things nor discuss things nor do things that could not be read nor discussed nor done by a Patrol all together. If you will think about this, you will see that it does not cut out anything that is really necessary, interesting or amusing. Nor does it mean that Scouts *should* never do anything except in Patrols; that would be ridiculous. But if they find they *could* not do so, they had better ask themselves why. When there is any doubt about this higher kind of cleanliness, Captains and Councillors may always be asked for advice and explanation.

SECTION III

ORGANIZATION OF THE GIRL SCOUTS

Lone Scout

The basis of the Girl Scout organization is the individual girl. Any one girl anywhere who wishes to enroll under our simple pledge of loyalty to God and Country, helpfulness to other people and obedience to the Scout Laws, and is unable to attach herself to any local group, is privileged to become a Lone Scout. The National Organization will do its best for her and she is eligible for all Merit Badges which do not depend upon group work.

Patrol

But the ideal unit and the keystone of the organization is the Patrol, consisting of eight girls who would naturally be associated as friends, neighbors, school fellows or playmates. They are a self selected and, under the regulations and customs of the organization, a self governing little body, who learn, through practical experiment, how to translate into democratic team-play, their recreation, patriotic or community work, camp life and athletics. Definite mastery of the various subjects they select to study is made more interesting by healthy competition and mutual observation.

Patrol Leader

Each Patrol elects from its members a Patrol Leader, who represents them and is to a certain extent responsible for the discipline and dignity of the Patrol.

Corporal

The Patrol Leader is assisted by her Corporal, who may be either elected or appointed; and as she is subject to re-election at regular intervals, the office is a practical symbol of the democratic basis of our American government and a constant demonstration of it.

Troop

From one to four of these Patrols constitute a Troop, the administrative unit of the organization. Girl Scouts are registered and chartered by troops, and the Troop meeting is their official gathering. The Troop has the privilege of owning a flag and choosing from a list of flowers, trees, birds, and so forth, its own personal crest and title.

Captain

Its leader is called a Captain. She must be twenty-one or over, and officially accepted by the National Headquarters, from whom she receives the ratification of her appointment and to whom she is responsible. She may be chosen by the girls themselves, suggested by local authorities, or be herself the founder of the Troop. She represents the guiding, friendly spirit of comradely leadership, the responsibility and discretion, the maturer judgment and the definite training which shapes the policy of the organization.

Lieutenants

She may, in a small troop, and should, in a large one, be assisted by a Lieutenant, who must be eighteen or over, and who must, like herself, be commissioned from National Headquarters, and if desired, by a Second Lieutenant, who must be at least sixteen.

Council

The work of the Girl Scouts in any community is made many times more effective and stimulating by the co-operation of the Council, a group of interested, public spirited citizens who are willing to stand behind the girls and lend the advantages of their sound judgment, broad point of view, social prestige and financial advice. They are not expected to be responsible for any teaching, training or administrative work; they are simply the organized Friends of the Scouts and form the link between the Scouts and the community. The Council is at its best when it is made up of representatives of the church, school, club and civic interests of the neighborhood, and can be of inestimable value in suggesting and affording means of co-operation with all other organizations, patronizing and advertising Scout entertainments, and so forth. One of its chief duties is that of finding interested and capable judges for the various Merit Badges, and arranging for the suitable conferring of such badges. The Council, or a committee selected from its members, is known for this purpose as the Court of Honor.

A Captain who feels that she has such a body behind her can go far with her Troop; and citizens who are particularly interested in constructive work with young people will find endless possibilities in an organized Girl Scout Council. The National Headquarters issues charters to such Councils and cooperates with them in every way.

National Organization

The central and final governing body is the National Council. This is made up of delegates elected from all local groups throughout the country, and works by representation, indirectly through large State and District sub-divisions, through the National Executive Board which maintains its Headquarters in New York.

National Directors

The National Director is in charge of these Headquarters and directs the administrative work under the general headings of Field, Business, Publication and Education.

Policy

From the youngest Lone Scout up to the National Director, the organization is democratic, self-governing and flexible, adjusting itself everywhere and always to local circumstances and the habits and preferences of the different groups. It is not only non-secretarian, but is open to all creeds and has the enthusiastic support of all of them. It offers no new system of education, but co-operates with the schools and extends to them a much appreciated recreational plan. It affords the churches a most practical outlet for their ideals for their young people. Its encouragement of the intelligent domestic interests is shown by the stress laid on every aspect of home and social life and by the great variety of Merit Badges offered along these lines. The growing interest in the forming of Girl Scout Troops by schools, churches and parents proves as nothing else could, how naturally and helpfully this simple organization fits in with the three factors of the girl's life; her home, her church, her school. And the rapid and never ceasing growth of the Girl Scouts means that we are able to offer, every year, larger and larger numbers of healthy and efficient young citizens to their country.

SECTION IV

WHO ARE THE SCOUTS?

In the early days of this great country of ours, before telephones and telegrams, railroads and automobiles made communication of all sorts so easy, and help of all kinds so quickly secured, men and women—yes, and boys and girls, too!—had to depend very much on themselves and be very handy and resourceful, if they expected to keep safe and well, and even alive.

Our pioneer grandmothers might have been frightened by the sight of one of our big touring cars, for instance, or puzzled as to how to send a telegram, but they knew an immense number of practical things that have been entirely left out of our town-bred lives, and for pluck and resourcefulness in a tight place it is to be doubted if we could equal them today.

"You press a button and we do the rest" is the slogan of a famous camera firm, and really it seems as if this might almost be called the slogan of modern times: we have only to press a button nowadays, and someone will do the rest.

But in those early pioneer days there was no button to press, as we all know, and nobody to "do the rest": everybody had to know a little about everything *and be able to do that little pretty quickly,* as safety and even life might depend upon it.

The men who stood for all this kind of thing in the highest degree were probably the old "Scouts," of whom Natty Bumpo, in Cooper's famous old Indian tales is the great example. They were explorers, hunters, campers, builders, fighters, settlers, and in an emergency, nurses and doctors combined. They could cook, they could sew, they could make and sail a canoe, they could support themselves indefinitely in the trackless woods, they knew

17

all the animals and plants for miles around, they could guide themselves by the sun and stars, and finally, they were husky and hard as nails and always in the best of health and condition. Their adventurous life, always on the edge of danger and new, unsuspected things, made them as quick as lightning and very clever at reading character and adapting themselves to people.

In a way, too, they had to act as rough and ready police (for there were no men in brass buttons in the woods!) and be ready to support the right and deal out justice, just as our "cow-boys" of later ranch days had to prevent horse-stealing.

Now, the tales of their exploits have gone all over the world, and healthy, active people, and especially young people, have always delighted in just this sort of life and character. So, when you add the fact that the word "scout" has always been used, too, to describe the men sent out ahead of an army to gain information in the quickest, cleverest way, it is no wonder that the great organization of Boy and Girl Scouts which is spreading all over the world today should have chosen the name we are so proud of, to describe the kind of thing they want to stand for.

Our British Scout-sisters call themselves "Girl Guides," and here is the thrilling reason for this title given by the Chief Scout and Founder of the whole big band that is spreading round the world today, as so many of Old England's great ideas have spread.

WHY "GUIDES"?

On the North-West Frontier of India there is a famous Corps of soldiers known as the Guides, and their duty is to be always ready to turn out at any moment to repel raids by the hostile tribes across the Border, and to prevent them from coming down into the peaceful plains of India. This body of men must be prepared for every kind of fighting. Sometimes on foot, sometimes on horseback, sometimes in the mountains, often with pioneer work, wading through rivers and making bridges, and so on. But they have to be a skilful lot of men, brave and enduring, ready to turn out at any time, winter or summer, or to sacrifice themselves if necessary in order that peace may reign throughout India while they keep down any hostile raids against it. So they are true handymen in every sense of the word, and true patriots.

When people speak of Guides in Europe one naturally thinks of those men who are mountaineers in Switzerland and other mountainous places, who can guide people over the most difficult parts by their own bravery and skill in tackling obstacles, by helpfulness to those with them, and by their bodily strength of wind and limb. They are splendid fellows those guides, and yet if they were told to go across the same amount of miles on an open flat plain it would be nothing to them, it would not be interesting, and they would not be able to display those grand qualities which they show directly the country is a bit broken up into mountains. It is no fun to them to walk by easy paths, the whole excitement of life is facing difficulties and dangers and apparent impossibilites, and in the end getting a chance of attaining the summit of the mountain they have wanted to reach.

Well, I think it is the case with most girls nowadays. They do not want to sit down and lead an idle life, not to have everything done for them, nor to have a very easy time. They don't want merely to walk across the plain, they would much rather show themselves handy people, able to help others and ready, if necessary, to sacrifice themselves for others just like the Guides on the North-west Frontier. And they also want to tackle difficult jobs themselves in their life, to face mountains and difficulties and dangers, and to go at them having prepared themselves to be skilful and brave; and also they would like to help other people to get their difficulties also. When they attain success after facing difficulties, then they feel really happy and triumphant. It is a big satisfaction to them to have succeeded and to have made other people succeed also. That is what the Girl Guides want to do, just as the mountaineer guides do among the mountains.

Then, too, a woman who can do things is looked up to by others, both men and women, and they are always ready to follow her advice and example. so there she becomes a Guide too. And later on if she has children of her own, or if she becomes a teacher of children, she can be a really good Guide to them.

In fact, if one caricatured a Guide one would draw her thus:— "Turn to the right and keep straight on." And for these reasons the name Guide has been given to them.

By means of games and activities which the Guides practise they are able to learn the different things which will help them to get on in life, and show the way to others to go on also. Thus camping and signalling, first aid work,camp cooking, and all these things that the Guides practise are all going to be helpful to them afterwards in making them strong, resourceful women, skilful and helpful to others, and strong in body as well as in mind, and what is more it makes them a jolly lot of comrades also.

"BE PREPARED!"

The motto of the Guides on which they work is "Be Prepared," that is, be ready for any kind of duty that may be thrust upon them, and what is more, to know what to do by having practised it beforehand in the case of any kind of accident or any kind of work that they may be asked to take up."

It is a great piece of luck for us American Scouts that we can claim the very first Girl Scout for our own great continent, if not quite for our own United States. A great Englishman calls her "the first Girl Scout," and every Scout must feel proud to the core of her heart when she thinks that this statue which we have selected for the honor of our frontispiece, standing as it does on British soil, on the American continent, commemorating a French girl, the daughter of our Sister Republic, joins the three great countries closely together, through the Girl Scouts! Magdelaine de Verchères lived in the French colonies around Quebec late in the seventeenth century. The colonies were constantly being attacked by the Iroquois Indians. One of these attacks occurred while Magdelaine's father, the Seigneur, was away. Magdelaine rallied her younger brothers about her and succeeded in holding the fort for eight days, until help arrived from Montreal.

The documents relating this bit of history have been in the Archives for many years, but when they were shown to Lord Grey about twelve years ago he decided to erect a monument to Magdelaine de Verchères on the St. Lawrence. It was Lord Grey who called Magdelaine "The First Girl Scout," and as such she will be known.

The following is taken from "A Daughter of New France," by Arthur G. Doughty who wrote the book for the Red Cross work of the Magdelaine de Verchères

Chapter of the Daughters of the Empire, and dedicated it to Princess Patricia, whose name was given to the famous "Princess Pat" regiment.

"On Verchères Point, near the site of the Fort, stands a statue in bronze of the girl who adorned the age in which she lived and whose memory is dear to posterity. For she had learned so to live that her hands were clean and her paths were straight. .. .... To all future visitors to Canada by way of the St. Lawrence, this silent figure of the First Girl Scout in the New World conveys a message of loyalty, of courage and of devotion."

Our own early history is sprinkled thickly with brave, handy girls, who were certainly Scouts, if ever there were any, though they never belonged to a patrol, nor recited the Scout Laws. But they lived the Laws, those strong young pioneers, and we can stretch out our hands to them across the long years, and give them the hearty Scout grip of fellowship, when we read of them.

THE EXPLORER

If we should ever hold an election for honorary membership in the Girl Scouts, open to all the girls who ought to have belonged to us, but who lived too long ago, we should surely nominate for first place one of the most remarkable young Indian girls who ever found her way through the pathless forests,—Sacajawea, "The Bird Woman."

In 1806 she was brought to Lewis and Clark on their expedition into the great Northwest, to act as interpreter between them and the various Indian tribes they had to encounter. From the very beginning, when she induced the hostile Shoshones to act as guides, to the end of her daring journey, during which, with her papoose on her back, she led this band of men through hitherto impassible mountain ranges, till she brought them to the Pacific Coast, this sixteen-year-old girl never faltered. No dangers of hunger, thirst, cold or darkness were too much for her. From the Jefferson to the Yellowstone River she was the only guide they had; on her instinct for the right way, her reading of the sun, the stars and the trees, depended the lives of all of them. When they fell sick she nursed them: when they lost heart at the wildness of their venture, she cheered them. Their party grew smaller and smaller, for Lewis and Clark had separated early in the expedition, and a part of Clark's own party fell off when they discovered a natural route over the Continental Divide where wagons could not travel. Later, most of those who remained, decided to go down the Jefferson River in canoes; but Clark, still guided by the plucky Indian girl, persisted in fighting his way on pony back overland, and after a week of this journeying, crowded full of discomforts and dangers, she brought him out in triumph at the Yellowstone, where the river bursts out from the lower cañon,—and the Great Northwest was opened up for all time!

The women of Oregon have raised a statue to this young explorer, and there she stands in Portland, facing the Coast, pointing to the Columbia River where it reaches the sea.

These great virtues of daring and endurance never die out of the race; though the conditions of our life today, when most of the exploring has been done, do not demand them of us in just the form the "Bird Woman" needed, still, if they die out of the nation, and especially, out of the women of the nation, something has been lost that no amount of book education can ever replace. Sacajawea, had no maps to study—she *made* maps, and roads have been built over her foot steps. And so we Scouts, not to lose this great spirit, study the stars and the sun and the trees and try to learn a few of the wood secrets she knew so well. This out-of-door wisdom and self-reliance was the first great principle of Scouting.

THE HOMEMAKER

But of course, a country full of "Bird Women" could not be said to have advanced very far in civilization. Though we should take great pleasure in conferring her well earned merit badges on Sacajawea, we should hardly have grown into the great organization we are today if we had not badges for quite another class of achievements.

In 1832, not so many years after the famous Lewis and Clark expedition, there was born a little New England girl who would very early in life have become a First Class Scout if she had had the opportunity. Her name was Louisa Alcott, and she made that name famous all the world over for the book by which the world's girls know her—"Little Women." Her father, though a brilliant man, was a very impractical one, and from her first little story to her last popular book, all her work was done for the purpose of keeping her mother and sisters in comfort. While she was waiting for the money from her stories she turned carpets, trimmed hats, papered the rooms, made party dresses for her sisters, nursed anyone who was sick (at which she was particularly good)—all the homely, helpful things that neighbors and families did for each other in New England towns.

In those days little mothers of families could not telephone specialists to help them out in emergencies: there were neither telephones nor specialists! But there were always emergencies, and the Alcott girls had to know what to put on a black-and-blue spot, and why the jelly failed to "jell," and how to hang a skirt, and bake a cake. and iron a table cloth. Louisa had to entertain family guests and darn the family stockings. Her home had not every comfort and convenience, even as people counted those things then, and without a brisk, clever woman, full of what the New Englanders called "faculty," her family would have been a very unhappy one. With all our modern inventions nobody has yet invented a substitute for a good, all-round woman, in a family, and until somebody can invent one, we must continue to take off our hats to girls like Louisa Alcott. Imagine what her feelings would have been if someone had told her that she had earned half a dozen merit badges by her knowledge of home economics and her clever writing!

And let every Scout who finds housework dull, and feels that she is capable of bigger things, remember this: the woman whose books for girls are more widely known than any such books ever written in America, had to drop the pen, often and often, for the needle, the dishcloth and the broom.

To direct her household has always been a woman's job in every century, and girls were learning to do it before Columbus ever discovered Sacajawea's great country. To be sure, they had no such jolly way of working at it together, as the Scouts have, nor did they have the opportunity the girl of today has to learn all about these things in a scientific, business-like way, in order to get it all done with the quickest, most efficient methods, just as any clever business man manages his business.

We no longer believe that housekeeping should take up all a woman's time; and many an older woman envies the little badges on a Scout's sleeve that show the world she has learned how to manage her cleaning and cooking and household routine so that she has plenty of time to spend on other things that interest her.

THE PIONEER

But there was a time in the history of our country when men and women went out into the wilderness with no nearer neighbors than the Indians, yet with all the ideals of the New England they left behind them: girls who had to have all the endurance of the young "Bird Woman" and yet keep up the traditions and the habits of the fine old home life of Louisa Alcott.

One of these pioneer girls, who certainly would have been patrol leader of her troop and marched them to victory with her, was Anna Shaw. In 1859, a twelve-year-old girl, with her mother and four other children she traveled in a rough cart full of bedding and provisions, into the Michigan woods and took up a claim there, settling down into a log cabin whose only furniture was a fire place of wood and stones.

She and her brothers floored this cabin with lumber from a mill, and actually made partitions, an attic door and windows. They planted potatoes and corn by chopping up the sod, putting a seed under it and leaving it to Nature—who rewarded them by giving them the best corn and potatoes Dr. Shaw ever ate, she says in her autobiography.

For she became a preacher and a physician, a lecturer and organizer, this sturdy little Scout, even though she had to educate herself, mostly. They papered the cabin walls with the old magazines, after they had read them once, and went all over them, in this fashion, later. So eagerly did she devour the few books sent them from the East, that when she entered college, years later, she passed her examinations on what she remembered of them!

They lived on what they raised from the land; the pigs they brought in the wagon with them, fish, caught with wires out of an old hoop skirt, and corn meal brought from the nearest mill, twenty miles way. Ox teams were the only means of getting about.

Anna and her brothers made what furniture they used —bunks, tables, stools and a settle. She learned to cut trees and "heart" logs like a man. After a trying season of carrying all the water used in the household from a distant creek, which froze in the winter so that they had to melt the ice, they finally dug a well. First they went as far as they could with spades, then handed buckets of earth to each other, standing on a ledge half way down, then, when it was deep enough, they lined it with slabs of wood. It was so well made that the family used it for twelve years.

Wild beasts prowled around them, Indians terrified them by sudden visits, the climate was rigorous, amusements and leisure scanty. But this brave, handy girl met every job that came to her with a good heart and a smile: she learned by doing. The tests and sports that we earn badges by mastering, were life's ordinary problems to her, and very practical ones. She never knew it, but surely she was a real Girl Scout!

It is not surprising to learn that she grew up to be one of the women who earned the American girl her right to vote. A pioneer in more ways than one, this little carpenter and farmer and well-digger worked for the cause of woman's political equality as she had worked in the Michigan wilderness and helped on as much as any one woman the great revolution in people's ideas which makes it possible for women today to express their wishes directly as to how their country shall be governed. This seems very simple to the girls of today, and will seem even simpler as the years go on, but, like the Yellowstone River, it needed its pioneers!

In the Great War which we have just passed through, the Scouts of all countries gave a magnificent account of themselves, and honestly earned the "War Service" badges that will be handed down to future generations, we may be sure, as the proudest possessions of thousands of grandchildren whose grandmothers (think of a Scout grandmother!) were among the first to answer their Country's call.

Let us hear what our British sisters accomplished, and we must remember that at the time of the war there were many Girl Guides well over Scout age and in their twenties, who had had the advantage, as their book points out, of years of training.

This is what they have done during the Great War.

In the towns they have helped at the Military Hospitals.

In the country they have collected eggs for the sick, and on the moors have gathered sphagnum moss for the hospitals.

Over in France a great Recreation and Rest Hut for the soldiers has been supplied by the guides with funds earned through their work. It is managed by Guide officers, or ex-Guides. Among the older Guides there are many who have done noble work as assistants to the ward-maids, cooks, and laundry women. In the Government offices, such as the War Office, the Admiralty, and other great departments of the State, they have acted as orderlies and messengers. They have taken up work in factories, or as motor-drivers, or on farms, in order to release men to go to the front.

At home and in their club-rooms they have made bandages for the wounded, and warm clothing for the men at the Front and in the Fleet.

At home in many of the great cities the Guides have turned their Headquarters' Club-Rooms into "Hostels." That is, they have made them into small hospitals ready for taking in people injured in air-raids by the enemy.

So altogether the Guides have shown themselves to be a pretty useful lot in many different kinds of works during the war, and, mind you, they are only girls between the ages of 11 and 18. But they have done their bit in the Great War as far as they were able, and have done it well.

There are 100,000 of them, and they are very smart, and ready for any job that may be demanded of them.

They were not raised for this special work during the war for they began some years before it, but their motto is "Be Prepared," and it was their business to train themselves to be ready for anything that might happen, even the most unlikely thing.

So even when war came they were "all there" and ready for it.

It is not only in Great Britain that they have been doing this, but all over our great Empire—in Canada and Australia, West, East and South Africa, New Zealand, the Falkland Islands, West Indies, and India. The Guides are a vast sisterhood of girls, ready to do anything they can for their country and Empire.

Long before there was any idea of the war the Guides had been taught to think out and to practise what they should do supposing such a thing as war happened in their own country, or that people should get injured by bombs or by accidents in their neigborhood. Thousands of women have done splendid work in this war, but thousands more would have been able to do good work also had they only Been Prepared for it beforehand by learning up a few things that are useful to them outside their mere school work or work in their own home. And that is what the Guides are learning in all their games and camp work; they mean to be useful in other ways besides what they are taught in school.

WHAT THE GUIDES DO.

As a Guide your first duty is to be helpful to other people, both in small everyday matters and also under the worst of circumstances. You have to imagine to yourself what sort of things might possibly happen, and how you should deal with them when they occur. Then you will know what to do.

I was present when a German aeroplane dropped a bomb on to a railway station in London. There was the usual busy scene of people seeing to their luggage, saying good-bye and going off by train, when with a sudden bang a whole carriage was blown to bits, and the adjoining ones were in a blaze; seven or eight of those active in getting into the train were flung down—mangled and dead; while some thirty more were smashed, broken, and bleeding, but still alive. The suddenness of it made it all the more horrifying. But one of the first people I noticed as keeping her head was a smartly dressed young lady kneeling by an injured working-man; his thigh was smashed and bleeding terribly; she had ripped up his trouser with her knife, and with strips of it had bound a pad to the wound; she found a cup somehow and filled it with water for him from the overhead hose for filling engines. Instead of being hysterical and useless, she was as cool and ready to do the right thing as if she had been in bomb-raids every day of her life. Well, that is what any girl can do if she only prepares herself for it.

These are things which have to be learnt in peace-time, and because they were learnt by the Guides beforehand, these girls were able to do their bit so well when war came.

FIRST AID.

When you see an accident in the street or people injured in an air raid, the sight of the torn limbs, the blood, the broken bones, and the sound of the groans and sobbing all make you feel sick and horrified and anxious to get away from it—if you're not a Girl Guide. But that is cowardice: your business as a Guide is to steel yourself to face it and to help the poor victim. As a matter of fact, after a trial or two you really get to like such jobs, because with coolheadedness and knowledge of what to do you feel you give the much-needed help.

The Value of Nursing.—In this war hundreds and hundreds of women have gone to act as nurses in the hospitals for the wounded and have done splendid work. They will no doubt be thankful all their lives that while they were yet girls they learnt how to to nurse and how to do hospital work, so that they were useful when the call came for them. But there are thousands and thousands of others who wanted to do the work when the time came, but they had not like Guides Been Prepared, and they had never learnt how to nurse, and so they were perfectly useless and their services were not required in the different hospitals. So carry out your motto and Be Prepared and learn all you can about hospital and child nursing, sick nursing, and every kind, while you are yet a Guide and have people ready to instruct you and to help you in learning.

In countries not so settled and protected as England and America, where the women and girls are taught to count upon their men to protect them in the field, the Girl Scouts have sometimes had to display a courage like that of the early settlers. A Roumanian Scout, Ecaterina Teodorroiu actually fought in the war and was taken prisoner. She escaped, traced her way back to her company, and brought valuable information as to the enemy's movements. For these services she was decorated "as a reward for devotion and conspicuous bravery" with the Order of Merit and a special gold medal for the Scouts, only to be given for services during the war. At the same time she was promoted to the rank of Honorary Second Lieutenant.

Can we wonder that she is known as the Joan of Arc of Roumania?

During the Russian Revolution the Girl Scouts were used by the Government in many practical ways, as may be seen from the following letter from one of them:

"The Scouts assisted from the beginning, from seven in the morning until twelve at night, carrying messages, sometimes containing state secrets, letters, etc., from the Duma to the different branches of it called commissariats, and back again. They also fed the soldiers that were on guard. The Scout uniform was our protection, and everywhere that uniform commanded the respect of the soldiers, peasants and workingmen.

"As great numbers of soldiers came from the front, food had to be given them. It was contributed by private people, but the Scouts had lots of work to distribute it. All the little taverns were turned into eating houses for the soldiers, and there we helped to prepare the food and feed them. As there were not enough Boy Scouts, the Girl Scouts helped in the same way as the boys.

"The Scouts also did much First Aid work. In one instance I saw an officer whose finger had been shot off. I ran up to him and bandaged it up for him. (All of us Scouts had First Aid kits hanging from our belts.)

"It was something of a proud day for us Scouts when the Premier after a parade, called us all before the Duma and publicly thanked us for our aid."

Indeed it was, and we heartily congratulate our Sister Scouts! But if we do our duty by our Patrol and the Patrols all do their duty by their Troop, that proud moment is going to come to every single Scout of us, when the town where we live tells us by its smiles and applause, when we go by in uniform, what it thinks of us.

We Scouts shall be more and more interested, as the years go on, to remember that in the great hours of one of the world's greatest crises we helped to make its history. Little instances like these are very exceptional; they could not occur to one in ten thousand of us; but we stay-at-homes can always remind ourselves that it was the obedience, the quickness, and the skill learned in quiet, every-day Scouting that made these few rise to their opportunity when it came.

War and revolution do not make Scouts either brave or useful: they only bring out the bravery and the usefulness that have been learned, as we are all learning them. every day!

All we have to do is to fix Scout habits in our hearts and hands, and then when our Country calls us, we shall be as ready as these little Russian Scouts were.

In France the Scouts, known as the Eclaireuses, have agreed with us that the "Land Army" is the best army for women. Rain or shine, in heat and cold, they have dug and ploughed and planted, and learned the lesson American girls learned long ago—that team work is what counts!

A bit of one of their reports is translated here:

· "The crops were fine—potatoes, radishes, greens and beans were raised. The crop of potatoes, especially, was so good that the Eclaireuses were able to supply their families with them at a price defying competition, and they always had enough besides for their own use on excursions. (Our hikes.)

"Such has been the reward of the care, given so perseveringly and intelligently to the gardening.

"And what an admirable lesson! Not a minute was lost in this out-of-door work; chest and muscles filled out; and at the same time the girls learned to recognize weather signs; rain or sun were the factors which determined the success or non-success of the planting. And each day, there grew in them also love and gratitude for the earth and its elements, without the assistance of wnich we could harvest nothing.

"Is this not the best method of preparing our youth to return to the land, to the healthy and safe life of the beautiful countryside of France; by showing them the interest and usefulness that lie in agricultural labor?

"So the Eclaireuse becomes a model of the new women, used to sports, possessing her First Aid Diploma, able to cook good simple meals, marching under orders, knowing how to obey, ready to accept her responsibilities, good-natured and lively in rain or sun, in public or in her home. . . . . They continue their courses in sewing, hygiene and gymnastics and assist eagerly at conferences arranged for them to discuss the duties of the Eclaireuses and what it is necessary to do to become a good Captain.

"To make themselves useful—that is the ideal of the Eclaireuses. They know that in order to do this it is becoming more and more necessary to acquire a broad and complete knowledge."

It is quite a feather in the cap of this great Scout Family of ours that we are teaching the French girl, who has not been accustomed to leave her home or to work in clubs or troops, what a jolly, wonder-working thing a crowd of girls, all forging ahead together, can be.

In our own country we were protected from the worst sides of the great war, but we had a wonderful opportunity to show how we could Be Prepared ourselves by seeing that our brave soldiers were prepared.

Our War Records show an immense amount of Red Cross supplies, knitting, comfort kits, food grown and conserved in every way, money raised for Liberty Loans and Thrift Stamps, war orphans adopted, home replacement work undertaken and carried through; all these to so great an amount that the country recognized our existence and services as never before in our history, the Government, indeed, employing sixty uniformed Scouts as messengers in the Surgeon General's Department.

Perhaps it is only the truth to say that the war showed

our Country what we could Be Prepared to do for her!
And it showed us, too.

It has been said that women can never be the same
after the great events of the last few years, and we must
never forget that the Girl Scouts of today are the women
of tomorrow.

FLAG RAISING AT DAWN

SECTION V

THE OUT-OF-DOOR SCOUT

Busy as the Girl Scout may be with learning to do in a clever, up-to-date way all the things to improve her home and town that the old pioneer girls knew how to do, she never forgets that the original Scouts were out-of-door people. So long as there are bandages to make or babies to bathe or meals to get or clothes to make, she does them all, quickly and cheerfully, and is very rightly proud of the badges she gets for having learned to do them all, and the sense of independence that comes from all this skill with her hands. It gives her a real glow of pleasure to feel that because of her First Aid practice she may be able to save a life some day, and that the hours of study she put in at her home nursing and invalid cooking may make her a valuable asset to the community in case of any great disaster or epidemic; but the real fun of scouting lies in the great life of out-of-doors, and the call of the woods is answered quicker by the Scout than by anybody, because the Scout learns just how to get the most out of all this wild, free life and how to enjoy it with the least trouble and the most fun.

One of our most experienced and best loved Captains says that "a camp is as much a necessity for the Girl Scouts as an office headquarters," and more and more girls are learning to agree with her every year.

Our British cousins are the greatest lovers of out-of-door life in the world, and it is only natural that we should look to our Chief Scout to hear what he has to say to his Girl Guides on this subject so dear to his heart that he founded Scouting, that all boys and girls might share his enthusiastic pleasure in going back to Nature to study and to love her and to gain happiness and health from her woods and fields.

HOW CAMPING TEACHES THE GUIDE LAW

Last year a man went out into the woods in America to try and see if he could live like the prehistoric men used to do; that is to say, he took nothing with him in the way of food or equipment or even clothing—he went just as he was, and started out to make his own living as best he could. Of course the first thing he had to do was to make some sort of tool or weapon by which he could kill some animals, cut his wood and make his fire and so on. So he made a stone axe, and with that was able to cut out branches of trees so that he could make a trap in which he eventually caught a bear and killed it. He then cut up the bear and used the skin for blankets and the flesh for food. He also cut sticks and made a little instrument by which he was able to ignite bits of wood and so start his fire. He also searched out various roots and berries and leaves, which he was able to cook and make into good food, and he even went so far as to make charcoal and to cut slips of bark from the trees and draw pictures of the scenery and animals around him. In this way he lived for over a month in the wild, and came out in the end very much better in health and spirits and with a great experience of life. For he had learned to shift entirely for himself and to be independent of the different things we get in civilization to keep us going in comfort.

That is why we go into camp a good deal in the Boy Scout and in the Girl Guide movement, because in camp life we learn to do without so many things which while we are in houses we think are necessary, and find that we can do for ourselves many things where we used to think ourselves helpless. And before going into camp it is just as well to learn some of the things that will be most useful to you when you get get there. And that is what we teach in the Headquarters of the Girl Guide Companies before they go out and take the field. For instance, you must know how to light your own fire; how to collect dry enough wood to make it burn; because you will not find gas stoves out in the wild. Then you have to learn how to find your own water, and good water that will not make you ill. You have not a whole cooking range or a kitchen full of cooking pots, and so you have to learn to cook your food in the simplest way with the means at your hand, such as a simple cooking pot or a roasting stick or an oven made with your own hands out of an old tin box or something of that kind.

NATURE STUDY

It is only while in camp that one can really learn to study Nature in the proper way and not as you merely do it inside the school; because here you are face to face with Nature at all hours of the day and night. For the first time you live under the stars and can watch them by the hour and see what they really look like, and realize what an enormous expanse of almost endless space they cover. You know from your lessons at school that our sun warms and lights up a large number of different worlds like ours, all circling round it in the Heavens. And when you hold up a shilling at arm's length and look at the sky, the shilling covers no less than two hundred of those suns, each with their different little worlds circling round them. And you then begin to realize what an enormous endless space the Heavens comprise. You realize perhaps for the first time the enormous work of God.

Then also in camp you are living among plants of every kind, and you can study them in their natural state, how they grow and what they look like, instead of merely seeing pictures of them in books or dried specimens of them in collections.

All round you, too, are the birds and animals and insects, and the more you know of them the more you begin to like them and to take an interest in them; and once you take an interest in them you do not want to hurt them in any way. You would not rob a bird's nest; you would not bully an animal; you would not kill an insect—once you have realized what its life and habits are. In this way, therefore, you fulfill the Guide Law of becoming a friend to animals.

By living in camp you begin to find that though there are many discomforts and difficulties to be got over, they can be got over with a little trouble and especially if you smile at them and tackle them.

Then living among other comrades in camp you have to be helpful and do good turns at almost every minute, and you have to exercise a great deal of give and take and good temper, otherwise the camp would become unbearable.

So you carry out the different laws of courteousness, of helpfulness, and friendliness to others that come in the Guide Law. Also you pick up the idea of how necessary it is to keep everything in its place, and to keep your kit and tent and ground as clean as possible; otherwise you get into a horrible state of dirt, and dirt brings flies and other inconveniences.

You save every particle of food and in this way you learn not only cleanliness, but thrift and economy. And you very soon realize how cheaply you can live in camp, and how very much enjoyment you can get for very little money. And as you live in the fresh, pure air of God you find that your own thoughts are clean and pure as the air around you. There is hardly one of the Guide Laws that is not better carried out after you have been living and practising it in camp.

Habits of Animals.—If you live in the country it is of course quite easy to observe and watch the habits of all sorts of animals great and small. But if you are in a town there are many difficulties to be met with. But at the same time if you can keep pets of any kind, rabbits, rats, mice, dogs or ponies you can observe and watch their habits and learn to understand them well; but generally for Guides it is more easy to watch birds, because you see them both in town and country; and especially when you go into camp or on walking tours you can observe and watch their habits, especially in the springtime.

Then it is that you see the old birds making their nests, hatching out their eggs and bringing up their young; and that is of course the most interesting time for watching them. A good observant guide will get to know the different kinds of birds by their cry, by their appearance, and by their way of flying. She will also get to know where their nests are to be found, what sort of nests they are, what are the colours of the eggs and so on And also how the young appear. Some of them come out fluffy, others covered with feathers, others with very little on at all. The young pigeon, for instance, has no feathers at all, whereas a young moorhen can swim about as soon as it comes out of the egg; while chickens run about and hunt flies within a few minutes; and yet a sparrow is quite useless for some days and is blind, and has to be fed and coddled by his parents.

Then it is an interesting sight to see the old birds training their young ones to fly by getting up above them and flapping their wings a few times until all the young ones imitate them. Then they hop from one twig to another, still flapping their wings, and the young ones follow suit and begin to find that their wings help them to balance; and finally they jump from one branch to another for some distance so that the wings support them in their effort. The young ones very soon find that they are able to use their wings for flying, but it is all done by degrees and by careful instruction.

Then a large number of our birds do not live all the year round in England, but they go off to Southern climes such as Africa when the winter comes on; but they generally turn up here at the end of March and make their nest during the spring. Nightingales arrive early in April; wagtails, turtle doves, and cuckoos come late in April; woodcock come in the autumn, and redpoles and fieldfares also come here for the winter. In September you will see the migrating birds collecting to go away, the starlings in their crowds and the swallows for the South, and so do the warblers, the flycatchers, and the swifts. And yet about the same time the larks are arriving here from the Eastward, so there is a good deal of traveling among the birds in the air at all times of the year."

How many of our American Scouts are able to supply from their observation all of our native birds to take the places of these mentioned in this lovely paragraph? Everyone should be able to.

Nature in the City.—This noticing of small things, especially in animal life, not only gives you great interest, but it also gives you great fun and enjoyment in life. Even if you live in a city you can do a certain amount of observation of birds and animals. You would think there is not much fun to be got out of it in a murky town like London or Sheffield, and yet if you begin to notice and know all about the sparrows you begin to find there is a great deal of character and amusement to be got out of them, by watching their ways and habits, their nesting, and their way of teaching their young ones to fly.

OBSERVATION.

"Stalking.—A Guide has to be sharp at seeing things if she is going to be any good as a Guide. She has to notice every little track and every little sign, and it is this studying of tracks and following them out and finding out their meaning which we include under the name of stalking. For instance, if you want to find a bird's-nest you have to stalk. That is to say, you watch a bird flying into a bush and guess where its nest is, and follow it up and find the nest. With some birds it is a most difficult thing to find their nests; take, for instance, the skylark or the snipe. But those who know the birds, especially the snipe, will recognize their call. The snipe when she is alarmed gives quite a different call from when she is happy and flying about. She has a particular call when she has young ones about. So that those who have watched and listened and know her call when they hear it know pretty well where the young ones are or where the nest is and so on.

"How to Hide Yourself.—When you want to observe wild animals you have to stalk them, that is, creep up to them without their seeing or smelling you.

"A hunter when he is stalking wild animals keeps himself entirely hidden, so does the war scout when watching or looking for the enemy; a policeman does not catch pickpockets by standing about in uniform watching for them; he dresses like one of the crowd, and as often as not gazes into a shop window and sees all that goes on behind him reflected as if in a looking-glass.

"If a guilty person finds himself being watched, it puts him on his guard, while an innocent person becomes annoyed. So, when you are observing people, don't do so by openly staring at them, but notice the details you want to at one glance or two, and if you want to study them more, walk behind them; you can learn just as much from a back view, in fact more than you can from a front view, and, unless they are scouts and look round frequently, they do not know that you are observing them.

"War scouts and hunters stalking game always carry out two important things when they don't want to be seen.

Background.—One is— they *take care that the ground behind them, or trees, or buildings, etc., are of the same colour as their clothes.*

"Freezing."—In that way a scout, even though he is out in the open, will often escape being noticed. This is called by scouts "Freezing."

And the other is—if an enemy or a deer is seen looking for them, *they remain perfectly still without moving so long as he is there.*

Tracking.—The native hunters in most wild countries follow their game by watching for tracks on the ground, and they become so expert at seeing the slightest sign of a footmark on the ground that they can follow up their prey when an ordinary civilized man can see no sign whatever. But the great reason for looking for signs and tracks is that from these you can read a meaning. It is exactly like reading a book. You will see the different letters, each letter combining to make a word, and the words then make sense; and there are also commas and full-stops and colons; all of these alter the meaning of the sense. There are all little signs which one who is practised and has learnt reading makes into sense at once, whereas a savage who has never learned could make no sense of it at all. And so it is with tracking.

TRACKING.

"Sign" is the word used by Guides to mean any little details, such as footprints, broken twigs, trampled grass, scraps of food, old matches, etc.

Some native Indian trackers were following up the footprints of a panther that had killed and carried off a young kid. He had crossed a wide bare slab which, of rock, of course, gave no mark of his soft feet. The tracker went at once to the far side of the rock where it came to a sharp edge; he wetted his finger, and just passed it along the edge till he found a few kid's hairs sticking to it. This showed him where the panther had passed down off the rock, dragging the kid with him. Those few hairs were what Guides call "sign."

This tracker also found bears by noticing small "sign." On one occasion he noticed a fresh scratch in the bark of a tree, evidently made by a bear's claw, and on the other he found a single black hair sticking to the bark of a tree, which told him that a bear had rubbed against it.

HORSES' TRACKS

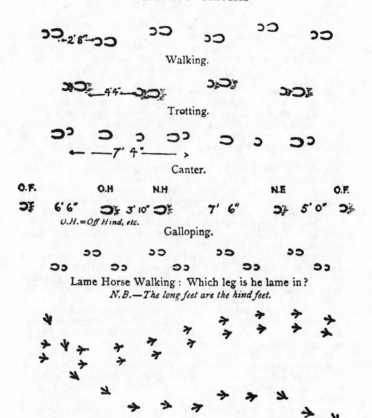

Walking.

Trotting.

Canter.

O.F.　　　　O.H　　　N.H　　　　　　　N.E　　　　O.F.

6' 6"　　　　3' 10"　　　　7' 6"　　　　5' 0"

O.H. = Off Hind, etc.

Galloping.

Lame Horse Walking : Which leg is he lame in?
N.B.—The long feet are the hind feet.

These are the tracks of two birds on the ground. One that lives generally on the ground, the other in bushes and trees. Which track belongs to which bird?

Details in the Country.—If you are in the country, you should notice landmarks—that is, objects which help you to find your way to prevent your getting lost—such as distant hills and church towers; and nearer objects, such as peculiar buildings, trees, gates, rocks, etc.

And remember in noticing such landmarks that you may want to use your knowledge of them some day for telling some one else how to find his way, so you must notice them pretty closely so as to be able to describe them unmistakably and in their proper order. You must notice and remember every by-road and foot-path.

Remembrance of these things will help you to find your way by night or in fog when other people are losing themselves.

Using your Eyes.—Let nothing be too small for your notice—a button, a match, a hair, a cigar ash, a feather, or a leaf might be of great importance, even a finger-print which is almost invisible to the naked eye has often been the means of detecting a crime.

With a little practice in observation you can tell pretty accurately a man's character from his dress.

How would you recognize that a gentleman was fond of fishing? If you see his left cuff with little tufts of cloth sticking up, you may be sure he fishes. When he takes his flies off the line he will either stick them into his cap to dry, or hook them into his sleeve. When dry he pulls them out, which often tears a thread or two of the cloth.

Remember how "Sherlock Holmes" met a stranger, and noticed that he was looking fairly well-to-do, in new clothes with a mourning band on his sleeve, with a soldierly bearing and a sailor's way of walking, sunburns, with tattoo marks on his hands, and he was carrying some children's toys in his hand. What would you have supposed that man to be? Well, Sherlock Holmes guessed correctly that he had lately retired from the Royal Marines as a sergeant, that his wife had died, and that he had some small children at home.

PRACTICE IN OBSERVATION.—*Instructor can take the finger-marks of each girl. Lightly rub the thumb on blacklead or on paper that is blacked with pencil, then press the thumb on paper and examine with magnifying glass. Show that no two peoples' prints are alike.*

IN TOWN.—*Practice your girls first in walking down a street to notice the different kinds of shops as they pass, and to remember them in their proper sequence at the end.*

Then to notice and remember the names on the shops.

Then to notice and remember the contents of a shop window after two minutes' gaze. Finally, to notice the contents of several shop windows in succession with half a minute at each. Give marks for the fullest list.

The Guides must also notice prominent buildings as landmarks, and the number of turnings off the street they are using.

IN THE COUNTRY.—*Take the patrol out for a walk and teach the girls to notice distant prominent features such as hills, church steeples, and so on; and as nearer landmarks such things as peculiar buildings, trees, rocks, gates, by-roads or paths, nature of fences, crops, different kinds of trees, birds, animals, tracks, people, vehicles, etc. Also any peculiar smells of plants, animals, manure, etc.; whether gates or doors were open or shut, whether any smoke from chimney, etc.*

Send Guides out in pairs.

It adds to the value of the practice if the instructor makes a certain number of small marks in the ground beforehand, or leaves buttons or matches, etc., for the girls to notice or to pick up and bring in as a means of making them examine the ground close to them as well as distant objects.

PRACTICES IN NATURAL HISTORY.—*Take out Guides to get specimens of leaves, fruits, or blossoms of various trees, shrubs, etc., and observe the shape and nature of the tree both in summer and in winter.*

Collect leaves of different trees; let Guides make tracings of them and write the name of the tree on each.

In the country make Guides examine crops in all stages of their growth, so that they know pretty well by sight what kind of crop is coming up.

Start gardens if possible; either a patrol garden or individual Guides' gardens. Let them grow flowers and vegetables for profit to pay for their equipment, etc.. Show all the wild plants which may be made use of for food. Find yew trees; report if any good branches to make archers' bows of.

Encourage the keeping of live pets, whether birds, animals, reptiles, insects. Show how to keep illustrated diary-records of plants, insects, birds, etc., giving dates when seen for comparison following year and showing their peculiar markings, etc.

If in a town take your Guides to the Zoological Gardens, menagerie or Natural History Museum, and show them particular animals on which you are prepared to lecture. Not more than half a dozen for one visit.

If in the country get farmer or shepherd to help with information on the habits of farm animals, e. g. how a cow lies down and when. How to milk, stalk rabbits, water voles, trout, birds, etc., and watch their habits.

SECTION VI

FORMS FOR SCOUT CEREMONIES
1. ENROLLMENT

Before a girl may become enrolled as a regular Girl Scout she must be at least ten years old, and must have attended the meetings of a Troop for at least a month, during which time she must have passed her Tenderfoot Test. The Captain must have prepared the candidate for enrollment by explaining the meaning of the Promise and the Laws and making sure that she fully understands the meaning of the oath she is about to make, and that she also comprehends the meaning of "honor." The following is a convenient form for enrollments.

(1) The Scouts stand in the form of a horseshoe with the officer who is to enroll at the open side facing Scouts.

(2) Officer addresses troops on the subject of what it means to be a Scout.

(3) Patrol Leader brings candidate to officer and salutes and returns to place.

(4) Officer addresses candidate in low tone: "What does your honor mean?"
Candidate answers.
Officer: "Will you on your honor, try: To do your duty to God and to your Country; to help other people at all times; to obey the Scout Laws?"
Candidate and officer both salute as candidate repeats Promise. Officer: "I trust you on your honor to keep this Promise."

(5) Officer pins Tenderfoot Badge on the new Scout, explaining what it stands for, that it symbolizes her Scout life, and so forth.

(6) Scout and officer salute each other. Scout turns

and troop salutes her, scout returning salute, and then goes alone to her place.

(7) All Scouts present repeat Promise and Laws. Troop then breaks ranks to take up some Scout activity.

When many scouts are to be enrolled, four at a time may be presented to the officer, but each should singly be asked and should answer the question: "What is your honor?" All four repeat the Promise together and the officer addresses all together in saying: "I trust you on your honor to keep this Promise," but speaks to each separately as she puts on the pin.

A Captain may perform this ceremony or she may ask some higher Scout officer to do so.

2. *Presentation of Other Badges*

The following form of ceremony was devised for special use in the presentation of the highest honor attainable by a Girl Scout, the Golden Eaglet, but the same outline may be followed for giving Merit Badges, and First and Second Class Badges, or any other medals or honors.

Presentation of Golden Eaglet.—As the presentation of the Golden Eaglet is an important occasion in the life of a Scout and her Troop, it should take place at a public Scout function, such as a District or Community Rally, a reception to a distinguished guest of the Scouts, or possibly at the time of a civic celebration.

The Court of Honor is responsible for all details of the meeting, and it is suggested that it invite parents, friends and other persons interested in the Scout movement to be present. The medal may be presented by the Chairman of the Court of Honor, some other member of that Committee or by a higher Scout officer.

Arrangements for the ceremony should be planned so that during the presentation of guests, the Court of

Honor, the Eaglet's troop and the Color Guard form a hollow square, with the Captain at her post three paces in front of the Troop, the Lieutenant at her post "center and rear" of the Troop. The ceremony should be rehearsed wherever possible, so that all action and form shall be as smart as possible.

1. The Court of Honor enters and takes its place at right angles to the assembled guests.

2. The Captain enters, takes post, and gives all commands.

3. The Color Guard (bearer of the American flag, bearer of the Troop flag, and two guards) followed by Troop to which the Eaglet belongs, enter and march two paces in front of the Court of Honor. The lieutenant is at the left of the leading file. The Troop marches in single file, by twos or in Squad formation according to the number, and the space available.

When the Troop is very large, or the space restricted, the Eaglet's Patrol may take the place of the Troop. As the Colors pass, the Court of Honor should rise, stand at attention, and if Scouts, salute.

4. When the Color Guard at the head of the column has passed the Court of Honor, the command "Column left, MARCH!" is given. When the last file has completed the movement, the following commands are given:

    (1) "Scouts, HALT!"
    (2) "Left, FACE," or
       "Squads, left, MARCH, Squads, HALT," according to the formation of the column.
    (3) "Right, DRESS, FRONT!"

5. At the command "Left, FACE," or "Squads left, MARCH, Squads HALT," the Color Guard makes a left turn, marches forward until on a line with the Court of Honor, again makes a left turn, immediately halts and grounds flags.

6. When the Troop and Color Guard are in position, the Captain gives the command "Patrol Leader and Eaglet, forward, MARCH!" The Patrol Leader escorts the Eaglet to the Captain, salutes the Captain and returns to her position in line.

7. The Chairman of the Court of Honor comes forward, the Captain faces her, salutes, and presents the Eaglet to her.

8. The Chairman after reading the list of Merit Badges which the Scout has earned in order to receive the Golden Eaglet, pins the medal on to the Eaglet's blouse, over the middle of the right pocket. The Eaglet salutes.

If desired, this is the opportunity for the Official presenting the badge to say a few words.

9. After the presentation, the Eaglet turns, and facing her Captain and Troop, stands at attention as the Colors are raised, the Scout flag dipped, and the Troop salutes. The Eaglet returns the salute and then marches to her position in line.

10. The Captain gives the command "Color Guard forward, MARCH." The Color Guard marches in front of the Captain and Troop who salute as the colors pass, make a right turn two paces in front of the Court of Honor and march out.

11. After the colors have left the "square" the Lieutenant takes her position at the left of the leading file.

The Captain gives the commands:

"Right, FACE, MARCH!" or Squads right, MARCH!"
"Column left, MARCH!"

and the Troop marches out. The Captain turns, salutes the Court of Honor and passes out.

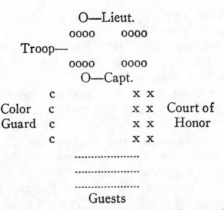

Where there is no Local Council or Court of Honor, Captains are asked to communicate with the National Headquarters concerning the ceremony of presentation of the Golden Eaglet.

ALTERNATE FORMS FOR SCOUT CEREMONIES

In the case of troops for which this formal procedure is not practical, and for the better assistance of Captains and Councils who feel the need of a more definite formulation of the Scout principles on these occasions, the following ceremonies are suggested. They are designed to meet the necessity for expressing at each stage of the Scout's progress, recognition of her achievement up to that point and appreciation of her future responsibilities.

1. Tenderfoot Enrollment

1. The Troop being assembled in any desired formation, the Captain calls forward those who have passed the test.

Captain: "Scout ——, do you think you know what

it means to be loyal to God and your Country, **to** help other people at all times, and to obey the Scout Laws?"

Scout: "I think I do, and I will try my best **not** to fail in any of them."

This is repeated to each Tenderfoot.

Captain: "Are you ready to make your Promise with your Troop?"

New Scouts *(together)*: "Yes."

Captain: "Scouts of Troop ———, repeat your promise."

All salute and repeat the Promise.

Captain: "I trust you on your honor to keep this Promise."

(Here, when practicable, investiture of hat, neckerchief, etc., takes place.)

Captain then pins on Tenderfoot pin. While attaching it, she says:

Captain: "This pin makes you a Girl Scout. It is yours, so long as **you** are worthy of it."

Captain dismisses recently enrolled Scouts to their Troop position.

(Here the Captain may add, if she wishes, anything in her judgment applicable to the Troop as a whole, or to the new Scouts individually.)

2. Conferring Second Class Badges

The Troop being assembled in any desired formation, the Captain calls forward those who have passed the test.

Captain: "Scout ———, you have learned what is necessary for a Second Class Scout to know. Do you think you can apply your knowledge, if the occasion should arise?"

Scout: "I think so, and I will always try to Be Prepared."

Captain: "Scouts *(reciting the candidates' names in order)*, do you think that the discpline and training you have gone through have made you more capable of doing your duty to God and to your Country, of helping other people at all times and of obeying the Scout Laws, than you were as a Tenderfoot?"

Scouts *(together)* : "Yes."

Captain *(pinning on each badge, and speaking to each Scout as she does so)*: "You are now a Second Class Scout, which means that though you have learned much, you have still much to learn."

Captain dismisses Second Class Scouts to their Troop position.

(Here the Captain may address the Troop at her discretion.)

3. Conferring First Class Badge

The Troop being assembled in any desired formation, the Captain calls forward those who have passed the test and presents them to the presiding Official.

Captain: "Commissioner ———, these Scouts of ——— Troop have passed their First Class Tests. I recommend them to you for First Class badges."

Official *(to each Scout separately, the Captain giving her the name)*: "Scout ———, you have passed the final Scout test. You should thoroughly understand by now the meaning of duty to God and Country, the privilege of helpfulness to others, and the seriousness of the Scout Laws. Are you sure that you do?"

Scout: "I am. And I realize that I must help other Scouts to see these things as I see them."

SCOUTING FOR GIRLS 51

Official: "Scouts ———— *(reading the candidates'* *names in order),* it has taken a great deal of thought and time and energy on the part of a great many people to enable you to wear this badge. Are you prepared to pay this back in generous service, when and where you can?"

Scouts *(together):* "Yes."

Official *(pinning on each badge and speaking to each Scout as she does so):* "You are now a First Class Scout. Remember that the world will judge us by you."

Official (to Captain): "I congratulate you, Captain ————, Troop ————, and the members of the Council, on these First Class Scouts, and I trust that the Town of ———— will have every reason to be proud of them and to feel that it can depend upon them as especially good citizens and loyal Americans."

Captain acknowledges this in suitable manner and dismisses First Class Scouts to Troop position. (Here the Official may address the audience at discretion.)

4. Conferring Merit Badges

The Troop being assembled in any desired formation, the Captain calls forward those who have passed the test and presents them to the presiding Official. (Note—The Merit Badges may be conferred by a member or members of the Council, if desired.)

Captain: "Members of the Girl Scout Council of ————, these Scouts have passed the various tests for their Merit Badges, and I recommend them to you for decoration accordingly."

Official: "Scouts *(reading the list),* you have fairly won the right to wear these badges we are about to present to you, and we are glad to do so. We take this opportunity of reminding you, however, that all good Scouts understand that they are far from having completely mastered the subjects represented by these badges. The symbols which you wear on your sleeve mean that you have an intelligent interest in the subjects you have chosen, understand the principles of them, and can give reasonable, practical proof of this. Do you realize that the Girl Scout Organization credits you with a good foundation and trusts to you to continue to build upon it intelligently?"

Scouts (*together*): "Yes."

Official (*pinning on badges and speaking to each girl separately*): "We congratulate you on your perseverance and wish you all success in your work."

Note—When more than one badge is to be presented to a Scout, they may be attached, for the ceremony, to a piece of ribbon and put on with one motion.)

Captain dismisses Scouts to Troop position.

(Here the official may address the audience at discretion.)

This ceremony being distinctly less formal and intimate than the regular class awards, Scout songs and cheers are in order.

5. Golden Eaglet Ceremony

The Troop being assembled in any desired formation, the Captain presents the Golden Eaglet to the Official who is to make the award.

Captain: "Commissioner ———, Scout ———, of Troop ———, of ———, has not only passed the twenty-one Merit Badge Tests required for the

honor of the Golden Eaglet, but is, in the judgment of her Troop, fully worthy of it. We therefore recommend her to you for the decoration."

Official: "What badges does Scout ——— offer?"

*Captain reads the list Badges earned by the
Candidate.*

Official: "Troop ———, do you agree that Scout
——— has fairly won this decoration and that
you are willing to have her represent you to your
National Organization as your Golden Eaglet?"

Troop *(together):* "Yes."

Official: "Members of the Council, do you agree
that Scout ——— has fairly won this decoration and that you are willing to have her represent you to your community as your Golden
Eaglet?"

Council *(rising if seated):* "Yes."

Official: "Scout ———, you have won the highest
honor in the gift of the Girl Scouts."

"If the Scout life meant nothing more to you
than a reasonable understanding of certain subjects, there would now be nothing more for the
Girl Scouts to teach you; but I am sure that your
training has not failed in this respect, and that
you understand now, even better than the average
Girl Scout, that your great principles of duty to
God and Country, helpfulness to others, and
obedience to the Scout Laws, are lessons that no
Scout can fully learn as long as she lives. Do
you agree to this?"

Golden Eaglet: "I agree to it thoroughly."

Official *(pinning on badge):* "I have the honor of
naming you a Golden Eaglet, and in the name of
the Girl Scouts I congratulate you heartily on
your fine achievement."

*Scout salutes or shakes the hand of the Official, as
desired, and returns to her troop position.*
*(Here the Official may address the audience at
discretion).*

The accompanying diagram of suggested relative positions in Scout ceremonies lends itself equally to a small
room, theatre, hall or open field. Whether the Scouts
form a troop or even one patrol; whether they make use
of strict military formation or informal grouping;
whether the visiting Scout dignitaries are many or limited to one member of the local Council, the Scout bodies
face each other, and the guest or guests of honor, equally
with the general audience, can observe the Troop and the
candidates easily from the side.

All Troops who are familiar with military drill can take
their usual positions in their usual manner and observe
all details of color guard, salutes, etc., to any desired extent. Troops and Captains not familiar with such procedure, by accustoming themselves to this general grouping, will always be able to present a dignified appearance.

Note: These suggestions for the various ceremonials
assume that the regular opening of the Scout meetings
has already taken place; therefore nothing is given but
the actual matter of the presentations, etc. In the case
of the Tenderfoot, Second Class and First Class awards,
the ceremonies constitute the special business of the meeting, and opening and closing should proceed as usual.
They are distinctly Scout business and are not, in general,
offered to the public.

The awarding of Merit Badges might with advantage
be connected with any local civic ceremony where interest
in young people may be created; and in the case of the
Golden Eaglet award it is distinctly desirable thus to
connect it. Any visiting dignitary, national or state, may
with propriety be asked to officiate; and where different

organizations are taking their various parts in a public function, it will not always be possible to claim the time nor the space for the regular Scout opening ceremonies, nor would this necessarily be advisable. It is, therefore, well to be provided with a form like the preceding, where a small delegation from the Troop, the Captain and a Councillor could, if necessary, represent the essential units of the organization among a number of other societies; and the words of the ceremony would explain the occasion sufficiently without much concerted action, and may be inserted at the proper place, preceded and followed by any Troop or local customs preferred.

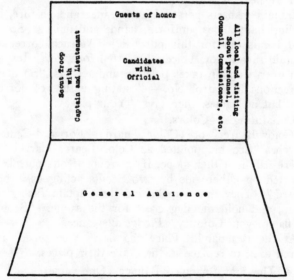

PLAN OF ASSEMBLY FOR GIRL SCOUT CEREMONIES

6. How to Conduct a Girl Scout Meeting

1. Calling to Order.

One long whistle blast: Silence (listen for orders).
Three short whistle blasts: "Fall In" three paces in
front of Captain.

Squad Formation:

5678   5678

1234   1234

0   0

Lieut. Capt.

Captain, lieutenant or patrol leader gives commands:

"Attention"   (See Scout Drill)

"Right Dress"

"Front"

2. Inspection.

Captain inspects personal appearance and posture, including hair, shoes, uniform, hands and nails. (Scouts
hold hands out for this purpose.)   At each correction
Captain says in low voice, "One step forward." Inspection over, Captain takes position and reports, "So many
corrections in Patrol No. —" stating nature of correction, but no names, then says, "Your places."

3. Saluting the Colors.

"Color Bearer" or (Color Guard) "Forward-Centers
March." Scout appointed as Color Bearer marches to
where flag is, either alone, if in troop of one patrol, or
escorted on either side by two Scouts acting as "Color
Guard." They draw up behind the Captain facing the
troop, and hold the flag erect for the salute.   "Scouts,
the flag of your Country.   Pledge allegiance."

At the command, "Place the flag," they wheel and
march back to replace it, then take their places.

4. The Star Spangled Banner (One verse)

5. Scout Promise, Salute.

6. Scout Laws, Repeat.

7. "Fall Out."

8. Business Meeting.

9. Discussion of one Scout Law.
10. Scout activities. Work for tests, games.

Closing Exercises

1. "Fall In."
2. America, or Battle Hymn of the Republic.
3. "Dismissed." Scouts salute Captain.

The form for opening and closing exercises suggested above takes only 20 minutes and is a practical method of ensuring uniformity when groups from different troops come together. Troops may use more elaborate forms, depending upon the amount of time which the girls wish to spend upon this type of work. For instance:

(a) In a troop composed of many patrols each Corporal forms her patrol and reports to the Lieutenant, who in turn reports to the Captain, "The company is formed," etc.

(b.) In dismissing, troops with a bugler may play "Taps" or may sing the same to words locally composed.

c. In some troops Corporals give commands. This is good because it emphasizes the patrol system.

But the form outlined is given as the minimum requirement, and troops using it need never feel at a loss in large rallies, for every ceremony necessary to express the Scout spirit with dignity is there.

No additions made locally should change the essential order of these exercises, all additions which are made being merely amplifications of it in detail, which may not be possible nor desirable in every community.

Business Meeting

The meeting opens with the Chairman, Secretary and Treasurer in place, with the Secretary at the right and the Treasurer at the left of the Chairman. The idea is to have every Scout in the troop learn to be the Chairman so that any and all could act in the capacity of a Business Chairman at any kind of meeting.

The meeting is called to order by the Chairman. "Will the meeting please come to order?"

The Chairman asks the Secretary to call the roll. "Will the Secretary call the roll? And will the Treasurer collect the dues?"

The Chairman calls for the Secretary's report. "Will the Secretary read the minutes of the last meeting?"

The Chairman calls for corrections of the minutes. "Are there any corrections?"

If there are none she says: "If not, the minutes stand approved."

If there are corrections the Chairman calls for further corrections, "Are there further corrections, etc. If not, the minutes stand approved as corrected."

Form of Secretary's report: "The regular meeting of Pansy Troop No. 5, held at the club house, on April 4th, was called to order at 3 o'clock. In the absence of the Chairman, Scout ——— took the chair. The minutes of the previous meeting were read and approved, dues collected amounted to ———. After ——— was discussed and voted upon, the meeting adjourned."

The Chairman calls for the Treasurer's report. "Will the Treasurer give her report?"

Form of Treasurer's report:

Balance on hand Jan. 1, 1919		$2.50
Members' dues	$1.00	
Fines	.30	1.30
Total		$3.80
Disbursements—		
Janitor	$1.00	$1.00
Balance on hand		2.80
Total		$3.80

The Chairman calls for corrections as before.

Then the Chairman calls for a discussion of old business, that is, anything discussed at previous meetings, that has been left undone or left to be decided at a later date. Any member of the meeting may bring up this old business, or the Chairman may start the discussion. "The business before the meeting is ————. What is your pleasure in regard to this," or "Will anyone make a motion?"

The member who wishes to make the motion says: "Madam Chairman, I move that—"

Another member who agrees to this says: "I second the motion."

If the motion is not seconded at once, the Chairman says: "Will anyone second the motion?"

After the motion has been moved and seconded the Chairman immediately states the question as, "It has been moved and seconded that the troop have a Rally on May 2. Are you ready for the question?" or "The question is now open for discussion." If no one rises, the Chairman proceeds to put the question. "All those in favor say aye, opposed no."

Then the Chairman says, "The motion is carried," or "The motion is not carried," as the case may be.

After the old business has been attended to, the Chairman calls for new business, saying, "Is there any new business to be discussed?"

The Chairman then dismisses the meeting by calling for a motion for adjournment.

Adjournment: "Will some one move that the meeting be adjourned?"

If this is moved and seconded it is not necessary to put it to a vote.

The Chairman says: "The meeting is adjourned.

SECTION VII

GIRL SCOUT CLASS TESTS

1. Tenderfoot Test

Before enrolling as a Tenderfoot a girl must be ten years old and have attended at least four meetings, covering at least one month in time. In addition to the material covered by the test, the Captain must have thoroughly explained to her the meaning of the Pledge of Allegiance to the Flag, the Scout Promise and the Scout Laws, and be sure of her general understanding of them as well as of her ability to respect them. This test is given by the Troop Captain.

Tenderfoot Test
Head

1. What are the Scout Promise and the Scout Laws? Give them as printed in Handbook.
2. Demonstrate the Scout Salute. When do Scouts use the Salute?
3. What are the Scout Slogan and the Scout Motto?
4. How is the respect due the American Flag expressed? Give the Pledge of Allegiance.
5. What are the words of the first and last stanza of The Star-Spangled Banner?
6. What is the full name of the President of the United States?
   What is the full name of the Governor of your State?
   What is the full name of the highest city, town or village official where you live?

Hands

7. Make or draw an American Flag, using correct proportions.

8. Tie the Reef, Bowline, Clove-hitch and Sheep-shank knots according to instructions given in Handbook, and tell use of each.

   Whip the end of a piece of rope. Indicate and define the three parts of a rope.

Helpfulness

9. Present record that you have saved or earned enough money to buy some part of the Scout uniform or insignia.

Recommended: Practice Setting-up Exercises, Scout positions and Tenderfoot Drill as shown in Handbook.

II. Second Class Test

While it is not necessary to devote any specified length of time to the training for this test, it is well to remember that if too long a time is taken, either because of lack of interest on the part of the Troop, or too inflexible standards on the part of the Captain, the possibility of winning Merit Badges is delayed and the feeling of steady progress is likely to be lost. The girls should be urged to keep together as a body, and reminded that regular attendance and team-work will be fairer to all. Quick learners can spend their extra time on private or group preparation for their Merit Badges, for which they become eligible as soon as they have passed the test, but not before.

This test may be given by the Troop Captain, or at her request by another Captain or competent authority, such as a registered nurse for bedmaking, health officer for First Aid, fire chief for fire prevention, and so forth.

Second Class Scout Test
Head

1. What is the history of the American Flag, and for what does it stand?

2. Describe six animals, six birds, six trees and six flowers.

3. What are the sixteen points of the compass? Show how to use a compass.

4. How may fire be prevented, and what should a Scout do in case of fire?

5. Send and receive the alphabet of the General Service or Semaphore Code.

6. Demonstrate ability to observe quickly and accurately by describing the contents of a room or a shop window, *or* a table with a number of objects upon it, after looking a short time, (not more than ten seconds); *or* describe a passer-by so that another person could identify him; *or* prove ability to make a quick rough report on the appearance and landmarks of a stretch of country, not to exceed one-quarter of a mile and to be covered in not more than five minutes. Report should include such things as ground surface, buildings in sight, trees, animals, etc.

   (Note: This territory must have been gone over by person administering the test. The test is not to be confused with the First Class requirement for map making. It may be made the object of a hike, and tested in groups or singly. Artificial hazards may be arranged.)

Hands

7. Lay and light a fire in a stove, using not more than two matches, or light a gas range, top burner, oven and boiler, without having the gas blow or smoke. Lay and light a fire in the open, using no artificial tinder, such as paper or excelsior, and not more than two matches.

8. Cook so that it may be eaten, seasoning properly,

one simple dish, such as cereal, vegetables, meat, fish or eggs in any other form than boiled.

9. Set a table correctly for a meal of two courses.

10. Make ordinary and hospital bed, and show how to air them.

11. Present samples of seaming, hemming, darning, and either knitting or crocheting, and press out a Scout uniform, as sample of ironing.

Health

12. Demonstrate the way to stop bleeding, remove speck from eye, treat ivy poisoning, bandage a sprained ankle, remove a splinter.

13. What do you consider the main points to remember about Health?

(Note: This is based on a knowledge of the section in the Handbook on Personal Health. It is suggested that a good way to demonstrate practically a knowledge of the main points is to keep for a month the Daily Health Record. This will incidentally complete one-third of the requirement for Health Winner's Badge.)

14. What are your height and weight, and how do they compare with the standard?

Helpfulness

15. Present to Captain or. Council the proof of satisfactory service to Troop, Church or Community.

16. Earn or save enough money for some part of personal or troop equipment.

Recommended: Practice Setting-up Exercises and Second Class Drill.

III. First Class Test

Work on this test should not be hurried. It is purposely made more thorough and more difficult, because it is designed for the older and longer trained Scout. The work for the Merit Badges, which all Scouts enjoy, should not be considered as interfering with this period, as such work is also the preparation for a possible Golden Eaglet degree. As a general rule, girls under fifteen are not likely to make thoroughly trained First Class Scouts, nor is the community likely to take their technical ability in the important subjects very seriously. The First Class Scout is the ideal Scout, of whom the organization has every right to feel proud; and ability to grasp a subject quickly and memorize details is not so important as practical efficiency, reliability and demonstrated usefulness to the Troop and the community. While the standard must not be set so high as to discourage the average girl, impatience to get through in any given time should not be encouraged, as this is not important.

First Class Scout Test
Head

1. Draw a simple map of one square mile of territory seen on hike or about camping place, according to directions in Handbook, using at least ten conventional map signs.
2. Demonstrate ability to judge correctly height, weight, number and distance, according to directions in Handbook.
3. Demonstrate ability to find any of the four cardinal points of the compass, using the sun or stars as guide.
4. Send and receive messages in the General Service or the Semaphore Code at the rate of thirty and sixty words a minute respectively.
5. Present the following Badges:
   Home Nurse

    First Aide
    Homemaker
and any two of the following:
    Child Nurse
    Health Winner
    Laundress
    Cook
    Needlewoman
    Gardener

Health

6. Take an overnight hike, carrying all necessary equipment and rations; *or*
Take a group of younger girls on a day time hike, planning the whole trip, including where and how to get the food, assigning to each girl her part in responsibility, directing transportation and occupation, and so forth; *or*
Be one of four to construct a practical lean-to; *or*
Demonstrate skating backwards, the outer edge, and stopping suddenly; *or*
Run on skiis; *or*
Show your acquaintance from personal observation of the habits of four animals or four birds.
7. Be able to swim fifty yards, *or* in case of inaccessibility to water, be able to shin up ten feet of rope, or in case of physical disability, earn any merit badge selected that involves out-of-door activity.

Helpfulness

8. Present a Tenderfoot trained by candidate.
9. Present to Captain or Council some definite proof of service to the community.
10. Earn or save one dollar and start a savings account in bank or Postal Savings, or buy Thrift Stamps.

Recommended: Practice Setting-up Exercises. Practice First Class Drill.

AMERICA THE BEAUTIFUL

Music by
WILL C. MACFARLANE
Municipal Organist, Portland, Maine

* Words by
KATHARINE LEE BATES

Maestoso

1. O beau - ti - ful for spa-cious skies, For am - ber waves of grain,
2. O beau - ti - ful for pil-grim feet, Whose stern, im-pas-sion'd stress
3. O beau - ti - ful for he-roes proved, In lib - er - at - ing strife.
4. O beau - ti - ful for pa-triot dream That sees be-yond the years

For pur - ple mountain majesties A-bove the fruited plain ! A-mer - i - ca ! A
A thor-oughfare for freedom beat A-cross the wil-der-ness ! A-mer - i-ca ! A
Who more than self their country loved, And mercy more than life ! Amer - i-ca ! A
Thine al a - bas-ter cit-ies gleam Undimm'd by human tears ! A-mer - i-ca ! A

mer - i - ca ! God shed His grace on thee, And crown thy good with brotherhood, From
mer - i - ca ! God mend thine ev'ry flaw, Con-firm thy soul in self-control, Thy
mer - i - ca ! May God thy gold re -fine, Till all success be no-ble-ness, And
mer - i - ca ! God shed His grace on thee, And crown thy good with brotherhood, From

REFRAIN Molto maestoso   ritard

sea to shining sea !   A, mer - i - ca ! A - mer -i-ca ! God shed His grace on thee !
lib er - ty in law !
ev - 'ry gain di-vine !
sea to shining sea !

SECTION VIII

WHAT A GIRL SCOUT SHOULD KNOW ABOUT THE FLAG

We take the star from Heaven, the red from our mother country, separating it by white stripes, thus showing we have separated from her, and the white stripes shall go down to posterity representing liberty.—George Washington.

The American flag is the symbol of the one-ness of the nation: when a Girl Scout salutes the flag, therefore, she salutes the whole country. The American Flag is known as "Old Glory," "Stars and Stripes," "Star-Spangled Banner," and "The Red, White and Blue."

The flag today consists of the field of red and blue stripes, with the blue field, sometimes known as the Union in the upper left-hand corner, with forty-eight white stars. The thirteen stripes stand for the thirteen original States—New Hampshire, Massachusetts, Rhode Island, Connecticut, New York, New Jersey, Pennsylvania, Delaware, Maryland, Virginia, North Carolina, South Carolina and Georgia. The stars stand for the States now in the Union.

The colors of the flag are red, representing valor; white, representing hope, purity and truth; blue, representing loyalty, sincerity and justice. The five-pointed star, which is used, tradition says, at Betsy Ross' suggestion, is the sign of infinity.

History of the American Flag

We think of ourselves as a young country, but we have one of the oldest written Constitutions under which a Nation operates, and our flag is one of the oldest in existence.

When our forefathers came from Europe to settle

in this country, which is now the United States, they brought with them the flags of their home countries, and planted them on the new territory in symbol of taking possession of it in the name of their liege kings and lands. Gradually the colonies came to belong to England, and the Union Jack became the flag of all, with the thirteen colonies represented by thirteen stripes and the Union Jack in the corner. This flag was known as the Grand Union or Cambridge Flag, and was displayed when Washington first took command of the army at Cambridge. It was raised on December 3, 1775, on the *Alfred,* flagship of the new little American Navy, by the senior Lieutenant of the ship, John Paul Jones, who later defended it gallantly in many battles at sea.

On July 4, 1776, the Declaration of Independence was signed in Philadelphia and the United Colonies dissolved all ties that bound them to England and became an independent nation—the United States. It was immediately necessary to adopt a new flag, as the new nation would not use the Union Jack. Tradition says that in the latter part of May, 1776, George Washington, Robert Morris and Colonel Ross called on Betsy Ross in Philadelphia to make the first flag, which they designed. They kept the thirteen stripes of the Colonial flag, but replaced the Union Jack by a blue field bearing thirteen stars, arranged in a circle.

The birthday of the flag was June 4, 1777, when Congress passed this resolution: Resolved: That the flag of the thirteen United States be thirteen stripes; alternate red and white; that the union be thirteen stars, white on a blue field, representing a constellation.

The first American unfurling the Stars and Stripes over a warship was John Paul Jones when he took command of the *Rayer* in June, 1777. Tradition says that this flag was made for John Paul Jones by the young ladies of Portsmouth Harbor, and that it was made for him from their own and their mothers' gowns. It was this flag, in February, 1778, that had the honor of receiving from France the first official salute accorded by a foreign nation to the Stars and Stripes.

It was first carried into battle at the Battle of Brandywine in September, 1777, when Lafayette fought with the Colonists and was wounded. This was the famous flag made out of a soldier's white shirt, a woman's red petticoat, and an officer's blue cloak. A famous flag now in the National Museum in Washington is the Flag of fifteen stars and stripes, which floated over Fort McHenry—near Baltimore—in the War of 1812, and which Francis Scott Key (imprisoned on a British ship) saw "by the dawn's early light" after watching through the night the "rocket's red glare, the bombs bursting in air" as proof that the fort had not fallen to the enemy. The next day he wrote "The Star-Spangled Banner."

It is said that peace has its victories as well as war, and Scouts will want to know that our flag flew from the first vessel ever propelled by steam—Robert Fulton's *Clermont*.

It was carried by Wilbur Wright on his first successful airplane flight in France.

It was the flag planted at the North Pole by Robert Peary.

It was the National emblem painted upon the first airplane to make the transatlantic flight, May, 1919.

At first, when states came into the Union, a new stripe and a new star were added to the flag, but it was soon evident that the added stripes would make it very unwieldly. So on April 4, 1818, Congress passed this act to establish the flag of the United States:

"Sec. 1. Be it enacted . . . That from and after the 4th of July next, the flag of the United States be thirteen horizontal stripes, alternate red and white; that the union have twenty stars, white on a blue field.

"Sec. 2. Be it further enacted, that, on admission of every new State into the Union, one star be added to the union of the flag; and that such addition shall take effect on the 4th day of July succeeding such admission."

In 1917 after the United States entered the World's War, the Stars and Stripes were placed with the flags of the Allies in the great English Cathedral of St. Paul's in London, and on April 20, 1917, the flag was hoisted beside the English flag over the House of Parliament as a symbol that the two great English-speaking nations of the world had joined hands in the cause of human brotherhood.

RESPECT DUE THE FLAG

1. The flag should be raised at runrise and lowered at sunset. It should not be displayed on stormy days or left out over night, except during war. Although there is no authoritative ruling which compels civilians to lower the flag at sundown, good taste should impel them to follow the traditions of the Army and Navy in this sundown ceremonial. Primarily, the flag is raised to be *seen,* and secondarily, the flag is something to be guarded, treasured, and so tradition holds it shall not be menaced by the darkness. To leave the flag out at night, unattended, is proof of shiftlessness, or at least carelessness.

2. At retreat, sunset, civilian spectators should stand at attention. Girl Scouts, if in uniform, may give their salute.

When the national colors are passing on parade or in

review, Scouts should, if walking, halt, and if sitting, rise and stand at attention. When the flag is stationary it is not saluted.

An old, torn, or soiled flag should not be thrown away, but should be destroyed, preferably by burning.

The law specifically forbids the use of and the representation of the flag in any manner or in any connection with merchandise for sale.

When the "Star-Spangled Banner" is played or sung, stand and remain standing in silence until it is finished.

The flag should, on being retired, never be allowed to touch the ground.

Regulations for Flying the Flag

1. The flag should not be raised before sunrise, nor be allowed to remain up after sunset.

2. In placing the flag at half mast, it should be raised first to full mast, and then lowered to the half mast position, from which it should again be raised to full mast before lowering.

3. The flag should never be draped.

4. When the flag is hung against a wall, the blue field should be in the upper left corner if the stripes are horizontal; in the upper right corner if the stripes are vertical.

5. In the case of flags hung across the street it is necessary to hang them by the points of the compass instead of right or left, because the right or left naturally varies according to whether the spectator is going up or down the street. When the flag is hung across a north and south street, the blue field should be toward the east, the rising sun, when across an east and west street, the field should be toward the north.

6. The flags of two or more nations displayed together should always be hung at the same level, and should be on separate staffs or halyards.

7. In the United States, when the American flag is carried with one other flag, it should be at the right. When it is carried with two other flags, it should be in the middle.

8. When the American flag is hung against a wall with other flags, it is placed at the spectator's right, if it is one of two; and in the middle, if it is one of three.

9. The flag at half mast is a sign of mourning.

10. The flag flown upside down is a signal of distress.

11. On Memorial Day, May 30, the flag is flown at half mast during the morning, and is raised at noon to full mast for the rest of the day.

Patriotic Songs for Girl Scouts

"The Star-Spangled Banner"

Oh, say, can you see, by the dawn's early light,
    What so proudly we hailed at the twilight's last
        gleaming,
Whose broad stripes and bright stars, through
        the perilous fight,
    O'er the ramparts we watched were so gallant-
        ly streaming!
And the rocket's red glare, the bombs bursting in
        air,
    Gave proof through the night that our flag was
        still there;
Oh! say, does that star-spangled banner yet
        wave,
    O'er the land of the free, and the home of the
        brave?

On that shore dimly seen through the mists of
        the deep,
    Where the foe's haughty host in dread silence
        reposes,

What is that which the breeze, o'er the towering
    steep,
  As it fitfully blows, now conceals, now dis-
    closes?
Now it catches the gleam of the morning's first
    beam,
  In full glory reflected now shines on the
    stream;
'Tis the star-spangled banner; Oh, long may it
    wave,
  O'er the land of the free, and the home of the
    brave!

O! thus be it ever, when freemen shall stand
  Between their loved homes and the war's deso-
    lation
Blessed with victory and peace, may the heav'n-
    rescued land
  Praise the power that hath made and preserved
    us a nation.
Then conquer we must, when our cause it is just,
  And this be our motto—"In God is our trust";
And the star-spangled banner in triumph shall
    wave
  O'er the land of the free, and the home of the
    brave.

              —*Francis Scott Key,* 1814.

The Star Spangled Banner was written in 1814 by
Francis Scott Key at the time of the bombardment of
Fort McHenry, near Baltimore, by the British. Key
had been sent to the British squadron to negotiate the
release of an American prisoner-of-war, and was detained there by the British during the engagement for
fear he might reveal their plans. The bombardment
lasted all through the night. In his joy the following
morning at seeing the American flag still flying over
Fort McHenry, Key wrote the first stanza of the *Star*

Spangled Banner on the back of an old letter, which he drew from his pocket. He finished the poem later in the day after he had been allowed to land. The poem was first printed as a handbill enclosed in a fancy border; but one of Key's friends, Judge Nicholson, of Baltimore, saw that the tune of *Anacreon in Heaven,* an old English drinking song, fitted the words, and the two were quickly united with astonishing success. The old flag which prompted the poem is still in existence; it was made by Mrs. Mary Pickersgill.

"America"

My country, 'tis of thee,
Sweet land of liberty,
   Of thee I sing;
Land where my fathers died,
Land of the Pilgrims' pride,
From every mountain side
   Let freedom ring.

My native country, thee,
Land of the noble free,
   Thy name I love;
I love thy rocks and rills,
Thy woods and templed hills;
My heart with rapture thrills
   Like that above.

Let music swell the breeze,
And ring from all the trees
   Sweet freedom's song;
Let mortal tongues awake,
Let all that breathe partake,
Let rocks their silence break,
   The sound prolong!

Our father's God, to Thee,
Author of liberty,
    To Thee we sing:
Long may our land be bright
With freedom's holy light;
Protect us by Thy might,
    Great God, our King.
            —Samuel F. Smith, 1832.

"America" was written in 1832 by Samuel Francis
Smith, a graduate of Harvard, at that time studying for
the ministry at Andover, Mass. The circumstances attending the writing of this hymn are told by the author in
the following letter:

    Newton Centre, Mass., June 5, 1887.
Mr. J. H. Johnson:

Dear Sir: The hymn "America" was not written with
reference to any special occasion. A friend (Mr. Lowell
Mason) put into my hands a quantity of music books in
the German language early in the year 1832—because, as
he said, I could read them and he couldn't—with the
request that I would translate any of the hymns and
songs which struck my fancy, or, neglecting the German
words, with hymns or songs of my own, adapted to the
tunes, so that he could use the music. On a dismal day
in February, turning over the leaves of one of these
music books, I fell in with the tune, which pleased me—
and, observing at a glance that the words were patriotic,
without attempting to imitate them, or even to read them
throughout, I was moved at once to write a song adapted
to the music—and "America" is the result. I had no
thought of writing a national hymn, and was surprised
when it came to be widely used. I gave it to Mr. Mason
soon after it was written, and have since learned that
he greatly admired it. It was first publicly used at a

Sabbath school celebration of Independence in Park Street Church, Boston, on the 4th of July, 1832.

Respectfully,

S. F. SMITH.

The tune of "America," which Samuel Smith took from a German song book, was originally a French air. This French air was borrowed in 1739 by an Englishman, Henry Carey, who recast it for the British national anthem, "God Save the King." Switzerland, Prussia and other German States, and the United States have used the music for their national hymns.

Letter and facts from The Encyclopedia Americana.

"Battle Hymn of the Republic"

Mine eyes have seen the glory of the coming of the Lord:
He is trampling out the vintage where the grapes of
    wrath are stored;
He hath loosed the fateful lightning of His terrible swift
    sword;
        His truth is marching on.

I have seen Him in the watch-fires of a hundred circling
    camps;
They have builded Him an altar in the evening dews and
    damps;
I can read his righteous sentence by the dim and flaring
    lamps:
        His day is marching on.

I have read a fiery gospel writ in burnish'd rows of steel:
"As you deal with my contemners, so with you my grace
    shall deal;
Let the Hero, born of woman, crush the serpent with his
    heel,
        Since God is marching on."

He has sounded forth the trumpet that shall never call
    retreat;
He is sifting out the hearts of men before His judgment-
    seat:
Oh, be swift my soul, to answer Him, be jubilant my
    feet!
        Our God is marching on.

In the beauty of the lilies Christ was born across the sea,
With a glory in His bosom that transfigures you and me;
As He died to make men holy, let us die to make them
    free,
        While God is marching on.
                —Julia Ward Howe.

How to Make an American Flag

The exact proportions of the American Flag have been
fixed by executive order; that is to say, by order of the
President, as have other features, such as the arrangement and position of the stars. The exact size of the
flag is variable, though the army has several regulation
sizes. The cut given below shows the dimensions of
one of the regulation army flags. The proportions fixed
by executive order on May 26, 1916, are as follows:

If the width of the flag be taken as the basis and
called 1, then

The length will be 1.9,

Each stripe will be 1/13 of 1,

The blue field will be .76 long and 7/13 of 1 wide.

Other features of the officially designed flag are as
follows: The top and bottom stripes are red. Each state
is represented by a five-pointed star, one of whose points
shall be directed toward the top of the flag.

Beginning with the upper left-hand corner and reading from left to right the stars indicate the states in order

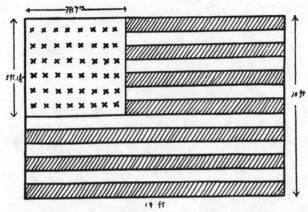

U. S. FLAG SHOWING OFFICIAL DIMENSIONS

To make a five-pointed star, take a square of cloth or paper and fold and cut in the way shown in the cut.

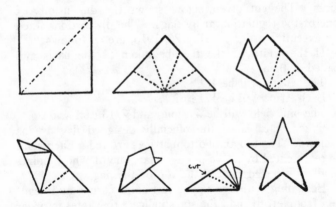

of their ratification of the Constitution and their admission to the Union. Find your State's star in the following list, and remember its number and line.

First Row

1—Delaware
2—Pennsylvania
3—New Jersey
4—Georgia

8—South Carolina
5—Connecticut
6—Massachusetts
7—Maryland

Second Row

11—New York
12—North Carolina
13—Rhode Island
14—Vermont

15—Kentucky
16—Tennessee
9—New Hampshire
10—Virginia

Third Row

17—Ohio
18—Louisiana
19—Indiana
20—Mississippi

21—Illinois
22—Alabama
23—Maine
24—Missouri

Fourth Row

25—Arkansas
26—Michigan
27—Florida
28—Texas

29—Iowa
30—Wisconsin
31—California
32—Minnesota

Fifth Row

33—Oregon
34—Kansas
35—West Virginia
36—Nevada

37—Nebraska
38—Colorado
39—North Dakota
40—South Dakota

Sixth Row

41—Montana
42—Washington
43—Idaho
44—Wyoming

45—Utah
46—Oklahoma
47—New Mexico
48—Arizona

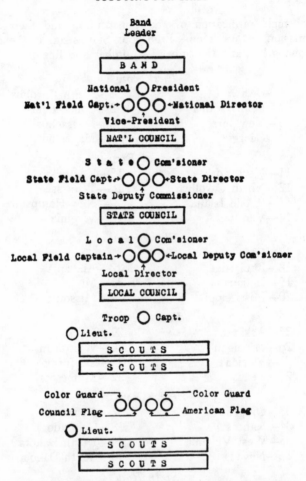

PARADE FORMATION FOR GIRL SCOUTS

The accompanying Cut 1 indicates a suggested formation
for patriotic, civic or Girl Scout parades when Scout officials
take part in the parade. It should be noted that the Scouts
are represented by a column of four ranks, the Color Guard

SIMPLE PARADE FORMATION

marching in the center of the column. Should a larger number of Scouts participate in the parade, the Color Guard must
be changed to a position in the center of the longer column.

Cut 2 indicates a more simple form of parade which has
been found of service and effectiveness. In this formation
the Color Guard follows the band or Scout buglers. The
local director or her representative marches directly behind
the Color Guard and is followed by the Scouts in column
formation, each double rank commanded by a captain, who
marches three paces in front of the front rank, and a lieutenant, who marches at the extreme left of the double rank.
one step ahead of the front rank. Front and rear ranks
march forty inches apart.

It is not usually possible, nor is it necessarily advisable, to
use one troop in forming a double rank. The important
thing is to have in each line the number of Scouts designated
by the person in charge of the parade. This number, determined by the width of the street and the number marching, will be either four, eight, twelve or sixteen. If girls of
the same height march together, the shorter preceding the
taller, the appearance of the column will be more uniform and
pleasing.

When Scout troop flags are used, they are carried in the
column at the extreme right.

GIRL SCOUT UNIFORM—ONE PIECE

SECTION IX

GIRL SCOUT DRILL

Although the simple exercises in opening and closing a meeting are the only formal work necessary for Scouts, the Scout Drill outlined in this Handbook is added for Captains as a suggestion for handling one or more Patrols in the club room, or on the street, in an orderly dignified manner.

Where the Troop and Captain are interested in this form of activity, it adds a great variety to the Scout meetings, and its value in giving an erect carriage, alert habit of obedience, and ability to think and act quickly are undoubted.

In case of rallies and parades it is practically the only way of handling large bodies of Scouts from different localities.

Every order and formation here recommended is taken from the United States Infantry Drill Regulations, and it is now possible for Captains in all localities to secure the assistance of some returned soldier glad to give a half hour occasionally to drilling the Scouts.

The simple formations selected have been divided into Tenderfoot, Second Class and First Class groups entirely for the convenience of the Captain; none of the work is too difficult for a Second Class Scout and there is nothing to prevent a Tenderfoot from taking all of it, if the troop should be particularly interested in drilling.

Commands are divided into two classes:

(a) The preparatory, to tell the Scout *what* to do, and

(b) The command of execution, to tell *how* to do it.

Tenderfoot Drill Schedule
"FALL IN"

At this command each Scout immediately takes her position in the Patrol to which she belongs, (the Captain having already assigned to each Scout her exact place) and without further order assumes the possition of *"Attention."*

'The position of *Attention* is: body and head erect, head, shoulders and pelvis in same plane, eyes front, arms hanging easily at the sides, feet parallel and about four inches apart; perfect silence to be maintained.

Patrol formation, two ranks (rows) of four Scouts each, forty inches between front and rear ranks. The patrol corresponds to the military unit of the squad.

Other patrols will fall in on the left of patrol No. 1 and on a line with it, in their numerical order. When assembled a troop of four patrols will be in the position indicated by the following diagram, and facing the captain.

5678	5678	5678	5678
1234	1234	1234	1234
	Lieut.	Capt.	

If the Captain prefers, and where there are only a few Scouts to be handled, they may be drawn up in a single rank facing the Captain. In either position they are now ready for the preliminaries of military drill.

1. *Right* (or left) *Dress.* 2. *Front.*

At the command *"Dress,"* whether to right or left, all Scouts place the left hand on the hip. Each Scout, except the base file, Scout on right or left end from whom the others take their alignment, when on or near the new line, executes *"Eyes Right!"* and taking steps of two or three inches, places herself so that her right arm rests lightly against the arm of the Scout on her right, and so that her eyes and shoulders are in line with those of the Scout on her right; the rear rank Scouts cover in file. The instructor verifies the alignment of both ranks from the right flank and orders up or back such Scouts as may be in rear or in advance of the line: only the Scouts designated move.

At the command *"Front,"* given when the ranks are aligned, each Scout turns her head and eyes to the front and drops the hand at her side.

To march the patrol or troop in column of twos, the preliminary commands would be as just given: 1. *Fall in.* 2. *Right Dress.* 3. *Front.*

The troop is then drawn up facing the Captain in two ranks as described. The Captain then commands:

1. *Right* (or left) *Face* (According to the direction in which the column is to proceed.)

2. *Forward.* 3. *March.*

At the command *"March,"* each Scout steps off smartly with the *left* foot.

Facings

To the flank: *"Right* (or left) *Face."*

Raise slightly the left heel and the right toe; face to the right, turning on the right heel, assisted by a slight pressure on the ball of the left foot; place the left foot by the side of the right. "Left Face" is executed on the left heel in the corresponding manner. Right (or left) Half Face is executed similarly, facing forty-five degrees.

To the rear: *About Face.*

Carry the toe of the right foot about half a foot length to the rear and slightly to the left of the left heel without changing the position of the left foot; face to the rear, turning to the right on the left heel and right toe; place the right heel by the side of the left.

Eyes Right or Left

1. *Eyes Right* (or left). 3. *Front.*

At the command "Right," turn the head to the right oblique, eyes fixed on the line of Scouts in, or supposed to be in, the same rank. At the command *"Front,"* turn the head and eyes to the front.

Being at halt, the commands for the different rests are as follows:

FALL OUT, REST, AT EASE and 1 PARADE, 2 REST.

At the command *Fall Out,* the Scouts may leave the ranks, but are required to remain in the immediate vicinity. They resume their former places, at attention at the command *"Fall In."*

At the command *"Rest"* each Scout keeps one foot in place, but is not required to keep silence or immobility.

At the command *"At Ease"* each Scout keeps one foot in place and is required to keep silence but not immobility.

1 Parade, 2 Rest.

Carry the right foot six inches straight to the rear, left knee slightly bent; clasp the hands, without constraint, in front of the center of the body, fingers joined, right hand uppermost, left thumb clasped by the thumb and forefinger of the right hand; preserve silence and steadiness of position.

To resume the attention: 1 *Squad (or Company)* 2 *Attention.*

Steps and Marchings

All steps and marchings executed from the halt, except right step, begin with the left foot.

The length of the full step in *"Quick Time,"* for a Scout is twenty inches, measured from heel to heel, and the cadence is at the rate of one hundred twenty steps per minute.

The length of the full step in *"Double Time,"* for a Scout, is about twenty-four inches; the cadence is at the rate of one hundred eighty steps per minute.

The instructor, when necessary, indicates the cadence of the step by calling "One, Two, Three, Four," or "Left,

Right, Left, Right," the instant the left and right foot, respectively, should be planted

All steps and marchings and movements involving march are executed in "Quick Time" unless the squad (or company) be marching in "Double Time."

Quick Time

Being at a halt, to march forward in quick time: *1 Forward, 2 March.*

At the command *"Forward,"* shift the weight of the body to the right leg, left knee straight.

At the command *"March,"* move the left foot smartly straight forward twenty inches from the right, sole near the ground, and plant it without shock; next, in like manner, advance the right foot and plant it as above; continue the march. The arms swing naturally.

Being at a halt, or in march in quick time, to march in double time; *1 Double time, 2 March.*

If at a halt, at the first command shift the weight of the body to the right leg. At the command *"March"* raise the forearms, fingers closed to a horizontal position along the waist line; take up an easy run with the step and cadence of double time, allowing a natural swinging motion to the arms.

If marching in quick time, at the command *"March,"* given as either foot strikes the ground, take one step in quick time, and then step off in double time.

To resume the quick time: *1 Quick Time, 2 March.*

At the command *March,* given as either foot strikes the ground, advance and plant the other foot in double time; resume the quick time, dropping the hands by the sides.

To Mark Time

Being in march: *1 Mark Time, 2 March.*

At the command *March,* given as either foot strikes the

ground, advance and plant the other foot; bring up the foot in rear and continue the cadence by alternately raising each foot about two inches and planting it on line with the other.

Being at a halt, at the command *March,* raise and plant the feet as described above.

The Half Step

1 Half Step, 2 March.

Take steps of ten inches in quick time, twelve inches in double time. *Forward, Half Step, Halt* and *Mark Time* may be executed one from the other in quick or double time.

To resume the full step from half step or mark time: *Forward March.*

Side Step

Being at halt or mark time: *1 Right (or left) Step, 2 March.* Carry and plant the right foot twelve inches to the right; bring the left foot beside it and continue the movement in the cadence of quick time.

The side step is used for short distances only and is not executed in double time.

Back Step

Being at a halt or mark time: *1 Backward, 2 March.* Take steps of twelve inches straight to the rear. The back step is used for short distances only and is not executed in double time.

To Halt

To arrest the march in quick or double time: *1 Squad* (or if the full troop is drilling, *Company), 2 Halt.*

At the command *Halt,* given as either foot strikes the ground, plant the other foot as in marching; raise and place the first foot by the side of the other. If in double time, drop the hands by the sides.

To March by the Flank

Being in march: *1 By the Right (or left) Flank, 2 March.*

At the command *March,* given as the right foot strikes the ground, advance and plant the left foot, then face to the right in marching and step off in the new direction with the right foot.

To March to the Rear

Being in march: *1 To the Rear, 2 March.*

At the command *March,* given as the right foot strikes the ground, advance and plant the left foot; turn to the right about on the balls of both feet and immediately step off with the left foot.

If marching in double time, turn to the right about, taking four steps in place, keeping the cadence, and then step off with the left foot.

Change Step

Being in march: *1 Change Step, 2 March.*

At the command *March,* given as the right foot strikes the ground, advance and plant the left foot; plant the toe of the right foot near the heel of the left and step off with the left foot.

The change on the right foot is similarly executed, the command *March* being given as the left foot strikes the ground.

SECOND CLASS DRILL

Fall In. (Described in Tenderfoot Drill.)

Count Off.

At this command all except the right file execute *Eyes Right,* and beginning on the right, the Scouts in each rank count *One, Two, Three, Four;* each turns her head and eyes to the front as she counts.

GIRL SCOUT UNIFORM—TWO PIECE

Alignments

1 Right (or left) Dress, 2 Front.   (Described in Tenderfoot Drill.)

To preserve the alignment when marching; *Guide Right (or left).* The Scouts preserve their intervals from the side of the guide, yielding to pressure on that side and resisting pressure from the opposite direction; they recover intervals, if lost, by gradually opening out or closing in; they recover alignment by slightly lengthening or shortening the step; the rear rank Scouts cover their file leaders at forty inches.

To Take Distance

(Formation for signalling or for setting-up exercises)

Being in line at a halt having counted off: 1 *Take Distance at four paces,* 2 *March;* 3 *Squad (or company), Halt.*

At the command *March,* each Scout in succession starting at four paces apart and beginning with No. 1 of the front rank, followed by 2, 3, 4 and 1, 2, 3, 4 of the rear rank, marches straight forward until the order Squad, Halt is given. The command *Halt* is given when all have their distances.

(Word to instructors: Where the floor space is limited it is advisable to have the Scouts take the half step in executing this formation or move at two paces.)

If more than one squad is in line, each squad executes the movement as above simultaneously.

Being at distances, to assemble the squad (or company):

1 *Assemble,* 2 *March.*

At the command *March,* No. 1 of the front rank stands fast; the other members move forward to their proper places in the line.

The Oblique March

For the instruction of the recruits, the squad being in column or correctly aligned, the instructor causes the Scouts to face half right and half left, points out to them their relative positions, and explains that these are to be maintained in the oblique march.

1 *Right (or left) Oblique,* 2 *March.*

At the command *March,* each Scout steps off in a direction forty-five degrees to the right of her original front. She preserves her relative position, keeping her shoulders parallel to those of the guide, and so regulates her steps that the ranks remain parallel to their original front.

At the command *Halt* the Scouts face to the front.

To resume the original directions: 1 *Forward,* 2 *March.*

The Scouts half face to the left in marching and then move straight to the front.

To Turn on Moving Pivot

Begin in line: 1 *Right (or left) Turn,* 2 *March.*

(This applies to the single squad; if the whole troop is drilling and is in column of squads, or twos, the command would be: 1 *Column Right (or left),* 2 *March.)*

The movement is executed by each rank successively and on the same ground. At the second command, the pivot Scout of the front rank faces to the right in marching and takes the half step; the other Scouts of the rank oblique to the right until opposite their places in line, then execute a second right oblique and take the half step on arriving abreast of the pivot Scout. All glance toward the marching flank while at half step and take the full step without command as the last Scout arrives on the line.

Right (or left) Half Turn is executed in a similar manner. The pivot Scout makes a half change of direction to the right and the other Scouts make quarter changes in obliquing.

To Turn on a Fixed Pivot

Being in line, to turn and march: 1 *Squad Right (or left),* 2 *March.*

At the second command, the right flank Scout in the front rank faces to the right in marching and marks time; the other front rank Scouts oblique to the right, place themselves abreast of the pivot, and mark time. In the rear rank the third Scout from the right, followed in column by the second and first, moves straight to the front until in the rear of her front rank Scout, when all face to the right in marching and mark time; the other number of the rear rank moves straight to the front four paces and places herself abreast of the Scout on her right. Scouts on the new line glance toward the marching flank while marking time and, as the last Scout arrives on the line, both ranks execute *Forward March* without further command.

Being in line to turn and halt: 1 *Squad Right (or left),* 2 *March,* 3 *Squad,* 4 *Halt.*

The third command is given immediately after the second. The turn is executed as prescribed in the preceding paragraph except that all Scouts, on arriving on the new line mark time until the fourth command is given, when all halt. The fourth command should be given as the last Scout arrives on the line.

Being in line to turn about and march: 1 *Squad Right (or left) About,* 2 *March.*

At the second command the front rank twice executes Squad Right initiating the second Squad Right when the Scout on the marching flank has arrived abreast of the rank. In the rear rank the third Scout from the right, followed by the second and first in column, moves straight to the front until on the prolongation of the line to be occupied by the rear rank; changes direction to the right; moves in the new direction until in the rear of her front rank Scout, when all face to the right in marching, mark time, and glance toward the marching flank. The fourth Scout marches on the left of the third to her new position; as she arrives on the line, both ranks execute *Forward March* without command.

FIRST CLASS DRILL

On right (or left) Into Line.

Being in columns of squads, to form line on right or left; 1 *On right (or left) into Line,* 2 *March,* 3 *Company,* 4 *Halt,* 5 *Front.*

At the first command the leader of the leading unit commands: *Right Turn.* The leaders of the other units command: *Forward,* if at a halft. At the second command the leading unit turns to the right on moving pivot. The command *Halt* is given when the leading unit has advanced the desired distance in the new direction; it halts; its leader then commands: *Right Dress.*

The units in the rear continue to march straight to the front; each, when opposite its place on the line, executes *Right Turn* at the command of its leader; each is halted on the line at the command of its leader, who then commands: *Right Dress.* All dress on the first unit on the line.

If executed in double time, the leading squad marches in double time until halted.

Front Into Line.

Being in columns of squads, to form line to the front: *Right (or left) Front Into Line,* 2 *March,* 3 *Company,* 4 *Halt,* 5 *Front.*

At the first command the leaders of the units in the rear of the leading one command: *Right Oblique.* If at a halt, the leader of the leading unit command: *Forward* At the second command the leading unit moves straight forward; the rear units oblique as indicated. The command *Halt* is given when the leading unit has advanced the desired distance; it halts; its leader then commands: *Left Dress.* Each of the rear units, when opposite its place in line, resumes the original direction at the command of its leader; each is halted on the line at the command of its leader, who then commands: *Left Dress.* All dress on the first unit in line.

To Diminish the Front of a Column of Squads

Being in column of squads: 1 *Right (or left) By Twos,* 2 *March.* At the command *March,* all files except the two right files of the leading squad execute *In Place Halt;* the two right files of the leading squad oblique to the right when disengaged and follow the right files at the shortest practicable distance. The remaining squads follow successively in like manner.

Being in columns of twos: 1 *Right (or left) By File,* 2 *March.* At the command *March,* all files evecute *In Place Halt,* except the right file of the leading two oblique successively to the right when disengaged and each follows the file on its right at the shortest practicable distance. The remaining twos follow successively in like manner.

Being in column of files of twos, to form column of squads; or being in column of files, to form column of twos: 1 *Squads (Twos) Right (or left) Front Into Line,* 2 *March.*

At the command *March,* the leading file or files halt. The remainder of the squad, or two, obliques to the right and halts on line with the leading file or files. The remaining squads or twos close up and successively form in the rear of the first in like manner.

The movement described in this paragraph will be ordered *Right* or *Left,* so as to restore the files to their normal relative positions in the two or squad.

SECTION X

SIGNALLING FOR SCOUTS

A. GENERAL SERVICE CODE

The General Service Code, given herewith, also called the Continental Code and the International Morse Code, is used by the Army and Navy, and for cabling and wireless telegraphy. It is used for visual signalling by hand, flag, Ardois lights, torches, heliograph, lanterns, etc., and for sound signalling with buzzer, whistle, etc.

The American Morse Code is used for commercial purposes only, and differs from the International Morse in a few particulars. A Scout need not concern herself with it because it would only be used by the Scout who eventually becomes a telegrapher, and for this purpose the Western Union Company offers the necessary training.

Wig Wag Signalling

GENERAL SERVICE CODE

The flag used for this signalling is square with a smaller square of another color in the center. It may be either white with the smaller square red, or red with the smaller square white. A good size for Scout use is 24 inches square with a center 9 inches square, on a pole 42 inches long and one-half inch in diameter.

There are but three motions with the flag and all start from, and are completed by, return to position, which means the flag held perpendicularly and at rest directly in front of the signaller.

Signaller should stand erect, well balanced on the arches of the feet. The butt of the flag stick is held lightly in the right hand; the left hand steadies and directs the flag at a distance from six to twelve inches above the right on the stick. The length of the stick will

determine the position of the left hand; the longer the stick the further apart must the hands be placed in order to obtain the best balance.

DOT: To make the dot, swing the flag down to the right until the stick reaches the horizontal and bring it back to Position.

DASH: To make the dash, swing the flag to the left until it reaches the horizontal and bring it back to Position.

INTERVAL: The third position is made by swinging the flag down directly in front and returning to Position.

In order to keep the flag from "fouling" when making these motions, make a sort of figure 8 with the point of the stick. A slight turn of the wrist accomplishes this result and becomes very easy after a little practice. Beginners should master the three motions of the flag, exaggerating the figure 8 motion before they attempt to make letters. *It is also best to learn the code*

THE GENERAL SERVICE CODE

(The International Morse or Continental)

Uses: Commercial wireless, submarine cables, Army and Navy. Methods: flags by day, torches, lanterns, flashlight, searchlight, by night, whistle, drum, bugle, tapping.

A .—	M ——	Y —.——
B —...	N —.	Z ——..
C —.—.	O ———	1 .————
D —..	P .——.	2 ..———
E .	Q ——.—	3 ...——
F ..—.	R .—.	4 ....—
G ——.	S ...	5 .....
H	T —	6 —....
I ..	U ..—	7 ——...
J .———	V ...—	8 ———..
K —.—	W .——	9 ————.
L .—..	X —..—	0 —————

Period	Colon ———...
Comma .—.—.—	Semicolon —.—.—.
Quotation Marks .—..—.	Interrogation ..——..

A convenient form for learning the letters is as follows:

DOTS	DASHES
E .	T —
I ..	M ——
S ...	O ———
H	

OPPOSITES

A .—	—. N	G ——.		.—— W	
B —...	...— V	F ..—.		.—.. L	
D —..	..— U	Y —.——		——.— Q	

SANDWICH LETTERS

K —.—   P .——.   X —..—   R .—.

LETTERS WITH NO OPPOSITES

Z ——..   C —.—.   J .———

before attempting to wig wag it, so that the mind will be free to concentrate upon the technique or correct managing of the flag.

Make no pause between dots and dashes in making a letter, but make a continuous swing from right to left, or left to right. A pause at Position indicates the completion of a letter.

One Interval (Front) indicates the completion of a word.

Two Intervals indicate the completion of a sentence.

Three Intervals indicate the completion of a message.

Do not try for speed. In all signalling, accuracy is the important thing, for unless the letters are accurately made they cannot be easily read, and the message will have to be repeated. Fall into a regular easy rhythm in sending. Speed comes with practice.

Signalling with a Flash Light: Use a short flash for the dot and a long steady flash for the dash. Pause the length of three dots between letters, and the length of five dots between words. A still longer pause marks the end of a sentence.

Signalling by Whistle: Use a short blast for the dot, and a long steady blast for the dash. Indicate the end of a letter, a word, and a sentence by the same pauses as explained in Flash Light Signalling.

Signalling with a Lantern: The motions used in signalling with a lantern are somewhat like those of the wig wag flag. For Position hold the lantern directly in front of the body; for the dot swing it to the right and back to Position; for the dash swing it to the left and back to Position; and for Interval move it down and up in a vertical line directly in front. A stationary light should be placed on the ground before the feet as a point of reference for the various motions.

B. SEMAPHORE SIGNALLING
SEMAPHORE CODE

The semaphore is a machine with two arms which may be moved into various positions to make letters. The semaphore code shown in the accompanying picture may also be employed by a person using two flags. It is the quickest method of flag signalling but is available for comparatively short distances, seldom over a mile, unless extra large flags are employed or there is some extraordinary condition of background or atmosphere.

The semaphore code is not adapted to as many uses as is the general service code, but for quick signalling over comparatively short distances, it is preferable in every way.

The regulation flag is 18 inches square, either divided diagonally into two triangles of white and red, or square of white with small square of red in the center, or red with small square of white. These flags are fastened on poles 24 inches long and ½ inch in diameter.

The flags must be carefully held so that the sticks make, as it were, a continuation of the arm bone; a bent wrist will cause the flags to make an entirely different angle, and consequently a different letter from the one intended.

Swing the arms smoothly and without hesitation from one letter to another. Hold each letter long enough to make it clear to the person receiving it. Every word begins and ends with "intervals," the hands crossed downward in front of the body, arms nearly straight, right hand always over the left.

Indicate the end of a sentence by one "chip-chop" made by holding both flags to the right, horizontally, and moving them up and down several times; not together, but one flag going down as the other comes up, making the "chopping" motion.

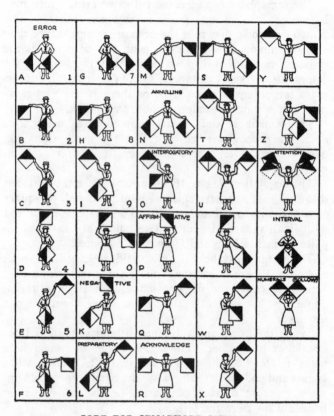

CODE FOR SEMAPHORE SIGNALLING

From the very beginning practice reading as well as sending. It is harder to do and requires more practice. Instructors should always face the class in giving a lesson; in this way the pupil learns to read at the same time as she is learning to make the letters. This principle applies to all visual signalling.

Whistle Signals

1. One blast, "Attention;" "Assemble" (if scattered.)
2. Two short blasts, "All right."
3. Three short, one long blast, calls Patrol Leaders
4. Alternate long and short blasts, "Mess Call."

Hand Signals

These signals are advisable when handling a troop in a street where the voice cannot be readily heard, or in marching the troop into some church, theatre, or other building where a spoken command is undesirable.

Forward, March:

Carry the hand to the shoulder; straighten and hold the arm horizontally, thrusting it in the direction of the march. (This signal is also used to execute quick time from double time.)

Halt:

Carry the hand to the shoulder; thrust the hand upward and hold the arm vertically.

Double Time, March:

Carry the hand to the shoulder, rapidly thrust the hand upward the full extent of the arm several times.

Squads Right, March:

Raise the arm laterally until horizontal; carry it to a vertical position above the head and swing it several times between the vertical and horizontal positions.

Squads Left, March:

Raise the arm laterally until horizontal; carry it downward to the side and swing it several times between the downward and horizontal positions.

Change Direction or Column Right (Left) March:

The hand on the side toward which the change of direction is to be made is carried across the body to the opposite shoulder, forearm horizontal; then swing in a horizontal plane, arm extended, pointing in the new direction

Assemble:

Raise the arm vertically to its full extent and describe horizontal circles.

SECTION XI
THE SCOUT AIDE
Introduction.

The six following subjects, Home Economics, Child Care, First Aid, Home Nursing, Public Health, and Personal Health are grouped together, and for proficiency in all of them a special badge called "Scout Aide" is awarded.

This badge will probably be regarded by the outside world as the most important decoration the Girl Scouts can win, and all Scouts who will try for it should realize that those who wear it will represent the organization in a very special sense and will be eager to prove their practical knowledge and ability in the important subjects it stands for.

No young child could pretend to represent all this medal stands for. Any grown girl or woman should be proud to own it.

Practical knowledge of Personal Health, Public Health and Child Care will add to the efficiency and happiness of this nation, and the women of today have a better chance to control these things than ever before.

Home Nursing and First Aid will save lives for the nation in the two great emergencies of illness and accident.

Household Economics, the great general business and profession of women, if it is raised to the level of the other great businesses and professions, and managed quickly, efficiently and economically will cease to be regarded as drudgery and take its real place among the arts and sciences.

When the girls of today have learned to do this, the women of tomorrow will be spared the criticism of waste and extravagance that our nation has had to bear. If Girl Scouts make good as far as this medal is concerned and become real "Scout Aides" the Scout reputation is secure.

1. THE HOME MAKER
BY SARA LOUISE ARNOLD
Dean Simmons College

The Keeper of the House. Every Girl Scout knows that good homes make a country great and good; so every woman wants to understand home-making. Of course that means "keeping" a house; and of course that means that Girl Scouts should try for the Housekeeper Merit Badge, the "Home Maker."

Now "making a home" doesn't mean just having it, owning it and holding its key. It means making it a good place to live in, or helping to make it so. This sounds like the House that Jack built; but all this belongs to the making of a home.

Planning Your House. When you plan a house of your own you must think what it needs most. You would choose, first of all, to have abundant air, fresh and clean; a dry spot where dampness will not stay; sunshine at some time of day in every room of the house, which you can have if your house faces southeast; and you must be able to get a good supply of pure water. You will want to make your house warm in the winter and cool in the summer, so you will look out for windows, doors and porches.

Think what must be done in a house: eating, sleeping, working, resting, by the whole family. How many rooms must you have? Draw a plan of some house in your neighborhood that seems good to live in. Make up your mind what you like best in that house.

Furnishing. Then houses must be furnished with the things that the family needs. The furniture will be for use. You must ask every piece what it is good for. What will you do with it? Could you get along without it? Some things you would use constantly, others once in a while. Which would you get first if you were planning carefully? How much would it cost to furnish the house for which you have drawn the plans: to furnish the kitchen, the living room, the bed rooms? Make a list of the furniture *needed* (not just *wanted*) for each room with the cost of each piece.

It is worth while for you to go to look at furniture in stores and to think about buying it. Then you will discover that a piece of furniture that looks well in the store might not look at all well in your house, for furniture must "suit" the house and the room into which it goes. It must "fit," we say. No other furniture will do. So the Girl Scout will make up her mind what will fit her house; and of course this means also what will fit the family purse. For the keeper of the house must not let into her house one single thing that she cannot afford to buy. She will take pride in that.

So when you make a list of furniture—with its price— make sure that everything you choose, suits, or fits, *your* house.

The Cellar. Most houses are built over cellars, for purposes of sanitation, heating and water supply, as well as for storage.

The Girl Scout who lives in the country probably knows all about cellars for they are much needed there.

The city girl may live in an apartment and may never think of a cellar.

Look at the cellars of two or three houses. How are they built? Did you plan for one in your house?

The cellar should be well ventilated, having light as well as air. Its windows should be screened; the floor should be dry and if possible made of cement; the walls should be whitewashed. Ashes should be kept in a galvanized iron barrel, to prevent fire.

A cellar should be a clean place, corners and all.

The Kitchen. The kitchen is a work-shop; it should be sunny and airy.

Look out for windows to let in the fresh air and sunshine. And while you are thinking of windows, be sure that they can open at the top and bottom to let sweetness in, and drive bad odors out.

Your kitchen should hold things that are necessary, and nothing else. It should be easy to keep clean, having painted walls, and the floor should be of hard pine or else covered with linoleum. When a Girl Scout takes care of the kitchen she is in honor bound to keep all the corners clean and to leave no dust nor crumbs of food anywhere about. She will take great pains to keep flies out of the kitchen and so will have her windows screened.

A good kitchen is provided with a sink and if possible with running water; and it must have a good stove, with a place for keeping wood or coal if either is used.

The Kitchen Floor. The floor of the kitchen should be made of hard wood. Maple or hard pine will make a good floor. A hard-wood floor can be dressed with shellac or with oil. The wood absorbs this dressing so that water will not soak in. A floor which has been shellacked should be wiped with warm water. Not much water will be needed. The oiled floor can be wiped and dried, then oiled lightly from time to time.

Linoleum or oilcloth may be used to cover an old floor. If the floor is rough it should be made even by planing before the linoleum is put down, and the cracks should be filled. If you can't get linoleum you can paint your floor with a hard floor paint. Be sure to get a paint that dries hard. The linoleum should be frequently washed with warm water and soap and then rinsed carefully before it is dried.

The Kitchen Stove. The chief business of the kitchen stove is to provide heat for cooking. It must hold a fire, and so must be made of something which will not burn. Stoves are usually made of iron. Fire will not burn without air, so a place must be arranged to let air into the stove, and just enough to make the fire burn clearly and furnish the right amount of heat. That is what the front dampers or slides are for. The fuel, wood or coal, is held in the fire-box. The heated air makes the top of the stove hot for frying, broiling or boiling, and the oven hot for baking.

The smoke and gases from the fire must not come out into the room to blind our eyes or suffocate us; the chimney is built to take care of the smoke and gases, and there must be a way for them to get into the chimney; the stove pipe is for this. But the game you have to play with your stove is to let the smoke and gases run up chimney, but to save all the heat you can for the work to be done. So your stove is supplied with dampers. When the fire is new, and there is much smoke or gas, you open the damper into the stove pipe, and in the stove pipe. Try to get a picture of the way the heated air goes from the fire-box up into the chimney. We call this direct draft. Of course a great deal of heat runs away through the chimney, and so your fuel is wasted. Now if you want to save heat, and particularly if you want to bake, and must have a hot oven, you will close the oven damper that has made the short easy way into the stovepipe. Then the heated air must find another way to get to the chimney, and it has to go around the oven to do this. While the hot air is finding its way around the oven, it heats it, ready for your baking. We call this the "indirect draft." Look over your kitchen stove and see how this happens. Take off the covers, open every door, and examine every part.

Stoves must be carefully managed. The fires must burn readily and the cooking must be done with the least possible amount of wood or coal. This means a clean stove, free from ashes and with a clear draft. Wood or coal will burn freely in the air. They will stop burning if there is no draft.

Learn to manage your draft. Remember that stoves are made with a damper, in order to control the current of hot air. If the oven damper is closed this heated air *must* pass over and around the oven before it gets to the chimney and so heat the oven. If it is open the hot air can immediately escape up the chimney.

When starting the fire leave the damper open. As soon as it is burning well, close it so that the oven will be heated. Your stove should also have a damper in the pipe, to save the heat which would otherwise run up the chimney. If there is none, have one put in. There are also dampers or slides in front of the stove to control the amount of air going in.

The housekeeper must learn how to manage her stove ; she must get acquainted with it, for every stove has its own way. Draw a picture or plan of the stove that you know best. See if you can tell plainly how to build a fire in your stove. If you use natural gas or a kerosene stove tell how that should be managed.

Gas and Oil Stoves. Cooking may be done on an iron stove with either coal or wood as fuel, or the stove may be planned for burning gas or kerosene. The coal fire must be fed several times a day with coal and the ashes must be removed to keep the fire burning clearly. Wood burns out quickly and must be replaced often. Both wood and coal stoves mean almost constant care for the housekeeper.

Gas gives less trouble. It comes in pipes from outside the house. This means that somebody else—the gas company—provides the supply. You turn on the gas when you want to use it and turn it off, if you are wise and thoughtful, the moment it is not needed. The gas company measures the amount of gas that you use by its meter, and you pay for every bit that you burn or waste. The important thing, then, is to use as little gas as possible in order to pay for as little as possible. You would rather pay twenty-five cents for a thrift stamp, than for gas that had burned simply because you had forgotten to turn it off. Be sure that gas is turned completely off at all places and never have a low light burning, as the flame may be blown out and the unburned gas escape. This would be dangerous and might even kill persons in the house.

The kerosene stove may be used instead of a gas stove in houses which are not piped for a gas supply. If wicks are used they must be carefully trimmed, so that they will be clean and even. A kerosene stove needs frequent cleaning. It should be kept free from dust and from drippings of oil.

The Fireless Cooker

When a Girl Scout gets to thinking about all the work to be done in a kitchen she will ask some very important questions. How much work is to be done? How long does it take to do it? Can time be saved by doing it in a better way? How can I save labor. Save time? Save money?

The Girl Scout will find the answers one at a time, if she does her own work. And if you do your own work you will at once call for a fireless cooker. The name sounds impossible, for you have always cooked with a stove, and, of course, a fire. How can you cook without a fire?

The women of Norway taught us how. When they went out to work in the fields or on the farm they took the hot kettle of soup off the stove and hid it away in a hay box. The hay kept the heat in the kettle instead of letting it escape; so the soup kept on cooking, and when the women came home from their work in the fields there it was, all steaming hot and ready for dinner.

Everyone has noticed how some things carry or conduct heat and other things don't. That's why we use a "holder," when handling a hot dish or stove lifter or tea-pot. The "holder" does not carry the heat to the hand; it keeps it away. So the hay packed around the hot kettle kept the heat in the kettle, refusing to "conduct" it away. Therefore the soup went on cooking.

Your English cousins use a "cosy" to cover the hot tea-pot or coffee pot. This "cosy" is made of quilted cotton; and looks like the quilted hood that your great-grandmother used to have. This keeps the heat in the tea or coffee, so that you can have a second cup for the asking.

America was slow to learn from her thrifty cousins, but at last she adopted the fireless cooker; and this is what it does:

The fireless cooker, a case packed with some material which refuses to conduct heat, is used to continue the cooking of foods after they have been made hot on the stove. When securely covered in the cooker they will go on cooking for several hours because the heat is retained by the protecting case. A Girl Scout may buy a fireless cooker, paying from $5 to $25 for it, or she may make one, which will cost less than one dollar. Of course this is a challenge to make one. You may be very sure that if you make a fireless cooker you will understand all about it. To make a fireless cooker you will need:

(1) *A cooker or container,* which should be an agate pail with a close fitting cover. No sides should be straight up and down, the bottom just as big as the top. You can choose a small one holding two quarts, or a gallon pail which would be large enough for anything an ordinary family would be likely to cook.

(2) *A case,* which must be at least eight inches wider than your container, for the packing must extend at least four inches around the pail on every side. You may use a round case like a big wooden candy pail, which you can usually get at the ten cent store for ten cents; or it may be a galvanized iron can with a cover like the one ordinarily used for garbage; or it may be a box shaped like a cube.

(3) For packing you may use crumpled newspapers tightly packed in; or ground cork, which is used in packing Malaga grapes, is fine, and you may be able to get it from a fruit store. Excelsior is good, and perhaps you will find that in the shed in some packing case; while, if you live in the country, you may be able to get Spanish moss. This should be dried, of course. And then there is hay—which our Norwegian cousins use.

Let us try paper. Pack the box or can four inches deep, with crumpled paper, making a very even layer. Put a piece of pasteboard much larger than the bottom of your pail upon this layer and set your pail in the middle of it. Now pack the paper tightly around the pail up to the very top, using a stick of wood or mallet to press it down.

Now you must make a cloth cover for your pail in the shape of a tall hat. The rim of the hat must reach out to the edges of your case and be tacked there. Take out your pail, fit this cloth cover into the hole and tack the edge evenly to the box.

You must now make a cushion to fill the rest of the box, packing it full of the crumpled paper. Make hinges for the lid of your box and put some sort of fastener on the front to keep the lid down tight.

Now you have your fireless cooker. When your oatmeal or your stew, or your chicken, or your vegetables have boiled ten or fifteen minutes on the stove in your agate pail, clap on its cover, set it into the nest, push the cushion into the top of the cooker, clamp down the lid, and your work is done, for the cooking will go merrily on all alone by itself in your fireless cooker.

While you are making your fireless cooker, remember that the thermos bottle is made on the same principle. And remember, too, that your non-conducting packing material will keep heat out just as well as it keeps heat in. In the summer time you may wish to keep your ice cream cold for a while in your fireless cooker. Perhaps you will see how this might help in a hot summer's day and what a comfort a fireless cooker might prove in a sick room.

The Ice Chest. How It Is Made

In taking care of food we must be provided with a cool place, for the storage of milk, butter, cream, and all cooked food that may spoil. In summer this is especially important; in an apartment, and in most city houses the ice chest is needed all the year around; in the country, it is needed only in the warm months.

The ice chest is built much as the fireless cooker is made. Its case is usually made of wood, its packing material must be non-conducting, and its lining must be some smooth surface through which water cannot pass. Some ice chests are lined with zinc and some with porcelain tiles. In some ice chests, food and ice are kept in the same box, which usually opens at the top; in other chests there is a separate chamber for the ice. From the ice chamber a drain pipe carries away the water which drips from the melting ice.

Every ice chest must be kept clean and sweet. It should be looked over every day and washed carefully at least once a week. No crumbs of food should be left on the shelves. If you spill anything, wipe it up *clean* at once.

The drain pipe must be kept clean. A long wire brush is used for this. If you are buying an ice box, get one with removable pipes, which are easily cleaned. If there is any odor from the chest, scald with water and soda, a teaspoonful of soda to a quart of water. Rinse with fresh cold water.

If your ice chest drips into a pan which must be emptied daily, have a regular time for emptying it. An overflowing pan in an apartment may damage the ceiling below. If it drips into a pan which drains itself, be sure that the drain is kept clean and the entrance to the pipe unclogged. Clean the drip pan whenever you clean the ice chest.

It is a good plan to keep food in closed containers like fruit jars. Wide dishes take up too much space. Containers should be tall rather than broad.

Put no hot dishes in the ice box; it wastes the ice.

The Iceless Refrigerator

An "iceless refrigerator" sounds like a "fireless cooker." This is an arrangement made to keep food cool in the summer when there is no ice. A wooden cage with shelves is covered with a cloth cover and placed near a window or out of doors. If in the house it should stand in a large pan to prevent the dripping of water on the shelf or floor.

A piece of the cloth cover should rest in a pan of water. If this is not convenient a strip of cloth can be sewed to the cover endwise and this piece should be placed in a pan or bowl of water which should be set on top of the cage. This water will be sucked throughout the cloth cover of the refrigerator until it is wholly wet. As the water evaporates from the cover the air inside the refrigerator is cooled.

The iceless refrigerator works well on days when dry air is moving about. It does not do well on damp, quiet days.

Another simple refrigerator which does very well for a little milk or a pat of butter is a clean, earthen flower pot, turned upside down in a shallow pan of water. This will keep very cool the food which it covers.

The Kitchen Sink

Next to the stove, the sink is the most important piece of kitchen furniture.

The best sinks are of enamel or are made of porcelain. They have a fine wire drainer so that nothing solid will go into the trap and plug the pipes. The Girl Scout uses boiling water, and plenty of it, to flush the sink. She takes pains that no grease gets into the drain to harden there. When grease is accidentally collected, soda and hot water will wash it away, but it should never collect in the pipes.

The Keeper of the House takes pride in a perfectly clean sink.

Taking Care of the House and the Things in It

Taking care of a house and its furniture means keeping the house clean, neat, and orderly, and keeping everything in good repair. This means a great deal of thought on the part of the Keeper of the House. For there are many sorts of work to be done, and there is a right way of doing every bit of it. By paying attention a Girl Scout may learn very fast, and become very helpful and competent.

First, there's the Dish Washing.

Dish Washing

In making ready for dish washing scrape every plate carefully to remove crumbs that would get into the dish water. Try using crumpled tissue paper to remove milk, grease, or crumbs before the dishes are put into the pan. Save tissue paper, and paper napkins for this.

Pile in separate piles, all dishes of each sort; wash first glass, then silver, then cups, saucers, plates, then the rest; do not put bone, ivory or wooden handles of knives into the water. Use hot water and soap for dish washing, then rinse with clean hot water.

Dish towels should be cleansed after every dish washing; wash clean in hot soapy water, then rinse all the soap away in clean water. Cooking utensils should soak in cold water until time for dish washing, unless they can be washed as soon as used.

Use a tray for carrying dishes to the closet or pantry instead of traveling with a handful back and forth. Strain the dish water before pouring it down the sink. Be sure that no greasy water is put into the sink. Let the grease rise and cool; skim it off and dispose of it after the dishes are washed.

Taking Care of Rooms

Keeping a house in order means having everything in its place in every room. It means sweet, fresh air in every room; it means removal of dust and litter. A good housekeeper "tidies" her rooms as she goes along, always

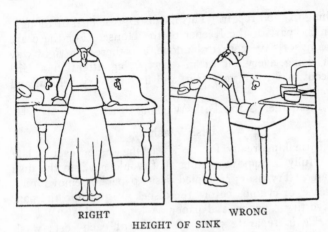

RIGHT   WRONG

HEIGHT OF SINK

picking up anything that is out of place and putting it where it belongs. But she also has an order for doing things. Perhaps she sweeps the entire house every day or every other day, or perhaps she puts one room in order on one day and another on another and so on. The important thing is to have a regular plan.

The Living Room

Taking care of a living room means cleaning the floor and the rugs; dusting the walls, the pictures; cleaning, dusting, and sometimes polishing the furniture. Open the windows top and bottom, dust and brush them inside and out; use a soft brush or a dust mop to take the dust from the floor. Use a carpet sweeper for the rugs unless you have electricity and can use a vacuum cleaner; collect the sweepings and burn them.

Dampen one quarter of your cheese-cloth duster and roll it inside the rest of the duster, then wring. This makes a dampish cloth for dusting the base-boards, window sills, and other woodwork as well as the furniture.

Where the furniture is highly polished, or would be injured by water, use oil on the duster instead. Dust after the dust has settled, not when it has been stirred into the air. Shake and replace doilies or covers.

Be sure that the pictures hang straight after dusting and that every piece of furniture is put in its right place. See how long it takes to clean the room; then study to find out how the time can be shortened.

Do not keep useless furniture nor have too many things in your room.

The Bathroom and the bath tub require daily cleansing. In the ordinary family every one who uses the tub should leave it perfectly clean for the next one who needs it. All the furnishings of the bathroom should be kept sweet and clean. Use a flush closet brush daily, scalding it after using it. And remember that fresh air and sunshine are cleansing agents. Get them to work for you.

The Bedroom. Your bedroom needs all the fresh air it can get. The Girl Scout sleeps with her windows open. As soon as you have dressed in the morning throw the windows wide open again, if they have been closed. Open the bed, so that both sheets may be reached by the fresh air. Shake up your pillows and put them on a chair near the window. Leave your night clothing spread or hung where it will be well aired. Let your room have a fresh air bath!

You know already how to make a bed. You will remember that all the bedclothing must be smooth and even, when the bed is made. You are lucky if you have a sister to help you make your bed, for this piece of work is easier for two than for one. You will see that the mattress is lying straight. Once a week you (the two of you) will turn the mattress, end over end one week, and side over side the next week. Then your mattress will wear evenly, and not have a hollow in the middle where you sleep all the time. Then you two will lay the mattress cover straight, and tuck it in firmly, so that you will have no hard wrinkles to sleep on. The under sheet, smooth and straight, must be tucked in all around. You will make that bed as smooth as the table. Now the upper sheet, which is the hardest thing to manage in bed-making, must be neatly tucked in at the foot. But you must allow eight inches at the top to be turned over the blankets and spread. Now the blankets, straight and smooth, and evenly tucked in at the foot. Then you may choose between tucking in the sides after folding the top sheet down over the blankets, and afterwards covering the whole bed with the spread, letting the sides and ends hang down; and laying the spread even with the blankets, tucking in the sides, and turning down the sheet over all. Try both ways.

Now, shake and pat the pillows, making them very smooth and quite square-cornered; then lay them or stand them neatly at the head of the bed, meeting exactly in the middle; and your bed is fit for a queen, or a tired Girl Scout after a tramp!

With the bed neatly made, everything must be put in its proper place. The furniture and window sills must be dusted with a clean cheese-cloth duster; and the bare floors must be nicely dusted with a dry floor-mop, or a cloth pinned over a broom. If there are rugs, use a carpet sweeper, if you have one, or a broom. If you do any broom sweeping, however, you will do it before you dust.

Now a last look to see that the room is tidy, every chair in place and the shades even at the windows, and your room is ready for the day. Of course any Girl Scout who wants a Homemaker's badge will *do* all these things;—not guess or suppose how others do them and how long it takes. That is the honest way to learn. So

find out how long it takes to put your own room in order
There is only one way to find out.

Fighting Germs

Keeping clean in these days means keeping free from
troublesome germs as well as visible dirt. Germs thrive
in dampness and darkness. They can be overcome by
sunshine. For thorough cleanness, the house needs fresh
air and sunshine as well as sweeping and dusting. The
Girl Scout must remember to let the fresh air blow
through every room in the house every day. She should
sleep with her windows open. She is fortunate if she
can sleep out of doors.

Of course she is in honor bound to have no dark, damp,
hidden, dirt-filled corners in any part of her house, not
even in shed or cellar. Let in the light and clean out
the dirt.

Fighting the House Fly and Mosquito

House flies carry disease. They breed in filth, human
waste, animal droppings, decayed animal or vegetable
matter, and are so made that they carry filth wherever
they go. Since the fly alights wherever it pleases, it
carries dirt from outside and distributes it wherever it
chooses.

Clean up all heaps of rubbish where flies may breed.
Keep your garbage pail *absolutely clean*. Disinfect outdoor water-closets and cover with gravel or slacked lime.
Get fly traps to set on your porches. Kill all flies that
come into the house, especially the early ones, in the
spring. Keep your windows and doors screened.

Fight mosquitoes just as you fight flies. Leave no
still water even in an old tin can, for the eggs of mosquitoes are deposited in still water and hatch there. The
mosquito, like many other insects, has an intermediate
stage between the egg and the grown mosquito. During

this stage it swims about in quiet water. Mosquitoes in great numbers may be growing in old cans or bottles, rain-filled and hidden away under the bushes in your yard. Watch for such breeding places; clean up your yard and banish the mosquito.

Taking Care of Waste

All waste must be carefully disposed of. It should never accumulate in the kitchen; but the important thing is to have *no real waste*. See that everything is put to the utmost use. If you live in the country, chickens and pigs will take the parings, the outer leaves of vegetables, etc., and you can bury or burn waste. If you live in the city the garbage man will collect all waste.

The garbage can must be kept thoroughly clean. It should be rinsed and scalded whenever it is empty, so that there will be no bad odors about the kitchen. Find out how garbage is taken care of in your town. How can you help to keep your neighborhood clean? What should be done if there is carelessness about garbage?

Taking Care of Woolen Things

Housekeepers must fight moths as well as flies. The clothes moth loves to lay its eggs in wool. It is very keen in searching out bits of wool and finding a place for its baby to thrive. Unless you have a care it will lay its eggs in your best winter dress which you forgot and left hanging in the hot summer days.

When the baby worm pokes its head out of the egg, it begins to feed upon the wool; and when some cold winter morning you get your dress you will find holes neatly cut where the little worm has gnawed, and beside the holes the little woven cradle which the tiny creature spun for itself, and in which the crawling worm changed to the flying, silvery moth.

The housekeeper must therefore, carefully brush and

pack away all woolen things before the moths arrive. After the garment is cleansed and brushed it may be folded in newspapers carefully pinned at the ends, so that no crack is left for the moth to get in, or it may be laid in a cedar box; or in any plain box with moth balls or camphor. Every box should be labelled so that you know without opening it what is in it.

Watch edges of carpets and rugs for the carpet beetle and the "Buffalo bug." The last bothersome creature may eat your cotton dresses in your closet. All clothing must have care.

Make a list of the woolen things that must be taken care of if the house is closed in summer and what personal clothing must be packed away for the summer even if the house is not closed.

Storage of Food

Taking care of food so that it will "keep" well is just as important as the careful buying of food. Much waste, and therefore loss of money and labor, comes from carelessness in the storage of food. The bright Girl Scout will keep her eyes open to see how foods are taken care of in the house; which foods must be kept in the cellar; which ones must be stored on the shelves of dry closets; which ones come in sealed parcels; which in paper bags; which in boxes; which in barrels. There must be a place in the house for keeping all these things. So you need to think which foods *must* be kept in the house and which must be bought from day to day. And in the house which you plan there must be ample space for closets and shelves, for keeping properly all that must be stored. No one can say which things must be kept in the house by every family. If the Girl Scout happens to live in a crowded city where rents are high, she will have little storage space, and will not keep so many things on hand. If she lives in the country, miles from a store, she must have a "store" of her own. So keep your eyes open, Girl Scout, and see what is being done in your part of the world. That is what eyes are made for.

Heating the House

A house may be heated by a furnace, by stoves, or even by open fires in the fireplace, as in old days. Heating the house makes the chimney necessary. This must be carefully arranged for in planning your house. Heating by stoves is the most common arrangement. In the large city or town, the furnace is used. This is merely a big stove in the cellar or basement, so planned that its heat is distributed through the house. By this means one big stove does the work of many little ones, and warms the whole house.

The furnace may use its heat to turn water into hot steam, which is sent through all the house through the iron pipes and radiators. Or the water in the boiler may be made quite hot, though not turned into steam, and sent through the house in the same way, by means of pipes. Or hot air from around this big stove or furnace may be sent through big pipes directly to the various rooms. This means dust and dirt, and we are learning to use steam and hot water instead of the hot air system.

The fireplace is almost a luxury. It is found oftenest in country houses where wood can be easily got and stored. The town or city home may have its open fire, however. Everyone loves an open fire; and when you plan your own house, you must manage to get one if you can. The hearth is the heart of the house.

Labor Saving

The housekeeper must learn how to do her work in the least possible time; she must save steps. Look at the house that you have planned and see whether everything you need to use is within easy reach. Look carefully at

the closets where you keep things. Are they big enough?
Are they in the right place? Suppose your water comes
from a well which is a long way from the house. What
difference will it make? What would you do about it?

The Water Supply

The water supply of every home should be carefully
guarded. If the water is defiled or contaminated by
germs of typhoid fever, diphtheria, or other diseases,
whose bacteria may be carried by water, the disease may
be spread wherever the water is used.

No earth closets or human or animal waste should be
in the neighborhood of the well. Water should come
from high ground and clean places with no possibility
of gathering infection on the way to the house. Great
pains should be taken to keep drinking water absolutely
clean. All drinking vessels should be washed and scalded
and the rims should never be handled.

In the country every home has a private water supply
and takes pains to guard it. In the city there is a common
water supply and everyone is responsible for keeping it
pure. Where does the water come from that supplies
your city or town? How is it kept clean? Who takes
care of it?

Whenever there is any question about the purity of
common drinking water, the table supply should be
boiled, for safety. Boiling will destroy any bacteria that
could produce disease. This boiled water should be used
for rinsing dishes as well as for drinking.

Girl Scouts will interest themselves in municipal or
neighborhood housekeeping, for that is a responsibility
which all share together.

Learning to take care of one's own home is a good
beginning, if one is to share in providing good conditions for the neighborhood.

Little Things Worth Remembering

The stove should be cleaned with crumpled newspaper whenever the kitchen is put in order. All ashes should be neatly brushed off.

In lifting ashes from the ash pan with a shovel use a newspaper to cover the pail into which the ashes are poured, so that the dust will not scatter over the room. Don't dump them and raise dust; and never put hot ashes into a wooden box or barrel.

Watch the floor of closets and see that no dusty corners are hidden out of sight.

Air and dry soiled clothing before putting it in the laundry basket. If damp clothes are hidden away they will mildew.

Learn to make out a laundry list and to check it when the laundry comes home.

Save soap chips and use in a soap shaker.

Get all the help you can from older housekeepers in your neighborhood. Ask them how they do things and why. Your mother may know something better than anybody else does.

The Girl Scout asks questions and learns why things are done as they are. She may think out a better way some day, but first she must pay attention to the old way.

Sing at your work; it goes better so. Besides, joy belongs with housekeeping and your song helps to keep her there. Always sing if the work drags, but let it be a lively song!

Making Things Clean and Keeping Clean

Making things clean is a most important duty of the Keeper of the House. But don't forget, Girl Scout, that keeping things clean is a constant duty. You know many a body who "cleans up" with a lot of stir once in a while, but who litters and spills and spreads dirt and lets dust collect in corners all the rest of the time.

"Keeping clean" is the housekeeper's regular business, and "cleaning up" never need stir up the whole house.

For keeping clean, soap and water must always be had. The soap loves to wrestle with grease. The water softens and rinses away both dirt and soap You will use a scouring soap or powder to clean stained or dirty metal or glass; and you should cover water-closets and other out-of-door places for refuse with clean slaked lime now and then to keep them clean.

Ten Ways of Removing Stains

1. When you have *raspberry* or *blueberry* or *strawberry* stains on your white handkerchief or blouse or skirt, do not be too much disturbed. Hold the stained part firmly over an empty bowl, with the spot well in the centre, and ask some one to pour boiling hot water over the spot and into the bowl. The stains will disappear like magic. Then the wet spot may be dried and pressed with a hot iron, and the damage is repaired.

2. *Peach* stains are much harder to remove, but they should be treated just as the others were treated. Often several applications of hot water are necessary for these stubborn stains. But you must not lose patience. And you must not use soap! The stain will fade out at last under the hot water.

3. *Ink* stains are a great bother, especially to the school girl who carries a leaky fountain pen. Do not let them get dry. They will be much harder to remove. Sometimes cold water, applied immediately, will remove the ink, if the spot is rinsed carefully. Use the cold water just as the hot water is used for the peach stain. If that does not remove it try milk. If the milk fails, let the spot soak in sour milk. Sometimes it must

soak a day or two; but it will disappear in the end, with rinsing and a little rubbing.

4. *Ink* stains on a carpet are a serious matter. Let us hope that no Girl Scout will be so unlucky as to upset an ink bottle on a friend's carpet or rug. If she does, she should know the best way to set about removing it. This should be done as quickly as possible before the ink dries, or "sets." Take cotton, or soft tissue paper or blotting paper, and absorb all that has not soaked in. You will see that the "sooner" *is* the "better" in this case. Try not to increase the size of the spot, for you must keep the ink from spreading. Then dip fresh cotton in milk, and carefully sop the spot. Do not use the cotton when it is inky; that will smear the carpet and spread the stain. Use fresh bits of cotton, dipped in clean milk, until the stain has disappeared. Then rinse with clean water in the same way, and dry with dry cotton.

5. The *spots* made on silk or woolen by *acids* may be removed by touching with ammonia or baking soda, dissolved in a little water. The bright yellow spot on a black dress will sometimes run away like lightning when touched by the wet cork of the ammonia bottle.

6. *Egg stains* on the napkin, or sometimes, unfortunately, on a dress front, must be removed before washing. Use cold water alone. The egg will dissolve and can be rinsed out. Hot water will cook the egg and it will be hard to remove.

7. *Liquid shoe blacking* is almost worse than ink. It must be treated in the same way, and *at once*.

8. *Coffee* and *tea stains* will wash out with either warm water or soap and water. A black coffee stain on a fresh table cloth may be removed like the berry stains, by the teakettle and bowl method.

9. *Grease spots* may be removed from washable fabrics by soap and water. For silk and woolen, gaso-

line should be used. Use gasoline in daytime only, to avoid lamps or gas in the neighborhood; and *never* near a fire. Use carbona instead of gasoline or benzine when possible, as it cannot burn. Remember that all grease or sugar spots should be removed before putting a woolen garment away. Moths always seek them out, and they will find them if you don't.

10. *Paint* can be removed by soaking the spot in turpentine. This dissolves it, and a bit of rubbing shakes it out. A brush helps, when the paint spot is on a woolen garment, after the turpentine has done its work.

Remember: All spots and stains should be removed before washing the garment.

GOOD MANNERS AND SOCIAL FORMS

It is easier to meet people socially if we are acquainted with the simple forms of introductions, meeting and parting, and so forth. A girl who is entertaining her friends will be more successful in doing so if she plans ahead how she can welcome them, and has all the necessary preparations for a substantial good time, at hand. This planning also makes it possible for her to be less occupied when the time comes, and to have a good time herself.

Stand where guests can see you at once when they enter.

Always introduce a younger person *to* an older one, as "Mrs. Smith, may I present Miss Jones, or Mr. Brown?" A man is always presented *to* a woman, or a girl, as "Miss Brewster, may I present Mr. Duncan?"

If you have many guests, ask some of your friends to join you in watching to be sure that no one is left out, so that the evening may be a success for every one. It is sometimes difficult for a hostess to do this alone.

If you ask other girls to help you, ask each to do a

definite thing, as to arrange for wraps, sing or play, pay special attention to some older person, etc. This saves confusion, as the Pine Tree patrol does in camp.

A few intimate friends need no plan to make them have a good time, but with a large number it is usually better to plan games, music, charades, or some other form of entertainment.

When invited to a house at a certain time, be prompt. Promptness is always a mark of courtesy, as it means consideration for the time and convenience of others. One should also watch carefully the time of leaving, and not stay about unless specially detained.

TABLE MANNERS

Accept what is offered or placed before you, with a quiet "Thank you." If you are asked what you prefer, it is proper to name it.

Do not drink while food is in the mouth.

Take soup quietly from the side of the spoon, dipping it into the plate *from* instead of towards you, to avoid dripping the soup.

Break bread or roll, and spread with butter only the piece which you are about to eat.

Use knife only as a divider, the fork to take food to the mouth. Where one can dispense with a knife, and use only the fork to divide the food, do so. When not using either, lay them together across the side of the plate, not resting on the table cloth.

A spoon should never be allowed to rest in a tall receptacle such as a cup or glass, as it is likely to overturn the receptacle. Place the spoon on plate or saucer.

At close of meal, fold napkin, that table may be left in orderly condition. When napkins are to be washed at once, or when they are paper napkins, they need not be folded.

Do not begin a course until all are served.

Sometimes it is better to serve the hostess first, and sometimes it is the custom to serve the guest first, that is the guest of honor who sits on the hostess' right. When the host or hostess does the serving, the guest is served first.

Do not be troubled if you use the wrong spoon or fork, and never call attention to anyone else's doing so. No matter how you feel, or what the blunder or accident may be, such as spilling something or dropping a plate, never show displeasure to either servant or guest. Good breeding and pleasant atmosphere are essential to all entertainment.

Good breeding means first of all thoughtfulness of others, and nothing shows lack of breeding so quickly as a lack of such politeness to those who happen to be serving us in hotels, at home, in shops, or when travelling, or anywhere else.

When acting as waitress, stand at the left of the person to be served, so that the portion may be taken with the right hand.

Preparing the Meal

Plan the cooking so that the food that is to be served may be kept hot; for instance, soup may be kept hot on the back of the stove or where there is less heat, while the meat or vegetables are being cooked. Food that is to be served cold, should be kept in the ice-box or standing in water until the last moment and served in chilled dishes. In placing the food on the dishes and platters care should be taken to make it look attractive.

Setting the Table

When setting the table keep in mind how many courses there will be, and therefore, how many knives, forks, and spoons are needed. Have everything clean, and lay every-

thing straight.   Air room well.   Wipe table, and if a
tablecloth is used, cover table with a felt silence cloth.
If a tablecloth is used, it should be laid with the fold
in the center of the table.   If a centerpiece and doilies
are used, they should be laid at even distances.   Clean
white oil cloth and paper napkins make an attractive
looking table.   At each cover the knife, edge in, is placed
at the right with the spoon, and the glass is placed at
the right in line with the end of the knife.   The fork is
at the left and bread and butter plate and small knife
are at the left opposite the glass.   Put the napkin between
the knife and fork.

Salt, pepper, water, bread and butter should be on the
table, and if necessary, vinegar, mustard, sugar, pickles,
etc.

When possible a few flowers add to the appearance of
the table.

Have as much ready as possible before sitting down
at the table.   See at least that (1), glasses are filled;
(2) butter portioned; (3) chairs placed.

Hard and fast rules as to table setting do not exist. Local customs, the amount of service at hand, and common sense must govern this. The captain, assisted by the council, must be the judges.

THE GIRL SCOUT COOK
By Ula M. Dow, A. M.
In charge of Division of Food, Simmons College

The Girl Scout who has earned the Cooking Badge may be a great help at home if she has learned to work quickly and neatly and may get much amusement both at home and on camping parties. If the first trial of a process is not a success, the Scout should have patience to try again and again until her result is satisfactory. If she has learned to prepare a few simple dishes well she should have courage to try unfamiliar recipes which are found in any good cook book. If she is to be ready to take responsibility when it is necessary, she should be able to plan the meals in such a way that nothing is wasted and that the family is satisfied and well-nourished.

When working in the kitchen the Scout should wear a clean, washable dress, or a washable apron which covers her dress. She should be sure that her hair is tidy, and she should remember to wash her hands before beginning work. She should try to use as few dishes as possible and not to spill or spatter. She should remember that her cooking is not finished until she has cleaned up after herself, has washed and put away the dishes, washed the dish towels and left the kitchen in order.

What to Have for Breakfast—Breakfast is in most families the simplest meal of the day and the easiest to prepare. Some people are satisfied with fruit, cereal, toast or muffins, coffee for the adults, and milk for the children. Many families, however, like the addition of a heartier dish, such as boiled or poached eggs, fish hash, or minced meat on toast. If a hearty dish is served at breakfast this is a good time to use up such left-overs as potato, fish, or meat.

SIMPLE BREAKFAST

Apple sauce or sliced peaches.
Oatmeal or cornmeal mush.
Toast or muffins.
Coffee (for adults).
Milk (for children).

HEARTY BREAKFAST

Apple sauce or sliced peaches.
Oatmeal or cornmeal mush.
Toast or muffins.
Coffee (for adults).
Milk (for children).
Poached eggs or minced lamb on toast.

FRUIT—Raw fruit should be carefully washed and prepared in such a way that it can be easily eaten. Berries may be cooked with no other preparation than washing. Fruits, such as apples and pears, should be washed, pared, quartered, and cored before cooking. Any fruit which becomes dark on standing after it is cut may be kept light colored by dropping the pieces into a pan of water until they are ready to be cooked. If this is done most of the water should be drained off before they are cooked.

Dried fruits, such as prunes, which have a wrinkled skin should be soaked for a short time in cold water before they are washed. Otherwise it is impossible to get them clean. After washing they should be covered with cold water and soaked over night, or until they are plump. They should be put on to cook in the water in which they are soaked and cooked until tender. **Sugar** should then be added if they are not sweet enough.

The most common method of cooking fresh fruit is to boil it gently with just enough water to prevent it from burning. Sugar should be added just before the cooking is finished, the amount depending on the acidity of the fruit and the taste of the family.

In sampling food, the cook should remember that the rest of the food is to be eaten by other people. She should never taste from the cooking spoon, but should transfer her sample to a tasting spoon which is not returned to the kettle.

CEREAL—Cereals, such as oatmeal, cornmeal, and cracked wheat, should be cooked in a double boiler. A double boiler can be improvised by setting a pail or pan into a kettle of boiling water. Cereals for breakfast may be cooked the day before and reheated in the double boiler, but should not be stirred while reheating. A tablespoonful or two of cold water on top will prevent a hard skin from forming while standing. All prepared cereals are better if cooked for a longer time than the package directions indicate. It is hardly possible to cook any grain too long. The fireless cooker is especially valuable for cooking cereals, but a longer period of time must be allowed than for cooking in a double boiler. A home-made fireless cooker, described in another place, is interesting to make. Ready-to-serve cereals are very expensive compared with those cooked at home.

Cracked wheat, ¼ cup to 1 cup water; 3-12 hours.

Rolled oats, ½ cup to 1 cup water; ½-3 hours.

Cornmeal, 3 tablespoonfuls to 1 cup water; 1-4 hours.

Use ½ teaspoonful of salt to each quart of water. Have the water boiling rapidly. Add the cereal gradually. Let the mixture cook directly over the fire 5 minutes. Place over boiling water or in the fireless cooker to cook slowly for a long time. Keep covered and do not stir. The time of cooking given in the table means that the cereal is eatable after the shorter time mentioned, but is better if cooked the longer time.

TOAST—Good toast is worth knowing how to make. The cook should not be satisfied with toast which is either white or burned.

Toast is most easily made from stale bread, which should be cut in one-third to one-half inch slices. A single slice of toast may be made by holding it over the fire on a fork. In camp a forked stick answers every purpose. The easiest way to make several slices is to put them in a wire toaster and hold them over hot coals. Begin carefully and hold the bread some distance away from the fire, turning it often until it dries. Then hold it nearer the coals until it is a golden brown on both sides. With a new coal fire or wood fire toast must be made on a toaster on the top of the stove to prevent the bread from being smoked. If the top of the stove is being used for other things, the drying may be done in the oven.

MUFFINS—Any good cook book has numerous recipes for muffins, most of which can be made easily if the directions are followed exactly.

Cornmeal Muffins (for four persons):

Four tablespoonfuls butter or oleomargarine, 3 tablespoonfuls sugar, 1 egg, 1 cup milk, 1 1-3 cups flour, 2-3 cup cornmeal, 3 teaspoonfuls baking powder.

Cream the butter, add the sugar and the egg well beaten. Sift the baking powder with the flour and cornmeal and add to the first mixture, alternating with milk. Bake in buttered muffin pans 25 to 30 minutes. This mixture makes good corn bread if baked in a shallow buttered pan.

COFFEE—If the family drink coffee, they will want

coffee for breakfast, no matter what other items of the menu may be varied. It should be served only to the grown-up members of the family. Coffee of average strength is made as follows:

One-half cup coffee finely ground, 4 cups cold water, 2 eggshells.

Mix the coffee, the crushed eggshell, and ½ cupful of cold water in a scalded coffee pot. Add the remainder of the water and allow the mixture to come gradually to the boiling point. Boil 3 minutes. Draw to the back of the range and keep hot for 5 minutes. Add ⅛ cupful of cold water and let stand 1 minute to settle. Strain into a heated coffee pot in which the coffee is to be served at the table.

A method for making coffee used by the guides in the White Mountains is as follows:

Boil the water in an ordinary pail, remove the pail from the fire, pour the dry coffee gently on the top of the water, cover tightly and move it near the fire where it will keep warm but will not boil again. In about thirty minutes the coffee will have become moistened and sunk to the bottom of the pail. If the coffee is slow in becoming moist, time may be saved by removing the cover for a moment and pressing gently with a spoon on the top of the coffee, but the mixture must not be stirred. It is essential that the water be boiling when the coffee is added, that the cover be absolutely tight, and that the coffee be kept hot without boiling. Half a cup of coffee to four cups of water makes coffee of average strength.

MILK—The little children of the family should have whole milk at every meal. The older children should have milk at breakfast and supper time. There is no food so good for children who want to be well and strong. A part of the family supply of milk is sometimes skimmed to give cream for use in coffee and on desserts. The cream contains most of the fat in the milk, but the skimmed milk which is left is still a very valuable food, containing the substances which make muscle and bone, and every bit of it should be used in the cooking or for making cottage cheese. The waste of milk is the worst possible extravagance.

Eggs—Eggs may be prepared in countless ways, and the ambitious cook will find much amusement in trying some of the suggestions in the cook books. Eggs are an entirely satisfactory substitute for meat and fish, and are therefore often served for the main dish at dinner or supper. Many people like an egg every morning for breakfast, but this is a rather extravagant habit. If eggs are served for breakfast they are usually cooked in the shell, poached or scrambled. The men of the family sometimes prefer their eggs fried, but this is not a good method for the children. Only fresh eggs can be poached successfully, so that this is a good test for freshness.

Poached Eggs—Oil the skillet and fill it within a half inch of the top with water. Break each egg into a saucer and let the water boil after the egg is placed in it. The egg is done when the white is jelly-like and a slight film is formed over the yolk. Remove the egg with a griddle cake turner to a piece of buttered toast. Sprinkle lightly with salt. If the eggs are not absolutely fresh, the white will scatter in the water. If the first egg to be cooked shows this tendency oiled muffin rings may be put in the pan to keep the rest of them in shape.

Soft Boiled Eggs—A soft boiled egg has much the same consistency as a poached egg. It is easier to manage because the shell is unbroken, but it is harder to get it of just the right consistency because the contents of the egg are invisible. Most people are very particular to have the egg just hard or soft enough to suit them, and it is necessary for the cook to practice to be sure of uniform results. Drop the eggs carefully into a kettle of boiling water, draw the kettle back on the stove so that the water does not boil again and (for a soft egg) allow the eggs to remain for five minutes. If the eggs are very cold they should remain longer.

USE OF LEFT-OVERS FOR BREAKFAST—If the family like a hearty breakfast this is a good meal at which to use bits of left-over meat which might otherwise be wasted. Meat may be chopped or ground, reheated in the gravy which was served with it, and served on toast. Lamb is especially good minced on toast. To make hash mix equal quantities of meat and chopped potato and brown nicely in a greased frying pan. Such mixtures should be tasted to make sure that they are salt enough. Some people like a very small amount of onion with any of these made-over meat dishes.

DINNER

WHAT TO HAVE FOR DINNER—If all the members of the family are at home at noontime it is usually more convenient to have dinner then, but if members of the family are away or hurried at noontime it may be better to have dinner at night. Dinner may consist of several courses, but if the mother or the daughter of the family prepares the meal, the family is usually perfectly satisfied with two courses.

The main course of a simple family dinner consists of meat, fish, eggs or a cheese dish served with potato, rice or macaroni, and a vegetable such as string beans, green peas, carrots, cabbage, tomatoes or corn. If the family like salad, the vegetables are often served as a salad. This is a very good way to use up small amounts of vegetables which are left from the day before. Often little remainders of two or more vegetables may be very attractively combined in this way.

Some families like hot bread at dinner, and hot breads, such as baking powder biscuit (described under supper), or corn bread (described under breakfast), are particularly good with some combinations. Examples are baking powder biscuit with meat stew or fricasseed chicken and corn bread with bacon and eggs or ham. If fish is served in a chowder, buttered and toasted crackers are usually served. An occasional chowder for dinner is an excellent way to use up any surplus of skimmed milk which may be on hand.

The kind of dessert served at dinner, besides depending on the taste of the family, depends on the amount of money which is spent for food and whether there are young children in the family. Pie and ice cream, which are favorite desserts in many families, are expensive. Little children should not have desserts which contain a good deal of fat, such as pie or doughnuts, or which are the least bit soggy, as some steamed puddings are inclined to be. The most economical desserts and those best suited to the children are baked puddings made with milk and cereal, such as Indian pudding, rice pudding, and those made with cereal and fruit, such as Apple Betty or peach tapioca. If there is skimmed milk on hand the possibility of using it in a milk pudding should be considered. Chocolate bread pudding and Apple Betty make a very attractive use of left-over bread. Dessert should always be chosen with reference to the heartiness of the first course. A main dish which is not very filling can be balanced by a more substantial dessert.

SIMPLE DINNERS:

   1. Hamburg steak.
      Baked potato.

Squash or baked tomatoes.

Apple Betty.

2. Roast chicken or roast lamb with dressing and currant jelly.

Mashed potato and gravy.

Peas or string beans.

Orange jelly and whipped cream.

MEAT—The best way to learn about cuts of meat is to go often to market and talk to the butcher whenever he has a minute to spare. Some cuts of meat are tough with coarse fibers and much connective tissue. They should be ground if, like Hamburg steak, they are to be cooked by a short process, such as broiling. If not ground, the tougher meats are usually cooked a long time with water and made into a stew, a pot roast, a meat pie, or a meat loaf. These cuts are cheaper, but require more care in preparation than the more expensive cuts. Examples are the bottom of the round, the shin, and the flank of beef. The more expensive cuts, such as the top of the round, tenderloin and sirloin, are more tender, more delicately flavored, and are used for broiling and roasting. Some cuts which seem inexpensive really cost more than they appear because they contain large amounts of bone or waste fat. The difference between lamb and mutton is a question of the age at which the animal was slaughtered. Lamb is much more tender than mutton, is more delicately flavored and more expensive. There is a similar difference between chicken and fowl. Fowl is much tougher than chicken and requires careful and long cooking to make it tender.

Pan Broiled Hamburg Steak—Hamburg steak may be bought already ground at the butcher's, or one of the cheap cuts of beef, such as bottom of the round or shin, may be bought and ground at home. Many people like a little salt pork or onion ground with the meat.

Make the meat into small, flat cakes and cook in a smoking hot frying pan which has been thoroughly rubbed over with a piece of fat. When one side is seared over nicely turn the cakes (a griddle cake turner or spatula is helpful) and broil on the other side. Place on a hot platter, sprinkle with salt and pepper, dot with bits of butter and garnish with a little parsley or watercress.

A rump or sirloin steak may be broiled in a hot frying pan in a similar way. Wipe and trim the steak, place in a smoking hot frying pan and sear both sides. Reduce the heat and turn the steak occasionally (about every 2 minutes) until it is cooked, allowing 8 minutes for a rare steak, 10 minutes for medium cooked steak, and 12 minutes for well done steak, for a steak 1 inch thick. Avoid puncturing the meat with a fork while cooking.

Many people prefer to broil a steak on a broiler. This is practical with gas or electricity or over a wood or coal fire which is reduced to clear coals without smoke or flame. It is very difficult indeed to cook Hamburg steak on a broiler.

Lamb chops may be broiled in either way.

Roast Leg of Lamb—Wash the leg of lamb, place it on the rack in a roasting pan and put in a hot oven with the roaster uncovered. When the roast is well seared (15 to 30 minute), draw from the oven, sprinkle with salt, pour a little water into the pan, and put on the cover. Finish cooking at a lowered temperature, allowing 20 or 25 minutes for each pound.

A dripping pan may be used in place of a roaster, using a pan of similar size for a cover. A rack may be improvised from a broiler, a toaster or a cake rack.

Beef is roasted in the same way, but is usually cooked

for a shorter time (15 to 20 minutes for each pound).
BEEF STEW (for four):

2½ pounds beef shoulder or shin.
2   cups diced potato.
1-3 cup turnip cut in half inch cubes.
1-3 cup carrot cut in half inch cubes.
 ¼   onion chopped.
2   tablespoons flour.
Salt and pepper.

Wash the meat, remove from the bone and fat and
cut in 1½ inch cubes. Sprinkle with salt and pepper
and dredge with flour. Sear the pieces of meat in the
frying pan in the fat cooked out from the trimmings
of fat. Put the meat in a kettle, and rinse the frying
pan with boiling water, so that none of the juices will
be lost. Add the bone, cover with boiling water and
boil five minutes. Lower the temperature and cook until the meat is tender (about three hours.) Add the
carrots, turnips, onions, pepper and salt in an hour, and
the potato in 15 minutes before the steak is to be served.
Remove the bone and any large pieces of fat. Stir
two tablespoons of flour to a smooth paste with a little
water and thicken the stew.

Such a stew may also be made with lamb, mutton, or
veal, using other vegetables as desired. Celery and
onion are better than turnip and carrot with veal.

CHICKEN—If a chicken is purchased at the market
it is usually delivered dressed. This means that the
head has been cut off, the entrails removed, and the
coarser pinfeathers pulled out. Many times, however,
it is necessary to know how to do this oneself.

To Dress and Clean a Chicken—Cut off the head and
draw out the pinfeathers. Remove hair and down by
holding the fowl over a flame (a gas flame, an alcohol
flame, or a piece of paper flaming in the wood or coal

range), constantly changing the position until all parts
of the surface have been exposed to the flame. Cut
off the feet. Wash the fowl thoroughly, using a small
brush, in water to which a little soda has been added.
Rinse and dry. Make a slit down the back of the neck.
Remove the crop and windpipe. Draw down the neck
skin long enough to fasten under the back. Make a
straight cut from ½ inch below the tip of the breast-
bone to the vent. Cut around the vent. Slip fingers
in carefully around and fully loosen the entrails. Carefully draw out the entrails. The lungs, lying in the
cavities under the breast, and the kidneys, in the hollow near the end of the backbone, must be taken out
separately. Remove the oil sack and wash the chicken
by allowing cold water to run through it.

To clean giblets (the gizzard, the heart, and the liver)
proceed as follows: Separate the gall bladder from
the liver, cutting off any portion of the liver that may
have a greenish tinge. Remove the thin membrane, the
arteries, the veins and the clotted blood around the
heart. Cut the fat and the membranes from the gizzard. Make a gash through the thickest part of the
gizzard as far as the inner lining, being careful not to
pierce it. Remove the inner sack and discard. Wash
the gizzard carefully and boil in water to use for giblet
sauce.

If the chicken comes from the market dressed it
should be washed carefully and any pinfeathers removed which were overlooked by the market man.

To Stuff, Truss and Roast a Chicken—When the
chicken is clean and prepared as directed, fill it with
stuffing (described later), a little in the opening at the
neck, the rest in the body cavity. Sew up the opening
with a few long stitches. Draw the skin of the neck
smoothly down and under the back, press the wings

close against the body and fold the pinions under, so that they will cross the back and hold down the skin of the neck. Press the legs close to the body. Thread the trussing needle with white twine, using it double. Press the needle through the wing at the middle joint, pass it through the skin of the neck and back, and out again at the middle joint of the other wing. Return the needle through the bend of the leg at the second joint, through the body, and out at the same point on the other side; draw the cord tight and tie it with the end at the wing joint. Thread the needle again and run it through the legs and body at the thigh bone and back at the ends of the drumsticks. Draw the drumstick bones close together, covering the opening made for drawing the chicken and tie the ends. Have both knots on the same side of the chicken. When cooked, cut the cord on the opposite side and draw out by the knots.

Lay the stuffed and trussed chicken on its back on a rack in a roasting pan. Lay a strip of salt pork on breast. Place in a hot oven until the chicken begins to brown, then lower the temperature and cook the chicken until very tender. Baste often with the drippings in the pan. From 3 to 4 hours will be required for a five-pound chicken. If a fowl is used it should be steamed for 3 or 4 hours and then roasted for ½ hour.

Stuffing—For a large chicken mix thoroughly 4 cups of finely broken stale bread, 1½ teaspoon of salt, ⅛ teaspoon of pepper, 1 teaspoon of poultry dressing and 4 tablespoons of fat. Pour over the mixture hot milk or water, stirring lightly until the mixture is moist.

Giblet Gravy—If the chicken was properly roasted the drippings in the pan should be nicely browned, but not burned. Make a gravy from these drippings and the water in which the giblets were boiled. To do this pour the water into the pan, set the pan over the fire and stir until the contents of the pan are dissolved. Thicken with a smooth paste of flour and water, using two tablespoons of flour for every cup of liquid. Boil until the flour tastes cooked. Strain. Add the giblets cut in small pieces.

VEGETABLES—All vegetables should be clean, crisp and firm when ready for cooking. Vegetables are prepared and cooked in a variety of ways, but almost all vegetables should be carefully washed as the first process. It is convenient to keep a small brush for washing the vegetables, like potatoes, sweet potatoes, and beets, which must be scrubbed to get them clean. Vegetables which are to be eaten raw, such as lettuce and celery, should be washed with special care, wrapped in a clean, wet cloth and put in the ice box to keep them crisp.

Baked Potato—Select smooth potatoes of even size. Scrub them carefully and bake them in a hot oven. The time required is from 45 to 60 minutes, depending on the size of the potatoes and the temperature of the oven. When the potatoes are done, slash each one with a knife to let the steam escape, and serve immediately.

Mashed Potato—Wash the potatoes, pare, cover with boiling salted water (1 level teaspoon of salt to a pint of water), and cook until tender (30 to 45 minutes). Drain off the water and return to the fire a moment to dry. Mash the potatoes, add butter, salt, pepper and hot milk, and beat vigorously until light and creamy. For three cups of potato use 2 tablespoons of butter and 4 tablespoons of hot milk. Pile lightly in a hot dish and serve immediately.

Steamed Squash—Wash and cut in one-inch slices. Steam until tender, scrape from the shell, mash thoroughly, season with salt, pepper and butter, and serve.

String Beans—Snap the ends from the beans, remove any strings, cut into short pieces, wash, cover with boiling salted water (1 level teaspoon to a pint) and cook until tender. The time required will vary from one hour to three hours, depending on the age and kind of bean. Drain the beans, season with salt and butter, and serve.

Canned string beans should be rinsed, reheated in as little water as possible, drained, and seasoned.

Baked Tomatoes—Select smooth tomatoes of even size. Wash the tomatoes, remove the thin slice from the stem end and remove a spoonful of pulp. Sprinkle with salt, pepper and scraped onion, fill the cavity with buttered crumbs, place in a pan (preferably one which can be used as a serving dish at the table), and bake in a moderate oven until the tomatoes are tender. Serve in the dish in which they were cooked or remove them carefully to the platter on which the Hamburg steak is being served, arranging them in a ring around the meat.

The buttered crumbs are prepared by melting a tablespoon of butter or oleomargarine and stirring in six tablespoonfuls of dry bread crumbs.

DESSERTS—Most desserts are easy to make if the directions given in the cook books are followed exactly. Many people take pride in making beautiful cake or pie, who are careless about making good toast or baking a potato well.

Apple Betty—Prepare well sweetened apple sauce and thin slices of lightly buttered bread cut in small triangles. Fill a shallow baking dish with alternate layers of apple sauce and toast, beginning with apple sauce and ending with toast. Sprinkle lightly with sugar and cinnamon and heat in the oven. Serve with cream.

Orange Jelly—Swell 1½ tablespoons of powdered gelatin in a half cupful of cold water. Mix 1 cupful of orange juice, ¼ cupful of lemon juice, ½ cupful of sugar and 1¼ cupfuls of boiling water. Add the gelatin and stir carefully until it is dissolved. Strain into a wet mould and chill until the jelly is firm. Unmould the jelly and serve with whipped cream or a custard sauce. To unmould the jelly, run the point of a knife around the edge of the mould, dip the mould quickly in warm water, place an inverted serving plate on top of the mould, turn both over and lift the mould carefully.

SUPPER OR LUNCH

WHAT TO HAVE FOR SUPPER.—Supper shows more variation between families than other meals of the day. Some men insist upon meat, even though meat is served for their dinner, but this is rather extravagant unless there is left-over meat which should be used. Hash and minced lamb on toast, which were suggested for the hearty breakfast, would be equally well liked by most families for supper. Many families prefer for supper some milk dish such as macaroni and cheese or a cream soup served with either stewed or fresh fruit or followed by a fruit or vegetable salad. Hot rolls or baking powder biscuits are a very attractive substitute for plain bread if someone has time to make them at the last minute. If the mother and daughter do all the work of the family, they usually like to have on hand cookies or cake, which can be used for supper rather than to have to prepare some special dessert. Cold meat has the advantage that it is ready to serve with little preparation, but many other dishes such as the macaroni and cheese and the creamed soup, suggested in the menus, may be made when dinner is being prepared and simply reheated for supper.

A hot drink at night usually seems desirable except on hot days in the summer. If tea is served for adults, the children should have cocoa or milk.

If dinner is served at night, luncheon is served in the middle of the day. The suggestions made in regard to supper apply equally well to luncheon.

Little children should have their hearty meal in the middle of the day and a light meal at night no matter what arrangement of meals the rest of the family may have.

SIMPLE SUPPERS

1. Macaroni and cheese or cold meat
   Stewed or fresh fruit
   Cookies
   Bread and butter
   Tea (for adults)
   Milk or cocoa (for children).
2. Cream of potato soup
   Vegetable or fruit salad
   Baking powder biscuit
   Tea (for adults)
   Milk or cocoa (for children).

Macaroni and Cheese.—For macaroni and cheese the macaroni must be cooked and white sauce prepared. Break three-quarters of a cup of macaroni in inch pieces and cook in two quarts of boiling water to which a tablespoon of salt has been added. The water must be boiling rapidly when the macaroni is added and must be kept boiling constantly. When the macaroni is tender, drain it in a strainer and run enough cold water through it to prevent the pieces from sticking together. To prepare the sauce, melt two tablespoons of butter or oleomargarine in the top of a double boiler, stir in two tablespoons of flour and a half teaspoon of salt and pour over the mixture a cup and a half of cold milk. Cook this mixture directly over the heat, stirring constantly until it begins to thicken. Then place the dish over the lower part of the double boiler, containing boiling water, and let it continue cooking for fifteen minutes. Put a layer of the boiled macaroni in a buttered baking dish and sprinkle with cheese, either grated or cut into small pieces. Pour on a layer of the sauce. Follow this by layers of macaroni, cheese and sauce until the dish is full. Cover with buttered crumbs and bake until the crumbs are brown. To make the buttered crumbs, melt one tablespoon of butter or oleomargarine and stir in six tablespoons of crumbs.

The macaroni and cheese may be prepared in the morning if desired and baked at supper time in a moderate oven. It should be left in the oven long enough to become thoroughly hot. If there are little children in the family a dish of creamed macaroni should be made for them without the cheese.

Cream of Potato Soup—

3 potatoes	1½ teaspoons salt
1 quart milk	¼ teaspoon celery salt
2 slices of onion	⅛ teaspoon pepper
3 tablespoons flour	2 tbsp. butter or oleomargerine

Cook the potatoes in boiling salted water. When soft rub through a sieve. Scald the milk with the onion in a double boiler, remove the onion, unless the family likes it left in, add the salt, celery salt and pepper. Melt the butter in a small sauce pan, stir the flour into it and then add this mixture to the hot milk, stirring briskly. Cook for ten minutes over boiling water in the double boiler.

A good creamed soup may be made from almost any vegetable, substituting vegetable pulp for the potato. Celery soup and corn soup are very good With these and most other vegetables, the celery salt should be omitted. Onion salt is very useful.

Creamed soups are very good made from skimmed milk if there is a supply in the house which should be used.

SALAD—The pleasure in a salad is in its crispness, attractiveness of arrangement, and pleasant combination of flavors. A salad may be arranged in a large dish and served at the table if it is the chief dish of the meal, such as chicken salad or fish salad, but it is usually arranged in individual portions and made to look as dainty and pretty as possible. All fresh vegetables and fruits used should be crisp and cold and thoroughly washed. Canned or leftover vegetables or fruit may often be used.

To wash lettuce.—Handle delicately. Remove leaf by leaf from the stalk, examining for insects. Pass the leaves backwards and forwards through clean water until all sand is removed. Fold in a wet cloth and keep in the ice-box until it is used. The lettuce leaves should be dried when they are used.

French Dressing.—Mix ¾ teaspoon of sugar, 1 teaspoon of salt and ½ teaspoon of paprika. Add oil and vinegar alternately, beating constantly with a fork until 5 tablespoons of vinegar and 10 tablespoons of oil have been used. A quick way to make French dressing is to mix all the ingredients in a bottle with a tightly fitting stopper and shake vigorously until the ingredients are blended. Some persons prefer less vinegar, and reduce the amount to 2½ tablespoons vinegar to 10 of oil.

Cooked Salad Dressing.—

¾ tablespoon sugar	¼ tablespoon flour
¼ tablespoon butter	⅛ teaspoon mustard
1 egg yolk	¼ teaspoon salt
¼ cup vinegar	Dash of red pepper.

Heat the vinegar in the upper part of double boiler over direct heat. Sift the flour, mustard, salt and pepper thoroughly. Pour the boiling vinegar gradually upon the mixture, stirring constantly. Return to the upper part of the double boiler and cook over hot water until the mixture thickens, stirring constantly. Add the butter and remove from the fire. Chill before using.

Mayonnaise.—

  1 egg yolk

  2 tablespoons lemon juice or 2 tablespoons vinegar

  ½ teaspoon mustard

2/3 teaspoon salt

  Dash of cayenne pepper.

2/3 cup of oil (olive oil, cotton seed oil or other edible oil).

Have the ingredients chilled. Place the mixing bowl in crushed ice. Mix the egg yolk, mustard, salt and cayenne pepper. Add a few drops of vinegar or lemon juice, then a teaspoon of oil, drop by drop, until all the ingredients are used. Constant beating is necessary throughout.

Fruit and Vegetable Salads.—Good combinations for salad are (1) potato and beet, (2) carrot and green peas, (3) tomato and celery, (4) asparagus and pimento. Combinations of fruit and vegetables are, (1) apple and celery, (2) orange and green pepper. Combinations of different kinds of fruit and nuts or cheese are especially good. Examples are, (1) pineapple and orange, (2) white cherries stuffed with nuts, (3) banana rolled in chopped nuts or (4) half pears (cooked or raw) with a ball of cream cheese and chopped nuts in the cavity made by the removal of the core.

Magazines which devote a page to cooking usually have in their summer numbers pictures of salads from which suggestions in regard to arrangement may be taken.

Baking Powder Biscuit.—

2 cups flour
4 teaspoons baking powder
1 teaspoon salt
3 tablespoons shortening
¾ to 1 cup milk or milk and water.

Sift the flour, baking powder and salt, twice. Put in the shortening, then add the milk gradually, mixing with a knife. The dough should be as soft as can be handled without sticking. Turn onto a lightly floured board, roll lightly ¾ inch thick and cut with a floured cutter. Bake in a hot oven 12 or 15 minutes.

*Tea.—*People who like tea have very decided ideas about how strong it should be and how long it should be steeped. The following gives tea of moderate strength.

Scald the teapot and put in 4 teaspoonfuls of tea leaves. Pour over them four cups of boiling water, cover and steep 3 minutes. Strain into a tea pot and serve at once.

*Cocoa.—*The children of the family should never have tea. On a cold night cocoa is a very pleasant variant from the usual glass of milk.

Mix 4 tablespoons of cocoa with 3 tablespoons of sugar and a little salt. Add 1 cup of boiling water and cook until the mixture is smooth and glossy. Add a quart of milk and heat to boiling. This may be done more safely in a double boiler. Just before serving beat with an egg beater.

General Suggestions

If the Girl Scout who is preparing for her examination will look back over the menus which have been suggested, she will notice that milk is emphasized. It is absolutely essential that the children in the family shall have milk. If the family do not like milk to drink, it should be remembered that every bit which is used in cooking serves the same purpose as if it were taken from a glass, but little children do not ordinarily get enough milk unless they drink some. Fruit should be served at least once a day and better twice, and some vegetable other than potato should be not only served but eaten by the family. Children who are not taught to like vegetables when they are little sometimes never learn to like them, and it is really important to eat vegetables, not only because they contain important substances for growth, but because it is only good manners to learn to like all the ordinary foods which are served. Anyone who has cooked knows how discouraging it is to feel that some member of the family does not like the food. There is a temptation in the city where fruit, vegetables and milk are high, to use too much meat and but little of these foods. It has been suggested recently that in forming an idea as to whether the money is being spent to the most advantage, the money spent for fruit and vegetables, for milk and cheese, and for meat and fish should be compared. In a well-balanced diet these amounts should be nearly equal. An increasing number of people are becoming lacto-vegetarians, which means that they eat no meat or fish, but balance their absence by using more milk, eggs and cheese.

Before starting to prepare a meal the Scout should not only have her menu in mind, but should have an idea how long it will take to prepare each dish so that everything will be ready to serve at the same time with all the hot dishes very hot and all the cold dishes very cold. If all the dishes of the meal require about the same length of time in their preparation the ones should be started first which can be most easily kept in good condition.

Enjoyment of a meal depends quite as much on neat and comfortable service as it does upon good food. The table cloth, napkins, dishes and silver should be clean and the dishes should be arranged so that there is as little danger as possible of accident. This is the reason, for example, for the rule that a spoon should never be left in a coffee or tea cup. The arrangement is usually more comfortable if nothing is placed on the table which is not going to be actually used at the meal, except that a few flowers or a little dish of ferns in the center of the table is very much liked by most people, if there is room for it. It often happens that the family see more of each other at meal times than at any other time in the day and everyone should try to make meal time a pleasant, restful, good humored time.

HOUSEHOLD WEIGHTS AND MEASURES

The careful housewife soon becomes skilled in weighing and measuring the various goods she buys and uses. At the store she is on guard against short measures, and if she does not market in person, she has machines at home to test what is delivered. The following table is given for frequent reference use by the Girl Scout while earning her badges in Homecraft. She will also find it useful in learning to judge weights and distances for her First Class test.

TABLE OF HOUSEHOLD WEIGHTS AND MEASURES
(Reprinted by permission of publisher from "House-wifery," by L. Ray Balderston, M. A.
J. B. Lippincott, 1919)

Linear Measure:

12 inches	= 1 foot
3 feet	= 1 yard
5½ yards	= 1 rod
320 rods	= 1 mile
1760 yards	= 1 mile
5280 feet	= 1 mile

Square Measure:

144 square inches	=	1 square foot
9 square feet	=	1 square yard
30¼ square yards	=	1 square rod
160 square rods	=	1 acre
1 square mile	=	1 section
36 square miles	=	1 township

Avoirdupois Weight:

27.3 grains	=	1 dram
16 drams	=	1 ounce (oz.)
16 ounces	=	1 pound (lb.)
100 pounds	=	1 cwt. (hundredweight)
2,000 pounds	=	1 ton

Liquid Measure:

4 gills	=	1 pint
2 pints	=	1 quart
4 quarts	=	1 gallon
31½ gallons	=	1 bbl.

Dry Measure:

2 pints	=	1 quart
8 quarts	=	1 peck
4 pecks	=	1 bushel
105 dry quarts	=	1 bbl. (fruit, vegetables, etc.)

Miscellaneous Household Measures:

4 saltspoonfuls	=	1 teaspoonful
3 teaspoonfuls	=	1 tablespoonful
16 tablespoonfuls	=	1 cupful
2 gills	=	1 cupful
2 cupfuls	=	1 pint
1 cupful	=	8 fluid ounces
32 tablespoonfuls	=	1 lb. butter
2 cups of butter	=	1 lb.
1 lb. butter	=	40 butter balls
4 cups flour	=	1 lb.

2 cups sugar   = 1 lb.
5 cups coffee   = 1 lb.
1 lb. coffee = 40 cups of liquid coffee
1⅞ cups rice = 1 lb.
2 2/3 cups oatmeal = 1 lb.
2 2/3 cups cornmeal = 1 lb.
1 cup of liquid to 3 cups of flour = a dough
1 cup of liquid to 2 cups of flour = a thick batter
1 cup of liquid to 1 cup of flour = a thin batter
1 teaspoonful soda to 1 pint sour milk
1 teaspoonful soda to one cup of molasses
1 teaspoonful cream of tartar plus ½ teaspoonful
   soda = 2 teaspoonfuls baking powder

2. THE CHILD NURSE

There always are and always will be children to be taken care of. There is no way in which a girl can help her country better than by fitting herself to undertake the care of children. A Girl Scout thinks for herself, and, knowing the Health Laws, she knows the important things to consider in caring for children:

1. The care necessary for the child's bones.
2. When it should exercise its muscles.
3. Its rest.
4. The air, sun and food and water which it needs.
5. How to keep it clean.

Bones—Great care must be taken in handling a baby. Its bones are soft and easily injured, and for this reason a baby should not be handled more than necessary. When very young its entire spine should be supported, and no undue pressure made upon the chest, as often happens if the baby is grasped under the arms. In lifting a young baby from its bed, the right hand should grasp the clothing below the feet, and the left hand should be slipped beneath the infant's body to its head. It is then raised upon the left arm. An older child should be lifted by placing the hands under the child's arms, and never by the wrists. If children are jerked or lifted by the arms, serious injury may be done to the bones. The bones, when a child is growing, are partly composed of soft tissue which is easily destroyed, and further growth is prevented. Many children are brought to the hospital with injuries done to their arms from being jerked across the street. Do not let a child walk too soon, especially a heavy child. Bow legs and knock knees come from standing and walking when the bones are soft.

Exercise—At least twice a day an infant should be allowed for fifteen or twenty minutes the free use of its limbs by permitting it to lie upon a bed in a warm room, with all clothing except the shirt and diaper removed. In cold weather leave on the stockings. Later, when in short clothes, the baby may be put upon a thick blanket or quilt, laid upon the floor, and be allowed to tumble at will.

Rest—Healthy children never sleep too much. A new born baby should sleep nine-tenths of the day. A child should have a nap during the day until four years old, and, if possible, until seven or eight years old. It should go to bed before six. It should have a crib or bed to itself, placed where it will have fresh air, but protected from draughts, and its eyes protected from direct rays of light.

Air and Sun—A little child is in its room so much it is very important that fresh air and sunlight should be brought to it there. Rooms may be well aired twice or three times a day, removing the baby to another room while the windows are open. The child may be placed in its crib or carriage before an open window, dressed as if for the street. After children are three months old they may be taken out, but the sunny part of the day should be chosen, between 10 a. m. and 3 p. m. in cold weather. At night the windows should be partly opened, but care should be taken that the infant does not become chilled. Be careful that sheet and blankets do not get over a baby's head. The clothes may be pinned to the side of the bed.

Food and Water—Even little babies should be given water twice a day. The water should be boiled, cooled and kept covered. It is hardly possible for children or older persons to drink too much water. During hot weather a child needs more water than during cold weather.

Mother's milk is the only perfect food for an infant during the first nine or ten months. If it is necessary to give artificial food from a bottle, the greatest possible care must be taken. The milk used should be the best obtainable. To obtain clean milk it is necessary that everything that touches it be clean, sterilized when possible, and that the cows, and men who handle the milk be healthy. In New York City all milk is classified according to its cleanliness and butter fat content. The cleanest and richest milk is called "certified milk" and is sold raw. The other milks are classified according to cleanliness. Grade A, B and C are all pasteurized. Only certified and Grade A should be used for infant feeding. You know that sterile means free from germs or bacteria. Milk or water may be made comparatively sterile by boiling. Pasteurized milk is milk which has been heated to 155° Fahrenheit, kept at that temperature for thirty minutes and cooled quickly by placing the bottles in cold running water.

Punctual feeding makes good digestion, and even if the baby takes an extra nap it is better to wake a healthy baby to give him his meals at regular hours than to let his digestion get out of order. Between meals a little water which has been boiled and cooled and kept covered will wash out its mouth as well as refresh the child. The average infant is fed every three hours until it is five months old. After that it is fed every four hours until it is fifteen or sixteen months old, when it is shifted to three meals a day with perhaps a cup of milk in long intervals. Solid food, such as zweiback and milk or cereal, is begun at seven months, and by thirteen or fourteen months the child will be eating cereal, bread, broth, beef juice, potato, rice, vegetables, etc. Candy is harmful for children, and even older children should eat candy only after meals. Raw fruit, except orange juice, is apt to be upsetting in summer.

Keep the baby and everything around him clean. The baby's food is the most important thing to keep clean. The cleanliness of the bottle, when it is necessary to feed the baby from one, is very important. Choose a bottle of fairly heavy glass with rounded bottom and wide mouth, so that it may be easily cleaned. Short rubber nipples which clip over the neck of the bottle and which can be easily turned inside out, should be selected, and discarded when they become soft, or when the openings become large enough for the milk to run in a stream instead of drop by drop. Remove the bottle from the baby's mouth as soon as empty, rinse at once in cold water and then fill with a solution of bicarbonate of soda (baking soda), about one teaspoonful to a pint of water. Before rinsing wash in hot soapsuds, using a bottle brush, rinse well in plain water, and boil for twenty minutes, placing a clean cloth in the bottom of the basin to protect the bottle from breaking. Before using new nipples they should be scrubbed inside and out and boiled for at least five minutes. After using they should be carefully rinsed in cold water and kept in a covered glass containing a solution of boric acid (one teaspoonful dissolved in a pint of boiling water), and at least once a day be turned inside out and thoroughly washed with soap and water, then rinsed. Nipples should be boiled twice a week.

Bath—A baby should have a bath every day, not sooner than one hour after feeding. The room should be warm; if possible there should be an open fire in the room. The temperature of the water for a baby up to six months old should be 98°. Then it should gradually decrease, next temperature being 95°, until at the age of two it should range between 85° to 90°. Before a baby is undressed the person who is bathing the baby must be sure that everything needed for the bath and dressing is at hand. The hand basin or small tub of warm water, a pitcher of hot water in case it is needed, castile or ivory soap, soft wash cloths, towels, brush, powder, fresh absorbent cotton, boric acid solution, and the baby's clothes laid out in the order in which they will be needed in dressing the child, the soft flannel bandage, the diapers, the shirt, flannel petticoat, dress and shawl.

For some people it is easier to handle a baby when laid on a bed or table than on one's lap, having under the child a soft bath towel or canton flannel large enough to be wrapped around it. Its nose may be cleaned with a bit of absorbent cotton rolled to a point, using a fresh piece for each nostril. To bathe the eyes use fresh pieces of absorbent cotton dipped in boric acid solution. Wash the baby's face carefully so that the water does not drip into its ears. Dry the face carefully. Wash the head gently and thoroughly with soap, being careful to rinse completely. Soap the baby's body before putting it into the bath. As a soapy little baby is difficult to hold, support him firmly all the time he is kicking and splashing, by placing the arm or hand at the baby's back between its shoulders. Wash particularly, under the arms, the creases in the back of the neck, between the legs, fingers and toes. The bath should be given quickly and the baby lifted out on the bath towel or flannel, covered and dried quickly, using a soft towel. Rub the baby very slightly. All the folds of the skin should be dried and well powdered: under the arms, behind the ears, about the neck, legs, etc. Do not put too much powder on, as it forms a paste. Dress the infant and lay it on its crib while putting away all the things used for its bath. It is perfectly proper for a baby to exercise its lungs by crying, so do not be alarmed, but be sure that its clothing is comfortable and that the child is clean. Garments worn at night should always be different from those worn during the day. The garments next to the skin should be of wool or part wool, except the diaper, which should be soft cotton, and when new, washed several times before using. Wet diapers should be rinsed in cold water and dried before using a second time; about every twenty-four hours diapers should be washed, scalded, rinsed in cold water and hung in the air to dry.

Daily Routine—Child Under Two Years of Age

6.00 A.M.   Feed warm milk.

7.30 A.M.   Seat on chair or hold over chamber not more than ten minutes. If the child has no movement of the bowels at this time, try later.

9.00 A.M.   Give bath, and immediately after, feed, then put to bed in a well ventilated room, darkened, or out of doors in carriage or crib. Be sure no strong light is in the child's eyes. Child should sleep until one o'clock.

1.00 P.M. Take up, make comfortable, and feed.

2.00 P.M. Take child out of doors again, but do not stay after 3 P.M. in winter time. Later in summer. Stormy days keep in house in crib or carriage, well wrapped up in room with window open.

3 to 5 P. M. Hold child, or let it stay in crib and play or kick.

6.00 P.M. Undress, rub with soft, dry towel, put on nightclothes, feed and put to bed in well ventilated room.

10.00 P.M. A young baby should be fed at this time, dried, and not fed again until 6 A.M.

A baby needs to be kept quiet. Do not make loud noises near it. Do not play with infant too much. Leave it to itself to grow. Keep the baby clean, everything about it tidy. Do not give a child pointed toys or playthings small enough to go into the infant's mouth. Tie toys to the crib or carriage so that they do not fall on the floor.

Things to Remember

Emphasize "tidy as you go," sleep, water, bowel movements, exercise for older children, especially in cold weather, nothing in mouth, do not use pacifiers, tying toys to crib or carriage, a baby over two years of age should not be fed oftener than every four hours.

Bowel Movements

At least once a day.

Should be medium soft, not loose, smooth, and when on milk diet, light in color.

If child is constipated, give one teaspoonful of milk of magnesia clear, at night.

See doctor if child is not well.

Feedings

Children from birth to five months should be fed every three hours.

Children over one and a half years old need three meals a day, dinner in the middle of the day.

Little children need to be kept very quiet. No confusion or loud noises around them. They will then grow better and stronger.

Colds

Never neglect a cold. Do not "pass it on" to a child by coughing, sneezing, talking or breathing into its face. Do not kiss anyone when you have a cold. Never allow the handkerchief used by a person with a cold to touch a child. If you must handle a child when you have a cold, wear a piece of gauze over your mouth and nose, and be sure to keep your hands clean. Be very careful with the handkerchiefs used; see that no one touches or uses them. It is preferable to use gauze or soft paper for handkerchiefs and burn them. When a child has a cold put it to bed. Keep quiet as long as there is any fever. Give a cathartic, such as castor oil, as soon as cold appears. Reduce the child's diet and give plenty of drinking water. Consult a doctor. Do not let the child go out until thoroughly well.

3. THE FIRST AIDE IN ACCIDENTS AND EMERGENCIES

General Rules

The sorrow and unhappiness of the world is increased enormously every year by injury and loss from accidents, more than half of which might be prevented if someone had not been careless, or if someone else had taken a little trouble to correct the results of that carelessness before they caused an accident.

It therefore becomes the plain duty of Girl Scouts not only to be careful but to repair, if possible, the carelessness of others which may result in accident.

Let us review briefly some of the many small things in our daily lives which cause accidents, and therefore suffering and loss.

1. *Carelessness in the Street.* As, for example, taking chances in getting across in front of a car or automobile; running from behind a car without looking to see if some vehicle is coming from another direction; catching a ride by hanging on to the rear end of cars or wagons; getting off cars before they stop; getting on or off cars in the wrong way; being too interested to watch for open manholes, cellarways, sewers, etc.; reckless roller skating in the street, throwing things like banana peels on the street or sidewalk where people are likely to slip on them; teasing dogs, or trying to catch strange ones; many dogs resent a stranger petting them and use their only means of defense—biting. Other examples will occur to you of carelessness in the streets which space does not allow us to mention here.

Wait until the car stops before trying to get off. In getting off cars you should face in the direction in which the car is going. A simple rule is to get off by holding a rod with the left hand and putting the right foot down first. This brings you facing the front of the car and prevents your being swept off your feet by the momentum of the car.

If you see any refuse in the street which is likely to cause an accident, either remove it yourself or report it to the proper authorities to have it removed at once.

2. *Carelessness at Home.* As, for example, starting the fire with kerosene; leaving gas jets burning where curtains or clothing may be blown into the flame; leaving clothing or paper too near a fire; throwing matches you thought had been put out into paper or other material which will catch fire easily; leaving oily or greasy rags where they will easily overheat or take fire spontaneously; leaving objects on stairs and in hallways which will cause others to fall; leaving scalding water where a child may fall into it or pull it down, spilling the scalding water over himself; leaving rags or linoleum with upturned edges for someone to fall over; and innumerable other careless things which will occur to you.

3. *Disobedience,* playing with matches; building fires in improper places; playing with guns; trying the "medicines" in the closet; throwing stones; playing with the electric wires or lights; playing around railroad tracks and bridges. We could multiply the accidents from disobedience indefinitely. Remember, a caution given you not to do something means there is danger in doing it, which may bring much sorrow and suffering to yourself and to others.

It is a very old saying that "An ounce of prevention is worth a pound of cure," but it is just as true today as it was hundreds of years ago.

After the Accident

When the time for prevention is past, and the accident has happened, then you want to know what is the best thing to do, and how best to do it in order to give the most help and relief immediately, before expert help can arrive, and to have the victim in the best condition possible for the doctor when he comes, in order that he may not have to undo whatever has been done before he can begin to give the patient relief from his suffering.

1. Keep cool. The only way to do this effectually is to learn beforehand what to do and how to do it. Then you are not frightened and can do readily and with coolness whatever is necessary to be done.

2. Send at once for a doctor, if you have a messenger, in all except the minor accidents. This book will help you learn to judge of whether a doctor will be necessary. If in doubt, send for the doctor anyway.

3. Prevent panic and keep the crowd, if there is one, at a distance. The patient needs fresh air to breathe, and space around him.

4. Loosen the clothing, especially any band around the neck, tight corsets or anything else that may interfere with breathing.

5. *Keep the patient flat on his back* if the accident is at all serious, with the head slightly down if his face is pale and he is faint, or slightly raised if his face is flushed and he is breathing heavily, as though snoring.

6. *If there is vomiting,* turn the head to one side in order that the vomited material may easily run out of the mouth and not be drawn into the windpipe and produce choking to add to the difficulties already present.

7. *Remove clothing,* if necessary, gently and in such manner as to give the patient the least amount of suffering. Move any injured part as little as possible. At the same time, as a secondary consideration, injure the clothing as little as possible. If, as often, it becomes necessary to cut off the clothing, it may be possible to rip up a seam quickly instead of cutting the cloth, but saving the clothing is always secondary to the welfare of the patient. Little or no consideration should be shown for clothing where it is necessary to keep the patient motionless, or where quick action is needed.

8. *Transportation.* There are three methods for

emergency transportation of accident victims which can be used according to the degree of the injury:

(a) *Fireman's Lift.* If it is necessary for one person to carry a patient, it is easily possible to lift and carry quite a weight in the following manner:

First, turn the patient on his face; then step astride his body, facing toward his head, and, with hands under his armpits, lift him to his knees; then clasp your hands over the patient's abdomen and lift him to his feet; then draw his left arm around your neck and hold it against the left side of your chest, the patient's left side resting against your body, and supporting him with your right arm about the waist. Then drop the patient's left hand and grasp his right wrist with your left hand and draw the right arm over your head and down upon your left chest; then stooping, clasp his right thigh with your right arm passed between the legs (or around both legs) and with a quick heave lift the patient to your shoulders and seize his right wrist with your right hand, and lastly, grasp the patient's left hand with your left hand to steady him against your body. (Work this out with a companion as you read it.)

(b) A seat made of four arms and hands (which you have no doubt used in your play), may be used for the lesser injuries. If the patient can, he supports himself by putting his arms around the necks of his carriers, each of whom in the meantime grasps one of his own wrists and one of his partner's. This makes a comfortable seat for carrying. If the patient needs supporting, a back may be improvised by each carrier grasping the other's arm below the shoulder to form the back and their other hands clasped to form the seat. A better seat may be made with three hands clasping the wrists, while the fourth arm is used as a back, by one clasping the other's arm below the shoulder. This does not provide a very secure back, however, as it is not easy to hold the arm against much of a weight from the patient's body.

(c) *Improvised Stretcher.* When the patient shows any sign of shock, is unconscious, has a serious fracture of some bone or bones, has a serious injury to any part of the body, or is bleeding excessively, he must be carried lying down. It may be that there will be no regular stretcher at hand. In that case one must be improvised. A serviceable one can be made from ordinary grain or flour bags by cutting the two corners at the bottom and running two poles inside the mouth of the bags and through the holes.

A workable stretcher can be made from coats by turning the sleeves inside out, passing the poles through the sleeves and buttoning the coat over the poles. This brings the turned sleeves on the inside. A five-bar gate or a door, if it can be gotten without delay, also make satisfactory emergency stretchers.

A stretcher may also be made out of dress skirts, with or without poles. Put the skirts together, bottoms slipped past each other, and slip the poles through, as with the bags. If no poles are available, roll the edges of the skirts over several times to form a firm edge, and carry with two or four bearers, as the size and weight of the patient make necessary.

Minor Injuries and Emergencies

Minor injuries may or may not need the aid of a doctor, and you must learn to use judgment as to the necessity of sending for one. We will consider these minor injuries in groups to remember them more easily.

1. (a) BRUISES; (b) STRAINS; (c) SPRAINS

(a) *A Bruise* is produced by a blow which does not break the skin, but does break the delicate walls of the capillaries and smaller veins, thus permitting the blood to flow into the surrounding tissues, producing the discoloration known as "black and blue."

(b) *A Strain* is produced by the overstretching of muscles or ligaments, or both, but not tearing them. It may or may not be accompanied by breaking of capillary walls with discoloration. Any muscle or ligament may be strained.

(c) *A Sprain* is produced by the overstretching of the muscles or ligaments or both about a *joint*. There may also be some tearing of the fibres or tearing loose from their attachments. This always breaks capillaries or small veins, making the surface black and blue. This discoloration usually appears some time after the accident, because the broken blood vessels are far below the surface.

Treatment—For bruises and strains it is seldom necessary to call a doctor. Apply cold, either by wringing cloths out of cold water and applying, or by holding the injured part under the cold water tap. Do this at intervals for several hours, until the pain is lessened. The cold may be alternated with hot water which must, however, be quite hot, just enough not to burn, as lukewarm water is almost useless. Some patients will prefer to use only hot water. The water followed by applications of tincture of arnica, witch hazel, or alcohol and water, half and half, and bandaging will be sufficient.

If, however, there has been no black and blue at first, as in a bruise, but it begins to show later, and the pain continues severe, and there is a good deal of swelling, then you should send for a doctor, as more than first aid is needed.

In case of *sprain,* send for a doctor, and in the meantime elevate the joint and apply hot or cold water, or alternate hot and cold, as patient prefers. This will give relief by contracting the blood vessels.

2. (a) BURNS; (b) SCALDS; (c) SUNBURN; (d) FROSTBITE

(a) *Burns* are produced by dry heat, as a fire, acids, alkalis, etc., and may be of all degrees, from a superficial reddening of the skin to a burning of the tissues to the bone.

(b) *Scalds* are produced by moist heat, and may be of the same degrees as those produced by dry heat.

(c) *Sunburn* is produced by the sun, and is usually superficial, but may be quite severe.

(d) *Frostbite* is produced by freezing the tissues and is usually not dangerous. The more severe types will be treated later under Freezing.

Treatment—(a) *Burns;* (b) *Scalds*

1. Except in the minor burns and scalds, send for the doctor at once.

2. The first thing to do is allay pain by protecting the injured part from the air, since the oxygen in the air keeps the fire burning in the flesh as it does in wood.

3. For a burn produced by fire, cover with a paste made of baking soda and water, or smear with grease —as lard, carron oil (mixture of linseed oil and lime water—half and half) or vaseline. Cover with a piece of clean cloth or absorbent gauze and bandage loosely or tie in place. Gauze prepared with picric acid, if at hand, is a most satisfactory dressing. It can be purchased and kept on hand for emergencies.

4. In burns from alkalis or acids, wash off as quickly as possible and neutralize (make inactive) the acids with baking soda, weak ammonia or soapsuds; the alkalis with vinegar or lemon juice. Afterward treat like other burns.

(c) *Sunburn* is an inflammation of the skin produced by the action of the sun's rays and may be prevented by gradually accustoming the skin to exposure to the sun. It is treated as are other minor burns.

(d) *Frostbite—Prevention—*1. Wear sufficient clothing in cold weather and keep exposed parts, such as ears and fingers, covered.

2. Rub vigorously any part that has become cold. This brings the warm blood to the surface and prevents chilling.

3. Keep in action when exposed to the cold for any length of time. The signs of danger are sudden lack of feeling in an exposed part, and a noticeably white area. Chilblain is an example of frostbite.

*Treatment—*The circulation of the blood through the frozen part must be restored gradually. This must be done by rubbing the part first with snow or cold water, which will be slightly warmer than the frozen part, and *gradually* warming the water until the circulation and warmth is fully restored. Then treat as a minor burn. If heat is applied suddenly it causes death of frozen parts.

3. SPLINTERS, SMALL CUTS, SCRATCHES AND PIN PRICKS

None of these injuries will usually require a doctor if properly treated in the beginning. The bleeding from any of them is not sufficient to be dangerous. But whenever there is a break in the skin or mucous membrane there is danger of infection by germs, and this is what makes the first aid treatment in these cases so important. A tiny scratch is sometimes converted into a bad case of blood poisoning by not being properly treated at first.

Splinters should be removed by using a needle (not a pin) which has been sterilized by passing it through a flame (the flame of a match will do if nothing better is at hand). After the splinter is out, the wound is treated like a cut or scratch.

The germs which produce poisoning do not float in the air, but may be conveyed by anything which is not sterile, as, for instance, the splinter or the instrument that did the cutting, scratching or pricking. They may be carried to the scratch by our hands, by water, or cloth used for dressings.

Treatment—Wash your own hands thoroughly with soap and water, using a nail brush. Clean the injured part well with disinfectant, as, for instance, alcohol and water, half and half, or peroxide of hydrogen—paint the spot with iodine, and cover with sterile gauze (if this is not to be had, use a piece of clean cloth that has been recently ironed), and bandage in place. If the bleeding is severe, a little pressure with the bandage over the dressing will stop it. Use the same precautions if the wound has to be re-dressed.

4. STINGS AND BITES OF INSECTS

The poison injected by the sting or bite of an insect is usually acid, and the part should be washed at once with a solution of ammonia or soda (washing soda) to neutralize the poison. Then apply a paste of soda bicarbonate (baking soda) or wet salt and bandage in place. If the sting is left in the wound it must be pulled out before beginning treatment.

5. FOREIGN BODIES IN THE (a) EYE (Cinder), (b) EAR (Insect), (c) NOSE (Button)

(a) *Eye*—If a cinder, eyelash, or any tiny speck gets into the eye it causes acute pain, and in a few minutes considerable redness.

Treatment—Do not rub the eye, as this may press the object into the tender cornea so that it can be removed only with difficulty and by a physician. First close the eye gently, pull the eyelid free of the ball, and the tears may wash out the speck. If this is not successful, close the eye, hold the lid free, and blow the nose hard. You may then be able to see the speck and remove it with a bit of clean cotton or the corner of a clean handkerchief. If the object is lodged under the lid, and the foregoing efforts do not dislodge it, proceed to turn the lid up as follows:

Ask the patient to look at the floor, keeping the eyeball as stationary as possible. Take a clean wooden toothpick or slender pencil, wrapped with cotton, place on the upper lid about one-fourth of an inch from the edge, grasp the eyelashes with the other hand, give a slight push downward toward the cheek with the toothpick, a slight pull upward on the lashes and turn the lid over the toothpick. Remove the speck and slip the lid back in position. Wash the eye with boric acid solution.

If you are still unable to dislodge the body, discontinue any further efforts, apply a cloth wet in cold boric acid solution and send for the doctor. Anything done to the eyes must be done with the greatest gentleness.

If an acid has entered the eye, neutralize it with a weak solution of soda bicarbonate in water. If an alkali (lime) is the offending substance, neutralize by a weak vinegar solution. Follow in each case with a wash of boric acid solution.

(b) *Ear* (Insect); (c) *Button in Nose*—Foreign bodies in the ear and nose are not very common.

But sometimes a child slips a button or other small object into these cavities, or an insect may crawl in. Drop in a few drops of sweet oil and if the object comes out easily, well and good. If not, do not keep on trying to extract it, for fear of greater injury. Send for the doctor.

6. IVY AND OAK POISONING

There are a poison ivy and a poison oak which are very poisonous to some people, and more or less so to all people. The poison ivy has a leaf similar to the harmless woodbine, but the leaves are grouped in threes instead of fives. The poison given off by these plants produces a severe inflammation of the skin. In the early stages it may be spread from one part of the body to another by scratching.

Treatment—Wash the irritated surface gently with soap and water, and then apply a paste of soda bicarbonate or cover quickly with carbonated vaseline. Another remedy is fluid extract *grindelia robusta,* one dram to four ounces of water. Sugar of lead and alcohol have also been found useful. For severe cases consult a doctor, especially if the face or neck or hands are affected.

7. (a) FAINTING; (b) HEAT EXHAUSTION

(a) *Fainting* is caused by lack of blood in the brain, and usually occurs in overheated, crowded places, from fright or from overfatigue.

Symptoms—1. The patient is very pale and partially or completely unconscious.

2. The pulse is weak and rapid.

3. The pupils of the eyes are normal.

Treatment—1. If possible put the patient flat on his back, with the head slightly lower than the rest of the body.

2. If there is not room to do this, bend the patient over with his head between the knees until sufficient blood has returned to the brain to restore consciousness.

3. Then get the patient into the fresh air as soon as possible.

4. Keep the crowd back.

5. Loosen the clothing about the neck.

6. Apply smelling salts to the nose.

7. When the patient has recovered sufficiently to swallow, give him a glass of cold water, with one-half teaspoonful of aromatic spirits of ammonia if necessary.

(b) *Heat Exhaustion* is exhaustion or collapse due to overheating where there is not sufficient evaporation from the surface of the body to keep the temperature normal.

Symptoms—1. The patient is usually very weak.

2. The face is pale and covered with a clammy sweat.

3. The pulse is weak and rapid.

4. The patient is usually not unconscious.

Treatment—1. Remove the patient to a cool place and have him lie down.

2. Loosen the clothing.

3. Give him a cold drink to sip.

4. Put cold cloths on his head.

5. Send for the doctor.

6. If necessary, give stimulant as in fainting.

8. (a) CHOKING; (b) HICCOUGH

(a) *Choking*—Choking is produced by something lodged in the throat, does not require artificial respiration, but a smart slap on the back to aid in dislodging whatever is blocking the air passage. It may be necessary to have the patient upside down, head lower than feet, to aid in getting out the foreign body. This is a comparatively simple matter with a child, but is not so easy with an adult. When the object is not too far down the throat it may be necessary for someone to use his fingers to pull out the offending substance to keep the patient alive until the doctor can arrive. In this case wedge the teeth apart with something to prevent biting before trying to grasp the object.

(b) *Hiccough*—This is usually due to indigestion or

overloading of the stomach. Holding the breath for one-half a minute will usually cure it, as it holds quiet the diaphragm (the large muscular and fibrous partition between the chest and abdomen), and overcomes its involuntary contractions which are causing the hiccoughs. A scare has the same effect sometimes. If the hiccoughs still continue troublesome after these simple remedies try to cause vomiting by drinking lukewarm water, which will get rid of the offending material causing the hiccough, and relieve the distress.

9. NOSE BLEED

The ordinary nose bleed will soon stop from the normal clotting of the blood and does not require treatment.

(c) Keep head elevated, with patient sitting up if possible. Do not blow the nose, as this will dislodge any clot which may have formed, and the bleeding will begin again. Any tight collar around the neck should be loosened.

(d) If the bleeding seems excessive, apply cloths wrung out of ice water to the back of the neck and over the nose.

(e) If the bleeding still continues and is abundant, pack the nostril with a cotton or gauze plug. Pack tightly (with the blunt end of a pencil if nothing else is at hand) *and send for the doctor at once.*

Major Injuries and Emergencies

1. (a) DISLOCATIONS; (b) FRACTURES

(a) *Dislocations*—In a dislocation the head of a bone is pushed or pulled out of its socket. A person may be falling and in trying to save himself catch hold of something in such a way that he feels a sharp, sudden, severe pain, and may even feel the head of the bone slip out at the shoulder or elbow.

Symptoms—1. When you look at the injured part it does not look like the other side.

2. If you attempt to move it you find it will no longer move as a joint does, but is stiff.

3. There is great pain and rapid swelling usually.

4. There may or may not be black and blue spots around the joint.

Treatment—Send for a doctor at once. While waiting for the doctor, place the patient in the easiest position possible, and apply hot or cold cloths, frequently changed, to the injured part.

In dislocation of the jaw it may be necessary for someone to try to replace it before the doctor arrives. The mouth is open and the jaw fixed. The patient may even tell you he has felt the jaw slip out of its socket. Wrap your thumbs in cloth to prevent biting when the jaw snaps back in place. Place the thumbs on the tops of the lower teeth on each side, with the fingers outside. and push firmly down until the head of the bone can slip over the edge of the socket into place. As you feel the bone slipping into place, slide your thumbs out to the inner side of the cheek to prevent biting when the jaws snap together with the reducing of the dislocation.

(b) *Fractures—Broken bones*—There are two classes of fractures:

1. *Simple*—In a *simple* fracture the bone is broken, but the skin is not broken; that is, there is no outward wound.

2. *Compound*—In a *compound* fracture not only is the bone broken, but the jagged ends pierce through the skin and form an open wound. This makes it more dangerous as the possibility of infection by germs at the time of the accident, or afterward, is added to the difficulty of the fracture.

Symptoms—As in dislocations, you should be familiar with the main symptoms of a broken bone.

1. When you look at the injured part it may or may not look like its mate on the other side. In the more severe fractures it usually does not.

2. When you try to move it you find more motion than there should be if the bone has broken clear through; that is, there will seem to be a joint where no joint should be.

3. The least movement causes great pain.

4. The swelling is usually rapid.

5. The discoloration (black and blue) appears later; not at once, unless there is also a superficial bruise.

6. The patient is unable to move the injured part.

7. You may hear the grate of the ends of the bone when the part is moved, but you should not move the injured bone enough to hear this, especially if the limb is nearly straight; the detection of this sound should be left for the doctor.

Treatment—Send for a doctor at once, and if it will be possible for him to arrive soon, make the patient as comfortable as possible and wait for him. However, if it will be some time before the doctor can arrive you should try to give such aid as will do no harm and will help the sufferer.

You must handle the part injured and the patient with the utmost gentleness to avoid making a simple fracture into a compound one, or doing other injury, and also to give him as little additional suffering as possible. You will need to get the clothing off the part to be sure of what you are doing. Rip the clothing in a seam if possible when the fracture is in an arm or leg, but if this cannot be done, you will have to cut the material. Do not try to move the broken bone trying to get off a sleeve or other part of the clothing.

With the greatest gentleness put the injured part, for instance, the arm or leg, as nearly as possible in the same position as the sound part, and hold it in that position by splints. Do not use force to do this. There is no great hurry needed to set a broken bone. The important point is to get it set right, and this may better be done after complete rest of several days, allowing for the passing of the inflammation.

The Most Important "What Not to Do Points" for Fractures Are:

1. If there is reason to think a bone *may* be broken try in all ways to prevent motion at *point* of fracture lest it be made compound.

2. Do not go hunting for symptoms of fracture (such as the false point of motion or the sound "crepitus") just to be sure.

3. The best treatment is to try to immobilize the part till the doctor comes.

Splints—Anything that is stiff and rigid may be used for splints. Shingles, boards, limbs of trees, umbrellas, heavy wire netting, etc. Flat splints are best, however. All splints should be padded, especially where they lie against a bony prominence, as, for instance, the ankle or elbow joint.

If the patient is wearing heavy winter clothing this may form sufficient padding. If not, then other cloth, straw or leaves may be used. Cotton batting makes excellent padding, but if this is not to be had quickly, other things can be made to do to pad the first rough splints which are applied until the patient can reach a doctor or the doctor arrives on the scene of the accident.

In applying splints remember they must extend beyond the next joint below and the next joint above, otherwise movement of the joint will cause movement of the broken part.

The splints are tied firmly in place with handkerchiefs, strips of cloth, or bandages, tied over splints, padding and limb. Do not tie tight enough to increase the pain, but just enough to hold the splints firmly. Do not tie directly over the break. There must be an inner and outer splint for both the arms and the legs.

2. (a) SERIOUS WOUNDS; (b) SERIOUS BLEEDING

Send for the doctor at once, and then stop the bleeding and keep as clean as possible till he arrives.

Dangers—1. In any wound with a break in the skin, there is the danger of infection or blood poisoning, as you have already learned.

2. In serious wounds through the skin, flesh and blood vessels there is also the danger of severe bleeding, with the possibility of the patient's bleeding to death.

Infection—You already know how the germs which can cause the blood poisoning get into the wound

(a) by the object that makes the wound

(b) from the clothing of the patient through which the wound is made

(c) from the rescuer's hands

(d) from water which has not been sterilized used in washing the wound

(e) from dirty dressings, that is, dirty in the sense that they have on them germs which can get into the wound and cause infection or blood poisoning.

The first two of these chances the Girl Scout will not be able to control. The last three she can to some extent prevent. *Do not wash, touch or put anything into a serious wound* unless a doctor cannot be found. Only this sort of thing justifies running risk of infection. Otherwise just put on a sterile dressing and bandage. In reality washing wounds only satisfies the aesthetic sense of the operator without real benefit to the patient in many cases. If a wound has to be cleansed before the doctor comes use boiled water; if this cannot be had at once, use water and alcohol half and half.

1. Always wash your hands thoroughly with water, soap and a nail brush, unless there is necessity for immediate help to stop bleeding which admits of no time to clean one's hands. Be sure your nails are clean.

2. Try not to touch the wound with your hands unless it is absolutely necessary.

3. Many wounds do not have to be washed, but dressing may be applied directly.

4. Apply sterile cloth for dressing, having cleansed the wound as best you can, or all that is necessary. This may be gotten at a drug store in a sterile package ready for use immediately, and is very satisfactory. If, however, these cannot be had, remember any cloth like a folded handkerchief that has been recently washed and *ironed* is practically sterile, especially if you unfold it carefully and apply the inside which you have not touched, to the wound. Bind the dressing on with a bandage to keep in place util the doctor arrives.

(b) *Serious Bleeding:*

It is important that you should learn what *is* serious bleeding and this will often help you to be cool under trying circumstances.

As you learned in your work in minor emergencies, the bleeding from the small veins and capillaries is not usually sufficient to be dangerous, and the pressure of the dressing when put on and bandaged in a place will soon stop it. It may sometimes be necessary to put more dressing outside of that already on (called re-in-

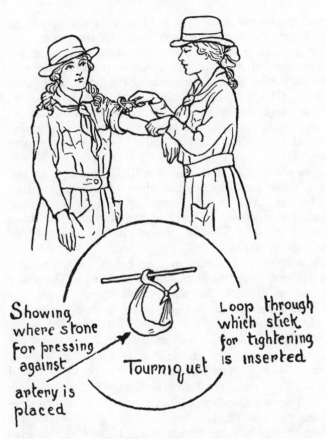

Showing where stone for pressing against artery is placed

Tourniquet

Loop through which stick for tightening is inserted

forcing it) and bandage again snugly. But if you have made sure first that there is no large vein or artery cut, you need not be troubled for fear there will be serious bleeding before the doctor arrives.

Bleeding from an Artery: If an artery is cut the blood spurts out, the size of the stream depending on the size of the artery cut. This is the most serious bleeding because the heart is directly behind, pumping the blood through the artery with all its power. If it is a small artery the pressure with the finger between the cut and the heart for a few minutes will give the blood time to clot behind the finger and form a plug. This will stop the bleeding aided by pressure of the bandage. If it is a larger vessel the force in the heart muscle pumping the blood will force out any plug formed by holding the finger there, as the finger tires too easily.

Tourniquet: In this case it will be necessary to put on a tourniquet to take the place of the finger until a clot can form in the vessel big enough and strong enough to prevent the force of the blood current from pushing it out. This of course can be used only on the legs or arms.

A tourniquet is something put on to make pressure on a blood vessel to stop serious bleeding. There are five points to remember about a tourniquet:

1. It must be long enough to tie around the limb— a big handkerchief, towel or wide bandage.

2. There must be a pad to make the pressure over the artery greater than on the rest of the limb—a smooth stone, a darning ball, a large cork, cloth folded into a large pad or a rolled bandage.

3. The pad must be so placed that the artery lies between pad and the bone on the limb, in order that the pressure may stop the flow of blood by forcing the walls of the artery together between the pad and the bone.

4. Unless the tourniquet is put on tight enough, its application increases bleeding. It is extremely rare to find a tourniquet put on tight enough. In almost every such case removing the tourniquet will stop or partly lessen bleeding. A short stick or handle is needed, about a foot long, with which to twist the tourniquet

sufficiently to cut the flow of blood. Usually it cannot be twisted tightly enough by hand alone. Tie the twisted part firmly so it will not slip, after it has been made tight enough to stop bleeding.

5. Remember, a tourniquet stops most of the circulation below it as well as in the cut artery, and must not be left in place too long for fear of injury to the rest of the limb by cutting off the circulation. *Usually it should not be left on for more than an hour.*

Bleeding from Veins—Bleeding from the veins is not so dangerous as from an artery. The blood from the heart has to go through the little capillaries before it gets into the veins, and therefore the force of the heart muscle on the blood in the veins is not so great as in the arteries. The blood does not spurt out, but flows out as it would from a bottle tipped on its side.

You have already learned what to do to stop the bleeding from the smaller veins, and that it is not serious. From the larger veins, however, it can be very serious, and it may be necessary for you to put on a tourniquet before the doctor arrives in order to save the patient's life.

Almost always bleeding from a vein can be controlled by clean gauze or handkerchief pad and pressure by hand directly over the bleeding wound. Tourniquets are almost never needed in bleeding from a vein. If necessary, it is wisest to apply them in the same way as for arterial hemorrhage and stop the circulation in the whole limb.

It is important to know in a general way where the blood vessels are in order to put the pad over them to stop the bleeding. Roughly speaking, the artery of the arm runs down about in a line with the inner seam of the coat. The large vein lies close beside it, carrying the blood back to the heart. The artery and vein of the leg run about in a line with the inside seam of a man's trousers.

Stimulants—In serious bleeding of any kind do not give stimulants until the bleeding has been stopped, as the stimulants increase the force of the heart and so increase the flow of blood. After the tourniquet is on and bleeding is stopped, if the patient is very weak, he may have a teaspoonful of aromatic spirits of ammonia in half a glass of water.

(a) SHOCKS; (b) APOPLEXY; (c) CONVULSIONS

(a) *Shocks*—In any injury, except the slight ones, the ends of the nerves in the skin are bruised or jarred. They send this jar along the nerves to the very delicate brain. The blood is drawn from the brain into the larger blood vessels, and the result produced is called shock. If you have jammed your finger in a door sometime, perhaps you have felt a queer sick feeling and had to sit down. A cold sweat broke out all over you, and you were hardly conscious for a moment or two. This was a mild case of shock. In more severe injuries a shock to the brain may be very serious.

Symptoms of Shock—1. The patient may or may not be unconscious, but he may take no notice of what is going on around him.

2. The face is pale and clammy.

3. The skin is cold.

4. The pulse is weak.

5. The breathing is shallow.

In any serious injury the shock is liable to be severe and will need to be treated before the doctor arrives.

Treatment—Send for the doctor if serious.

1. Lay the patient flat on his back with head low, so that the heart can more easily pump the blood back into the brain.

2. Cover warmly; if they can be gotten, put around him several hot water bottles or bricks, being extremely careful to have them covered so that they will not burn him. Persons suffering from shock are more easily burnt than usual. Do not put anything hot next him unless it can be held against your own face for a minute without feeling too hot.

3. Rub the arms and legs, toward the body, but under the covers.

4. Give stimulants only after the patient has recovered enough to swallow, and when there is no serious bleeding.

Stimulants—Strong, hot coffee, or a half teaspoonful of aromatic spirits of ammonia in a half glass of warm water. The latter may be given if the coffee is not ready.

(b) *Apoplexy*—When a person has a "stroke" of apoplexy send for the doctor at once.

This condition resembles shock only in that the patient is unconscious. The blow to the delicate brain does not come from the outside along the nerves, but from the inside by the breaking of a blood vessel in the brain, letting the blood out into the brain tissue and forming a clot inside of the brain, and thus making pressure which produces the unconsciousness.

Symptoms of Apoplexy—1. The patient is unconscious.

2. The face is usually flushed—red.

3. The skin is not cold and clammy.

4. The pulse is slow and full.

5. The breathing is snoring instead of shallow.

6. The pupils of the eyes are usually unequally dilated.

Treatment—1. Lay the patient flat on his back with head slightly raised.

2. Do not give any stimulants.

3. Wait for the doctor.

(c) *Convulsions*—This condition resembles the fore-going shock and apoplexy in that the patient is unconscious.

Symptoms of Convulsions—1. The patient is unconscious.

2. The face is usually pale at first, but not so white as in shock, and later is flushed, often even purplish.

3. The skin is not usually cold.

4. The breathing may be shallow or snoring.

5. There are twitchings of the muscles of the face and body or a twisting motion of the body.

6. The pulse may be rapid, but is usually regular.

7. The mouth may be flecked with foam.

8. The pupils of the eyes may be contracted or equally dilated.

Treatment—Convulsions come from various causes, and are always serious, therefore send for the doctor at once.

1. Put a wedge of some kind between the teeth if possible, the handle of a spoon protected by a cloth cover, or a rolled napkin does well. This is to prevent biting the tongue, which the patient is apt to do in unconsciousness with convulsive movements.

2. Lay the patient flat on his back, and prevent him from hurting himself in his twisting, but do not try to stop convulsive movement. It will do no good.

3. No stimulant is needed.

(a) SUNSTROKE; (b) FREEZING

(a) *Sunstroke*—Sunstroke is caused by too long exposure to excessive heat, or to the direct rays of the sun, and is much more serious than heat exhaustion, which you have already studied.

Prevention—Do not stay out in the direct sunlight too long on a hot summer day. Wear a large hat which shades the head and face well, if obliged to be in the hot sun for any length of time. Do not wear too heavy clothing in the hot weather. Leaves or a wet sponge in the top of the hat will help to prevent sunstroke. Drink plenty of cool water between meals.

Symptoms of Sunstroke—1. The patient is unconscious.

2. The face is red.

3. The pupils large.

4. The skin very hot and dry, with *no* perspiration.

5. The pulse is full and slow.

6. The breathing is sighing.

Treatment—1. Get the patient into the shade where it is as cool as possible.

2. Send for the doctor.

3. Remove the greater part of the clothing.

4. Apply cold water or ice to the head, face, chest and armpits.

Often the patient recovers consciousness before the doctor arrives; give cold water to drink; never stimulants.

(b) *Freezing*—This is a much more serious condition than frost bite, which you have studied, but only because more of the body is frozen and the tissues are frozen deeper. Much more care must therefore be taken to prevent bad effects after the thawing-out process.

Symptoms of Freezing—1. The patient may or may not be unconscious.

2. The frozen parts are an intense white and are without any feeling or motion.

Treatment—Send for the doctor at once.

1. Take the patient into a cold room.

2. Remove the clothing.

3. Rub the body with rough cloths wet in cold water.

4. Very gradually increase the warmth of the water used for rubbing.

5. Increase the temperature of the room gradually.

6. When the patient can swallow, give him stimulants.

7. When the skin becomes more normal in color and the tissues are soft, showing that the blood is once more circulating properly through the frozen flesh, cover the patient warmly with hot bottles or bricks outside of the bed clothing, or wraps, and give hot drinks. In using hot water be sure it is not too hot.

MAD DOG AND SNAKE BITES

The wounds made by the bite of a mad dog or a poisonous snake are not so important as wounds, as because of what gets into the wound from the dog's teeth or the fangs of the snake. In both cases the poison from the bite is quickly absorbed and affects the brain of the victim. The poison from the snake is much quicker in its results than that from the mad dog, but not more sure.

Treatment—This is similar in both cases. To prevent absorption of the poison as much as possible, immediately tie a handkerchief or bandage or string tightly above the bite; that is, between the bite and the heart. Do not leave on too long. This, of course, could be done only on the limbs, but fortunately most bites, especially snake bites, are on the arms or legs.

Soak the wound in hot water and squeeze or suck the poison out; sucking the poison out is not dangerous unless one has cuts or sores about one's mouth. In that case do not do it. Otherwise, remember you may save a life by doing it.

Then burn the wound with strong ammonia. This is not aromatic spirits of ammonia, but the stronger ammonia. Most households use it diluted for cleaning, and you can usually find some at the nearest house.

When it is a snake bite, stimulants should be given; if a grown person, whiskey, one or two tablespoonfuls, or aromatic spirits of ammonia, one or two teaspoonfuls, in water. Send for the doctor at once, but carry out these instructions while you wait for him.

WATER ACCIDENTS

When it is possible, Girl Scouts should learn to swim well. It is fear when suddenly thrown into the water that causes many of the deaths by drowning, and learning to swim well takes away this fear. A Girl Scout should also learn how to prevent accidents, and how best to help the victims of accidents in the water.

PREVENTION

Below are five rules for preventing drowning accidents.

1. Do not change seats in a canoe or rowboat.

2. Do not rock the boat.

3. Do not go out alone in a canoe, rowboat or sailboat unless you are thoroughly competent to manage such a boat, even in a sudden squall or storm.

4. Very cold water exhausts a swimmer much quicker than warm water, therefore do not take any chances on a long swim in cold water unless a boat accompanies you to pick you up in case of necessity.

5. Be careful not to get too far out when there is a strong undertow; that is, a strong current below the surface of the water flowing relentlessly out to sea.

RESCUE

When a person gives up the struggle in the water, the body goes down, and then because of its bouyancy it comes to the surface and some air is expelled from the lungs, making the body less bouyant. It immediately sinks again, this time a little lower, and again comes to the surface, and more air is expelled. This process may be repeated several times, until sufficient water is taken into the stomach and lungs to overcome the buoyancy of the body and it no longer appears at the surface; but the buoyancy is barely overcome, and therefore the

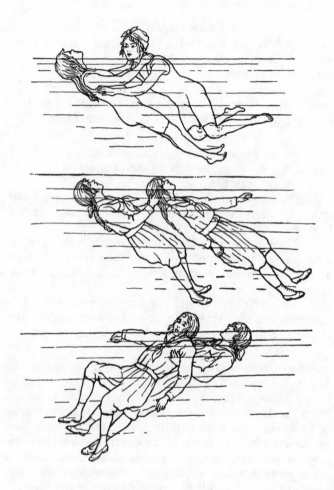

body will float easily. This can be easily utilized in saving the drowning person by making the water carry most of the weight of the body.

To do this, place the hands on either side of the drowning person's head, and tow him floating on his back with the face above the surface of the water, while you swim on your back and keep the body away from you. Remember, if possible, to go with the current and thus save necessary strength. In some cases it may be easier and safer to grasp the drowning person by the hair instead of trying to clasp the head.

EMERGENCIES

Grips—A drowning person is always a frightened person, and is governed by a mad instinct to grab anything which subconsciously he thinks may save his life. Usually he is past any reasoning. He grabs his would-be rescuer with a death grip that is hard to break, but remember he instinctively grabs what is above the surface and will not try to grab below the shoulders.

Wrist Grip—If the drowning person grasps the rescuer's wrists, the rescuer throws both hands above his head, which forces both low in the water, and then turns the leverage of his arms against the other's thumbs and breaks the grip.

Neck Grip—To release a grip around the neck and shoulders from the front, immediately cover the mouth of the other with the palm of the hand, holding the nose between the first two fingers, and at the same time pull the other body toward you with the other hand, meanwhile treading water. Then take a full breath and apply your knee to the other's stomach quickly, thus forcing him to expel any air in his lungs and preventing him from getting more air by the hand on mouth and nostrils.

If the grip of the drowning person does not allow use of the arms, then try to raise your arms to the level of the shoulder, thus slipping his arms to the neck and leaving your own arms free to use, as described.

Back Grip—This strangle hold is perhaps the most difficult to break, and it is necessary to break it instantly if the rescuer is not also to be in the rescued class.

Grasp the wrists of the other and push sharply back with the buttocks against the abdomen of the other, and thus make room to slip suddenly out of the encircling arms.

If this is not successful, do not despair, but throw the head suddenly back against the nose of the drowning person and then slip out of the grip before he recovers from his daze.

It is often necessary to dive from the surface in rescuing a drowning person, and this requires practice, and should be learned thoroughly before the necessity for saving a life is presented. Remember that to dive from the surface to a depth of more than ten feet will usually require a weight in addition to the weight of the body. Carry a stone or other heavy object in diving. Then when wishing to rise to the surface, drop it and push against the bottom with the feet. This will send the swimmer to the surface in short order.

In carrying a weight in the water, carry it low on the body, close to the waist line, leaving one hand and both feet free for swimming. Or if for any reason it is necessary to swim on the back, it leaves both feet free to use as propellers.

ARTIFICIAL RESPIRATION

If the apparently drowned person is to be saved, no time must be lost in the rescue from the water or in getting the water out of him, and breathing re-established after he is brought to land.

If there is a messenger handy send for the doctor at

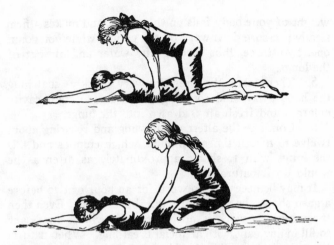

once, but in the meantime lose no time in attempting restoration.

The best method for getting the water out of the lungs and breathing re-established is the *Schaefer Method,* because it is the simplest, requires only one operator and no equipment. It can be kept up alone for a long time.

1. Every moment is precious. Immediately lay the patient face downwards, with the arms extended above the head and the face to one side. In this position the water will run out and the tongue will fall forward by its own weight, and not give trouble by falling back and closing the entrance to the windpipe. Be sure there is nothing in the mouth, such as false teeth, gum, tobacco, etc. Do not put anything under the chest. Be sure there is no tight collar around the neck.

2. Kneel astride of the patient facing toward his head.

3. Place your hands on the small of the patient's back, with thumbs nearly touching and the hands on the spaces between the short ribs.

4. Bend slightly forward with arms rigid so that the

weight of your body falls on the wrists, and makes a firm steady pressure downward on the patient while you count one, two, three, thus forcing any water and air out of the lungs.

5. Then relax the pressure very quickly, snatching the hand away, and counting one-two—the chest cavity enlarges and fresh air is drawn into the lungs.

6. Continue the alternate pressing and relaxing about twelve to fifteen times a minute, which empties and fills the lungs with fresh air approximately as often as he would do it naturally.

It may be necessary to work for an hour or two before a gasp shows the return of natural breathing. Even then the rescurer's work is not over, as it will be necessary to fill in any gaps with artificial breathing. When natural breathing is established, aid circulation by rubbing and by wrapping him in hot blankets and putting hot bottles around him, being careful that they are protected to prevent burning the patient.

If at any time it is necessary to pull the tongue forward and to hold it to prevent choking, remember to put a wedge between the teeth to prevent biting. Do not give anything liquid by mouth until the patient is conscious and can swallow readily. Aromatic Spirits of Ammonia or Spirits of Camphor may be used on a handkerchief for the patient to smell. The patient should be carefully watched for an hour or two even after he is considered out of danger.

ICE RESCUE

Prevention: Below are two rules for preventing ice accidents:

1. Do not skate or walk on thin ice.

2. Watch for air holes.

Rescue: In trying to rescue a person who has broken through the ice, always tie a rope around your own body and have this tied to some firm object on shore. Do not try to walk out to the rescue as the ice will probably break again under the weight of your body on so small an area as the size of your feet. Always get a long board, ladder, rail or limb of a tree, and either crawl out on this, which will distribute the weight of your body over a larger surface of ice, or lie flat on your stomach and crawl out, pushing the board ahead of you so that the person in the water may reach it. If you yourself break through the ice in attempting a rescue, remember that trying to pull yourself up over the edge of the ice only breaks it more. If rescuers are near it is much wiser to support yourself on the edge of the ice and wait for rescue.

After getting the person out of the water use artificial respiration if necessary and bend every effort to get the patient warm and breathing properly.

ASPHYXIATION

Prevention: Below are seven rules for preventing asphyxiation:

1. When coal stoves and furnaces are freshly filled with coal, coal gas may escape if the dampers are not properly regulated. See that all dampers in coal stoves and furnaces are correctly arranged before leaving them for any long time, as the for the night.

2. Do not go to sleep in a house or room with a gas jet or gas stove turned low. The pressure in the pipes may change and the flame go out, or a breeze may blow out the flame leaving the gas leaking into the room.

3. Do not blow out a gas jet.

4. Be careful to turn off gas jet completely.

5. Report gas leaks promptly.

6. Charcoal stoves and braziers are especially dangerous from escaping gas and should not be used in sleeping rooms.

7. Do not go into unused wells or underground sewers without first lowering a lighted candle which will go out at once if the air is very impure, because of lack of oxygen to keep it burning.

Rescue: 1. Remove the patient *at once* to the fresh air. Gas is lighter than air, and therefore will not be found close to the floor and it will often be possible to crawl out when one would be overcome by the gas if he tried to walk out. For this reason it is sometimes best in trying to rescue anyone already unconscious from gas to tie the wrists together with a handkerchief, put his arms around your neck, and crawl out on all fours, dragging the insensible body with you, under your own body. If you attempt to walk out and carry the patient, cover your mouth and nose with a wet handkerchief, go very quickly, and do not breathe until you reach the fresh air.

2. If there is a messenger handy, send for the doctor at once, but in the meantime if necessary, perform artificial respiration as outlined under the Schaefer System in the preceding paragraphs, until the patient is restored to normal breathing.

ELECTRIC SHOCK

This is caused by some part of the body coming in contact with a live electric wire. The seriousness of the

SCOUTING FOR GIRLS 199

shock depends on how heavy a charge of electricity the wire is carrying at the time.

The patient is usually unable to release himself from the wire. The first thing to be done, if possible, is to turn off the current by means of the switch, but if this cannot be done *at once,* the patient must be rescued by pulling him away from the wire.

Remember his body will easily carry the charge to yours while he is against the wire. Therefore you must "insulate" yourself—that is, put on your hands something that will not let the electricity into your body—or stand on something that will "insulate" you; for instance, rubber gloves or rubber tobacco pouches, dry silk handkerchiefs, other silk garments or newspapers used in place of gloves if necessary. Stand on a rubber mat or on *dry boards,* or glass, or in dire necessity *dry* clothes can be used to stand on. They must not be wet as then they will carry the electric current through your body and you must also be rescued instead of rescuing.

Prevention: 1. Do not touch the "third rail" of electric railways.

2. Do not catch hold of swinging wires, they may be "live wires."

3. Report broken wires to the right authorities.

Treatment:

1. Get patient loose from the current.

2. Send for the doctor.

3. Lay the patient flat on his back.

4. Loosen the clothing, and perform artificial respiration according to Schaefer method if necessary.

5. Give first aid treatment to the burns.

FIRE ACCIDENTS

The first thought about a fire is to get it put out before it spreads any further. There are methods which will do this work effectually and Girl Scouts should learn these methods beforehand thoroughly, in order that when the emergency arises they may act quickly, coolly and effectively.

FIRE IN CLOTHING

If this happens in your own clothing, do not run for help, as the draft made by the motion of your body will only fan the flames to burn more fiercely.

Grab the nearest thing that will cover you; overcoat, blanket, rug, wrap it tightly around you at the neck first to prevent flames from burning the face and lie down and roll over and over. This will smother the flames quickly. If you can get nothing to wrap around you, lie down and roll slowly over and beat the fire with your hands covered by some part of your clothing not on fire.

If the fire is in the clothing of another, wrap him in the nearest thing available, lay him on the floor and roll him over, smothering the flames as described before.

Woolen material will not catch fire as easily as cotton, therefore, if you have a chance to choose, take woolen material for smothering the flames.

RESULTS

Results of fire in the clothing are sure to be more or less serious burns.

When you have discovered the extent of the burn, if it is at all serious, send for the doctor at once, and in the meantime treat the burn as you have already learned to do in minor burns.

FIRE IN BUILDINGS

Keep cool, in order to remember what to do, and do it quickly.

Turn in a fire alarm at once. Send some one else if possible who may not know what to do to the fire. The quickest way is by telephone call, "Fire Department," and tell them the exact address of the building where the fire is. Or you may go to the nearest alarm box, smash the glass, open the door, and pull down the hook that sounds the alarm. (Generally the directions are printed on the box.) If you cannot sound the alarm alone, call upon the nearest person to help you. *Wait there until the firemen arrive and direct them to the fire.* When the firemen come do just as they tell you, for they know exactly what to do.

People trying to escape from a burning building often get frightened and then there is a panic. Panic kills more people than fire. Keep cool, and others will follow your example.

Never jump from a window unless the flames are so close that it is your only means of escape. If outside a burning building put mattresses and bedding piled high to break the jumper's fall and get a strong hold on a rug to catch the jumper, and let many people hold the rug.

If the fire is just beginning, it can easily be put out by smothering with a rug or blanket; sand, ashes, salt, or a few pails of water will answer the same purpose.

Keep the doors and windows closed if possible to prevent draughts from fanning the flames to fiercer effort.

Remember this point when you go into a burning building, and leave some responsible person guarding the door, in order that it may not be left open by some one in excitement and the flames fanned beyond control.

If you need fresh air in your search for people in a burning building, open a window, put out your head and draw your lungs full of fresh air and then close the window again. In any case it is best to tie a wet handkerchief or towel over the nose and mouth while in a burning building, as this will prevent you from breathing a good deal of smoke.

In searching for persons remember always to begin

at the top of the building if possible, and search every room. When on stairs keep to wall side, where air is relatively free from flames and smoke. If a room is locked, try to rouse the people by pounding and calling and then break in the door if unsuccessful in rousing them, and you suspect there is some one there.

Remember, the air within six inches from the floor is usually free from smoke, and if the smoke makes breathing too difficult, you can still accomplish your end by crawling along the floor and dragging the rescued one with you as you learned to do in gas rescue.

Form a bucket brigade from the fire to the nearest water supply; passing the filled pails from one to another rapidly, the last throwing the water on the fire and passing the empty pails back along *another* line to be filled again and passed on as before.

FIRES FROM KEROSENE, GASOLINE, BENZINE

Prevention.—1. Do not light a fire with kerosene.

2. Do not clean gloves or clothing with gasoline or benzine in a room with a lamp or gas jet lighted.

3. Do not try to dry clothing that has been cleaned with gasoline or benzine near a hot stove or lighted gas jet.

Extinction.—Do not use water to put out a fire of kerosene, benzine, or gasoline, as that only scatters the flames. Smother with blankets, rugs, sand, ashes, salt, or anything which is at hand and can be used; remember that woolen will not catch fire as easily as cotton.

COMMON POISON AND ANTIDOTES

Poisoning—Cases of poisoning happen most often because people do not examine the bottles before taking medicines from them.

Prevention—Disinfectants, liniments and medicines.

Bottles and boxes should be correctly and plainly labelled.

Bottles containing a poisonous substance should be rough outside, or with notched corks or marked with something beside the label stating that their contents are poison.

Treatment—1. *Send for the doctor at once,* telling him what kind of poison you think the patient has taken in order that he may bring the right antidote and the right implements to give the quickest and most effective relief.

2. Give demulcent or mucilaginous drinks, as for example, milk, raw egg, one or two tablespoonsful of salad oil, sweet oil, or barley water—whichever can be obtained most readily.

3. Give something to produce vomiting, provided the lips are not burned or stained as they are with an acid or alkali. A simple but effectual emetic can be made by mixing two teaspoonsful of salt or a tablespoon of mustard in a glass of lukewarm water. This may be repeated if necessary.

4. If the patient seems drowsy, suspect opium and keep patient awake at all costs till the doctor arrives.

5. If delirium threatens, dash cold water on the patient's head and face to try to prevent the fit from coming on.

6. When the poison taken has been acid, the antidote should be an alkali, but different poisons require different antidotes, and it would be unwise to trust to one's memory as to the proper one to take in each case. It would be well to have a list of the more common poisons and their antidotes attached to the First Aid Kit, but do not trust to the memory. If a Girl Scout does not know, and if the patient's lips are *not* stained or burned, give an emetic.

Bandages

Bandages form the most convenient way of keeping dressings on wounds and for making pressure when necessary. They are also used to correct some deformities, but you will not need to concern yourselves with the latter, as this is in the province of doctors.

There are three varieties of bandages which you will need to use and with which you should be familiar: the roller, trangular and four-tailed. The materials used for bandages are absorbent gauze, muslins or flannels. The kind you will use most will be gauze and muslin. The gauze is best to use in dressing wounds because it is pliable and absorbent, and muslin, if you may choose, in applying pressure, because it is firm. In an emergency there will usually be little chance to choose. Anything at hand, as underclothing, sheets, blankets, etc., may be torn into strips or triangles and used. Have the material which is used clean if possible.

The width of the roller bandage depends on the part of the body to be bandaged, from one inch for the little finger to four inches for the body. They can be rolled very well by hand with a little practice, and every Girl Scout should learn to do this or to improvise a bandage roller by running a very stiff wire through a small wooden box and then bending one end on the outside of the box like a handle.

A bandage must be rolled sufficiently tight so that the center will not fall out. By folding one end back and forth a few times to make a core, and then laying the bandaging over one's knees lengthwise of the thigh with the core uppermost, it can be rolled quite tightly and answer every purpose for emergencies.

Learn to put on all bandages smoothly and securely, but not too tightly.

Triangular Bandages—These bandages have advantages for first aid work. They can be quickly made, easily applied and are not apt to be put on too tightly even by a beginner.

The size of the piece of cloth varies with the part to be bandaged. Take a square piece of cloth (it should not be less than 34 to 38 inches), fold it diagonally from corner to corner and cut across the fold, making two bandages.

The bandage may be applied unfolded or folded into a narrow strip, called cravat bandage.

To fold the cravat bandage, the point of the triangle is brought to the middle of the diagonal side and the bandage folded lengthwise to the desired width.

The cravat bandage is convenient to use in bandaging the hand, foot, head, eyes, throat and jaw; for trying on splints; for tying around the limb in case of snake bite, and in making a tourniquet.

Always tie the bandage with a square knot to prevent slipping. Care must be used in applying the triangular

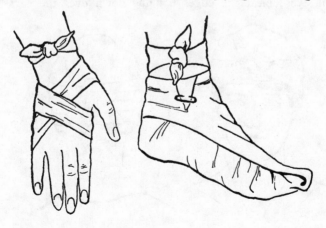

bandage to have it smooth and firm, folding the loose ends into pleats evenly.

Bandage for Hand—For wound of the palm, lay cravat in straight line, place palm across it at the middle. Fold ends over the back of hand, carry around wrist and tie. Reverse the order for injury to the back of the hand.

To cover entire hand, unfold cravat, lay flat with point of triangle beyond the fingers. Fold the point of the bandage over the fingers, cross the ends, and pass around wrist and tie at the back.

Bandage for Foot—Place foot on the smooth triangle with the point extending beyond the toes several inches. Fold the point back over the instep, cross the ends, carry around the ankle and tie.

Bandage for the Head—The bandage may be used flat or as a cravat, according to the nature of the injury and the part to be bandaged.

For a cap bandage, fold over the edge of the diagonal edge, place on the head with the folded edge just above the eyes; pleat the edges hanging down over the ears

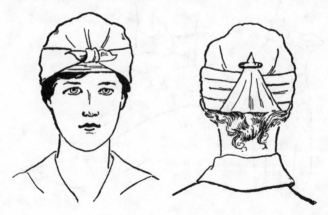

into small folds so that the bandage lies smoothly; carry the ends around the head; cross at the back, and tie in a square knot in front. The cravat bandage may be used to hold on small dressings where the whole head does not need to be covered.

For the eyes, jaw and throat the triangular bandage is used by folding smoothly into a cravat and tying securely over the part to be covered.

Arm Sling.—The triangular bandage makes the best arm sling to support the forearm or for supporting injuries to the elbow or shoulder.

An arm sling is firmer and more satisfactory if the triangle is double; that is, simply fold over the square diagonally, but do not cut it along the fold. An arm sling will need to be about a yard square before folding.

To adjust the arm sling, put one end over the shoulder on the uninjured side; slip the point of the triangle under the injured arm, so that it will extend beyond the elbow a few inches; then take the end of the bandage over the arm, carry around the back of the neck on the injured side, meeting the other end; and tie securely. To prevent slipping, pin the point of the bandage around the arm just above the elbow.

A temporary sling can be made by pinning the sleeve of the injured arm to the dress or coat in such a way as to support the arm.

The Four-tailed Bandage—This bandage is useful for bandaging the head, and especially in fracture of the jaw. Use a piece of cloth about six or eight inches wide and a yard long. Cut each end into two equal parts, leaving about three or four inches in the middle uncut.

When the bandage is applied, the split ends are crossed so that they may be tied over different parts of the head and thus hold the bandage more securely

in place. For instance, in the jaw bandage the uncut middle part is placed over and under the chin, the ends crossed, and two ends tied at the back of the neck and two over the top of the head.

Roller Bandages—Roller bandages are a little more difficult to put on so that they will stay on, and at the same time be smooth and have a uniform pressure on the part of the body bandaged. This last point is most important.

Rules for applying roller bandages:

1. Lay external surface of bandage against the part to be bandaged, holding the roll in the right hand, unless you are left-handed, unrolling it as a roll of carpet unrolls to show you a pattern in the shops.

2. Hold the loose end with the left hand and catch it with two or three turns of the bandage before beginning to put on the bandage. Never have more than four or five inches of the bandage unrolled at once.

3. Be careful to have the same pressure from every turn of the bandage. This is most important if the bandage is to stay on and be comfortable and not interfere with the circulation of the blood. Judgment of the pressure is only acquired by practice, and therefore you should practise enough to acquire this before the real emergency happens.

4. Do not bandage too tightly. Blueness of the skin above or below the bandage always means the bandage must be loosened. Remember in applying a bandage immediately after an injury that considerable swelling may occur later, and apply your bandage more loosely than if bandaging after the swelling has gone down. Always loosen a bandage that is tight enough to cause pain or blueness.

5. Bandage from below upward. That is, from the tip of a finger or toe toward the hand or foot. From

the hand or foot toward the shoulder or groin. This is in the general direction of the return of the circulation.

6. Bandage over a splint and not under it.

7. Bandage arms, legs, fingers, etc., in the position the patient is to keep the part in when the bandaging is completed. For instance, bend the elbow to a right angle before putting on the arm bandage. This will be more comfortable for the patient, allowing him to carry the arm easily in a sling and also permit him to use the hand to some extent if the nature of the injury will permit. In bandaging a leg both above and below the knee, the bandage must be put on with a view to the necessary bending of the knee in walking and sitting, if the patient is expected to use the leg.

8. Never apply a wet bandage, as you cannot judge of just how much pressure will be exerted when the bandage dries, because of the shrinkage of cloth with drying; much greater in some cloth than in others.

Kinds of roller bandages:

1. Circular for parts uniform in size, as the body.

2. Spiral for conical surfaces, as fingers or toes.

3. Reverse for more conical surfaces, as arms and legs.

Circular Bandages—Any part of the body which is of uniform size may be covered with a circular bandage. Each turn covers about two-thirds of the previous turn. This holds each turn firmly and prevents slipping and exposing the dressing or wound underneath. Bandage in general direction of the return of the blood to the heart. Fasten the bandage with a strip of adhesive plaster or safety pin. If there is possibility of restlessness or much activity on the part of the patient, it is best to run several narrow strips of adhesive plaster along the whole width of the bandage when finished to prevent possible slipping of the turns of the bandage when the muscles move under it with the activity of the patient. This is especially true of a body bandage.

Spiral Bandage—A conical part, if not too conical, may be covered with a spiral bandage. Each turn ascends at a slight angle, with one edge of the bandage a little tighter than the other. In putting on this kind of bandage it is necessary to learn to have the tight edges all of a uniform pressure and each turn overlap the turn below in such a way that these tight edges make the uniform pressure without regard to the upper edge underneath, which is covered in each turn by the tighter edge of the turn above it.

Reverse Bandages—The reverse bandage is a modification of the spiral one, in order to cover the gapping between spirals which occurs when the surface is very conical, as, for instance, on the leg.

In putting on this bandage the loose end is caught by two or three turns first as in other bandages. Then start to make a spiral turn, but at the mid point of the front of the part being bandaged place the thumb of the left hand, and fold the bandage down so that it lies smoothly and continue the turn around to that same point. Repeat the process with each turn. (See illustration.) Each turn covers two-thirds of the one below in order to hold firmly. The pressure must be uniform when the bandage is finished. Fasten the ends as described under circular bandages, or divide the end of the bandage into two parts for several inches—long enough to wind around the part bandaged. Tie a single knot at the base to prevent further dividing, and wrap the ends around the part in different directions; tie in a hard knot to hold firmly.

Bandaging Fingers and Toes—In bandaging fingers and toes it is usually best to bandage the whole of the injured member. Cover the end of the finger, for in-

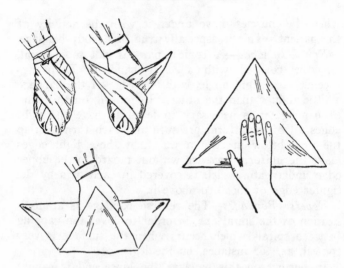

stance, by passing the end of the half inch or one inch
bandage several times the whole length of the finger,
over the end and to the base of the other side. Hold
this in place with one hand, start the spiral at the end
of the finger, and bandage smoothly toward the hand.
The spiral or the reverse spiral may be used.

Bandaging Two or More Fingers or Toes—It is sometimes necessary to bandage two or more fingers, for
instance, at once, as in case of a burn, where it is necessary always to have the burned fingers separated while
healing to prevent the raw places from growing together.

Pass a finger bandage twice around the wrist and
pass obliquely to the base of the thumb. Carry to the
and of the thumb and bandage as described above.
When the thumb is bandaged, carry the bandage back
to the wrist; pass around the wrist in one or two circular turns, and carry the bandage to the first finger

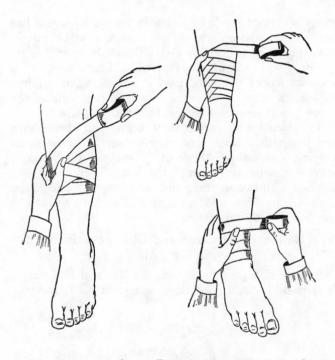

and bandage as before. Repeat this until all the fingers
are bandaged. Carry the bandage back to the wrist,
after the last finger you wish to bandage is done; make
one or two turns around the wrist and fasten.

In bandaging the foot, carry the bandage to the ankle
to make secure and hold in place.

Bandaging Arms and Legs—The reverse spiral is
usually best for bandaging these, because of the conical
shape. Practice alone can teach you to put this on
smoothly, firmly, not too tightly, and at the same time
quickly. A reverse bandage will not stay in place on
the leg of the person walking around unless pinned in

many places or stuck by sizing in the cloth (which has been wet), plaster, etc. Only a figure eight caught over the top of the calf, in each alternate loop, will do so.

The Figure Eight Bandage—The figure eight is a modification of the spiral used in bandaging over joints in such a way as to permit some motion and at the same time keep the bandage firm and in place.

The bandage is carried first below and then above the joint; then below and then above, the turns overlapping the usual two-thirds of the width of the bandage, leaving the joint free until the last. Then it may be covered with two or three circular turns of the bandage. This admits of considerable motion without disturbing the bandage to any extent.

The National Red Cross and Girl Scout Instruction in First Aid

By special arrangement with the National Red Cross, it is possible for a Girl Scout completing satisfactorily

the requirements for the First Aid Proficiency Badge to secure with slight additional work the Red Cross certificate in First Aid. Or the course may be taken entirely under Red Cross auspices, though arranged by Scout officials, in which case the Scout may receive both the Proficiency Badge and the Red Cross certificate. The conditions of this co-operation between the Girl Scouts and the National Red Cross are as follows:

Classes are to be organized with not less than four or more than twenty-five in a class. The best size is ten to fifteen. *Scouts must be at least sixteen years of age to be admitted to these classes.*

The instructor must be a physician appointed by the Chairman of the First Aid Committee of the local chapter of the Red Cross. He or she may be supplied upon request by the Chapter, or chosen by the class and the name submitted to the Chapter for appointment.

The Red Cross class roll must be sent in to the local Chapter early in the course.

A Secretary to handle the records should be chosen, and where the class is made up of Scouts, the officials should be preferably a Scout Captain or Scout Official.

The examiner must be a physician appointed by the local Red Cross chapter and is preferably some one other than the instructor, but this is not necessary. Like the instructor, the examiner may be supplied by the Chapter or chosen by the class.

The Red Cross examination roll, which may be obtained from the Chapter, should be used in giving examinations and then returned to the Chapter, who will issue the certificates. Follow the directions on the roll carefully.

If a Scout holds a First Aid Proficiency Badge she may complete the course in seven and one-half hours. If she does not hold a Proficiency Badge in First Aid then fifteen hours will be required. A Girl Scout holding a Proficiency Badge in First Aid and taking a school course held under Red Cross auspices which she passes with a mark of at least seventy-five per cent, can, when the school principal certifies to this, get the Red Cross certificate without further examination by applying to the local Red Cross Chapter.

Advanced Courses

Advanced courses are open to those who have the Red Cross certificate. There must be an interval of at least six months after the elementary course before an advanced course can be taken, and the same interval between repetitions of it. The course of instruction is seven and one-half hours, mainly practical demonstrations. A Red Cross medal is given on completion of this course. Each time it is repeated, up to three times, a bar (engraved with year) is given to be added to the medal.

Fees

A fee of fifty cents is required for the elementary course. The local Red Cross Chapter has the right to reduce this fee.

The fee for the advanced course is one dollar, which covers the cost of certificate, examination and medal. The fee for bar and engraving is fifty cents. These fees cannot be reduced.

These fees cover the cost to the Red Cross of postage, certificates, medals, bars, and so forth, but do not cover that of instructor, examiner, or classroom supplies, which the Red Cross requires the class to take care of.

Information

Where there is no local Girl Scout organization refer to the local Red Cross Chapter; or if there is none, either to the Girl Scout National Headquarters, 189 Lexington

Avenue, New York, N. Y., or to the Department of First Aid, American Red Cross National Headquarters, Washington, D. C.

4. THE HOME NURSE

The Girl Scout who has earned the Home Nurse Badge may be of great help where there is illness. But, she should remember that only such people as doctors and trained nurses who have knowledge and skill gained by special training and thorough practice are fitted to care properly for those who are very ill.

If the Scout with the badge keeps her head and shows herself steady, reliable and willing, when called upon for help in illness or emergencies, she proves herself a true Scout who is living up to the Scout motto of "BE PREPARED."

To earn the badge she should know:

How to keep the sick room clean and comfortable.

How to make a bed properly.

How to prepare for and help a sick person in taking a bath.

How to make a sick person comfortable in bed, changing position, etc.

How to take temperature, pulse and respiration.

How to prepare and serve simple, nourishing food for the sick.

How to feed a helpless person.

How to prepare and use simple remedies for slight ailments.

How to occupy and amuse the sick.

When helping about the sick, the Scout should wear a wash dress or an apron which covers her dress. She should be very neat and clean. She should wash her hands frequently, *always* before her own meals, and after coming into contact with the sick person and after handling utensils, dishes, linen, etc., used in the sick room.   Great cleanliness is necessary not only for her own protection but to prevent illness spreading.

She should move quickly and quietly, but without bustle or hurry, taking care not to let things fall, not to bump against the furniture, not to jar the bed, not to slam doors, in fact not to make any unnecessary noises, as sick people are not only disturbed but may be made worse by noises and confusion.   If a door is squeaky the hinges should be oiled.   Too much talking, loud talking and whispering are to be avoided.   Only cheerful and pleasant subjects should be talked of, *never* illnesses either that of the patient nor of others.

The best nursing aims not only to bring relief and comfort to those already sick, but to guard against *spreading* sickness.

We know, now, that many diseases are spread by means of *germs* which are carried from person to person by various means, such as air, water, milk, and other food; discharges from the mouth, nose, bowels, bladder, wounds; clothing; the hands; the breath, and so forth.

It has been found that great heat, intense cold, sunshine and some powerful drugs called disinfectants kill germs.   Germs thrive and multiply in dirt, dampness and darkness.   That is why it is important to have fresh air, sunshine and cleanliness in order to keep well, and to help in curing those who get sick.

The Room, Its Order and Arrangement

The hangings and furniture of a sick room should be of a kind that can be washed and easily kept clean.   Plain wooden furniture is better than upholstered furniture which collects and holds the dust.   If there is a rocking chair it should be for the use of the sick person only. Seeing and hearing other people rock may be very disturbing.

If carpets are movable, so much the better, as they can be taken out to be cleaned.

The room should be bright and attractive. Sick people like flowers and pretty things, but the flowers should not have a strong perfume, and there should not be too many ornaments around to collect dust and to take up too much room. Flowers should be taken out of the room every night and the water changed before returned to the room in the morning. Never have faded flowers around.

The room should be kept neat—a place for everything and everything in its place.

Neatness and attractiveness are not only pleasing to the sick person and those who come into the room but may really make the sick person feel better.

Medicines should not be kept in sight. All dishes and utensils not in use should be taken away and should be washed immediately after use.

Ventilating and Lighting the Room

The room of a sick person should be so situated that it will get plenty of sunlight and be easily aired. A room that has two or more windows can be better ventilated than a room with only one. When there is only one window, it should be opened both top and bottom. If there is not a screen, one can be made by hanging a shawl or a blanket over a clothes horse or a high-backed chair, or over a line stretched across the lower part of the window. A fire place or a stove keeps the air circulating—the air being constantly drawn up the chimney—and so helps in ventilating a room.

When "airing" the room great care must be taken to keep the sick person free from draughts.

Unless special orders have been given to the contrary there should be plenty of sunshine let in. The eyes of the sick person should be protected from the glare by a screen.

If possible there should be a thermometer in the room. The proper heat is between 65 and 70 degrees. If the temperature of the room is as high as 70 degrees and the sick person is cold, it is better to give her a hot water bag and to put on more covers than to shut the windows, thus keeping out the fresh air. Cool air acts as a tonic for the sick.

Cleaning the Room

The carpet should be gone over every day to remove the surface dust. Use the carpets sweeper, being careful not to knock the furniture nor to jar the bed. Raise as little dust and make as little noise as possible. Torn-up wet paper scattered on a small part of the carpet at a time and lightly brushed up into a dustpan with a whisk broom, or a broom, cleans the carpet very well without raising dust.

If the carpet cannot be taken out to be swept or beaten but requires thorough sweeping, an umbrella with a sheet over it may be hoisted over the head of the sick person to keep the dust from her nose and nostrils. The bare parts of the floor should be gone over with a damp duster or a damp mop.

The dusting should be done with a damp or oiled duster also, so that the dust may not be scattered. A basin of soapy water should be at hand and the duster washed in it frequently while dusting, so that the dust collected on it from one surface will not be carried to another. While dusting special attention should be paid to the door-knobs and that part of the door around them.

When the dusting is finished the dusters should be

thoroughly washed and scalded and hung out of doors
to dry.

The Bed

A metal bedstead is better than a wooden one, as wood
holds odors and moisture, and is apt to have more cracks
and crevices for germs or bugs to lodge in. It should be
white, for then it shows when it needs cleaning and bed
bugs keep away from white surfaces which show them
up easily.

If possible, have the bed in a part of the room, where
the drafts will not strike the patient every time a door
or window is opened, and where the light does not shine in
the eyes. If it can be placed so that the patient can see
from the window so much the better.

To Make an Unoccupied Bed

Remove pillows and bedclothes, one at a time, being
careful not to let corners drag on the floor, and put to
air. Turn the mattress over from end to end one day,
and from side to side next day. If the patient does not
have to return to bed at once leave to air for at least half
an hour.

An old blanket, old spread or a quilted pad, spread over
the mattress not only protects the mattress but prevents
the sheets from wearing out, and may make the bed more
comfortable. These should be kept clean.

The bed for a sick person is frequently made with a
rubber sheet and a draw sheet. The draw sheet is so
called because its proper use is to be drawn through under
the patient without greatly disturbing her and give her
a cool fresh place to lie on. Therefore it should be long
enough to tuck in sufficiently under one side to allow
of this being done. An ordinary sheet folded in two
from top to bottom and placed with folded edge toward
the head of the bed may be used. It should entirely

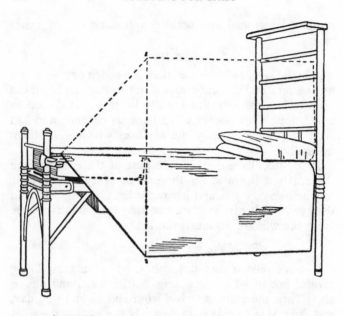

cover the rubber sheet, which is usually put on between
the bottom and the draw sheet.

When the mattress is sufficiently aired, put on the pro-
tective covering. Over this spread the lower sheet so
that the middle fold of the sheet lies up and down the
centre of the mattress from head to foot. Keep perfectly straight. The sheet should be long enough to
have at least fourteen inches over at ends and sides to
tuck in. Tuck ends under mattress at head and foot
drawing tightly so that it will be smooth and firm. Now
tuck under at one side, folding neatly at corners, so that
they will be mitred when finished. If there is no rubber
nor draw sheet to put on, go to the other side of the bed
and tuck in firmly at corners. Then, pulling the middle of
the sheet very tightly with one hand, push the mattress

with the other and tuck the sheet under. This under sheet should be very smooth without a wrinkle in it. If it is not long enough to tuck in well at both head and foot, leave plenty at the head to tuck in securely and tuck in at the sides tightly rather than risk having it come loose at the head. Be sure, however, that the mattress is entirely covered.

When Rubber and Draw Sheets Are Used

Before going around to the other side, lay the rubber sheet over the bed, so that the top edge will be well above where the lower edge of the pillow will come. Put the draw sheet over it. Tuck both well under the mattress on that side. Then, go to the other side and tuck in the corners of the lower sheet as directed, then stretching draw, rubber, and under sheet very tightly, tuck in separately.

Next spread the upper sheet, wrong side up, leaving as much at the head to turn back over the blankets as you left in the under sheet to tuck in. Have the middle fold over that of the lower sheet. Spread the blankets so that their upper edges will be even with the upper edge of the mattress. If the blankets are not long enough to reach as far up as they should, and yet tuck under firmly at the foot, place the lower one as directed, and the upper one so that there will be enough to tuck under at the foot, and hold the others in place. Tuck all in at once at foot and lower corners, mitring the corners as you did those of the lower sheet. Pull and straighten the sheet at the top and turn back smoothly over the blankets. If the bed is not to be occupied right away, tuck in both sides, stretching well so that it will have a smooth surface. Put on the spread, having the top edge even with the top of the covers. Tuck in neatly at foot and lower corners, letting the sides hang. Shake and beat the pillows thoroughly, make smooth and even, and put in place.

To Change the Under Sheet When the Patient Is in Bed

Loosen the bedclothes, without jarring the bed. Take off covers one at a time, until only one blanket and sheet remain. (If the patient feels cold, leave as many blankets as necessary to keep her warm.) Holding blankets with one hand or having patient hold it by the top, draw off the upper sheet, being careful not to uncover the patient. Remove the pillows. Have the patient as near the side of the bed as is safe, on her side, and facing the side on which she is lying. Roll the under sheets on the side of the bed close to the patient's back, making them as flat as possible. Pleat about half of the fresh under sheet lengthwise, and place close to the soiled sheets. Tuck in the other half, at the head, foot and side, draw the rubber sheet back over this fresh sheet, arrange the fresh draw sheet in place, tuck both in at that side and roll the free part close up to the patient's back. Now lift the patient's feet over the roll of fresh and soiled linen to the freshly made part, then have her roll her body over that side. Going to the other side of the bed, remove all the soiled linen and tuck the fresh sheets in, pulling tightly, being sure that there are no wrinkles under the patient. All the time keep the patient well covered. Now, spread the upper sheet and blankets over the covering the patient has had on while the lower sheets were being changed and, having the patient hold the coverings you have just put on, draw off the others, just as you took off the top sheet at first. Finish making the bed as you would an unoccupied one.

If the Bed Is to Be Occupied at Once

If the bed is to be occupied at once the coverings should

be tucked in only at foot, corners and one side, then turned back diagonally from the head to foot.

The bed clothes should never be drawn too tightly over a person in bed, or they may irritate the skin, especially at the knees and toes. Bed sores may be started in this way. Perhaps the commonest cause of bedsores is from wrinkles in the under sheets. If the spread is heavy it should not be used over a patient. Use a sheet instead to protect the blankets.

Bathing

Bathing is more important for the sick than for the well. It not only keeps the skin clean and in condition to do its work, but it is soothing to the nerves, makes the sick person rest better and is refreshing.

If the room is the right temperature and the bath is carefully taken there is no danger of a sick person taking cold. On the other hand bathing helps to keep people in condition to *avoid* taking colds. (See Red Cross Text Book on Home Hygiene and Care of the Sick, page 156.)

When a patient is very sick or helpless, the bath should be given by someone who is able to do it deftly and quickly, with the least exertion to the patient.

Very often, however, a person in bed is quite able to bathe herself, with a little help, if the necessary things are brought to her.

To Prepare for a Bath in Bed

Have the room warm and free from draughts. A good temperature is 70 degrees. An old person or a baby may have it warmer.

Bring into the room everything needed. This will include:

An extra blanket to wrap around the sick person.
Two or more bath towels.

Two wash cloths—one for the face and another for the rest of the body.

Soap—Ivory or castile are good.

Pitcher of good hot water, and slop jar.

Alcohol and toilet powder if you have it.

Nail file and scissors.

Comb and brush.

Clean bed linen and nightgown. In cold weather these may be hung near the fire or radiator to warm.

A basin of water of a temperature that the sick person finds comfortable.

When everything is ready the Scout can help by loosening the bedclothes, arranging the extra blanket, removing the nightgown, and in holding the basin and towels, in changing the water or in any way that will make the bath easier for the sick person, perhaps washing the feet and back, being careful to keep all the rest of the body covered and warm, and in protecting the bed by bath towels spread under the part being washed. When doing this the wash cloth should not be so wet that it will drip and wet the bed. It should be held so that the corners do not touch against the bedclothes. There should not be too much soap used as it makes the skin feel sticky. Every part should be dried thoroughly. Warm towels are a great help in this.

When the bath is finished alcohol or witch hazel may be used to rub the parts where there is most pressure as the back, shoulder blades, hips, buttocks, elbows, knees and ankles. This not only gives comfort but it prevents bedsores.

If a sick person gets a bath, so that it does not disturb nor tire her nor make her chilly she will usually enjoy it. By getting everything ready, by helping where needed, and by clearing up nicely the Girl Scout may make the bath a pleasure instead of something to be dreaded.

Sometimes sick people are able to go to the bath room to take their own baths, if everything is gotten ready for them beforehand, so that they will not get tired doing so. People who are not well should never be allowed to lock themselves in the bathroom alone.

Getting Ready a Tub Bath

The bathroom should be well aired but warm. The water in the bath tub helps to warm it up. A bath towel or bath mat should be spread beside the tub on the floor and a chair with a blanket and a bath towel on it for the person to sit on while she is drying herself. The water should be about 105 degrees or a temperature that the person finds comfortable. Always let a patient try it herself with her hand and arm before getting in. Five to ten minutes is long enough to stay in the water. The towels should be within easy reach and the bathrobe, night gown and slippers placed ready to put on.

The bed should be put to air and left as long as possible, but if the patient has to get back in it immediately after her bath, it should be made—care being taken that it is warm enough. If necessary put in hot water bags and spread a blanket over the under sheet to wrap around her if she needs it. People chill easily after a bath if they are exposed to sudden cold.

Foot Baths

Foot baths are often used in the home as remedies for colds, headaches, sleeplessness and to give relief at the monthly period.

If there is not a regular foot tub a pail that is large enough to put the foot in is better than a basin as it lets the water come up around the ankles. A person may sit in a chair or on the side of the bed. Have tub about half full of water and at first of a heat that feels comfortable, putting more hot water in from time to time, until it is as hot as it can be stood. When adding hot water the feet should be away from the part of the tub where the water is poured in, and it should be added slowly to prevent possibility of burning. A person getting a foot bath should be kept very warm. Wrap a blanket around the knees so that the legs will be protected front and back. After fifteen or twenty minutes the feet should be removed from the water and dried without rubbing. They should be kept well covered for an hour or more. No one should go out immediately after a foot bath.

If mustard is to be added, mix it first in a cup and mix it gradually so that it does not lump. Two tablespoonfuls of mustard to a foot bath is about enough.

Changing of position, and supporting different parts of the body, give both rest and comfort to anyone in bed. This may be done by turning a patient and by the proper arrangement of pillows and other supports.

To turn a patient toward you place one hand over her shoulder and the other hand over her hip and draw toward you. Bend her knees, go to the other side of the bed, put both hands under her hips and draw toward you. Place a pillow lengthwise at her back, from her shoulder to waist for support.

A pillow, placed under or between the knees, often gives much relief and comfort. Small air pillows that can be placed under or against the small of the back relieve strain and rest the muscles. Anyone lying on her back will be rested by arranging pillows lengthwise at the sides to support arms. Rubber rings and air cushions are also used to relieve pressure and give support. They should always be covered, using towel or pillow case, if they have not their own fitted covers.

Rings of any size may be made of cotton wound with

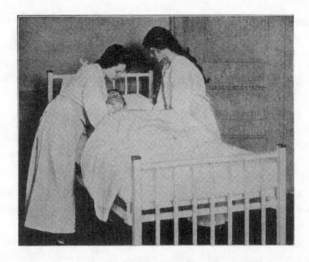

bandage. These are frequently needed under the heels, particularly for a patient lying on her back.

Sitting Up in Bed

When a patient is allowed to sit up in bed and a bed-rest is not available a straight chair placed bottom-up behind the patient makes a good support for the pillows. If there is no other support, at least six pillows are needed to make a patient comfortable. The pillows should be so arranged that the head is not thrown forward and that there is proper support for the back, and the arms.

Raising a Patient Who Has Slipped Down in Bed

Have the patient draw up the knees until the soles of the feet are firmly on the bed. Place your right arm under the far shoulder in such a way that the patient's head rests in your bent elbow. Place the left arm under the thighs. Hold your back stiff. Have the patient clasp her

hands around your waist. Lift without jerking. **When** *two* persons are doing the lifting, one should stand on either side of the bed. The person on the left side of the bed should place the right arm as though she were doing the lifting alone. Place the other arm under the small of the patient's back.

The person on the right side will place her left arm beside her companion's, and her right arm under the thighs. If able, the patient may place a hand on the shoulder of each lifter.

Lift in unison without jerking.

A pillow rolled in a sheet, placed under the body and tied to the head or sides of the bed will prevent slipping down in bed.

It is usually better to shake up and rearrange the pillows after raising the patient as the moving disarranges them somewhat.

To Change the Pillows

Slip the right arm under the shoulders in such a way that the neck and head are supported in your bent elbow; with the left hand gently draw out one pillow at a time, from above. In replacing, stand the pillows on the side at the head of the bed, lift the shoulders, and grasping the pillow by the middle draw down under the patient's head.

Another way is to have the patient near one side of the bed and lifting in the same way draw the pillows one at a time away from you. In replacing put the fresh pillows on the far side and again lifting the head pull them toward you.

The pillow should support the neck and shoulders. A small down or hair pillow placed under the back of the neck from time to time, rests and supports.

To Change the Nightgown

The nightgown should be loose enough to change easily. If there is an opening in the front, this may be made larger or the gown may be split up the back.

These openings may be sewn up again without in any way damaging the gown.

Have the gown well drawn up around the shoulders and neck.

Slip one hand through the arm hole of the gown, and bend the patient's arm. With the other hand draw off the sleeve.

Draw the hand through the corresponding sleeve of the fresh gown and lifting the head just as for changing the pillow, slip the soiled and fresh gown over the head at the same time. Pull away the soiled gown. Put your hand through the sleeve and draw the patient's hand through, then raising again draw the gown down under the back and hips.

Combing the Hair

The hair should be combed at least once a day. If this is done from the very beginning of an illness it will not get badly tangled.

Spread a towel over the pillow. Have the patient turn head on one side so that the back of the head is exposed. Part the hair in the middle from the forehead to the nape of the neck. Comb only a small strand at a time. If there are tangles, comb from ends toward the scalp. Avoid pulling by twisting the strand around the finger and holding loosely between the comb and the scalp. When the hair on one side has been combed, braid it, having the top of the braid near the ear. Do the other side the same way. If very much tangled a little oil or alcohol rubbed in makes it easier to comb.

Wash the comb and brush in soap and water once a week.

Wash the hands after combing the hair.

Be careful in removing the towel not to scatter the loose hairs and dandruff it may hold.

Getting Patient Up in Chair

If possible have a chair with arms.

Place beside the bed.

Put cushions on seat and fresh pillow at back.

Throw a blanket over all corner-wise, to wrap around the patient when she sits down.

While in bed put on stockings, slippers, bath robe (and under-drawers or flannel petticoat in winter).

Have the patient sit up in bed, and help her to swing her feet over the edge.

Stand in front of her, and have her place her hands on your shoulders. Place your hands under her arm pits, and let her slip off the bed with her feet firmly on the floor. Turn and let her sit down slowly

Place a stool for her feet.

Place the chair so that she will be out of drafts and so that the light does not shine directly into her face.

When patients become restless and nervous they may often be made more comfortable by rearranging the bed clothes, by fanning, by changing position, by rubbing the back and legs, by putting hot water bags at the feet, back and neck, or small of back. In summer try very cold water instead of hot water in the bags. Cold compresses may be applied to the back of the neck, the spine, the forehead, or wherever they may give comfort. A foot bath, a hot or cool sponging will not only quiet restlessness but will ofen make a patient sleepy. In using any wet application be sure not to get the pillows or bed clothes wet. Continued rubbing at the back of the neck or stroking of the forehead gently is soothing and quieting.

Temperature, Pulse, Respiration

The temperature of the average person in health is 98.6° Fahrenheit. This is called the *normal* temperature.

A temperature below 98.0 degrees is said to be sub-normal. A healthy person may have a sub-normal temperature in the early morning. People with a continuous low temperature, say around 97 (this is often the case with old people and those who are recovering from illness) need careful attention. If in bed, they should be kept warmly covered and supplied with hot water bags. If up, they should be warmly clothed, and protected from drafts, and sudden changes of temperature. Usually, in the early morning before daylight, the temperature is at the lowest. That is why it is important to watch sick people and babies and to put an extra cover over them at that time.

Any temperature above 100 degrees, if it continues, is serious. A temperature above 101 degrees is a fairly high one, and 103 degrees or above is very high.

The temperature is taken with a clinical thermometer placed in the mouth or in the armpit. For babies, and people who might break the thermometer if it were placed in the mouth, place the thermometer in the armpit. Temperatures of babies and very ill people are taken in rectum, but the Girl Scout should not attempt this. Always wash the thermometer in cold water before using. Wash in cold water and disinfect by wiping off with alcohol after using. Hot water will break it. When the thermometer is being used every day it may be kept in disinfectant. Never lay down a thermometer that has been used until after it has been washed and disinfected.

To Take the Temperature in the Mouth

Cleanse the thermometer.

Shake down so that the mercury is below 96 degrees.

Have patient moisten lips.

Place the thermometer with bulb under tongue. Lips must be closed while holding it.

Hold two or three minutes, in this position.

Be sure that nothing hot or cold has been in the mouth for at least five minutes before taking temperature.

To Take Temperature in the Armpits

Wipe out armpit.

Insert the thermometer.

Place arm across the chest so that the thermometer is held securely. It should remain so for four or five minutes.

Pulse

The pulse may be counted on the thumb side of the inside of the wrist, at the temples, the ankles, and other parts of the body where the arteries are near the surface.

The pulse shows the number of times per minute which the heart beats or pumps.

A normal pulse for a man is around 72, for a woman 80, for a child 90, and for a baby 100 degrees.

A very rapid or a very slow pulse shows that there is something wrong that should be reported. It takes a good deal of practice to learn to count the pulse.

Place two or three fingers on the beating artery, just touching firmly enough to feel the beats, and count for a half minute, then multiply by two to find the number of beats per minute. Be sure that the patient's hand is in a comfortable position while counting.

Respiration

Respiration is another word for breathing. An average normal person when sitting or lying still, breathes from twelve to twenty times per minute, and when moving about 24 times. We all know that quick moving makes quick breathing.

Respiration above 40 or below 8 is a danger sign. If

the respiration is very fast, or difficult, or wheezy, or in any way very unusual, we can tell it at a glance. People who are breathing hard are frequently relieved by being propped up in bed.

To count the respiration. It is better to do this without the person's knowledge. It may be counted by watching the rise and fall of the chest or of the shoulders. Another way is to hold the person's hand as though taking the pulse, having her rest her hand and fore-arm lightly on the chest and count the rise and fall.

Dishes

Dishes used by patients with any of the contagious diseases, and this includes colds and sore throats, should be kept separate, and washed separately from the family dishes. They should be scalded after washing and have special dish cloths. Using separate utensils, and separate room for the sick person are two of the surest ways to prevent the spread of the disease.

In such diseases as measles, scarlet fever, colds, mumps, influenza, dishes should be boiled every day. Put them in a large kettle in cold water and let them come to a boil. Even the thinnest glass will not break if treated in this way. Let the dishes stay in the water until cool enough to handle.

Dish cloths and dish mops should be thoroughly washed in good hot water and soap, and put in the sun to dry. They should be boiled regularly.

If it is necessary to disinfect linen put it all in a bag and leave in cold water to soak for some hours before putting it on to boil. Put a little washing soda in the water. After boiling hard for fifteen or twenty minutes it may be washed with the other garments.

Stains should be washed out before putting linen in the wash.

Utensils and Their Care

All utensils should be kept clean and ready for instant use. The bedpan should always be warmed before being used. Running warm water in and on it is usually the easiest way to do this. It should be thoroughly dried on the outside so that it will not wet the bed. It is a good plan to have a piece of rubber sheet or several thicknesses of old newspapers covered with a bath towel to put under the bed pan in bed. When carrying away, keep covered. Use cold water first, and after washing with soapy water, rinse and dry before putting away.

Basins in constant use, especially if they are used to hold disinfectant, need to be well scoured with sapolio from time to time. Nothing is more shiftless looking than to see a dark rim of dirt or stain around a basin.

Hot water bags should be emptied when not in use and hung upside down. The stoppers should be kept fastened to them.

Ice caps should be dried inside and out and stuffed with cotton or tissue paper to keep the sides from sticking together.

Hot and Cold Applications

Hot applications are used to relieve pain, to supply heat, and to bring down temperature. Both moist and dry heat are used. Hot water bags, metal heaters, electric pads, hot flannels are the commonest forms of dry heat. Fomentations, poultices, and baths are the simplest forms of moist heat.

In applying heat, one should be ever on the watch to avoid burning a patient. The skin of babies, children, old people, and of those who have been ill a long time, is very easily burned. Again, the same heat that is easily tolerated by one person, may burn another.

Hot water bags or their substitute, electric pads or metal heaters should always be wrapped in towels *or* have their own coverings. Never fill a hot water bag more than two-thirds full. The water should not be hot enough to scald a patient if the bag should spring a leak. Before putting in the cork, expel the air by twisting the upper part between the neck and the level of the water before putting in the cork. Be sure to cork tightly. If the bag is to be where the patient will bear the weight, put in a very little water and renew from time to time. Where there is no hot water bag, stone bottles may be used, or bags of salt or sand may be heated in the oven. The practice of using ordinary glass bottles is an unsafe one, as the corks are not always to be depended on to stay tight and the glass breaks easily. When bags of salt or sand are used the coverings should be thick enough to prevent the particles from sifting through. Pieces of flannel the right size may in some cases supply all the heat that is necessary. They should be covered with another flannel to keep in the warmth.

To make a mustard plaster. Have ready a piece of old muslin (a piece of an old nightgown will do) two inches wide and two inches longer than twice the length of the poultice required. On one end of it, with a margin of an inch on three sides, place a piece of oiled paper or shelf paper or a piece of clean paper bag, the size you wish the poultice to be. Mix one tablespoonful of mustard with 8 tablespoonfuls of flour, before wetting. Have water about as hot as the hand can stand. Do not use boiling water. Stir the water into the mustard and flour gradually so that it will not lump. Make the paste stiff enough to spread thinly on the paper, about a quarter of an inch thick. Turn the margins of the cloth over the paste. Fold the long end over so that all the paste is covered and tuck the end under the turned-in edges of the sides. Fold it and take it to the patient in a hot towel or between hot plates. The skin where it is to be placed

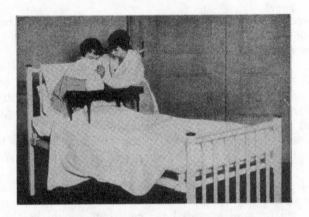

ADMINISTERING AN INHALATION

should be oiled. Test the heat by holding it against the
back of your own hand. Put on slowly and leave for two
minutes. Watch and remove sooner if the skin becomes
reddened or if it is uncomfortable. After removing wipe
away the moisture from the skin and cover with a soft
piece of muslin, and place a piece of flannel over that.
A blister after a mustard paste shows very careless nursing. Never let a patient go to sleep with a mustard
plaster on.

Fomentations or stupes are pieces of flannel wrung
out of very hot water and placed on the skin. They
should be two or three times as large as the part to be
treated, and should be applied as hot as the patient can
bear them, without burning the skin. Have two sets,
so that one set will be ready to put on when the other
is taken off. The stupes should be wrung as dry as
possible and as they must be very hot to do any good,
a fomentation wringer is a great protection for the
hands. One may be made by putting halves of a broom
handle through the ends of a short roller towel in the

middle of which the fomentation has been placed. By twisting the sticks in the opposite direction the fomentation can be wrung very dry. Take it to the bed in the wringer and do not open until ready to place on the skin, as it will lose its heat very quickly. Put a little oil or vaseline on the skin and apply the fomentation gradually. Cover with a dry flannel and put wadding over that. A piece of oiled skin or oiled paper between the wadding and the dry flannel helps to keep in the heat and moisture. Hold in place with a towel or binder pinned tightly.

Cold is applied by means of ice bags and by cold compresses. In filling an ice bag the ice should be in small pieces, and the bag not too full. Expel the air as from a hot water bag. Cover with a towel or a cover for the purpose. Never put the rubber near the skin, it may freeze if so left. Besides, the cover absorbs the moisture that collects on the outside as the ice melts.

Cold compresses are a common remedy for headache. Old handkerchiefs are excellent for this purpose. Fold in frayed edges, two or three thicknesses will be heavy enough, and have two, large enough to cover the forehead. Wring one out of ice water so that it will not drip, and put on the forehead. Keep the other on a piece of ice and change the two applications frequently. When applied to the neck a dry cloth should be placed outside to protect the pillow or the patient's clothing. Cold compresses for inflamed eyes should be of one thickness only, and a little larger than the eye. Have a number and change very often. Use a separate compress for each eye. If there is a discharge a compress should not be used a second time. The discarded compresses should be collected in a paper bag or wrapped in newspapers and burned.

When cold compresses are applied to the head there should be a hot water bag at the feet.

Gargles, sprays, and inhalations are often ordered for sore throats and colds.

Salt or soda added to water in the proportion of a teaspoonful to a pint makes an excellent gargle.

A very cold gargle or one as hot as can be held without burning is better than a tepid one.

Do not go out in the cold air directly after using a hot gargle.

Use at least six separate mouthfuls each time you gargle, and hold long enough at the back of the throat for the gargle to reach every part.

A spray should not be used for the nose without a special order from the doctor. The liquid sometimes gets into the passage leading to the ear and causes earache.

Always wipe the nozzle of the atomizer before using. It should be cleaned after each use and boiled, if another patient is to use it. Always boil the nozzle and clean out the bottle when the atomizer is to be put away. Keep it in a box where dust will not reach it.

Inhalations are useful to relieve difficult breathing and for loss of voice or hoarseness. Fill a pitcher, bowl, or basin, two-thirds full of boiling water. Wrap with a towel to prevent burning if it should touch a patient. Usually drugs such as peppermint spirits, oil of eucalyptus, or tincture of benzoin, in dose of a teaspoonful to the hot water contained in the receptacle, is enough. If no drug is at hand, the steam itself may be depended upon to do some good. Pin one end of a bath towel around the face below the eyes and spread the other over the pitcher inhaling the steam as it rises. It may not be possible to induce a child to do this, in which case make a tent of an open umbrella with a sheet thrown over it at the head of the bed, leaving the front a little open. Place the pitcher so that the child will get the steam and hold the pitcher carefully all the time. Do not let the pitcher touch the patient.

Another means of inhalation is to hold a funnel, made of a piece of folded paper in the nose of a kettle of very hot water, near the patient so that the steam can be inhaled. Be very careful not to scald the patient. After a steam inhalation one should not go out in the cold air nor have the windows opened for an hour or more.

Common Medicines and Other Remedies

It is a very safe rule *never* to take medicines oneself without a doctor's orders. Above all, never advise others, even when you know from experience that certain medicines have helped yourself or others. Medicines should be taken upon prescription from the physician, should be measured accurately, and given at the exact hour ordered.

Read carefully the label or box from which you take the medicine before and after opening or uncorking, and read the name again when putting back in its place. Many people have been poisoned by not reading the label. Have all glasses and spoons, etc., thoroughly cleansed before and after using.

Accuracy, attention, cleanliness, regularity should be watchwords.

In giving either food or medicine, the following measures are helpful:

1 teaspoonful measures 50 grains.
2 teaspoonfuls make 1 dessertspoonful.
2 dessertspoonfuls make 1 tablespoonful.
2 tablespoonfuls make 1 ounce.
8 ounces make 1 cupful or glassful.
16 ounces make one pint.
   (This applies to either liquid or dry measure.)

In giving pills, capsules, tablets give a drink of water first to moisten the tongue and throat. This helps them to slip down more easily.

If there is danger of a pill or tablet choking the patient, crush the pill or tablet between two spoons.

When medicines are taken by spoon, the spoon should be licked by the patient in order to get the full amount.

Nearly all medicines should be mixed with water, and should be followed with a drink of water unless orders are given to the contrary.

Keep all medicines tightly corked.

Buy medicines only in small quantities, as most of them lose their strength in time.

In buying vaseline or cold cream it is better to have it in a tube than in jars. Being opened and dipped into constantly soon makes the contents of a jar unclean.

Common Remedies

Such remedies as the following are to be found in many homes.

Castor oil, clove oil, vaseline, baking soda (this is the same thing as bi-carbonate of soda or saleratus), salt, lime water, alcohol, camphorated oil, spirits of camphor, flaxseed, aromatic spirits of ammonia. Do not confuse this latter remedy with ammonia water used for cleansing things.

Castor oil should be taken in these doses:

Baby, 1 to 2 teaspoonfuls.

Older children: 1 tablespoonful.

Adult: 1 to 2 tablespoonfuls.

There are many ways of taking castor oil. Heat the glass or spoon, put in some orange or lemon juice, then the oil, then more juice. Open the mouth wide and put the oil far back. Have more juice at hand to swallow immediately after. Chilling the mouth by holding a piece of ice in it for a few minutes also helps to disguise the taste. A couple of tablespoonfuls of lemon or orange juice with a quarter of a teaspoonful of soda mixed thoroughly with the oil will make it effervesce so that it is not unpleasant to take.

If the dose is vomited, wait a little while, then give another. Do not give directly before nor directly after a meal.

Olive oil is often taken in doses of one or two teaspoonfuls after meals to regulate the bowels or to help people gain weight or when the appetite is small. It is also used to rub into the skin of under-nourished babies and to rub sick people, especially if the skin is very dry. After rubbing with oil always wipe the skin with a towel.

Vaseline is used to grease sore and chafed parts. A little may be inserted into the nostrils for a cold. Camphorated vaseline is especially good for this. In case of an irritating cough that keeps a child from sleeping, a little plain pure vaseline may be put in the mouth, and it will be found very soothing.

Vaseline is also used to grease such utensils as nozzles and to put on the parts to which poultices or fomentations are to be applied.

Soda may be used for burns (moisten and apply as a paste), as a gargle (one teaspoonful to a pint of water), an an enema (the same proportion), for colds (a teaspoonful in a quart of water to be taken internally in the course of each day), and in bilious attacks, water with this amount of soda may be given. Also to get a person to vomit, in which case the water should be slightly warm.

Salt may be used as a gargle in the same way as soda, and even mixed with the soda, also for enemas. Coarse salt, when heated and put into bags, may be used when there is no hot water bag.

Lime water is used in mixing the baby's milk and is put in the milk for sick people when they cannot take full strength milk. The usual proportion is two table-spoons of lime water to a half glass of milk, which makes about 1 part of lime water to 3 parts of milk.

Alcohol may be used to disinfect the more delicate utensils as the thermometer. *Most alcohol now obtainable is wood alcohol or denaturated; that is, mixed with powerful poisons, so that it should never touch the mouth.* Never place a bottle of alcohol near a flame. If it is ever necessary to use an alcohol lamp, use the solid alcohol. It is much safer.

Camphorated oil is often used to rub the chest and neck with in case of colds. It should be warmed and rubbed in thoroughly. Protect the bedclothes and the patient's clothes with towels. After rubbing, wipe and cover the part with a flannel, to prevent chill.

Spirits of camphor or aromatic spirits of ammonia, a few drops on a handkerchief or piece of cotton, held five or six inches from the nose, relieves faintness. Inhaling the camphor in this way will often make it easier to breathe through the nose in case of a head cold. Fifteen drops of aromatic spirits of ammonia in a table-spoonful of water may be given to anyone recovering from a faint or to relieve nausea.

Flaxseed tea is an old-fashioned remedy for coughs. Pour a quart of boiling water over two tablespoonfuls of flaxseed and let it simmer for two to three hours, or until reduced to about a pint of tea. Strain through a fine strainer several times so that it will not be stringy, flavor with lemon, and add honey or sugar. Put in a covered jar, and take a teaspoonful at a time to relieve irritation in the throat.

The Daily Clean-Out.—People, sick or well, should have a bowel movement once or twice a day. Taking medicine for this purpose is a very bad habit. If healthy people have the proper exercise and food, and drink plenty of good water, medicine is not necessary. Eating coarse grained food, as bran muffins, corn meal porridge, fruits, and vegetables, drinking plenty of water, exercising in the open air, and having a regular time for going to the lavatory (immediately after breakfast and the last thing at night before retiring are suggested times) are habits that are usually sufficient to keep the bowels in good order.

If the waste matter is not carried off by the bowel movements, the body will in time become poisoned by the decayed substance in the intestines, and illness follows. Many headaches, "tired feelings," "blues," and even appendicitis may be caused by constipation.

People who are sick and therefore deprived of taking exercise to help in keeping their bowels regular, need to have very special attention paid to their diet and to have plenty of drinking water always at hand. Also they should have bed-pan or whatever other attention they need *regularly,* and when asked for, *immediately.*

Chill, if due to exposure, may be treated by giving a warm bath or a foot bath, and putting to bed between warm blankets and with hot water bags. Rub briskly under the covers and give a warm drink such as tea, coffee, milk, etc.

Some Common Ills and Their Treatment

When a chill is not merely due to being cold, give the same treatment except the rubbing, take the temperature, and if there is fever, send for the doctor, as it may be the beginning of an illness.

Colds or cramps, or pain in the bowels may be caused by constipation, by gas, by undigested food, by the monthly period or more serious causes. Apply heat (hot water bag or fomentation), sip hot water in which is a little baking soda (one-half teaspoonful to a cup), or a few drops of peppermint. Try a hot foot bath. Lie down and keep very quiet with a hot water bag at feet. If pain continues, except in the case of the monthly illness, empty the stomach either by putting the finger down the throat or by drinking warm water and soda until vomiting starts. Take an enema or a dose of castor oil. If the pain still continues, send for a doctor.

Convulsions. Send for a doctor at once. Loosen all clothing, undress if possible. Watch and prevent patient from hurting herself. Do not try to restrain. Try to force a spoonhandle wound with a bandage between the teeth, to prevent biting of tongue. Keep lying down with head slightly raised. As soon as possible, administer enema or dose of castor oil. Put ice bag on head and hot water bottle to feet. Keep warm. A child may be put into a warm bath and held until convulsions subside. Keep very quiet and handle as little as possible when the convulsion is over, as handling may cause a repetition of the twitching.

Croup. Give steam inhalation. Keep a kettle of very warm water in the room. If this is not possible, fill the bathroom with steam by turning on the hot water, and take the patient there. Put hot fomentations to neck, chest, and abdomen. Send for doctor, who will usually order medicine to make the child vomit, which brings some relief.

Earache. Use hot applications against the ear. A heated glass or a cup in which there is a cloth wrung in very hot water, held against the ear may be found very comforting. Never put drops nor anything else into the ear canal. Either send for the doctor or take the patient to him, as there may be a developing abscess which needs to be opened.

Fever. Patient should go to bed in a well ventilated room and keep quiet. The bowels should move freely and plenty of water be taken. Bathing the hands, face and neck or rubbing with alcohol gives relief, especially if there is restlessness. Only liquid food should be given, and even that should not be urged.

Headaches. The commonest causes of frequent head-aches are eye-strain and indigestion. The cure is being fitted with glasses and taking a proper diet. Rest and quiet, careful eating, cold compresses to the head, a hot water bag to the feet, or a foot bath will usually relieve an ordinary headache. Sometimes, as when there is constipation, a dose of castor oil is necessary. An enema will often give instant relief. Never take headache medicines unless a doctor has specially ordered it. These medicines may contain powerful poisons. The danger of taking them is that while for the time being they may relieve the headache, the *cause* of the headache *remains,* and the headache returns unless the cause, such as eye-strain or indigestion, is removed.

Hiccoughs can be usually stopped by drinking a glass of water in sips while holding the breath. They are usually caused by eating too fast or by some form of indigestion.

Colds, Their Prevention and Care

Everybody knows that colds are "catching." People who are over-tired or under-fed, who stay too much in either under-heated or over-heated rooms, or who do not bathe regularly, or who do not get exercise enough in the open air, are those most likely to catch cold.

If you have a cold yourself, stay away from others if possible, and do all in your power to prevent others coming close to you. Cover the mouth when coughing or sneezing, use paper or old rags instead of handkerchiefs and then burn them; wash your hands before touch-ing things others are to use, and use separate dishes, which should be kept entirely apart from the family dishes and washed separately. If such precautions are taken by the first member of the family to take cold, it would seldom spread through the family.

When people around you have colds, avoid getting close to them, gargle often, take deep breaths of fresh air whenever possible, wash your hands often and keep them away from your nose and mouth.

You do not need to be told that the handkerchief used by anyone with a cold is full of germs. It should be kept from touching other things and should never be left lying around.

If, at the first signs of a cold, a good dose of castor oil is taken, a glass of hot lemonade and a hot bath before going to bed, a cold may be "broken up," as we say. In mild weather, the windows may be left open, but if the weather is very cold it is better to air the room from another room, in order to keep an even temperature, but there should be good ventilation.

If the throat is sore, gargling and a cold compress to the neck will bring relief. If there is fever and headache, you have already been told what to do. Anyone with a cold should eat very lightly and drink plenty of water. They should be as quiet as possible and get all the rest and sleep possible.

Camphorated or plain vaseline may be put in the nostrils, and if there is a cough, plain vaseline may be taken internally—placed on the tongue at the back of the mouth. A spoonful of flaxseed tea taken as often as necessary to relieve irritation may bring relief. Inhalations are helpful in hoarseness. Never give any cough medicines except what are ordered by a doctor.

If the symptoms continue after the first night it is advisable to call a doctor, as what seems a slight cold may be the beginning of a serious illness, as measles, scarlet fever, pneumonia, etc. If there is earache, rapid breathing, great weakness or sleepiness the doctor should be called at once.

Any symptom that lasts after a cold, as pain in one part, weakness, or high temperature, needs a doctor's attention.

Food for the Sick

Food for the sick should be light and easily digested. Generally the doctor says what may be eaten. Such foods as the following are included is so-called invalid foods: Milk, milk soups, eggs, raw and soft-cooked, rennet, custards, ice creams, albumin water, well cooked cereals, gruels, broths, toasts, milk toast, jellies made with gelatine, such as lemon and wine jelly; macaroni, spaghetti, well-cooked bread (never fresh bread), tea, coffee, cocoa.

Sick people should have their meals as regularly as possible, at regular hours and promptly and attractively served. The tray, the dishes, the tray-cloth, should be spotlessly clean, and the tray should not be over-loaded with dishes or food. If it is necessary to bring all the food for a meal to the room on the tray at once in order to save steps, remove some of it, perhaps the dessert, until the patient is ready for it.

Before leaving the room to prepare the tray, arrange everything so that the patient may eat the food as soon as it is brought. As a rule it is better for the sick member of the family to have her meals served before the family sits down to the table, so that she may have her food fresh and hot, and not get tired waiting.

Try to have food that the patient likes, if possible. If she does not like what may be served her, it may be served so attractively that her appetite may be tempted.

All food should be tasted before serving. Serve hot food hot, and cold food cold.

Milk is the most nourishing of liquid foods. If it is

to be heated, do not let it boil. Always take the chill off milk served to children.

Generally speaking, cooked food is better than uncooked, even fruits. Baked apples or apple sauce, for example, are safer to give the sick than raw apples.

Toast is better than bread. Toast upon which the butter has melted should not be given to a sick person. Have the toast hot, and butter each mouthful as eaten. Bread should be at least one day old before given to a sick person. Hot breads, such as fresh rolls and biscuits, are not good foods for ill people. Fried foods should be kept from invalids and children.

The best way to prepare a potato for an invalid is to bake it. It should be served when it is light and mealy, and never after it has become soggy.

The best way of cooking meat is to broil it, having the outside well browned, and the inside soft and juicy, never dry and hard.

A Tray for Liquid and Soft Food

The tray should be large enough to hold two glasses or a cup and saucer and a glass, as well as salt or sugar. Put two spoons on the tray, and if the patient is using a tube or a feeder, put that on the tray. One of the glasses should contain fresh water. Offer a glass of water before and after the nourishment.

The tray for soft solids. Suppose the meal is to be boiled rice, or other cereal, and toast. The tray should have a fresh doilie, salt, sugar (covered), a glass of water, two teaspoons, a knife, if butter is allowed on the toast, and a small pitcher of milk or cream for the rice. Put the cereal in a deep saucer or small bowl, cover with a plate or saucer and rest on another plate. Spread a small napkin on another plate. Put the toast on it, then wrap the napkin around it to keep hot.

Sick people should have plenty of water to drink.

Besides having a pitcher of fresh water and a glass where it may be easily reached, always put a glass of fresh cool water on the tray when food or medicine are brought. While ice water is bad for both sick and well people, the water should be cool enough to be agreeable and refreshing. Water that is chilled to the right temperature by being kept in the ice chest, bottled, is preferable. It should be drunk slowly and not gulped down. Water standing in the room should be kept covered at all times.

Feeding Helpless Patients

A patient is often so weak that she cannot lift her head in order to eat. In this case she would be given liquids through straws or by spoon or "feeder." Sometimes by putting a small quantity of liquid in a glass, two tablespoonfuls, a patient is enabled to drink without spilling a drop.

If necessary, slip one hand under the pillow, raise the head a little, holding the glass to the lips with the other. Anyone lying down should take food very slowly. If solid, it should be cooked, especially well, as there is danger of choking.

Tubes should be washed immediately after using. If used continuously they should be cleaned with a tube brush made for that purpose. Straws should be burned or destroyed. If feeding with a spoon, be careful that neither the food nor the spoon burns the lips or mouth. Feed slowly and a little at a time, allowing plenty of time between mouthfuls.

Occupying and Amusing the Sick

When people are recovering from an illness, or when they are what we call chronic invalids, they often enjoy and are helped by being amused or occupied. At this time a Girl Scout may be very helpful. First of all, she should be cheerful herself. Then she should be able to play two or three quiet games, such as cards, dominoes, checkers, and be able to read aloud and to tell cheerful and amusing stories. Children may often be kept quiet and happy by hearing little rhymes recited. It might be a good idea for every Girl Scout to be able to tell three short stories and three funny stories, know three conundrums and three short poems, play three quiet games of cards, play checkers, play dominoes and know three puzzles.

Excitement is always bad for sick people and they become tired easily, so they should not be read to, talked to, nor played with for too long an interval, even if they seem to wish it themselves. The Scout must always remember that these things are being done for the pleasure of the sick person, and she must be very patient, to let the games or stories be of their own choosing if they wish it, and to avoid being noisy herself.

Daily Routine

There should be a regular daily routine. Have regular hours for feeding, bathing, giving treatment and medicines, giving the bedpan, etc. Be punctual.

Usually the first thing to do in the morning is to close or open the window as necessary, and to give the patient a bed-pan. Have it warm. Take temperature, pulse and respiration and record them. Bring a basin of warm water, soap, towel, etc., to wash hands and face, and a glass of water to brush teeth. Tidy the hair. Straighten up the room a little. Prepare and serve patient's breakfast. After an hour the bed bath may be taken, but a tub bath should not be taken until two hours after breakfast.

Make the bed. Clean up the room. If the patient is well enough, let her read or see visitors after this. Serve the dinner. After dinner, open the windows, lower the shades, and let the patient rest and sleep if possible for at least an hour. Sick people need more rest than well people and should have a regular hour for rest in the daytime. If they sleep, so much the better, as it has been proved that patients who take a nap during the day sleep better at night. After four o'clock give a drink of some kind of hot or cold substance, as needed or desired —broth, milk, lemonade. In the late afternoon sick people are often tired and restless. Change of position, re-arrangement of the pillows or a good rub give comfort and relieve the restlessness. Diversion of some kind, nothing noisy or exciting, may serve the same purpose. It may be found wise to delay the bath until this time of day as bathing has a soothing effect.

Between supper and bedtime the sick person should be kept from excitement. This is a good time for reading aloud or allowing them to read for themselves, but a very poor time to see visitors.

Preparations for the Night. Bring in all the necessities for washing the hands and face and brushing the teeth and combing the hair, and help where needed. Change the nightgown (it is better to have a gown for the day and one for the night), brush the crumbs from the bed, make the sheet smooth, shake up the pillows and straighten out the bedclothes, having extra covers handy in case of need. Fill the hot water bag, attend to the fire, if there is one, and arrange everything in the room just as it will be needed for the night. Give a warm drink, and allow the patient to rinse the mouth (or, if wished, the brushing of the teeth may be delayed until this time). The last thing to do for the sick person is to give a good rub, paying special attention to the bony parts (lower end of spine, shoulder-blades, hips, knees, ankles). Then arrange the ventilation.

Before settling a sick person for the night, be sure that everything about the room is done, as any moving about after she is prepared to sleep may tend to disturb her and prevent her from going to sleep

5. PUBLIC HEALTH

Has the town you live in a free swimming pool with instructors and well arranged hours for little children, older girls and boys and grown-ups? Can you step out after school and have a couple of hours on a well kept tennis court? Is there a good golf course reasonably near, with convenient trolley service? Are there plenty of playgrounds, so that the children are off the streets? And, since grounds are not enough, are there friendly young play-leaders connected with them, to get the children together and teach them all sorts of games and sports?

If none of these things are to be found, or not enough of them, wouldn't you like to have them?

"Of course I should," you reply, "but what can I do about it? I am only a girl, and I can't get all these things by just wishing for them!"

But that's just what you can do.

All these things in a town mean that the town is looking out for the health of its young people. Exercise is one of the most important means of preserving health, and most of the large cities nowadays are working hard to see that no child shall be out of the reach of a good park, a good swimming pool and a good playground.

This all comes under the city government and as this is a democratic form of government, these things are all arranged by vote. That is, the citizens vote to use the public money for such things and vote for the officials who shall spend the money for them. Now, a great many women have the vote today: by the time the present Girl Scouts are twenty-one, a great many more will have it, beyond any doubt. Do you see that if you make up your mind now about the village improvements you want, you can vote for them and get them?

Women are naturally interested in all that happens

to children, and if all the women of a community should get together and vote for everything that concerned the health and happiness and good education of children, can't you see what happy days their school-days would be?

If you saw "Public Health" at the head of a chapter, you might not think it looked very interesting; but when you once get the idea that if your mother had had her say on the Public Health Board you would have had a fine skating pond with a good skate-house, last winter, and sunny, well-aired school rooms to study in, with a big gymnasium for basket ball in bad weather, you may be more interested in the merit badge for Public Health called "Health Guardian!"

Remember that Public Health is simply good house-keeping, applied to the community.

It is a subject which women are sure to take up more and more, and a Girl Scout who has given the matter a little thought and study is going to make a good citizen later on, and will be certain to have her advice asked—and taken—in the matter of making her town healthy and happy.

For instance, if the desks in the public schools are not of the right height and shape, the children are bound to suffer in their health and hygiene.

It is the business of the state to see that all public buildings, schools, theatres, factories, etc., have a certain amount of light and air to the cubic foot, because so much is necessary for health.

It is the business of the state to see that only a certain number of hours a day should constitute a day's work. This is because a certain amount of rest is a necessity for all citizens.

It is the business of the state to see that food and water can be brought into the community. Also that they be kept pure, both in transportation and after they reach the community. This includes the policing of all reservoirs and the filtering of the water; the refrigerating of meat and milk; the condemning of rotten fruit and vegetables; the collecting and disposal of all garbage and waste.

It is the business of the state to prevent spitting in public places, (one of the greatest sources of public infection); to prevent the use of common drinking utensils, towels, etc.; to insist on the isolation of contagious diseases and the placarding of the houses where they occur.

In order to carry on these great wise policies the state should offer free clinics where citizens can find out what is the matter with them and how to prevent it, and trained community nurses for the sick.

Do you see what a wonderful power an intelligent woman can be in the community she lives in? Women ought to be much better, really, in this public housekeeping than men, because most of them have had to learn to do it on a small scale, and know how necessary light, air, rest, exercise and cleanliness are.

But, you may say, in my state women have no vote, as yet, and I am too young for it, anyway; what can I do?

The answer is very simple: every citizen, whether she is young or old, whether she has a vote or not, can find out the laws of the town she lives in and help to enforce them!

And the most important of these laws are those which affect the public safety and the public health. Whether there is a Public Health Commissioner or a Town Board or a Village Superintendent or only a District Nurse to appeal to, there is sure to be somebody whose business it is to listen to violation of the law.

If every troop of Girl Scouts knew the health laws of

their town, *and helped to get them obeyed,* there would be a wonderful lessening of epidemics and a wonderful advance in the health and beauty of our towns.

If the Girl Scouts stood, all over the country, for the intelligent guardianship of the public health and recreation, they would rapidly become one of the greatest and most respected organizations in America, for this reason alone.

6. THE HEALTH WINNER

". . . For since a little self-control, since a clean and elementary diet, pure water, openness of the body to sun and air, a share of honest work, and some degree of mental peace and largesse, are the simple conditions of health, and are or ought to be, accessible to everybody—

"To neglect these is sheer treason."

—*Toward Democracy, by Edward Carpenter.*

Five Points of Health for Girl Scouts

A cheerful Scout, a clean Scout, a helpful Scout, is a well Scout. She is the only Scout that really *is prepared.* She not only knows the laws of health, she lives them: she stands tall, she plays daily in the open air, she rests and sleeps at night, and conserves her energy at all times, she is careful to get the right amount of air, water, sun and food each day, and perhaps most important of all, she keeps clean.

1. *Stand Tall*—Every Scout should be recognized a long way off, not only by her uniform, but by her erect carriage. In sitting, the lower back should be against the back of the chair. In bending forward to read or

write, bend straight from the hips. At Scout meetings practice sitting without support for the back. When "at ease" during drill, stand with feet apart and parallel and with hands hanging free. When resting, lie flat on the back without pillows. Correct posture is obtained by balancing the different parts of the body—hips, head, chest in a straight line, so that the bony framework bears the weight. The muscles and ligaments will not then be strained, and the bones will not be forced into an abnormal position. Two rules to remember are: "Stand tall" and "Keep your spine long."

2. *Take Exercise*—If you have watched soldiers obey commands in drill you know how quickly their joints and muscles work. The setting-up exercises given in the Handbook have been planned to preserve the power of joints and muscles, and to prevent them from becoming like rusty machines. These exercises should be taken with windows open, if not out of doors. Clothing should be light and loose, and corsets removed. These exercises are not to be considered a substitute for vigorous outdoor work or play, but only as supplementary to or when these are impossible. The day should be planned to include at least an hour and a half of vigorous activity in the open air. This will take different forms, according to the place and season, so that in the summer one may swim, row or paddle, or play tennis or any other game outdoors, and in the winter skate, coast or snowshoe. However, the best all year round exercise, and the simplest and easiest to get is walking. Five miles a day is an adequate average. Even walking alone is good exercise, but walking in a group or two and two is better, because keeping step, singing, whistling and talking and laughing together add enormously to the exhilaration of motion and of sun, wind or rain in the face.

A Girl Scout should avoid unusual exercise before

during and immediately following menstruation. However, she should remember that a reasonable amount of exercise at this time is quite normal and beneficial, except where there is an actual disorder of some sort. In this case a physician should be consulted.

3. *Rest and Conserve Energy*—Go to bed early and sleep from eight to eleven hours, according to age. Sleep with windows open all the year round. Rest sometime during the day, flat on the back if possible, but even five minutes sitting quietly with hands in the lap and eyes closed is better than nothing. The following table shows the number of hours of sleep that are needed at different ages:

Age	Hours of Sleep
10 and 11 years	9½ to 11
12 and 13 years	9 to 10½
14 and 15 years	8½ to 10
16 and 17 years	8 to 9½
18 and 19 years	8 to 9
20 and over	at least 8

Save Your Eyes

The reason it is important to rest and to sleep enough is because it is while at rest that the body regains energy lost during activity, and stores it up for future work and play. There are other ways of saving energy, and one of them is by keeping the body in such good repair that like a good machine it does its work with a minimum expenditure of force and heat. This is the main reason for the setting-up exercises, or indeed for any sort of exercises. Perhaps the single best way to save energy is by saving your eyes. There is almost no work or play that does not involve the use of our eyes. If people are blind they can learn to do many things without vision, but it is infinitely harder than with it. Modern life, especially in cities, makes a constant demand on our eyes, and more than this, the demand is on one part of the eyes—the muscles concerned in near work. The best way to rest the eyes, and one which not only rests the tired parts but exercises the parts that are not used, is by doing things that will involve *distant vision*. Walking and looking far ahead and far away on every side rests the eyes best of all, and this is one reason why a good walk will often clear up a headache. Another way to insure distant vision is by riding backward in a car. Then as the landscape flows past you, your eye muscles relax to the position needed for distant vision. If you cannot walk or ride and are doing close work, like sewing or reading, look up and "at nothing" every once in a while.

The following are some important rules to remember in saving your eyes:

Rest your "near" eye muscles by looking at distant objects and places.

Do not work facing a light or where the rays from a light cross your field of vision directly.

Work so far as possible by indirect or reflected light.

If you must work near uncovered artificial lights, wear an eye-shade.

When sewing or writing have the light at your left, unless you are left-handed. This is to keep the shadow of your hands from the work.

Avoid a glare or light that is in streaks or bars of alternate dark and bright. Diffused, even light is best.

Have your eyes examined by a competent oculist immediately:

If you have headaches,

If the eyes sting or burn after using,

If print or other objects dance or blur,

If you must get close to your work to see it,

If near work tires your eyes or you,

If there is the slightest irritation or soreness about the lids or other parts.

How to Avoid Muscle Strain

Girls and women in attempting to live an outdoor life or indeed when trying to do many of the things numbered among the Scout activities, such as First Aid, Home Nursing and Hiking, often give themselves quite unnecessary pain and fatigue from lifting, pulling and carrying weights in the wrong way. Ability to carry and lift or move is not so much dependent upon absolute strength as it is on knowing how. The whole body, so far as it is a physical mechanism, may be thought of as a series of levers, of which the muscles, bones, and joints make up the parts and are fulcrum, power arm or weight arm as the case may be. Without going into the details of bodily structure or even knowing the names of the different bones and muscles, it is possible to learn a few simple things about the right use of these levers that will be useful at all times.

Certain parts of the body are more able to do heavy work than others, and the first thing to remember is that the upper part of the back, the shoulders and the upper arms are stronger than the lower back, the abdomen and the lower arms. Therefore, whenever you are trying to lift or move an object, see if you cannot use these stronger parts. If the arms are held away from the body when lifting, pulling, throwing or pushing, the muscles of the upper arm, the shoulders and the upper back will be brought into play. If the arms are held close to the body, the lower-arm muscles are unduly taxed and in trying to help them out, pressure is made on the abdominal and pelvic muscles, which are not fitted to bear this sort of strain. Therefore, in carrying a bag or suitcase, where this is absolutely unavoidable, try to swing the arm free from the body, so as to use the upper arm and back muscles for the weight.

Another important way to save strain is by pushing instead of pulling. It is almost impossible to push anything so hard as to injure your back or abdominal muscles. It is almost impossible, on the other hand, to pull even a relatively light weight without some strain. If you will think of how a horse in harness actually exerts his strength in drawing a wagon, you will see that what he does is to *push* against the straps, and it is the straps that *pull* the wagon. Even the strongest horse could not pull a wagon with his teeth very far, or pull something tied only to the back leg muscles. *Get behind and push* is the rule to remember, and never resort to *pulling* until you have tried every device for pushing instead.

If you *must* pull, try to use heavy muscles, such as *leg* muscles, to do it with. Often a weight may be lifted or pulled by getting the foot under or in back and using the arms only to steer with. This applies particularly to objects like trunks or bureaus.

Always take advantage of any natural leverage that you can and if you must move something heavy, do not lift it at once and attempt to carry it, but lift one end and swing or shove it and then lift the other end and shove it. If you will watch expressmen at work you will notice that they roll boxes and trunks, holding them almost on end and tipping them just enough to turn them along their shortest axis. In this way the boxes carry themselves, so far as their main weight is concerned.

Carrying a weight on the head or shoulders is another way of converting a pull into a push, and this is taken advantage of by peasant women in Europe, who often are seen carrying heavy weights to market in baskets perched on their heads, while they stride along arm-free.

A knapsack strapped on to the shoulders is not only more convenient because it leaves the arms and hands free to swing naturally or use for other purposes, but because the weight is distributed and is carried by means of heavy muscles pushing up under the strap. A weight should be distributed over a set of muscles as evenly as possible, and this is the reason for suspending a knapsack from two shoulders instead of one, when possible.

Finally, in doing any sort of lifting or pulling, if the muscles that are to be used are contracted before grasping the weight they will be able to do their work with far less effort. Try lifting a small weight like a book in two ways—first, have your hand and fingers relaxed and limp when you grasp it, and see how heavy it seems and how hard it is to contract your muscles properly while lifting it. Then drop the book and go at it again, this time anticipating its weight and contracting your hand and finger muscles before grasping it. See how easily it comes up. Try this same thing with heavier weights, and learn *always to contract the muscle before taking the load*. In carrying a weight for any distance it is well to shift it from one arm to another, always preparing the muscles by contracting them before the weight is assumed.

Using the muscles so as to take advantage of their lever-like qualities in the best way, contracting them before loading, and pushing instead of pulling, go to make up what is sometimes called "getting a purchase."

4. *Supply Daily Need for Air, Sun, Water and Food* —Besides exercise and rest there are other controllable factors upon which health depends. These are air, heat and light of the sun, water and food. To grow and work properly the body needs plenty of each of these.

Air—If you cannot work or play outdoors you can still bring out of doors in by opening your windows at frequent intervals. You will find that work goes better, and that you do not tire so easily if you make it a rule to open the windows and doors and move about the room for five minutes every hour or two. Sleep with windows open or out of doors. Camp and hike as often as possible. Work in the garden. Play out-of-door games.

Heat—The proper temperature of the body is between 98 and 99 degrees Fahrenheit. Human life depends upon the maintenance of this temperature at all times, and very slight changes either up or down interfere seriously with all the other life processes. The main source of heat is from food consumed, or really burned, in the body. Artificial heating in houses helps conserve the body heat, as does clothing. But clothes and shelter may make you overheated, which is nearly as bad as being cold; they may also shut out fresh air. Clothes should not be too heavy nor too tight. Shoes should have soles straight on the inner side, and be broad enough to allow the toes full play, and have low heels. Shoes that are comfortable to hike in are apt to be the best for all the time wear.

At night the clothes worn during the day should be aired and dried thoroughly. This will help much in maintaining the right body temperature, because clothes become damp from wearing, and dampness uses up body heat.

Sunlight—Sunlight is one of the best health bringers known. Little children—and grown people, too—suffering from the most serious form of tuberculosis, that of the bones, get well if they are kept in the sunlight. In one of the finest hospitals for children in the world, in Switzerland, the main treatment is to have the children play outdoors without clothes in the sunlight, and they do this even when there is heavy winter snow on the ground. Human beings droop and die without the sun, just as plants do, though it takes longer to kill them. It is a gloomy person who does not feel happier in the sun, and a happy and cheerful person is generally healthy. So get into the sun whenever you can. Walk on the sunny side of the street, and open your windows to the sun whenever you can. However, in hot climates and in the warmest summer days, remember that the sun can injure as well as help, and do not expose the head or body unnecessarily.

Water—As about three-quarters of our body weight is water, the solid portions of bone, muscle, and so forth, constituting only one-quarter, and as considerable water is given off each day by evaporation from skin and lungs and with excreta, the loss must be made up. In addition to the water taken with meals and contained in the food a Girl Scout should drink at least six tumblers of water daily. This is a quart and a half. One glass should be taken on arising and before breakfast, two between breakfast and lunch, two between lunch and dinner, and one before going to bed. Be sure the water is pure, and boil any water the purity of which is doubted in the slightest. Water kept cool in the ice chest, or in a jar with a moist cover, is better than ice water, both because cool water actually quenches thirst more easily, being more readily absorbed than ice cold water, and because it is difficult to control the purity of ice.

Food—Food should be clean and kept clean. Growing girls can tell whether they are eating enough of the right sort of food, and if they are getting the best out of it, by seeing whether they are up to the right weight for their height and age. A chart is given at the end of this section showing the standard weight for each height at each age. The following are good rules to follow in making your daily food habits:

Do not eat between meals.

Eat slowly and chew food thoroughly.

Eat freely of coarse cereals and breads.

Eat meat only once a day.

Have green vegetables, salad or fruit every day.

Drink as much milk as possible, but no coffee or tea.

If you do not have at least one bowel movement a day it is a sign of constipation, which means the accumulation of waste material from food in the intestine. Exercise. especially walking, eating coarse vegetables, coarse bread and coarse cereals, and fruit, and drinking enough water will help the bowels to move properly. Constipation is not only an unclean habit of the body, but it is dangerous, because the waste matter decays and poison is carried all over the body. Headaches, indigestion, bad breath and chronic fatigue are some of the results.

5. *Keep Clean*—A Girl Scout should be sure that the air, water and food that she allows to enter her body are clean. Be sure that they are pure when they reach her, and keep them so by keeping her body, clothes and room clean with the help of sun, soap and water. You have probably heard of germs, microbes and bacteria. These are names for the same organisms, which are tiny forms of plant life unseen by the eye, and of which our unaided senses give us no knowledge. They exist everywhere and in many forms. Most of them are harmless to human life, and many of them are useful, as, for example, one that grows on the roots of peas and beans and helps the plants to extract nitrogen from the air. Some bacteria, however, are harmful, and these are known as disease germs, as they are active in producing diseases, especially those diseases which we know as contagious. The dangerous germs nearly all live in dust and dirt and in dark places. When we clean house and dispose of waste material and bring air and sunlight into dark and dirty places we are doing more than re-

moving unpleasant sights and smells, we are destroying the breeding places of disease.

Every girl wants a clear skin. Proper food, water and exercise give this; but it is also necessary to keep the surface clean by taking a hot bath with soap at least twice a week, and a cold or tepid sponge and rubdown the other days. Besides the loose dirt which comes on the body from the outside, perspiration and oil come from the inside through the skin pores, and when accumulated give a disagreeable odor. Special attention is needed to guard against this odor, particularly under the armpits, and soap and water should be used daily. A hot bath is relaxing and opens the pores. A cold bath is stimulating and closes the pores. A hot bath is best taken at night, or if taken in the morning, follow by a cool sponge or shower. Do not take a cold plunge bath unless advised to do so by a physician.

Always wash the hands immediately before handling or preparing food and before eating. Always wash hands after going to the bathroom. Keep nails short, and clean with nail brush each time the hands are washed and with orange stick when necessary.

During menstruation it is particularly important to keep the body and clothes scrupulously clean, by bathing or washing with plenty of water.

Hair—Air and a good brushing every day will keep the hair in good condition. It should be washed once in two weeks. Wash with hot soapsuds and rinse thoroughly, using first hot, then cooler, and finally cold water. Keep the hair brush clean by washing in cold water and soap and a little ammonia at least once a week. The brush should be dried in the sun, not by artificial heat.

Ears—Keep the outer surfaces of the ears clean, but

leave the inner part alone. Do not poke for wax nor put oil in the ear.

Feet—Bathe the feet in hot water at night, when tired. In the morning bathe with cold water after hot, to harden them for walking. Keep the toenails clean, and cut evenly.

Teeth—Next to a fresh, sweet skin the most beautiful feature of a truly beautiful woman is her teeth. The basis of beautiful teeth is a clean mouth. Teeth should be brushed at least twice a day. The best times are after breakfast and the last thing before going to bed. A brush with medium soft bristles should be used. Clean a new brush thoroughly with soap and water and soak in cold water to set the bristles. A toothbrush should be cleansed and aired and if possible sunned every day. Never use a brush that has begun to lose its bristles, or which has become caked or yellow. Paste or powder that are not gritty should be used. Always brush away from the gums; that is, brush the upper teeth down, and the lower teeth up. Clean the roof of the mouth and the tongue.

It is a good plan to have the teeth examined at least every six months. Then any repairs or cleaning that may be needed can be easily attended to and much future pain, trouble and expense saved.

Eyes—Wash eyes carefully for "sleepers" in the morning. Bathing with alternate hot and cold will rest and strengthen the muscles.

Do not use public towels or drinking cups.

Do not use towels, handkerchiefs or other toilet articles or glasses or cups or table utensils used by others.

Avoid sneezing or coughing into another person's face.

Measurements

Every Girl Scout should know her measurements, including her height, her weight, her waist measure, her chest girth and her chest expansion. Not only are these things convenient to know when ordering uniforms and buying clothes, but any physical director, gymnasium teacher or doctor can tell her if these are in good proportion for her age and general development and advise her as to how she may go about to improve them if they need it.

The accompanying table (given in the last section of the Health Record) shows the right height and weight for girls at different ages. The way to consult it is as follows:

First, find your height by measuring yourself without shoes against a wall. The best way to do is to have someone lay a ruler on top of your head so that it extends to the wall and touches it at right angles. Then the place should be marked and the distance measured with a yard stick or tape. Count a half inch as the next highest inch; thus if you measure 59½ inches call this 60. If you measure 59¼ count it as an even 59. Stand with heels against the wall, and head high: "Stand Tall."

Second, find your weight with only indoor clothes on. Take the weight to the nearest pound, counting as before a half pound or three-quarters as the next highest and disregard the amounts less than one-half.

Then take your card and look along the top row for the age to which you are nearest, counting six months past one year mark as the next year. Thus, if you are within six months of being 13, count yourself 13.

Then look at the left-hand upright row of figures and find your height in inches.

Then with a rule or paper find the corresponding number of pounds for your height and age.

You will see that a girl may be any number of inches tall within wide limits, but her weight must correspond to her height rather than simply to her age.

A girl should be within ten per cent of the proper weight for her age and height. If you find that you are underweight, do not be frightened or discouraged, as it is quite easy to get up to normal by following the health rules, particularly those relating to food, water and sleep. Drink as much milk as possible, and eat fresh vegetables and don't spoil your appetite by eating too many sweets or nibbling between meals. If you find that after a month you are still more than ten per cent underweight, then ask your parents if you can see the doctor or consult the school physician.

A Health Record Chart for Girl Scouts

Girl Scouts who are working for the "The Health Winner" badge should keep an account of their progress for three months, and a good way to do it is to have a Health Chart to fill out daily and bring the record for each week to their Captain, at troop meeting. The chart given below is suggested as a model, and copies will be obtainable from National Headquarters, but troops can make up their own.

Every Scout is naturally a Health Crusader ,and she can use the blanks provided by the National Modern Health Crusade if she so desires.

In this case the first two points can be combined, which relate to washing hands and face, and an additional point inserted in place of the second, to the effect that "I ate no sweets, candy, cake or ice cream between meals today."

DAILY RECORD OF POINTS

1. I did my setting-up exercises . . . .
2. I walked, worked or played outdoors at least a half-hour
      2a. Time spent walking . . . .
      2b. Distance walked . . . .
3. I went to bed early last night, and slept at least 8 hours
4. I slept with my window open . . . .
5. I drank six glasses of water between meals . . . . .
6. I ate no sweets, candy, cake, sweet drinks or ice cream, except as dessert . . . .
7. I ate green vegetables or fruit or salad . . . . .
8. I drank no tea or coffee . . . .
9. I drank milk or had milk in some other form . . . .
10. I had a bowel movement . . . .
11. I washed my hands before eating, and after going to the bathroom . . . .
12. I had a bath (at least two a week must be recorded) . .
13. I brushed my teeth twice during the day . . . . .
14. I brushed my hair night and morning . . . . . .
15. I shampooed my hair (at least once every four weeks)

Scout. . . . .

Checks for Week Commencing Monday. . . . . No. . . . .

Pt.	Mon.	Tues.	Wed.	Thurs.	Fri.	Sat.	Sun.
1							
2							
2a							
2b							
3							
4							
5							
6							
7							
8							
9							
10							
11							
12							
13							
14							
15							

Date handed to Captain. . . . .

Captain's Comment. . . . .

THE GIRL SCOUTS HEALTH RECORD

RIGHT HEIGHT AND WEIGHT FOR GIRLS

Hght. ins.	10 yrs.	11 yrs.	12 yrs.	13 yrs.	14 yrs.	15 yrs.	16 yrs.	17 yrs.	18 yrs.
47	53								
48	55								
49	57								
50	59	56							
51	62	58	61						
52	65	60	64						
53	68	63	67						
54	70	66	69	70					
55	73	68	72	73					
56	77	71	75	76	77				
57	81	74	79	80	81	86			
58	85	78	83	84	85	90	91		
59	89	82	87	88	89	95	96	98	
60		86	91	93	94	100	102	104	106
61		90	95	97	99	106	108	109	111
62		94	101	102	104	111	113	114	115
63		99	106	107	109	115	117	118	119
64		104	111	112	113	119	120	121	122
65		109	115	117	118	122	123	124	125
66			117	119	120	124	126	127	128
67			119	121	122	127	128	129	130
68				124	124	130	132	133	134
69				126	126	133	135	136	137
70				129	128	136	138	139	140
71					134	140	142	143	144
72					138	145	147	148	149

RECORD FOR WHOLE PERIOD

1. Posture at beginning:
   (Comment by Captain)..............
2. Posture at end:
   (Comment by Captain)..............
3. Total distance walked..............
   (Must be at least 75 miles)
4. At least three shampoos..............
5. Any colds during period?..............
6. Constipation during period?..............
7. Answered correctly the following questions:
   How do you care for your teeth properly?...
   Why is it important to care for your eyes?...
   How can you rest them?..............
   What are points to remember about light for work?..............
   What is the difference in effect between a hot and a cold bath?..............
   How do you care for feet on a hike?..............
8. Height in inches at beginning of period..............
   Weight in pounds at beginning of period..............
   Standard weight for height and age?..............
   Difference plus or minus in your weight..............
   Height in inches at end of period..............
   Standard weight for height and age..............
   Difference plus or minus in your weight..............
   If growth is shown what rate is this per month? Standard?..............

PREPARED BY DR. THOMAS D. WOOD

About what a Girl should gain each month

AGE		AGE	
8 to 11	8 oz.	14 to 16	8 oz.
11 to 14	12 oz.	16 to 18	4 oz.

Weights and measures should be taken without shoes and in only the usual indoor clothes.
Used by courtesy of the Child Health Organization, 156 Fifth Avenue, New York City.

THE GIRL SCOUTS HEALTH RECORD

SECTION XII

SETTING-UP EXERCISES FOR GIRL SCOUTS

Our bodies are like machines that need frequent oiling and testing to see that all parts are working right.

Or they are like instruments that must be tuned before they are played.

If this is not done, the machinery gets rusty and clogged, or the instrument gets out of tune and makes horrid noises.

That is the way it is with our bodies; our muscles and joints should be bent and stretched every day to take the kinks out, and keep them strong and flexible.

The best way is to tune up every morning for just a few minutes before you put on your clothes, and then again at night to rest the tired parts and exercise the parts that have not been used, so you can even things up.

The Right Position

First of all try to stand in the right position.

Stand with the feet side by side, a few inches apart and pointed straight ahead. Many people think you should turn out your toes because they think it looks better. This is not natural. If you stand on a step with one foot even with the edge, and let the other foot hang over the step below, it will hang parallel with the foot you are standing on. That is the way it is meant to go, and people who turn out their toes do so much

walking sideways that they have to travel much farther than if they kept their feet pointed in the direction they want to go.

Then your legs should come up straight from your ankles; don't stand either on your heels or your toes, but right over the highest part of the arch, which is the strongest part, and best fitted to bear your weight when you are standing still, and brings your hips up to just the right place to hold your body.

In the lower part of your body are some big heavy bones shaped somewhat like a bowl. This bowl is balanced on the top of your legs, and holds most of your organs. If this bowl is balanced just right, the organs remain in place, the way they are meant to be, but if it is not balanced right, the contents are tipped so that they would come tumbling out if the muscles intended for other work did not hold them in. This is hard on these muscles which have their own work to do, and if they are used to hold up things that should keep their own balance, sooner or later they give way, and there is a sad accident, or a general slump. Then instead of saying, "That foolish person always stood in the wrong position and of course her insides got out of place," we say, "Poor dear so-and-so has given out from overwork and has acute indigestion, or a 'floating kidney,' or 'a bad liver.' How could it have happened?"

If your underpinning is all right it is not difficult to be straight above.

Let your shoulders hang easily in a straight line under your ears, in the position they will naturally take if from side stretch (fig. 3) the arms drop easily to the side. *Don't arch your chest and throw your shoulders back!* This is not a slump and does not mean to let your back bow out. If your shoulders are easy you can straighten your back and your head will balance itself, and there you are: a straight upstanding Scout, ready for what comes next.

Remember: a) Feet pointing straight ahead.

b) Body balanced on legs coming up
straight from ankles.

c) Shoulders easy under ears.

This gives a straight line from top of head through
shoulders and hips to between ankles.

General Rules

Stretch to the very tips of your middle fingers—stretching makes your muscles flexible.

Breathe in as arms rise and out as they fall.

Stand tall.

Sit tall.

Remember the straight line that comes from the top
of your head down to between your ankles.

Keep limber, don't let your knees grow stiff.

Sit crosslegged on the floor. Sit on your heels.

Rise without help from your hands.

The Exercises

New tune up: begin by repeating each exercise four
times; then increase to 8, 12, or 16; never more than 16.

1. Stretch arms down (fig. 1). Swing them forward
   and stretch up and slightly forward (fig. 2), breathing deep. Let them fall breathing out. Do this
   slowly counting, up 1 down 2.

2. From (fig. 1) swing arms forward and up (fig. 2)
   and out to side stretch (fig. 3) coming to full deep
   breath and stretch as far as you can—count 3. Up
   1—side 2—down 3—breathing out. Don't hurry,
   take time to breathe deep.

3. Stretch arms down, without bending anywhere. Two
   counts; down 1—relax 2.

4. From arms down (fig. 1) to side stretch (fig. 3).
   Two counts; to side 1—down 2. This may be done
   quickly with vigor.

5. From side stretch palms up to upward stretch (fig.
   2)—two counts—up 1—side 2.

6. From arms down roll shoulders and arms out and back, stretching arms back and down (fig. 4). Two counts out and down 1—back to position 2.

7. Hands palms down, tips of middle fingers touching, thumbs touching chest, elbows level with shoulders (fig. 5); jerk elbows back keeping them up even with shoulders (fig. 6). Two counts,—jerk 1—back to place 2.

8. From upward stretch (fig. 2) bend slowly from side to side (fig. 7), keeping arms close to ears and stretched to tip of middle fingers. Don't twist your body; just bend to each side alternately. Count slowly side 1—up 2—side 3—up 4.

9. From side stretch (fig. 3) twist body from waist up, without moving hips (fig. 8). Twist from side to side. Two counts—twist 1—front 2—twist 1—front 2.

10. From side stretch (fig. 3) bend body from side to side keeping straight line from tip of one middle finger to tip of other (fig. 9). Two counts—bend 1—back to position 2—alternate sides.

11. Bend right knee and kick yourself (fig. 10); left knee same. Two counts—kick right 1—kick left 2. Repeat slowly then double quick (running in place).

12. Bend right knee and hip, bringing knee nearly up to chest without bending body (fig. 11); left same— slowly. Then double quick bringing knee only as high as hip.

13. Place hands at back of neck (fig. 12) and rise on toes, bend knees (fig. 13) and rise keeping body upright (do not spread knees or touch heels. If this exercise is too difficult balance with arms side stretch, bring arms down to touch floor as you bend,

and to upward stretch as you rise). Count 4:—on toes 1—bend 2—up on toes 3—standing position 4.

14. From upward stretch (fig. 2) bend and touch floor in front of toes (fig. 14). Count two slowly: down 1—up 2. Breathe out as you come down—in as you come up.

15. *Neck Exercises.* Sit crosslegged on floor—hands on knees: head up—chin parallel with the floor.

   a) turn head to right and then to left—4 counts—right 1—front 2—left 3—front 4.

   b) droop head from side to side (fig. 15); four counts—right 1—up 2—left 3—up 4.

   c) drop chin forward (fig. 16); straighten and drop head back (fig. 17). Count 4—down 1—up 2—back 3—up 4.

   d) turn head and face right (fig. 18) drop chin 1—up 2—back 3 (fig. 19) up 4; keep looking in same direction only up and down; same to left.

   e) goose-neck; facing front stretch chin out as far as possible (fig. 20); then down and in and up. Count 4—out 1—down 2—in 3—to straight position 4.

16. Lie down on your back and raise first one foot and then the other without bending the knee, two counts —up 1—down 2.

17. Raise both feet without bending knees and touch the floor over your head (fig. 21). Lower slowly.

18. Raise body without bending back, and (if you can) without helping yourself with your hand, and touch your toes with your hands, and your knees with your forehead, without bending your knees (fig. 22).

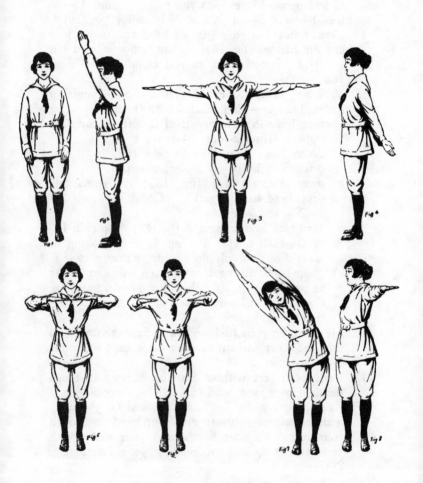

SETTING-UP EXERCISES (Figs. 1-8)

SETTING-UP EXERCISES (Figs. 9-22)

SECTION XIII

WOODCRAFT

Reprinted from the Woodcraft Manual for Girls by permission of the Woodcraft League.

TWELVE SECRETS OF THE WOODS

Do you know the twelve secrets of the woods?

Do you know the umbrella that stands up spread to show that there is a restaurant in the cellar?

Do you know the "manna-food" that grows on the rocks, summer and winter, and holds up its hands in the Indian sign of "innocence," so all who need may know how good it is?

Do you know the vine that climbs above the sedge to whisper on the wind "There are coconuts in my basement"?

Can you tell why the rabbit puts his hind feet down ahead of his front ones as he runs?

Can you tell why the squirrel buries every other nut and who it was that planted those shag-barks along the fence?

Can you tell what the woodchuck does in midwinter and on what day?

Have you learned to know the pale villian of the open woods—the deadly amanita, for whose fearful poison no remedy is known?

Have you learned to overcome the poison ivy that was once so feared—now so lightly held by those who know?

Have you proved the balsam fir in all its fourfold gifts —as Christmas tree, as healing balm, as consecrated bed, as wood of friction fire?

Do you know the wonderful medicine that is in the sky?

Have you tasted the bread of wisdom, the treasure that

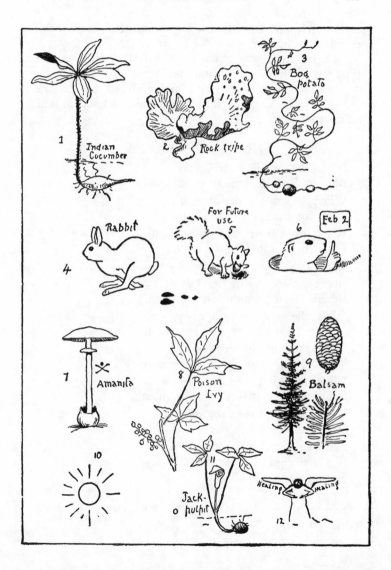

cures much ignorance, that is buried in the aisle of Jack-o-Pulpit's Church?

Can you tell what walked around your tent on the thirtieth night of your camp-out?

Then are you wise. You have learned the twelve secrets of the woods. But if you have not, come and let us teach you.

WEATHER WISDOM

When the dew is on the grass,
Rain will never come to pass.

When the grass is dry at night,
Look for rain before the light.

When grass is dry at morning light,
Look for rain before the night.

Three days' rain will empty any sky.

A deep, clear sky of fleckless blue
Breeds storms within a day or two.

When the wind is in the east,
It's good for neither man nor beast.

When the wind is in the north,
The old folk should not venture forth.

When the wind is in the south,
It blows the bait in the fishes' mouth.

When the wind is in the west,
It is of all the winds the best.

An opening and a shetting
Is a sure sign of a wetting.

(Another version)
Open and shet,
Sure sign of wet.

(Still another)
It's lighting up to see to rain.

> Evening red and morning gray
> Sends the traveler on his way.
> Evening gray and morning red
> Sends the traveler home to bed.

Red sky at morning, the shepherd takes warning;
Red sky at night is the shepherd's delight.

If the sun goes down cloudy Friday, sure of a clear Sunday.

If a rooster crows standing on a fence or high place, it will clear. If on the ground, it doesn't count.

> Between eleven and two
> You can tell what the weather is going to do.
> Rain before seven, clear before eleven.

Fog in the morning, bright sunny day.

If it rains, and the sun is shinning at the same time, the devil is whipping his wife and it will surely rain tomorrow.

If it clears off during the night, it will rain again shortly.

Sun drawing water, sure sign of rain.

A circle round the moon means "storm." As many stars as are in circle, so many days before it will rain.

Sudden heat brings thunder.

A storm that comes against the wind is always a thunderstorm.

The oak and the ash draw lightning. Under the birch, the cedar, and balsam you are safe.

East wind brings rain.

West wind brings clear, bright, cool weather.

North wind brings cold.

South wind brigs heat.   (On Atlantic coast.)

The rain-crow or cuckoo (both species) is supposed by all hunters to foretell rain, when its "Kow, kow, kow" is long and hard.

So, also, the tree-frog cries before rain.

Swallows flying low is a sign of rain; high, of clearing weather.

The rain follows the wind, and the heavy blast is just before the shower.

OUTDOOR PROVERBS

What weighs an ounce in the morning, weighs a pound at night.

A pint is a pound the whole world round.

Allah reckons not against a man's allotted time the days he spends in the chase.

If there's only one, it isn't a track, it's an accident.

Better safe than sorry.

No smoke without fire.

The bluejay doesn't scream without reason.

The worm don't see nuffin pretty 'bout de robin's song. —(Darkey.)

Ducks flying over head in the woods are generally pointed for water.

If the turtles on a log are dry, they have been there half an hour or more, which means no one has been near to alarm them.

Cobwebs across a hole mean "nothing inside."

Whenever you are trying to be smart, you are going wrong. Smart Aleck always comes to grief.

You are safe and winning, when you are trying to be kind.

WHEN LOST IN THE WOODS

If you should miss your way, the first thing to remember is like the Indian, "You are not lost; it is the teepee that is lost." It isn't serious. It cannot be so, unless you do something foolish.

The first and most natural thing to do is to get on a hill, up a tree, or other high lookout, and seek for some landmark near the camp. You may be sure of these things:

You are not nearly as far from camp as you think you are.

Your friends will soon find you.

You can help them best by signalling.

The worst thing you can do is to get frightened. The truly dangerous enemy is not the cold or the hunger, so much as the fear. It is fear that robs the wanderer of his judgment and of his limb power; it is fear that turns the passing experience into a final tragedy. Only keep cool and all will be well.

If there is snow on the ground, you can follow you back track.

If you see no landmark, look for the smoke of the fire. Shout from time to time, and wait; for though you have been away for hours it is quite possible you are within earshot of your friends. If you happen to have a gun, fire it off twice in quick succession on your high lookout then wait and listen. Do this several times and wait plenty long enough, perhaps an hour. If this brings no help, send up a distress signal—that is, make two smoke fires by smothering two bright fires with green leaves and rotten wood, and keep them at least fifty feet apart, or the wind will confuse them. Two shots or two smokes are usually understood to mean "I am in trouble." Those in camp on seeing this should send up one smoke, which means "Camp is here."

In a word, "keep cool, make yourself comfortable, leave a record of your travels, and help your friends to find you."

EDIBLE WILD PLANTS

No one truly knows the woods until he can find with certainty a number of wild plants that furnish good food for man in the season when food is scarce; that is, in the winter or early spring.

During summer and autumn there is always an abundance of familiar nuts and berries, so that we may rule them out, and seek only for edible plants and roots that are available when nuts and berries are not.

Rock Tripe. The most wonderful of all is probably the greenish-black rock tripe, found on the bleakest, highest rocks in the northern parts of this continent. There is a wonderful display of it on the cliffs about Mohonk Lake, in the Catskills. Richardson and Franklin, the great northern explorers, lived on it for months. It must be very carefully cooked or it produces cramps. First gather and wash it as clear as possible of sand and grit, washing it again and again, snipping off the gritty parts of the roots where it held onto the mother rock. Then roast it slowly in a pan till dry and crisp. Next boil it for one hour and serve it either hot or cold. It looks like thick gumbo soup with short, thick pieces of black and green leaves in it. It tastes a little like tapioca with a slight flavoring of licorice. On some it acts as a purge.

Basswood Browse or Buds. As a child I ate these raw in quantities, as did also most of my young friends, but they will be found the better for cooking. They are particularly good and large in the early spring. The inmost bark also has food value, but one must disfigure the tree to get that, so we leave it out.

Slippery Elm. The same remarks apply to the buds and inner bark of the slippery elm. They are nutritious, acceptable food, especially when cooked with scraps of meat or fruit for flavoring. Furthermore, its flowers come out in the spring before the leaves, and produce very early in the season great quantities of seed which are like little nuts in the middle of a nearly circular wing. These ripen by the time the leaves are half grown and

Wild Food - Plants

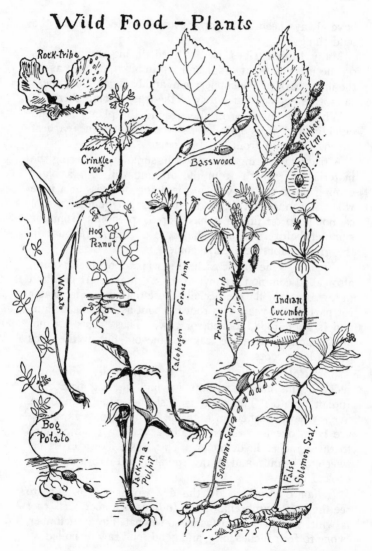

Rock-tribe

Crinkle-root

Basswood

Slippery Elm.

Hog Peanut

Wahato

Calopogon or Grass-Pink

Prairie Turnip

Indian Cucumber

Bog Potato

Jack-in-a-Pulpit

Solomon Seal

False Solomon Seal.

have always been an important article of food among the
wild things.

Many Indian tribes used to feed during famine times
on the inner bark of cedar and white birch, as well as on
the inner bark of the slippery elm and basswood, but these
cannot be got without injury to the tree, so omit them.

When the snow is off the ground the plants respond
quickly, and it is safe to assume that all the earliest
flowers come up from big, fat roots.

A plant can spring up quickly in summer, gathering the
material of growth from the air and soil, but a plant
coming up in the early spring is doing business at a time
when it cannot get support from its surroundings, and
cannot keep on unless it has stored up capital from the
summer before. This is the logic of the storehouse in
the ground for these early comers.

Wapato. One of the earliest is wapato, or duck potato,
also called common Arrowleaf, or Sagittaria. It is found
in low, swampy flats, especially those that are under water
for part of the year. Its root is about as big as a walnut
and is good food, cooked, or raw. These roots are not
at the point where the leaves come out but at the ends
of the long roots.

Bog Potato. On the drier banks, usually where the
sedge begins near a swamp, we find the bog potato, or
Indian potato. The plant is a slender vine with three,
five, or seven leaflets in a group. On its roots in spring
are from one to a dozen potatoes, varying from an inch
to three inches in diameter. They taste like a cross between a peanut and a raw potato, and are very good
cooked or raw.

Indian Cucumber. In the dry woods one is sure to
see the pretty umbrella of the Indian cucumber. Its root
is white and crisp and tastes somewhat like a cucumber,
is one to four inches long, and good food raw or boiled.

Calopogon. This plant looks like a kind of grass with an onion for a root, but it does not taste of onions and is much sought after by wild animals and wild people. It is found in low or marshy pleaces.

Hog Peanuts. In the early spring this plant will be found to have a large nut or fruit, buried under the leaves or quite underground in the dry woods. As summer goes by the plant uses up this capital, but on its roots it grows a lot of little nuts. These are rich food, but very small. The big nut is about an inch long and the little ones on the roots are any size up to that of a pea.

Indian Turnip or Jack-in-the-Pulpit. This is well known to all our children in the East. The root is the most burning, acrid, horrible thing in the woods when raw, but after cooking becomes quite pleasant and is very nutritious

Prairie or Indian Turnip, Bread-root or Pomme-blanche of the Prairie. This is found on all the prairies of the Missouri region. Its root was and is a staple article of food with the Indians. The roots are one to three inches thick and four to twelve inches long.

Solmon's Seal. The two Solomon's Seals (true and false) both produce roots that are long, bumpy store-houses of food.

Crinkle-root. Every school child in the country digs out and eats the pleasant peppery crinkle-root. It abounds in the rich dry woods.

MUSHROOMS, FUNGI OR TOADSTOOLS

We have in America about two thousand different kinds of Mushrooms or Toadstools; they are the same thing. Of these, probably half are wholesome and delicious; but about a dozen of them are deadly poison.

There is no way to tell them, except by knowing each kind and the recorded results of experience with each kind. The story about cooking with silver being a test has no foundation; in fact, the best way for the Wood-craft Boy or Girl is to know definitely a dozen dangerous kinds and a score or more of the wholesome kinds and let the rest alone.

Sporeprint. The first thing in deciding the nature of a toadstool is the sporeprint, made thus: Cut off the stem of the toadstool and lay the gills down on a piece of gray paper under a vessel of any kind. After a couple of hours, lift the cap, and radiating lines of spores will appear on the paper. If it is desired to preserve these, the paper should be first covered with thin mucilage. The *color* of these spores is the first step in identification.

All the deadly toadstools have *white* spores.

No black-spored toadstool is known to be poisonous.

POISONOUS TOADSTOOLS

The only deadly poisonous kinds are the Amanitas. Others may purge and nauseate or cause vomiting, but it is believed that every recorded death from toadstool poisoning was caused by an Amanita, and unfortunately they are not only widespread and abundant, but they are much like the ordinary table mushrooms. They have, however, one or two strong marks: their stalk always grows out of a *"poison cup,"* which shows either as a cup or as a *bulb;* they have *white* or *yellow* gills, a ring around the stalk, and *white spores.*

Deadly Toadstools

All the deadly toadstools known in North America are pictured on the plate, or of the types shown on the plate.

The Deadly Amanita may be brownish, yellowish, or white.

The Yellow Amanita of a delicate lemon color.

The White Amanita of a pure silvery, shiny white.

The Fly Amanita with cap pink, brown, yellow, or red

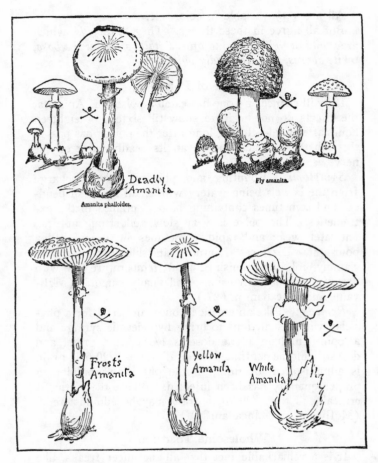

Deadly Amanita

Amanita phalloides.

Fly amanita.

Frost's Amanita

Yellow Amanita

White Amanita

in the centre, shaded into yellow at the edge, and patched with fragments of pure white veil.

The Frosty Amanita with yellow cap, pale cadmium in centre, elsewhere yellowish white, with white patches on warts.

All are very variable in color, etc.

But all agree in these things. They have *gills,* which are *white* or *yellow, a ring on the stalk,* a *cup at the base, white spores,* and are *deadly poison.*

In Case of Poisoning

If by ill chance any one has eaten a poisonous Amanita, the effects do not begin to show till sixteen or eighteen hours afterward—that is, long after the poison has passed through the stomach and began its deadly work on the nerve centres.

Symptoms. Vomiting and purging, "the discharge from the bowels being watery with small flakes suspended, and sometimes containing blood," cramps in the extremeties. The pulse is very slow and strong at first, but later weak and rapid, sometimes sweat and saliva pour out. Dizziness, faintness, and blindness, the skin clammy, cold, and bluish or livid; temperature low with dreadful tetanic convulsions, and finally stupor. (McIlvaine and Macadam p. 627.)

Remedy: "Take an emetic at once, and send for a physician with instructions to bring hypodermic syringe and atropine sulphate. The dose is 1/180 of a grain, and doses should be continued heroically until 1/20 of a grain is administered, or until, in the physician's opinion, a proper quantity has been injected. Where the victim is critically ill the 1/20 of a grain may be administered." (McIlvaine and Macadam XVII.)

Wholesome Toadstools

It is a remarkable fact that all the queer freaks, like clubs and corals, the cranks and tomfools, in droll shapes and satanic colors, the funny poisonous looking Morels, Inkcaps, and Boleti are good wholesome food, but the deadly Amanitas are like ordinary Mushrooms, except that they have grown a little thin, delicate, and anæmic.

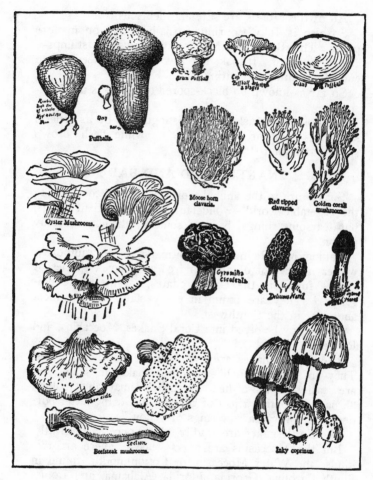

All the Puffballs are good before they begin to puff, that is as long as their flesh is white and firm.

All the *colored* coral toadstools are good, but the *White Clavaria* is said to be rather sickening.

All of the Morels are safe and delicious.

So also is Inky Coprinus, usually found on manure piles. The Beefsteak Mushroom grows on stumps—chiefly chestnut. It looks like raw meat and bleeds when cut. It is quite good eating.

So far as known no black-spored toadstool is unwholesome.

The common Mushroom is distinguished by its general shape, its pink or brown gills, its white flesh, brown spores, and solid stem.

SNAKES GOOD AND BAD

Snakes are to the animal world what toadstools are to the vegetable world—wonderful things, beautiful things, but fearsome things, because some of them are deadly poison.

Taking Mr. Raymond L. Ditmars* as our authority, we learn that out of one hundred and eleven species of snakes found in the United States, seventeen are poisonous. They are found in every state, but are most abundant in the Southwest.

These may be dived into Coral Snakes, Moccasins, and Rattlers.

The Coral Snakes are found in the Southern States. They are very much like harmless snakes in shape, but are easily distinguished by their remarkable colors, "broad alternating rings of red and black, the latter bordered with very narrow rings of yellow."

The Rattlesnakes are readily told at once by the rattle.

But the Moccasins are not so easy. There are two kinds: the Water Moccasin, or Cotton-mouth, found in South Carolina, Georgia, Florida, Alabama, and Louisiana, and the Copperhead, which is the Highland, or

---

*This article is chiefly a condensation of his pamphlet on "Poisonous Snakes of the United States," and is made with his permission and approval.

Types of Poisonous Snakes

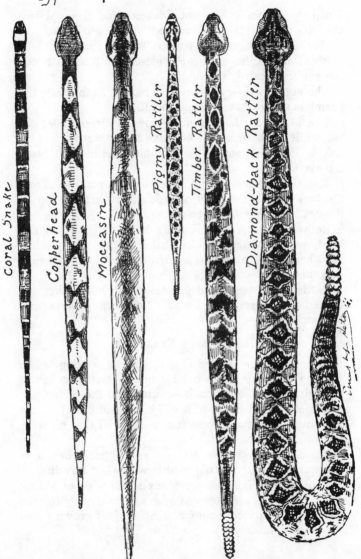

Coral Snake

Copperhead

Moccasin

Pigmy Rattler

Timber Rattler

Diamond-back Rattler

Northern Moccasin or Pilot Snake, found from Massachusetts to Florida and west to Illinois and Texas.

Here are distinguishing marks: The Moccasins, as well as the Rattlers, have on each side of the head, between the eye and nostril, a deep pit.

The pupil of the eye is an upright line, as in a cat; the harmless snakes have a round pupil.

The Moccasins have a single row of plates under the tail, while the harmless snakes have a double row.

The Water Moccasin is dull olive with wide black transverse bands.

The Copperhead is dull hazel brown, marked across the back with dumb-bells of reddish brown; the top of the head more or less coppery.

Both Moccasins and Rattlers have a flat triangular head, which is much wider than the thin neck; while most harmless snakes have a narrow head that shades off into the neck.

Rattlesnakes are found generally distributed over the United States, southern Ontario, southern Alberta, and Saskatchewan.

How Does a Snake Bite

Remember, the tongue is a feeler, not a sting. The stinging" is done by two long hollow teeth, or fangs, through which the poison is squirted into the wound.

The striking distance of a snake is about one-third the creature's length, and the stroke is so swift that no creature can dodge it.

The snake can strike farthest and surest when it is ready coiled, but can strike a little way when traveling.

You cannot disarm a poisonous snake without killing it. If the fangs are removed others come quickly to take their place. In fact, a number of small, half-grown fangs are always waiting ready to be developed.

In Case of Snake Bite

First, keep cool, and remember that the bite of American snakes is seldom fatal if the proper measures are followed.

You must act at once. Try to keep the poison from getting into the system by a tight bandage on the arm or leg (it is sure to be one or the other) just above the wound. Next, get it out of the wound by slashing the wound two or more ways with a sharp knife or razor at least as deep as the puncture. Squeeze it—wash it out with permanganate of potash dissolved in water to the color of wine. Suck it out with the lips (if you have no wounds in the mouth it will do you no harm there). Work, massage, suck, and wash to get all the poison out. After thorough treatment to remove the venom the ligature may be removed.

"Pack small bits of gauze into the wounds to keep them open and draining, then dress over them with gauge saturated with any good antiseptic solution. Keep the dressing saturated and the wounds open for at least a week, no matter how favorable may be the symptoms."

Some people consider whiskey or brandy a cure for snake bite. There is plenty of evidence that many have been killed by such remedies, and little that they have ever saved any one, except perhaps when the victim was losing courage or becoming sleepy.

In any case, send as fast as you can for a doctor. He should come equipped with hypodermic syringe, tubes of anti-venomous serum and strychnine tablets.

Harmless Snakes

Far the greatest number of our snakes are harmless, beautiful, and beneficient. They are friendly to the farmer, because, although some destroy a few birds, chickens, ducklings, and game, the largest part of their food is mice and insects. The Blacksnake, the Milk Snake, and one or two others, will bite in self-defence, but they have no poison fangs, and the bite is much like the prick of a bramble.

THE STARS AS THE CAMPER SEES THEM

(See Plate of Stars and Principal Constellations)

So far as there is a central point in our heavens, that point is the Pole-star, Polaris. Around this star all the stars in the sky seem to turn once in twenty-four hours.

It is easily discovered by the help of the Big Dipper, *a part of the* Great Bear, known to every country boy and girl in the northern half of the world. This is, perhaps, the most important star group in our sky, because of its size, peculiar form, the fact that it never sets in our latitude, and that of its stars, two, sometimes called the Pointers always point out the Pole Star. It is called the Dipper because it is shaped like a dipper with a long, bent handle.

Why *(the whole group)* is called the Great Bear is not so easy to explain. The classical legend has it that the nymph, Calisto, having violated her vow, was changed by Diana into a bear, which, after death, was immortalized in the sky by Zeus. Another suggestion is that the earliest astronomers, the Chaldeans, called these stars "the shining ones," and their word happened to be very like the Greek *arktos* (a bear) Another explanation is that vessels in olden days were named for animals, etc. They bore at the prow the carved effigy of the namesake, and if the Great Bear, for example, made several very happy voyages by setting out when a certain constellation was in the ascendant, that constellation might become known as the Great Bear's constellation. Certainly, there is nothing in its shape to justify the name. Very few of the constellations indeed are like the thing they are called after. Their names were usually given for some

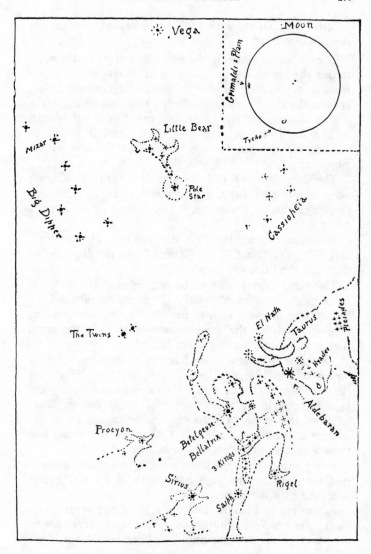

fanciful association with the namesake, rather than for resemblance to it.

The Pole-star is really the most important of the stars in our sky; it marks the north at all times; all the other stars seem to swing around it once in twenty-four hours. It is in the end of the Little Bear's tail; this constellation is sometimes called the Little Dipper. But the Pole-star, or Polaris, is not a very bright one, and it would be hard to identify but for the help of the Pointers of the Big Dipper.

The outside stars (Alpha and Beta) of the Dipper point nearly to Polaris, at a distance equal to five times the space that separates these two stars of the Dipper's outer side.

Indian names for the Pole-star are the "Home Star," and "The Star That Never Moves," and the Big Dipper they call the "Broken Back."

The great Bear is also to be remembered as the hour-hand of the woodman's clock. It goes once around the North Star in about twenty-four hours, the same way as the sun, and for the same reason—that it is the earth that is going and leaving them behind.

The time in going around is not exactly twenty-four hours, so that the position of the Pointers varies with the seasons, but, as a rule, this for woodcraft purposes is near enough. The bowl of the Dipper swings four-fifths of the width of its own opening in one hour. If it went a quarter of the circle, that would mean you had slept a quarter of a day, or six hours.

Every fifteen days the stars seem to be an hour earlier; in three months they gain one-fourth of the circle, and in a year gain the whole circle.

According to Flammarion, there are about seven thousand stars visible to the naked eye, and of these twenty are stars of the first magnitude. Fourteen of them are visible in the latitude of New York, the others (those starred) belong to the South Polar region of the sky. The following table of the brightest stars is taken from the Revised Harvard Photometry of 1908, the best authority on the subject.

THE FIRST TWENTY STARS IN ORDER OF BRIGHTNESS

1. Sirius, the Dog Star.
2. *Canopus, of the Ship.
3. *Alpha, of the Centaur.
4. Vega, of the Lyre.
5. Capella, of the Charioteer.
6. Arcturus, of the Herdsman.
7. Rigel, of Orion.
8. Procyon, the Little Dog-star.
9. *Achernar, of Eridanus.
10. *Beta, of the Centaur.
11. Altair, of the Eagle.
12. Betelgeuze, of Orion's right shoulder.
13. *Alpha, of the Southern Cross.
14. Aldebaran, of the Bull's right eye.
15. Pollux, of the Twins.
16. Spica, of the Virgin.
17. Antares, of the Scorpion.
18. Fomalhaut, of the Southern Fish.
19. Deneb, of the Swan.
20. Regulus, of the Lion.

OTHER CONSTELLATIONS

Orion (O-ri-on), with its striking array of brilliant stars, Betelgeuze, Rigel, the Three Kings, etc., is generally admitted to be the first constellation in the heavens.

Orion was the hunter giant who went to Heaven when he died, and now marches around the great dome, but is seen only in the winter, because, during the summer, he passes over during daytime. Thus he is still the hunter's constellation. The three stars of his belt are called the "Three Kings."

Sirius, the Great Dog-star, is in the head of Orion's Hound, the constellation *Canis Major,* and following farther back is the Little Dog-star, Procyon, the chief star of the constellation *Canis Minor.*

In old charts of the stars, Orion is shown with his hounds, hunting the bull, Taurus. This constellation is recognizable by this diagram; the red star, Aldebaran, being the angry right eye of the Bull. His face is covered with a cluster of little stars called the *Hyades,* and on his shoulder are the seven stars, called *Pleiades.*

PLEIADES

Pleiades (Ply-a-des) can be seen in winter as a cluster of small stars between Aldebaran and Algol, or, a line drawn from the back bottom, through the front rim of the Big Dipper, about two Dipper lengths, touches this little group. They are not far from Aldebaran, being in the right shoulder of the Bull. They may be considered the seven arrow wounds made by Orion.

Serviss tells up that the *Pleiades* have a supposed connection with the Great Pyramid, because "about 2170 B. C., when the beginning of spring coincided with the culmination of the Pleiades at midnight, that wonderful group of stars was visible just at midnight, through the mysterious southward-pointing passage of the Pyramid.

Cassiopeia

On the opposite side of the Polar-star from the Big Dipper and nearly as far from it, is a W of five bright stars. This is called the *Cassiopeia's Chair.* It is easily found and visible the year round on clear nights.

Thus we have described ten constellations from which

the Woodcrafter may select the number needed to qualify, namely, the Little Bear, or Little Dipper, the Big Dipper or Big Bear, Cassiopeia's Chair, the Bull, Orion's Hound, Orion's Little Dog, the Pleiades and the Hyades; the Lyre (later).

The Moon

The moon is one-fourth the diamenter of the earth, about one-fiftieth of the bulk, and is about a quarter of a million miles away. Its course, while very irregular, is nearly the same as the apparent course of the sun. It is a cold solid body, without any known atmosphere, and shines by reflected sunlight.

The moon goes around the earth in twenty-seven and a quarter days. It loses about fifty-one minutes in twenty-four hours; therefore it rises that much later each successive night on the average, but there are wide deviations from this average, as, for example, the time of the Harvest and Hunter's moons in the fall, when the full moon rises at nearly the same time for several nights in succession.

According to most authorities, the moon is a piece of the earth that broke away some time ago; and it has followed its mother around ever since.

The Stars as Tests of Eyesight

In the sky are several tests of eyesight which have been there for some time and are likely to be. The first is the old test of Mizar and Alcor. Mizar, the Horse, is the star at the bend of the handle of the Dipper. Just above it is a very small star that astronomers call Alcor, or the rider.

The Indians call these two the "Old Squaw and the Papoose on Her Back." In the old world, from very ancient times, these have been used as tests of eyesight. To be able to see Alcor with the naked eye means that one had excellent eyesight. So also on the plains, the old folks would ask the children at night, "Can you see the papoose on the old Squaw's back?" And when the youngster saw it, and proved that he did by a right description, they rejoiced that he had the eyesight which is the first requisite of a good hunter.

One of the oldest of all eye tests is the Pleiades. Poor eyes see a mere haze, fairly good see five, good see six, excellent see seven. The rarest eyesight, under the best conditions, see up to ten; and, according to Flammarion, the record with unaided eyes is thirteen.

Vega of the Lyre

If one draw a line from through the back wall of the Dipper, that is, from the back bottom star, through the one next the handle, and continue it upward for twice the total length of the Dipper, it will reach Vega, the brightest star in the northern part of the sky, and believed to have been at one time the Pole-star—and likely to be again. Vega, with the two stars near it, form a small triangle. The one on the side next the North Star is called Epsillon. If you have remarkably good eyes, you will see that it is a double star.

The Nebula in Orion's Sword

Just about the middle of Orion's Sword is a fuzzy light spot. This might do for blood, only it is the wrong color. It is the nebula of Orion. If you can see it with the naked eye, you are to be congratulated.

On the Moon

When the moon is full, there is a large, dark, oval spot on it to the left, as you face it, and close to the east rim, almost halfway up; this is the Plain of Grimaldi; it is about twice the size of the whole State of New Jersey; but it is proof of a pair of excellent eyes if you can see it at all.

SIGNS AND BLAZES

Signs in Stones

| This is the Trail | Turn to the Right | Turn to the Left | Important Warning |

Signs in Twigs

| This is the Trail | Turn to the Right | Turn to the Left | Important Warning |

Signs in Grass

| This is the Trail | Turn to the Right | Turn to the Left | Important Warning |

Signs in Blazes

| This is the Trail | Turn to the Right | Turn to the Left | Important Warning |

Code for Smoke Signals

| Camp is Here | I am lost. Help! | Good News | All come to Council |

Some Special Blazes used by Hunters & Surveyors

| A Trap to Right | A Trap to Left | Camp is to Right | Camp is to Left | Special | Adirondack Special | Surveyors Line Here |

Blazes

First among the trail signs that are used by Wood-crafters, Indians, and white hunters, and most likely to be of use to the traveler, are axe blazes on tree trunks. Among these some may vary greatly with locality, but there is one that I have found everywhere in use with scarcely any variation. That is the simple white spot meaning, *"Here is the trail."*

The Indian in making it may nick off an infinitestimal speck of bark with his knife, the trapper with his hatchet may make it as big as a dollar, or the settler with his heavy axe may slab off half the tree-side; but the sign is the same in principle and in meaning, on trunk, log, or branch from Atlantic to Pacific and from Hudson Strait to Rio Grande. "This is your trail," it clearly says in the universal language of the woods.

There are two ways of employing it: one when it appears on back and front of the trunk, so that the trail can be run both ways; the other when it appears on but one side of each tree, making a *blind trail,* which can be run one way only, the blind trail is often used by trappers and prospectors, who do not wish any one to follow their back track.

But there are treeless regions where the trail must be marked; regions of sage brush and sand, regions of rock, stretches of stone, and level wastes of grass or sedge. Here other methods must be employed.

A well-known Indian device, in the brush, is to break a twig and leave it hanging. (*Second line.*)

Among stones and rocks the recognized sign is one stone set on top of another (*top line*) and in places where there is nothing but grass the custom is to twist a tussock into a knot (*third line*).

These signs also are used in the whole country from Maine to California.

In running a trail one naturally looks straight ahead for the next sign; if the trail turned abruptly without notice one might easily be set wrong, but custom has provided against this. The tree blaze for turn "to the right" is shown in No. 2, fourth row; "to the left" in No. 3. The greater length of the turning blaze seems to be due to a desire for emphasis as the same mark set square on, is understood to mean "Look out, there is something of special importance here." Combined with a long side chip means "very important; here turn aside." This is often used to mean "camp is close by," and a third sign that is variously combined always with the general meaning of "warning" or "something of great importance" is a threefold blaze. (No. 4 on fourth line.) The combination (No. 1 on bottom row) would read "Look out now for something of great importance to the right." This blaze I have often seen used by trappers to mark the whereabouts of their trap or cache.

Surveyors often use a similar mark—that is, there simple spots and a stripe to mean, "There is a stake close at hand," while a similar blaze on another tree nearby means that the stake is on a line between.

Stone Signs

These signs done into stone-talk would be as in the top line of the cut.

These are much used in the Rockies where the trail goes over stony places or along stretches of slide-rock.

Grass and Twig Signs

In grass or sedge the top of the tuft is made to show the direction to be followed; if it is a point of great importance three tufts are tied, their tops straight if the trail goes straight on; otherwise the tops are turned in the direction toward which the course turns.

The Ojibways and other woodland tribes use twigs for

a great many of these signs. (See second row.) The hanging broken twig like the simple blaze means "This is the trail." The twig clean broken off and laid on the ground across the line of march means, "Here break from your straight course and go in the line of the butt end," and when an especial *warning* is meant, the butt is pointed toward the one following the trail and raised somewhat, in a forked twig. If the butt of the twig were raised and pointing to the left, it would mean "Look out, camp, or ourselves, or the enemy, or the game we have killed is out that way." With some, the elevation of the butt is made to show the distance of the object; if low the object is near, if raised very high the object is a long way off.

These are the principal signs of the trail used by Woodcrafters, Indians, and hunters in most parts of America. These are the standards—the ones sure to be seen by those who camp in the wilderness.

Smoke Signals

There is in addition a useful kind of sign that has been mentioned already in these papers—that is, the Smoke Signal. These were used chiefly by the Plains' Indians, but the Ojibways seem to have employed them at times.

A clear hot fire was made, then covered with green stuff or rotten wood so that it sent up a solid column of black smoke. By spreading and lifting a blanket over this smudge the column could be cut up into pieces long or short, and by a preconcerted code these could be made to convey tidings.

But the simplest of all smoke codes and the one of chief use to the Western traveler is this:

One steady smoke—"Here is camp."

Two steady smokes—"I am lost, come and help me."

I find two other smoke signals, namely:

Three smokes in a row—"Good news."

Four smokes in a row—"All are summoned to council."
These latter I find not of general use, nor are they so
likely to be of service as the first two given.

Signal by Shots

The old buffalo hunters had an established signal that
is yet used by the mountain guides. It is as follows:

Two shots in rapid succession, an interval of five seconds by the watch, then one shot; this means, "where
are you?" The answer given at once and exactly the
same means "Here I am; what do you want?" The reply to this may be one shot, which means, "All right; I
only wanted to know where you were." But if the reply
repeats the first it means, "I am in serious trouble; come
as fast as you can."

Totems in Town

A totem is an emblem of a man, a group of men, or
an idea. It has no reference to words or letters.

Before men knew how to write they needed marks to
indicate ownership. This mark must be simple and legible and was chosen because of something connected with
the owner or his family. Later some of the trades adopted a symbol; for instance the barbers in the early days
were "blood letters" and were closely associated with the
medical profession. Their totem indicated their business
and we have the red and white barber pole of today. It
was among the Indians along the West coast of America
that the science and art of totems reached its highest
development, though they have a world-wide usage and
go back in history to the earliest times.

Out of this use of totems as owner marks and signs
grew the whole science of heraldry and national flags.

Thanks to the fusion of many small armies into one
or two big armies, that is, of many tribes into a nation,
and also to modern weapons which made it possible to
kill a man farther off than you could see the totem on

Northern Pacific R. R.   Salt Lake R. R.   Santa Fé R. R.   Traffic Squad   Bell Telephone

Pawnshop   Liberty   Army   Druggist   Ireland

Woodcraft   Navy   Sea Power   Optician

Union Pacific R. R.   Islamism   Skating   Star Union Lines   New York City

Penna. R. R.   The Power of the People   Canadian Pacific R. R.   Barber   Scotland

Totems Often Seen

his shield, national flags have replaced the armorial devices, and are the principal totems used today.

But a new possibility has been discovered in modern times. Totems will serve the ends of commerce, and a great revival of their use is now seen.

The totem is visible such a long way off and is understood by all, whether or not they can read or know our language, is copyrightable and advertisable, so that most of the great railway companies, etc., now have totems.

There are not less than one hundred common totems used in our streets today. Among the familiar ones seen are the American eagle, with white head and tail, the Austrian eagle with two heads, the British lion, the Irish harp, the French fleur de lis, etc. Among trades the three balls of the pawnbroker, the golden fleece of the drygoods man, the mortar and pestle of the druggist, and others are well known. Examples of these and others are given in the illustration but any wideawake Woodcraft Girl will be able to find many others by careful observation.

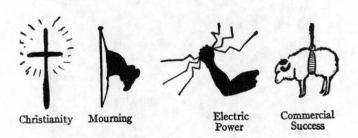

Christianity   Mourning   Electric   Commercial
                                 Power   Success

"AFOOT AND LIGHT-HEARTED"

SECTION XIV

CAMPING FOR GIRL SCOUTS
SONG OF THE OPEN ROAD

Afoot and light-hearted I take to the open road,
Healthy, free, the world before me,
The long brown path before me leading wherever I
*   choose.*

Henceforth I ask not good-fortune—I myself am good-
*   fortune;*
Henceforth I whimper no more, postpone no more,
*   need nothing,*
Strong and content, I travel the open road. . . . .

. . . . .

Now I see the secret of the making of the best persons,
It is to grow in the open air, and to eat and sleep with
*   the earth.   —Walt Whitman.*

A Girl Scout likes to hike and camp. She learns
to know the stars, and becomes acquainted with the
plants and animals about her. She gains independence from her ability to help herself, and health and
strength from exercise in the sunshine and fresh air.

These are the good things of camping. The bad
things are catching cold from damp ground, or insuffi-
cient bedding, uncomfortable nights, and weary feet.
But a wise Scout does not rough it. She knows how
to make herself comfortable by a hundred little dodges.
The aim of camping is to make things simpler for the
camper. She must make up her mind whether she is

---

[1] The passages in this section, from "Camping and Woodcraft," by Horace Kephart, are used by permission of the author and the publisher, the Macmillan Company, and are copy-
righted, 1916, by the Macmillan Company.

ready for an overnight hike, a week-end trip or a good vacation in the open air, and plan accordingly.

For a walking trip a Girl Scout must travel light and learn to do with a minimum amount of clothing, utensils and food. On the other hand, if she is going to spend the week out, why not be as comfortable as possible? This requires more of an outfit, but it is worth it. To know how to do this one must, of course, have first learned the simple rules of camping in Girl Scout training.

Hiking

Hikes are a good way to get this training. Extreme heat, or a downpour of rain is the only kind of weather which should interfere with a hike. Soft rains or snowstorms are very pleasant to hike in.

Skirts are dangerous for cross-country travel on account of brambles, rock work and climbing over brooks. Knickerbockers or bloomers should be worn.

In the city when starting off for a hike use squad or double file formation through the streets, railroad stations, ferries, etc. Silence is maintained in this formation.

Hiking Order—In the country, even along unused roads, hike in single file on the left side of the road. The advantage of this formation is that all danger from passing traffic in any direction is averted. It is *not* necessary to keep step, and talking, laughing, singing, etc., may be indulged in. Permission to break this order is only given when in woods, or fields, where there is no danger.

When returning home use Scout's Pace if weary. This helps to make the distance seem shorter.

Scout's pace is a walking and running device which serves to increase endurance when covering a long distance. It consist in taking a certain number of walking steps followed immediately by the same number of running steps, returning to the walking steps, and so forth. The number of steps may vary, according to the place, nature of the road and object of the walk Fifty steps walking, fifty steps running and alternating steadily for twelve minutes will take one a mile, and this is one of the measures of distance that is useful to know. For ordinary use on hikes the use of twenty steps running and walking is preferable.

Feet

With a little knowledge as to the care of her feet the city girl can make a good showing at her first camp. Prepare feet by brushing vigorously with a dry flesh brush. Strengthen muscles by standing on toes in bare feet, raising body gradually fifty or seventy-five times. Frequent changes of stockings, bathing of tired feet in hot water at night and cold water in the morning, will overcome most of the hiker's troubles. The cold water hardens the skin. Boric acid powder is good for naturally damp feet. Blisters should be cleansed with iodine, then carefully pricked with a sterile needle to let out the water (hold the needle in the flame of a match), then washed with iodine and covered with a few layers of sterile gauze and fastened with adhesive plaster.

It is desirable to change the stockings every day. Wash them at night and hang them out to dry and keep them well darned. Two pairs at least are necessary. Never risk your health by putting on stockings even slightly damp with dew. A hole will cause a blister. Woolen stockings are preferable. For very long hikes it helps to wear two or three pairs, and to lather the outside of the stocking with a cake of soap slightly moistened.

Shoes

Shoes should be the shape of the feet and have low, wide heels. It rests the feet to take the shoes off once or twice during a long tramp. Grease the shoes every few days with mutton fat or other grease. There is no such thing as waterproof leather, but it can be made so by being greased. After being wet, shoes should be well dried and greased, but should not be dried in a hot place, for this would ruin the leather. These may seem trifling details, but remember, "no army is stronger than its feet."

Things to Remember

Keep the feet straight when walking. If a Girl Scout notices the tracks of an Indian, the first hikers in this country, she will find them invariably straight forward. Scientists have agreed that the dancing school habit of turning out toes is one of the causes of flat feet, which disqualified so many men for army service.

Start the walk slowly. Keep the pace of the slowest of the party. "Slow and easy goes far in a day." Practice deep breathing. Inhale for five steps, hold your breath for five counts, and let it out, again counting five.

Take short steps when climbing. Do not run down hill. It causes stiffness, for which a hot bath and another walk the next day are the best cure.

When lunch is carried it should be divided among the troop. Each Scout should carry her knapsack on her back, to leave the hands free. It is a great mistake to start on a hike with one's arms laden.

Do not plan to go too great a distance in the time at your disposal. Remember that aside from the time you need for going and coming you expect to enjoy yourselves cooking and eating, and you need time for both. For an over-night hike, when you carry your equipment select a spot not more than two miles distant.

Good things to carry in one's pocket are a drinking cup, a geological survey map (ten cents), a small pocket compass, a camper's knife, a small soap stone to sharpen it, a match box, and a note book and pencil.

Plan a definite object for the hike. Note how many kinds of trees, wild flowers or birds one can find.

Practice building fires for cooking, or getting material for a bed such as balsam, etc. Inquire for points of historical interest and make them the goal of the hike. There is hardly a town that has not some place connected with the early history of the nation.

Personal Equipment

Spending the nights under the stars is one of the great fascinations of camping. Each person requires two waterproof ground cloths or ponchos, two pairs of light wool blankets, safety pins, heavy cord, sleeping garments, rain coat, and toilet articles, including such things as soap, toilet paper, sewing kit, electric flashlight, mirror, first aid kit, provision for mosquitoes or flies, five yards of bar netting, and oil of citronella.

In order to ensure protection from the rain spread one waterproof covering or poncho on the ground using half underneath so that the upper half may be folded over the head in case of rain. Put blankets *under* as well as *over* you, and a second waterproof covering over the blankets.

Clothing

When living out of doors, one may make shift for shelter, or even go hungry for a space, but there is no substitute for comfortable clothing that is safe to use if one would keep well. Horace Kephart, the master camper, devotes much space to this subject, and we can do no better than to follow his advice from Camping and Woodcraft.

"* * * One soon learns that the difference between comfort and misery, if not health and illness, may depend on whether he is properly clad. Proper, in this case does not mean modish, but suitable, serviceable, proven by the touchstone of experience to be best for the work or play that is in hand. When you seek a guide in the mountains, he looks first in your eyes and then at your shoes. If both are right, you are right.

"The chief uses of clothing are to help the body maintain its normal temperature and to protect it from sun, frost, wind, rain and injuries. *To help*, mind you—the body must be allowed to do its share.

"Perspiration is the heat-regulating mechanism of the body. Clothing should hinder its passage from the skin as little as possible. For this reason one's garments should be *permeable* to air. The body is cooled by rapid evaporation, on the familiar principle of a tropical water bag that is porous enough to let some of the water exude. So the best summer clothing is that which permits free evaporation—and this means all over, from head to heel. In winter it is just the same, there should be free passage for bodily moisture through the underclothes, but extra layers or thickness of outer clothing are needed to hold in the bodily heat and to protect one against wind; even so all the garments should be permeable to air. * * *"

"Underclothing, for any season, should be loosely woven, so as to hold air and take up moisture from the body. The air confined in the interspaces is a non-conductor, and so helps to prevent sudden chilling on the one hand, and over-heating on the other. A loose texture absorbs perspiration, but does not hold it—the moisture is free to pass on to and through the outer garments. In town we may endure close woven underwear in summer, if thin enough, because we exercise little and can bathe and change frequently. In the woods we would have to change four times a day to keep * * * as dry.

"*Wool versus Cotton*—Permeability also depends upon material. Ordinary cotton and linen goods do not permit rapid evaporation. They absorb moisture from the skin, but hold it up to the limit of saturation. Then, when they can hold no more, they are clammy, and the sweat can only escape by running down one's skin.

"After hard exertion in such garments, if you sit down to rest, or meet a sudden keen wind, as in topping a ridge, you are likely to get a chill—and the next thing is a 'bad cold' or lumbago, rheumatism, or something worse.

"Wool, on the contrary is permeable. That is why (if of suitable weight and loose weave) it is both cooler in summer and warmer in winter than cloth made of vegetable fibre. 'One wraps himself in a woolen blanket to keep warm—to keep the heat *in*. He wraps ice in a blanket to keep it from melting—to keep the heat *out*.' In other words, wool is the best material to maintain an equable normal temperature."

Camp Site

"The essentials of a good camp site are these:

1. Pure water.
2. Wood that burns well. In cold weather there should be either an abundance of sound down wood, or some standing hard wood trees that are not too big for easy felling.
3. An open spot level enough for the tent and camp fire, but elevated above its surroundings so as to have good natural drainage. It must be well above any chance overflow from the sudden rise of a neighboring stream. Observe the previous flood marks. . . . .
7. Exposure to direct sunlight during a part of the day, especially during the early morning hours.
8. In summer, exposure to whatever breezes may

blow; in cold weather, protection against the prevailing wind.

9. Privacy.

"Water, wood, and good drainage may be all you need for a "one-night stand," but the other points, too, should be considered when selecting a site for a fixed camp.

Water—Be particularly careful about the purity of your water supply. You come, let us say, to a mountain brook, that issues from thick forest. It ripples over clean rocks, it bubbles with air, it is clear as crystal, and cool to your thirsty throat. 'Surely that is good water.' But do you know where it comes from? Every mountain cabin is built close to a spring-branch. Somewhere up that branch there may be a clearing; in that clearing, a house; in that house, a case of dysentery or typhoid fever. I have known several cases of infection from just such a source. It is not true that running water purifies itself.

"When one must use well-water let him note the surrounding drainage. If the well is near a stable or out house, or if dish water is thrown near it, let it alone. A well in sandy soil is more or less filtered by nature, but rocky or clayey earth may conduct disease germs a considerable distance under ground. Never drink from the well of an abandoned farm: there is no telling what may have fallen into it.

"A spring issuing from the living rock is worthy of confidence. Even if it be but a trickle you can scoop out a basin to receive it that soon will clear itself.

"Sometimes a subaqueous spring may be found near the margin of a lake or river by paddling close in shore and trailing your hand in the water. When a cold spot is noted, go ashore and dig a few feet back from the water's edge. I have found such spring exit in the Mississippi some distance from the bank, and by weighting a canteen, tying a string to it and another to the stopper, have brought up cool water from the river bed.

"Disease germs are of animal, not vegetable origin. Still waters are not necessarily unwholesome, even though there is rotten vegetation in them. The water of cedar and cypress swamps is good to drink wherever there is a deep pool of it, unless polluted from some outside source. Lake water is safe if no settlements are on its border; but even so large a body as Lake Champlain has been condemned by state boards of health because of the sewage that runs into it.

"When a stream is in flood it is likely to be contaminated by decayed animal matter.

"*Alkaline Water*—When traveling in an alkali country carry some vinegar or limes or lemons, or (better) a glass stoppered bottle of hydrochloric acid. One teaspoonful of hydrochloric (muriatic) neutralizes about a gallon of water, and if there should be a little excess it will do no harm but rather assist digestion. In default of acid you may add a little Jamaica ginger and sugar to the water, making a weak ginger tea.

"*Muddy Water*—I used to clarify Mississippi water by stirring corn meal in it and letting it settle, or by stirring a lump of alum in it until the mud began to precipitate, and then decanting the clear water. Lacking these, one can take a good handful of grass, tie it roughly in the form of a cone six or eight inches high, invert it, pour water slowly into the grass and a runnel of comparatively clear water will trickle down through the small end.

"*Stagnant Water*—A traveler may be reduced to the extremity of using stagnant or even putrid water; but this should never be done without first boiling it. Some charred wood from the camp fire should be boiled with the water; then skim off the skum, strain, and set the

COOKING THE FIRST MEAL

water aside to cool. Boiling sterilizes, and charcoal deodorizes. * * *"

Arriving at Camp

As soon as the camp site is decided upon locate the tent. (This should be done in advance when the party is of any size). Each tent should be about twenty-five feet from the next, on a dry place and easy to drain in case of rain, and so placed as to have the sun in the morning and the shade in the afternoon. Each tent should be trenched and placed at some distance from the water supply and from the latrine.

Tents

"For fixed camps, situated where there are wagon roads or other adequate ways of transportation, the best cloth shelter is a wall tent, rectangular or square, of strong and rather heavy material. * * * The best all-round size of wall tent for two people, if weight and bulk and cost are of any consequence, is the so-called 9 x 9 or a 9 x 12, built with 3½-foot walls, instead of 3-foot, and 8-foot center, instead of 7½-foot. For four

persons a 12 x 14 is commonly used; but a 14 x 14 with
4-foot walls and 9-foot center has double the head-room
of the standard 12 x 14, and 2½ feet more space between
cots, if these are set lengthwise of the tent, two on a side.

"Before selecting a tent, consider the number of people
to occupy it, and their dunnage, and the furniture. Then
draw diagrams of floor and elevation of various sizes,
putting in the cots, etc., according to scale; so you can
get just what you want, no more, no less.

Camp Sanitation

"Nothing is cleaner, sweeter, wholesomer, than a wild-
wood unspoiled by man, and few spots are more disgust-
ing than a "piggy" camp, with slops thrown everywhere,
empty cans and broken bottles littering the ground, and
organic refuse left festering in the sun, breeding disease
germs, to be spread abroad by the swarms of flies. I
have seen one of nature's gardens, an ideal health resort,
changed in a few months by a logging crew into an
abomination and a pest hole where typhoid and dysentery
wrought deadly vengeance.

"*Destroy at once all refuse that would attract flies.*
Or bury it where they cannot get at it.

"Fire is the absolute disinfectant. Burn all solid
kitchen refuse as fast as it accumulates. When a can
of food is emptied toss it on the fire and burn it out, then
drop it in a sink hole that you have dug for slops and un-
burnable trash, and cover it with earth or ashes so no
mosquitoes can breed in it after a rainfall.

"The sink should be on the down hill side of camp,
and where it cannot pollute the water supply. Sprinkle
kerosene on it or burn it out frequently with a brush
fire. * * *"

The Latrine

One of the first tasks of the camper is to dig a trench
for a latrine and build a screen around it. The latrine

should be on a lower level than the camp, away from the water supply and in the opposite direction from which the prevailing winds come toward the camp, two hundred feet from sleeping and mess tents. Bushes or a tent fly may be used as a screen and shelter. A small lean-to serves admirably. Dig trenches four feet long, one foot wide and two feet deep. Allow six inches (length) per day for a Scout. Cover after using with fresh dirt. It is imperative to fill and re-sod all trenches dug. Whether you camp only for lunch or for the summer leave no trace that you have been there. Remember the animals, how they scratch the soil and cover up any waste that they leave, and be at least as clean as they.

Lime does not keep the flies away. Plenty of fresh dirt is better.

Team Work

Only as each and every member does her part will the camp be a complete success. The daily tasks should be assigned to individuals or groups, as in:

The Pine Tree Patrol System

The chief advantage of this system is that wherever the need for work of any description arises, there is always someone whose duty it is to perform that particular task, thus avoiding the inevitable question of "Who will do it?" The Pine Tree Patrol system does not in the least interfere with regular schedule of Scout activities; on the contrary, it saves time since more than one hand on each spoke of the wheel keeps it in continual motion. When the system seems too complicated for a small camp, the captain can simplify it to suit the circumstances.

Each girl in the Patrol is assigned a number which requires of her:

1. Certain well defined duties to perform for her Patrol.

2. Certain specific knowledge expected of her in the exercise of her "specialty."

3. Proper care of her special "station gear."

4. Willingness to teach her understudy all she knows

5. Willingness to learn the duties of the next higher numbers.

The front rank (Reds) is in touch with and under the Senior (Patrol Leader); the rear rank (Blues) is in touch with and under the Junior. The Senior receives her orders from the Captain and transmits them not only to 3, 5 and 7, but to Junior as well. The Senior and ranking Patrol officer keeps an eye on the Junior and her rear rank. The Captain, of course, is the general overseer, but the Senior has charge of all routine troop duties, superintends camp details and is virtually a first Lieutenant to the Captain. The Junior is a second Lieutenant and assists the Senior in the supervision of the camp.

The Senior (No. 1) looks after the flags, tentage, blankets, equipment and personal baggage, while the Junior (No. 2) has charge of food, fires, water, cooking, and kitchen work. They appease the demands of the outer and inner man.

The Scribe (No. 3)—She is secretary, bookkeeper, log writer, recorder, correspondent, tent pitcher and First-Aid Scout.

The Baker (No. 4) is the Junior's first aid. She is charged with the care and use of cereal foodstuffs all the way from corn on the cob to flap-jacks and "sinkers," and the cooking outfit and kitchen fire.

The Lighter (No. 5) has care of the lamps, lanterns, candles, matches, oils and all "leaky" stuff. She understands telegraphy and electricity and is chief signal Scout and assistant tent pitcher. She must keep the camp well illuminated.

The Water Scout (No. 6) locates water for all purposes and carries it to camp. She acts as Fire Chief and Fire Watchman. She provides and cooks meat, vegetables and "greens."

The Handy Scout (No. 7) is field engineer, carpenter, bridge builder, the general maker, mender, patcher, splicer and tinker; cares for tools and trek-cart, mends the tents and clothing, and makes the furniture.

The Wood Scout (Patrol Mascot) (No. 8) is usually the youngest girl. She keeps fires well fed, the rations dry and the garbage burned. She carries a spade, pick axe and cutting axe.

This system may be used in either a small or large camp; if the latter, corresponding numbers of each Patrol work together.

TEAM WORK AND DAILY ROUTINE

6:30 A. M. Junior Baker, Water Scout and Wood Scout report half an hour before Mess.

8:00 A. M. Tent inspection.

8:30 A. M. Senior, Scribe, Lighter and Handy Scout report.

8:30-9:30 A. M. Main work for day accomplished by both Senior and Junior groups.

Caution in Use of Knife and Axe

The Knife

1. Always whittle away from you.

2. Keep your fingers behind the blade.

3. Keep saying to yourself: "If this knife slips, can it cut my fingers?

4. Learn how to sharpen your knife and keep it sharp.

The Chopping Block

"A chopping block is the first thing needed about a camp. The axe, when not in use, should always be stuck in that particular block, where one can find it when wanted, and where it will not injure men or dogs."

The Axe

"Do not let the axe lie outdoors on a very cold night; the frost would make it brittle, so that the steel might shiver on the first knot you struck the next morning. . . ."

The axe is a most dangerous tool, and a glancing blow may cripple one for life.

1. Do not put your foot on a stick you are chopping.

2. Always have in mind where a glancing blow may throw the axe, and keep your foot away from that danger.

3. In splitting short sticks for kindling hold them by one end flat on the chopping block and strike the blade into the other end.

4. Do not hold the stick on end in one hand while splitting it.

5. Cut or split small wood on a chopping block or log. Never let the axe strike into the ground, as a hidden stone may ruin the edge.

The Camp Fire

"The forest floor is always littered with old leaves, dead sticks and fallen trees. During a drought this rubbish is so tinder-dry that a spark falling in it may start a conflagration; but through a great part of the year the leaves and sticks that lie flat on the ground are too moist, at least on their under side, to ignite readily. If we rake together a pile of leaves, cover it higgledy-piggledy with dead twigs and branches picked up at random, and set a match to it, the odds are that it will result in nothing but a quick blaze that soon dies down to a smudge. Yet that is the way most of us tried to make our first outdoor fires.

"One glance at a camper's fire tells what kind of a woodsman he is. It is quite impossible to prepare a good meal over a heap of smoking chunks, a fierce blaze,

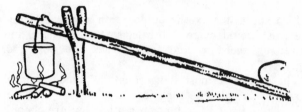

LUNCHEON FIRE

or a great bed of coals that will warp iron and melt everything else.

"If one would have good meals cooked out of doors, and would save much time and vexation; in other words, if he wants to be comfortable in the woods, he must learn how to produce at will either (1) a quick, hot little fire that will boil water in a jiffy, and will soon burn down to embers that are not too ardent for frying; or (2) a solid bed of long-lived coals that will keep up a steady, glowing, smokeless heat for baking, roasting, or slow boiling; or (3) a big log fire that will throw its heat forward on the ground, and into a tent or lean-to, and will last several hours without replenishing.

"*Luncheon Fire*—For a noonday lunch, or any other quick meal, when you have only to boil coffee and fry something, a large fire is not wanted. Drive a forked stake into the ground, lay a green stick across it, slanting upward from the ground, and weight the lower end with a rock, so that you could easily regulate the height of a pot. The slanting stick should be notched, or have the stub of a twig left at its upper end, to hold the pot bail in place, and to be set at such an angle that the pot swings about a foot clear of the ground.

"Then gather a small armful of sound, dry twigs from the size of a lead pencil to that of your finger. Take no twig that lies flat on the ground, for such are generally damp or rotten. Choose hard wood, if there is any, for it lasts well.

"Select three of your best sticks for kindling. Shave each of them almost through, for half its length, leaving lower end of shavings attached to the stick, one under the other. Stand these in a tripod, under the hanging pot, with their curls down. Around them build a *small* conical wigwam of the other sticks, standing each on end and slanting to a common center. The whole affair is no bigger than your hat. Leave free air spaces between the sticks. Fire requires air, and plenty of it, and it burns best when it has something to climb up on; hence the wigwam construction. Now touch off the shaved sticks, and in a moment you will have a small blast furnace under the pot. This will get up steam in a hurry. Feed it with small sticks as needed.

"Meantime get two bed-sticks, four or five inches thick, or a pair of flat rocks, to support the frying pan. The firewood will all drop to embers soon after the pot boils. Toss out the smoking butts, leaving only clear, glowing coals. Put your bed-sticks on either side, parallel and level. Set the pan on them, and fry away. So, in twenty minutes from the time you drove your stake, the meal will be cooked.

"*Dinner Fire*—First get in plenty of wood and kindling. If you can find two large flat rocks, or several small ones of even height use them as andirons; otherwise lay down two short cuts off a five or six inch log, facing you and about three feet apart. On these rocks or billets lay two four foot logs parallel, and several inches apart, as rests for your utensils. Arrange the kindling between and under them, with small sticks laid across the top of the logs, a couple of long ones lengthwise, then more short ones across, another pair length-

CAMP CRANE

wise, and thicker short ones across. Then light it. Many prefer to light the kindling at once and feed the fire gradually; but I do as above, so as to have an even glow under several pots at once, and then the sticks will all burn down to coals together.

"This is the usual way to build a cooking fire when there is no time to do better. The objection is that the supporting logs must be close enough together to hold up the pots and pans, and, being round, this leaves too little space between them for the fire to heat the balance evenly; besides, a pot is liable to slip and topple over. A better way, if one has time, is to hew both the inside surfaces and the tops of the logs flat. Space these supports close enough together at one end for the narrowest pot and wide enough apart at the other for the frying pan.

"If you carry fire-irons much bother is saved. Simply lay down two flat rocks or a pair of billets far enough apart for the purpose, place the flat irons on them, and space them to suit the utensils.   ,

"If a camp grate is used, build a crisscross fire of short sticks under it.

"Split wood is better than round sticks for cooking; it catches easier and burns more easily.

"*Camp Crane*—Pots for hot water, stews, coffee, and

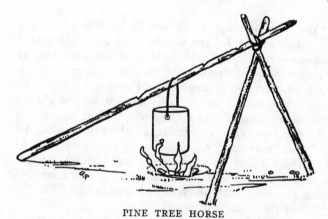

PINE TREE HORSE

so on, are more manageable when hung above the fire.
The heat can easily be regulated, the pots hanging low
at first to boil quickly, and then being elevated or shifted
aside to simmer.

"Set up two forked stakes about five feet apart and
four feet to the crotches. Across them lay a green
stick (lug-pole) somewhat thicker than a broomstick.
Now cut three or four green crotches from branches,
drive a nail in the small end of each, or cut a notch
in it, invert the crotches, and hang them on the lug-pole
to suspend kettles from. These pothooks are to be of
different length so that the kettle can be adjusted to
different heights above the fire, first for hard boiling,
and then for simmering. If kettles were hung from
the lug-pole itself, this adjustment could not be made,
and you would have to dismount the whole business in
order to get one kettle off.

"If forked stakes are not easily found in the neighborhood, drive straight ones, then split the tops, flatten
the ends of the cross poles and insert them in the clefts
of the stakes.

"You do not want a big fire to cook over. Many and many a time I have watched old and experienced woodsmen spoil their grub, and their tempers, too, by trying to cook in front of a roaring winter campfire, and have marveled at their lack of common sense. Off to one side of such a fire, lay your bed logs as above; then shovel from the campfire enough hard coal to fill the space between the logs within three inches of the top. You now have a steady, even heat from end to end; it can easily be regulated; there is level support for every vessel; and you can wield a short-handled frying pan over such an outdoor range without scorching either the meat or yourself.

"Fire for Baking—For baking in a reflector, or roasting a joint, a high fire is best, with a backing to throw the heat forward. Sticks three feet long can be leaned against a big log or a sheer-faced rock, and the kindlings started under them.

"Often a good bed of coals is wanted. The campfire generally supplies these, but sometimes they are needed in a hurry, soon after camp is pitched. To get them, *take sound hardwood,* either green or dead, and split it into sticks of uniform thickness (say, 1¼-inch face). Lay down two bed-sticks, cross these near the end with two others, and so on up until you have a pen a foot high. Start a fire in this pen. Then cover it with a layer of parallel sticks laid an inch apart. Cross this with a similar layer at right angles, and so upward for another foot. The free draught will make a roaring fire, and all will burn down to coals together.

"The thick bark of hemlock, and the hard woods generally, will soon yield coals for ordinary cooking.

"To keep coals a long time, cover them with ashes, or with bark which will soon burn to ashes. In wet weather a bed of coals can be shielded by slanting broad strips of green bark over it and overlapping them at the edges.

"*Fire in a Trench*—In time of drought when everything is tinder-dry, or in windy weather, especially if the ground be strewn with dead leaves or pine needles, build your fire in a trench. This is the best way, too, if fuel is scarce and you must depend on brushwood, as a trench conserves heat.

"Dig the trench in line with the prevailing wind. The point is to get a good draught. Make the windward end somewhat wider than the rest, and deeper, sloping the trench upward to the far end. Line the sides with flat rocks if they are to be found, as they hold heat a long time and keep the sides from crumbling in. Lay other rocks, or a pair of green poles. along the edges to support vessels. A little chimney of flat stones or sod, at the leeward end, will make the fire draw well. If there is some sheet-iron to cover the trench a quite practical stove is made, but an open trench will do very well if properly managed.

"*The Indian's Fire*—Best where fuel is scarce, or when one has only a small hatchet with which to cut night wood. Fell and trim a lot of hardwood saplings. Lay three or four of them on the ground, butts on top of each other, tips radiating from this center like the spokes of a wheel. On and around this build a small hot fire. Place butts of other saplings on this, radiating like the others. As the wood burns away, shove the sticks in toward the center, butts on top of each other as before. This saves much chopping, and economizes fuel. Build a little wind break behind you and lie close to the fire. Doubtless you have heard the Indian's dictum (southern Indians express it just as the northern ones do): 'White man heap fool; make um big

fire—can't git near; Injun make um little fire—git close.
Uh, good.'

Kindling

"The best kindling is fat pine or the bark of the paper
birch. Fat pine is found in the stumps and butt cuts
of pine trees, particularly those that died on the stump.
The resin has collected there and dried. This wood is
usually easy to split. Pine knots are the tough, heavy,
resinous stubs of limbs that are found on dead pine
trees. They, as well as fat pine, are almost imperish-
able, and those sticking out of old rotten logs are as
good as any. In collecting pine knots go to fallen trees
that are almost rotted away. Hit the knot a lick with
the pole of the axe and generally it will yield; if you
must chop, cut deep to get it all and to save the axe
edge. The knots of old dead balsams are similarly
used. Usually a dead stump of pine, spruce, or balsam,
all punky on the outside, has a core very rich in resin
that makes excellent kindling.

"Hemlock knots are worthless and hard as glass—
keep your axe out of them.

"The thick bark of hemlock is good to make glowing
coals in a hurry; so is that of hard woods generally.
Good kindling, sure to be dry underneath the bark in all
weather, is procured by snapping off the small dead
branches, or stubs of branches, that are left on the trunks
of small or medium-sized trees, near the ground. Do
not pick up twigs from the ground, but choose those
among the downwood that are held up free from the
ground. Where a tree is found that has been shivered
by lightning, or one that has broken off without uproot-
ing, good splinters of dry wood will be found. In every
laurel thicket there is plenty of dead laurel, and, since
it is of sprangling growth, most of the branches will be

free from the ground and snap-dry. They ignite readily and give out intense heat.

"The bark of all species of birch, but of paper birch especially, is excellent for kindling and for torches. It is full of resinous oil, blazes up at once, will burn in any wind, and wet sticks can be ignited with it.

"Making Fire in the Wet—It is a good test of one's resourcefulness to make a fire out of doors in rainy weather. The best way to go about it depends upon local conditions. If fat pine can be found, the trick is easy; just split it up, and start your fire under a big fallen log. Dry fuel and a place to build a fire can often be found under big up-tilted logs, shelving rocks, and similar natural shelters, or in the core of an old stump. In default of these, look for a dead softwood tree that leans to the south. The wood and bark on the under side will be dry; chop some off, split it fine, and build your fire under the shelter of the trunk.

"Lighting a Match—When there is nothing dry to strike it on, jerk the tip of the match forward against your teeth.

"To light a match in the wind, *face* the wind. Cup your hands, with their backs toward the wind, and hold the match with its head pointing toward the rear of the cup; *i. e.,* toward the wind. Remove the right hand just long enough to strike the match on something very close by; then instantly resume the former position. The flame will run up the match stick, instead of being blown away from it, and so will have something to feed on.

"Fire Regulations—On state lands and on national forest reserves it is forbidden to use any but fallen timber for firewood. Different states have various other restrictions, some, I believe, not permitting trampers to

light a fire in the woods at all unless accompanied by a
registered guide.

"In New York the regulations prescribe that fires
will be permitted for the purposes of cooking, warmth
and insect smudges; but before such fires are kindled
sufficient space around the spot where the fire is to be
lighted must be cleared from all combustible material;
and before the place is abandoned fires so lighted must
be thoroughly quenched.

"In Pennsylvania forest reserves no fire may be made
except in a hole or pit one foot deep, the pit being en-
circled by the excavated earth. In those of California,
no fire at all may be lighted without first procuring a
permit from the authorities.

"Fire regulations are posted on all public lands, and
if campers disregard them they are subject to arrest.

"These are wise and good laws. Every camper who
loves the forest, and who has any regard for public interest, will do his part in obeying them to the letter.
However, if he occupies private property where he may
use his own judgment, or if he travels in the wilderness
far from civilization, where there are no regulations,
it will be useful for him to know something about the
fuel value of all kinds of wood, green as well as dead,
and for such people the following information is given:

"The arts of fire building are not so simple as they
look. To practice them successfully in all sorts of wild
regions we must know the different species of trees
one from another, and their relative fuel values, which,
as we shall see, vary a great deal. We must know
how well, or ill, each of them burns in a green state,
as well as when seasoned. It is important to discrim-
inate between wood that makes lasting coals and such
as soon dies down to ashes. Some kinds of wood pop
violently when burning and cast out embers that may

burn holes in tents and bedding or set the neighborhood afire; others burn quietly, with clear, steady flame. Some are stubborn to split, others almost fall apart under the axe. In wet weather it takes a practiced woodsman to find tinder and dry wood, and to select a natural shelter where fire can be kept going during a storm of rain or snow, when a fire is most needed.

"There are several handy little manuals by which one who has no botanical knowledge can soon learn how to identify the different species of trees by merely examining their leaves, or, late in the season, by their bark, buds and habit of growth.

"But no book gives the other information that I have referred to; so I shall offer, in the present chapter, a little rudimentary instruction in this important branch of woodcraft.

"It is convenient for our purpose to divide the trees into two great groups, hard woods and soft woods, using these terms not so loosely as lumbermen do, but drawing the line between sycamore, yellow birch, yellow pine, and slippery elm, on the one side, and red cedar, sassafras, pitch pine and white birch, on the other.

"*As a general rule,* hard woods make good, slow-burning fuel that yields lasting coals, and soft woods make a quick, hot fire that is soon spent. But each species has peculiarities that deserve close attention.

"*Best Fuel*—Best of all northern fire woods is hickory, green or dry. It makes a hot fire, but lasts a long time, burning down to a bed of hard coals that keep up an even, generous heat for hours. Hickory, by the way, is distinctly an American tree; no other region on earth produces it. The live oak of the south is most excellent fuel; so is holly. Following the hickory, in fuel value, are chestnut, oak, overcup, white, blackjack, post and basket oaks, pecan, the hornbeams (ironwoods), and dogwood. The latter burn finely to a beautiful white ash that is characteristic; apple wood does the same. Black birch also ranks here; it has the advantage of 'doing its own blowing,' as a Carolina mountaineer said to me, meaning that the oil in the birch assists its combustion so that the wood needs no coaxing. All of the birches are good fuel, ranking in about this order: Black, yellow, red, paper, and white. Sugar maple was the favorite fuel of our old-time hunters and surveyors because it ignites easily, burns with a clear, steady flame, and leaves good coals.

"Locust is a good, lasting fuel; it is easy to cut, and, when green, splits fairly well; the thick bark takes fire readily and the wood then burns slowly, with little flame, leaving pretty good coals; hence it is good for night wood. Mulberry has similar qualities. The scarlet and willow oaks are among the poorest of the hard woods for fuel. Cherry makes only fair fuel. White elm is poor stuff, but slippery elm is better. Yellow pine burns well, as its sap is resinous instead of watery like that of the soft pines.

"In some respects white ash is the best of green woods for campers' fuel. It is easily cut and split, is lighter to tote than most other hard woods, and is of so dry a nature that even the green wood catches fire readily. It burns with clear flame, and lasts longer than any other free-burning wood of its weight. On a wager, I have built a bully fire from a green tree of white ash, one match, and no dry kindling. I split some of the wood very fine and 'frilled' a few of the little sticks with my knife.

"*Soft Woods*—Most of the soft woods are good only for kindling, or for quick cooking fires, and then only when seasoned. For these purposes, however, some of them are superior, as they split and shave readily and catch fire easily.

"Liquidambar, magnolia, tulip, catalpa, and willow are poor fuel. Seasoned chestnut and yellow poplar make a hot fire, but crackle and leave no coals. Balsam fir, basswood, and the white and loblolly pines make quick fires, but are soon spent. The grey (Labrador) or jack pine is considered good fuel in the far north, where hard woods are scarce. Seasoned tamarack is good. Spruce is poor fuel, although, being resinous, it kindles easily and makes a good blaze for 'branding up' a fire. Pitch pine, which is the most inflammable of all woods when dry and 'fat,' will scarcely burn at all in a green state. Sycamore and buckeye, when thoroughly seasoned, are good fuel, but will not split. Alder burns readily and gives out considerable heat, but is not lasting.

"The dry wood of the northern poplar (large-toothed aspen) is a favorite for cooking fires, because it gives an intense heat, with little or no smoke, lasts well, and does not blacken the utensils. Red cedar has similar qualities, but is rather hard to ignite and must be fed fine at the start.

"The best green soft woods for fuel are white birch, paper birch, soft maple, cottonwood, and quaking aspen.

"As a rule, the timber growing along the margins of large streams is softwood. Hence, driftwood is generally a poor mainstay unless there is plenty of it on the spot; but driftwood on the sea coast is good fuel.

"*Precautions*—I have already mentioned the necessity of clearing the camp ground of inflammable stuff before starting a fire on it, raking it toward a common center and burning all the dead leaves, pine needles and trash; otherwise it may catch and spread beyond your control as soon as your back is turned. Don't build your fire against a big old punky log; it may smoulder a day or two after you have left and then burst out into flame when the breeze fans it.

"*Never* leave a spark of fire when breaking camp, or when leaving it for the day. Make absolutely sure

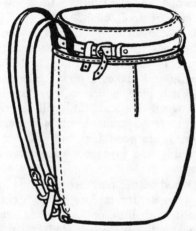

HAVERSACK FOR CARRYING KITCHEN UTENSILS.

of this by drenching the campfire thoroughly, or by smothering it completely with earth or sand. Never drop a lighted match on the ground without stamping it out. Have you ever seen a forest fire? It is terrible. Thousands of acres are destroyed and many a time men and women and children have been cut off by a tornado of flame and burned alive. The person whose carelessness starts such a holocaust is worse than a fool—he is a criminal, and a disgrace to the good earth he treads."

Cooking Devices

When it is convenient carry a hatchet. Scouts should carry a small folding grate. The best form of grate is one with folding legs.

After laying the fire the legs of the grate are driven into the ground. As the fire burns down, the grate may be lowered by driving the legs in deeper. This is a very useful utensil for supporting hot water pails or frying pan.

When no forks can be found use the "Pine Tree Horse," as shown in cut.

In order to boil water hard it will only be necessary to slip the kettle down the pole, holding it in place by graduated notches.

Equipment and supplies for one meal may be carried in one or two haversacks like the one shown. Indeed, a meal may be cooked without any equiment whatever other than a knife which every Scout should be provided with.

Improvised Grate—A few sticks ½ inch in diameter laid about 2 inches apart and about 2 inches above the coals form a good enough broiler. Steak and chops cook perfectly well if laid right on the coals.

Cooking kits allow for more variety, as they provide a frying pan, in which bacon and potatoes can be cooked, and a small pail for boiling water. It is convenient for each Scout to carry her own cup, knife, fork and spoon. The cooking kit and supplies can then be divided among the party.

At a permanent camp a frying board is a great convenience. It is simply a flat, smooth board with a pointed end which can be driven into the ground. Fish, meat, game and "Injun" bread can be cooked on this board better than in any other way, as the food receives the heat without becoming charred, and is much more wholesome than when fried in a pan. As long as the board is to windward of the flame, a constant heat is maintained without smoke. A small fire will cook a very large fish in a short time. An old canoe

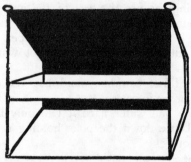

THE FOLDING BAKER.

paddle may be used for this purpose. The food is hung
on nails driven in the board, a strip of bacon, hung
above the fish and dripping on it would improve the
flavor.

It is a good plan to use a separate frying board when
cooking fish, as the juice from the fish seeps into the
board and it is practically impossible to remove it by
cleaning. The flavor of fish is not pleasant on other
food. If it is not practicable to carry two frying boards
one can be careful to reserve the same side of one
board for cooking fish.

A long cooking spoon for dishing vegetables out of
the pots is very useful. A roll of paper towels for drying dishes and for use as napkins, or cloth dish towels
and paper napkins are also useful. Other useful articles are a dish mop with a wooden handle, and a pan-
cake turner.

The Folding Baker—The baker may be placed before
the blazing fire. It is a perfect arrangement for baking
biscuits and roasting meats.

Friction Top Cans—It is well to have these varying
in capacity from one to three quarts. Use one
quart size for washing soda, powdered soap, and sugar.

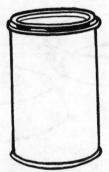

FRICTION TOP CAN.

The larger sizes should carry flour, cornmeal, etc. Eggs may be placed in the one used for the cornmeal.

Where convenient to provide a large equipment the following utensils are suggested:

Camp grate, 3 wire toasters (one for meat, one for fish, one for bread), 2 frying boards (one for meat, one for fish), 6-quart pail for reserve water, 9-quart pail for boiling vegetables, agate or paper plates, agate or paper cups, knives, forks, spoons, kit knife, paper towels, dish mops, powdered soap, cotton gloves for handling hot or smoky pots, candles, matches (in waterproof packages), non-rusting wire ⅛ inch thick for hanging pots, etc.

A large permanent camp may add greatly to the pleasure of its members, and make a delightful break in the day, by sending off troops of, say, eight girls to cook a camp lunch at a place about a mile distant. For this purpose, when a group plans to do a great deal of camping the above equipment is suggested. It could all be packed in the pack basket, and the girls could take turns carrying it.

Such a basket without a canvas cover costs about $8

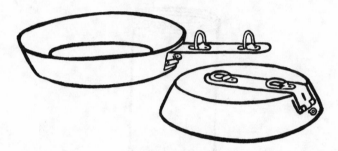

FOLDING FRYING PAN.

and is extremely useful in permanent camp equipment.

Utensils Required for a Party of Eight and their Uses

If the group of girls plans for a camping trip of several days and transport is available, all the following utensils will be found useful. These may be purchased in any sporting goods store.

Three Wire Toasters—One for meat, one for fish, one for toast.

In cooking meat or fish, and in making toast before a blazing fire, stand the wire toaster upright before the fire and prop it up with a stick, thus:

A board may be used in the same manner. It is often desirable to do this in order to avoid the delay of waiting for the fire to burn down.

Cooking Pots—Size 5 quarts, for boiling vegetables; size 6½ quarts, for boiling vegetables; size 9 quarts, for hot water; size 15 quarts, for reserve cold water.

Each of these pots nests in the next larger size, making one package. A cocoa pot of this type nests into the 5-quart pail.

Two Frying Pans—The handles fold in and the pans pack in a case with the nest of cooking pots. In addition to their usual uses, the frying pans are also used

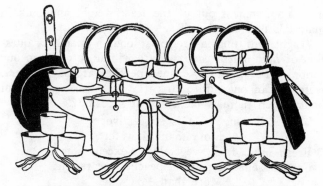

COMPLETE COOKING OUTFIT FOR EIGHT SCOUTS.

as dish-washing pans, one for the washing and one for the rinsing.

A heaped teaspoon of washing soda dissolved in hot water will so perfectly clean the frying pans as to permit their use as dish-pans.

Eight agate plates, or aluminum if possible; eight agate cups, or aluminum if possible; eight knives, forks and spoons; one large, long-handled cooking spoon.

The complete cooking outfit may be nested together and packed in a canvas bag and takes up about as much space as a water pail.

Provisions

"When a party camps where fresh meat and farm products can be procured as they are wanted, its provisioning is chiefly a matter of taste, and calls for no special comment here. But to have good meals in the wilderness is a different matter. A man will eat five or six pounds a day of fresh food. That is a heavy load on the trail. And fresh meat, dairy products, fruit and vegetables are generally too bulky, too perishable. So it is up to the woodsman to learn how to get the most nourishment out of the least weight and bulk in materials that 'keep' well.

"Light outfitting, as regards food, is mainly a question of *how much water* we are willing to carry in our rations. For instance, canned peaches are 88 per cent. water. Can one afford to carry so much water from home when there is plenty of it at camp?

"The following table is suggestive:

More than ¾ water

Fresh milk, fruit, vegetables (except potatoes).
Canned soups, tomatoes, peaches, pears, etc.

More than ½ water

Fresh beef, veal, mutton, poultry, eggs, potatoes.
Canned corn, baked beans, pineapple.
Evaporated milk (unsweetened).

More than 1/3 water

Fresh bread, rolls, pork chops.
Potted chicken, etc.
Cheese.
Canned blackberries.

Less than 1/3 water

Dried apples, apricots, peaches, prunes.
Fruit jelly.

Less than 1/5 water

Salt pork, bacon, dried fish, butter.
Desiccated eggs, concentrated soups.
Powdered milk.
Wheat flour, cornmeal, etc., macaroni.
Rice, oatmeal, hominy, etc.
Dried beans, split peas.
Dehydrated vegetables.
Dried dates, figs, raisins.
Orange marmalade, sugar, chocolate.
Nuts, nut butter.

"Although this table is good in its way, it is not a

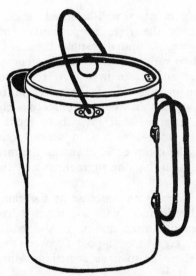

FIVE QUART PAIL TO NEST CANS.

fair measure of the relative value of foods. Even the solid part of some foodstuffs contains a good deal of refuse (potatoes 20 per cent), while others have none.

"*Nutritive Values*—The nutritive elements of foodstuffs are protein, a little mineral matter, fats, and carbohydrates. Protein is the basis of muscles, bone, tendon, cartilage, skin and corpuscles of the blood. Fats and carbohydrates supply heat and muscular energy. In other words, the human body is an engine; protein keeps it in repair; fats and carbohydrates are the fuel to run it.

"Familiar examples of proteids are lean meat and white of egg. The chief food fats are fat meat, butter, lard, oil and cream. Carbohydrates are starchy foods (flour, cereals, etc.) and sugar (sweets of almost any kind).

"The problem of a well-balanced ration consists in supplying daily the right proportion of nutritive elements in agreeable and digestible form, The problem of a campaign ration is the same, but cutting out most of the water and waste in which fresh foods abound. However, in getting rid of the water in fresh meats, fruits and vegetables we lose, unfortunately, much of the volatile essences that give these foods their good flavor. This loss—and it is a serious one—must be made up by the camp cook, changing the menu as often as he can by varying the ingredients and the processes -- cooking.

"*Variety* is quite as welcome at the camp board as anywhere else, in fact, more so; for it is harder to get. Variety need not mean adding to the load. It means *substituting*, say, three 5-pound parcels for one 15-pound parcel, so as to have something 'different' from day to day.

"*Digestibility*—We must bear in mind the adage that 'we live not upon what we eat but upon what we digest.' Some foods rich in protein, especially beans, peas, and oatmeal, are not easily assimilated, unless cooked for a longer time than campers generally can spare. A considerable part of their protein is liable to putrefy in the alimentary canal, and so be worse than wasted. An excess of meat or fish will do the same thing. Other foods of very high theoretical value are constipating if used in large amounts, as cheese, nuts, chocolate.

"*Food Components*—Let us now consider the material of field rations, item by item.

"*Bacon*—Good old breakfast bacon worthily heads the list, for it is the campaigner's standby. It keeps well in any climate, and demands no special care in packing. It is easy to cook, combines well with almost anything, is handier than lard to fry things with, does just as well to shorten bread or biscuits, is very nutritious, and nearly everybody likes it. Take it with you from home, for you can seldom buy it away from railroad towns. Get the boneless, in 5 to 8 pound flitches. Let canned bacon alone; it lacks flavor and costs more than it is worth. A little mould on the outside of a flitch does no harm, but reject bacon that is soft and watery, or with yellow fat, or with brownish or black spots in the lean.

"*Smoked Ham*—Small ones generally are tough and too salty. Hard to keep in warm or damp weather; moulds easily. Is attractive to blow-flies, which quickly fill it with 'skippers' if they can get at it. If kept in a cheesecloth bag and hung in a cool, airy place a ham will last until eaten up and will be relished. Ham will keep, even in warm weather, if packed in a stout paper bag so as to exclude flies. It will keep indefinitely if sliced, boiled or fried and put up in tins with melted lard poured over it to keep out air. * * *

"*Canned Soups*—These are wholesome enough, but their fluid kinds are very bulky for their meager nutritive value. However, a few cans of consomme are fine for 'stock' in camp soups or stews, and invaluable in case of sickness. Here, as in canned meat, avoid the country grocery kind.

"*Condensed Soups*—Soup powders are a great help in time of trouble—but don't rely on them for a full meal. There are some that are complete in themselves and require nothing but 15 to 20 minutes' cooking; others take longer, and demand (in small type on the label) the addition of ingredients that generally you haven't got. Try various brands at home till you find what you like.

"*Cured Fish*—Shredded codfish and smoked halibut,

sprats, boneless herring are portable and keep well. They will be relished for variety's sake.

"Eggs—To vary the camp bill of fare, eggs are simply invaluable, not only by themselves, but as ingredients in cooking. * * *

"When means of transportation permit, fresh eggs may be carried to advantage. A hand crate holding 12 dozen weighs about 24 pounds, filled.

"Eggs can be packed along in winter without danger of breakage by carrying them frozen. Do not try to boil a frozen egg; peal it as you would a hard-boiled one and then fry or poach.

"To test an egg for freshness, drop it into cold water; if it sinks quickly it is fresh; if it stands on end it is doubtful; if it floats it is surely bad.

"To preserve eggs, rub them all over with vaseline, being careful that no particle of shell is uncoated. They will keep good much longer than if treated with lime water, salt, paraffine, water-glass or any of the other common expedients.

"On hard trips it is impracticable to carry eggs in the shell. Some campers break fresh eggs and pack them in friction-top cans. The yolks soon break and they keep but a short time. *A good brand* of desiccated eggs is the solution of this problem. It does away with all risk of breaking and spoiling and reduces bulk very much. Desiccated eggs vary a great deal in quality, according to material and process employed. Desiccated eggs made of the yolks are merely useful as ingredients in cooking.

"Milk—Sweetened condensed milk (the 'salve of the lumberjacks') is distasteful to most people. Plain evaporated milk is the thing to carry—and don't leave it out if you can practicably tote it. The notion that this is a 'baby food' to be scorned by real woodsmen is

nothing but a foolish conceit. Few things pay better for their transportation. It will be allowed that Admiral Peary knows something about food values. Here is what he says in *The North Pole:* 'The essentials, and the only essentials, needed in a serious Arctic sledge journey, no matter what the season, the temperature, or the duration of the journey—whether one month or six—are four: pemmican, tea, ship's biscuit, condensed milk. The standard daily ration for work on the final sledge journey toward the Pole on all expeditions has been as follows: 1 lb. pemmican, 1 lb. ship's biscuit, 4 oz. condensed milk, ½ oz. compressed tea.'

"Milk, either evaporated or powdered, is a very important ingredient in camp cookery.

"*Butter*—This is another 'soft' thing that pays its freight.

"For ordinary trips it suffices to pack butter firmly into pry-up tin cans which have been sterilized by thorough scalding and then cooled in a perfectly clean place. Keep it in a spring or in cold running water (hung in a net, or weighted in a rock) whenever you can. When traveling, wrap the cold can in a towel or other insulating material.

"If I had to cut out either lard or butter I would keep the butter. It serves all the purposes of lard in cooking, is wholesomer, and beyond that, it is the most concentrated sauce of energy that one can use with impunity.

"*Cheese*—Cheese has nearly twice the fuel value of a porterhouse steak of equal weight, and it contains a fourth more protein. It is popularly supposed to be hard to digest, but in reality it is not so if used in moderation. The best kind for campers is potted cheese, or cream or 'snappy' cheese put up in tinfoil. If not so protected from air it soon dries out and grows stale.

A tin of imported Camembert will be a pleasant surprise on some occasion.

"*Bread Biscuits*—It is well to carry enough yeast bread for two or three days, until the game country is reached and camp routine is established. To keep it fresh, each loaf must be sealed in waxed paper or parchment paper (the latter is best, because it is tough, waterproof, greaseproof). Bread freezes easily; for cold weather luncheons carry toasted bread.

"*Hardtack* (pilot bread, ship biscuit) can be recommended only for such trips or cruises as do not permit baking. It is a cracker prepared of plain flour and water, not even salted, and kiln-dried to a chip, so as to keep indefinitely, its only enemies being weevils. Get the coarsest grade. To make hardtack palatable toast it until crisp, or soak in hot coffee and butter it, or at least salt it.

"Swedish hardtack, made of whole rye flour, is good for a change.

"Plasmon biscuit, imported from England, is the most nutritious breadstuff I have ever used. It is a round cracker, firm but not hard, of good flavor, containing a large percentage of the protein of milk, six of the small biscuits holding as much proteid as a quarter of a pound of beef.

"*Flour*—Graham and entire wheat flours contain more protein than patent flour, but this is offset by the fact that it is not so digestible as the protein of standard flour. Practically there is little or no difference between them in the amount of protein assimilated. The same seems to be true of their mineral ingredients.

"Many campers depend a good deal on self-raising flour because it saves a little trouble in mixing. But such flour is easily spoiled by dampness, it does not make as good biscuit or flapjacks as one can turn out in camp by doing his own mixing, and it will not do for thickening, dredging, etc.

"Flour and meal should be sifted before starting on an expedition. There will be no sieve in camp.

"*Baking Powder*—Get the best, made with pure cream of tartar. It costs more than the alum powders, and does not go so far, bulk for bulk; but it is much kinder to the stomach. Baking soda will not be needed on short trips, but is required for longer ones, in making sour-dough, as a steady diet of baking-powder bread or biscuit will ruin the stomach if persisted in for a considerable time. Soda also is useful medicinally.

"*Cornmeal*—Some like yellow, some prefer white. The flavor of freshly ground meal is best, but the ordinary granulated meal of commerce keeps better, because it has been kiln-dried. Cornmeal should not be used as the leading breadstuff, for reasons already given, but johnnycake, corn pancakes, and mush are a welcome change from hot wheat bread or biscuit, and the average novice at cooking may succeed better with them. The meal is useful to roll fish in before frying.

"*Breakfast Cereals*—These according to taste, and for variety's sake. Plain cereals, particularly oatmeal, require a long cooking, either in a double boiler or with constant stirring, to make them digestible; and then there is a messy pot to clean up. They do more harm than good to campers who hurry their cooking. So it is best to buy the partially cooked cereals that take only a few minutes to prepare. Otherwise the 'patent breakfast foods' have no more nutritive quality than plain grain; some of them not so much. The notion that bran has remarkable food value is a delusion; it actually makes the protein of the grain less digestible. As for mineral matter, 'to build up bone and teeth and brawn,' there is enough of it in almost any mixed diet, without swallowing a lot of crude fiber.

"Rice, although not very appetizing by itself, combines so well in stews or the like, and goes so well in pudding, that it deserves a place in the commissariat.

"*Macaroni*—The various paste (pas-tay, as the Italians call them) take the place of bread, may be cooked in many ways to lend variety, and are especially good in soups which otherwise would have little nourishing power. Spaghetti, vermicelli, and noodles all are good in their way. Break macaroni into inch pieces and pack so that insects cannot get into it. It is more wholesome than flapjacks and it 'sticks to the ribs.'

"*Sweets*—Sugar is stored-up energy, and is assimilated more quickly than any other food. Men in the open soon get to craving sweets.

"Maple sugar is always welcome. Get the soft kind that can be spread on bread for luncheons. Syrup is easily made from it in camp by simply bringing it to a boil with the necessary amount of water. Ready-made syrup is mean to pack around.

"Sweet chocolate (not too sweet) has remarkable sustaining power.

"When practicable, take along some jam and marmalade. The commissaries of the British Army were wise when they gave jam an honorable place in Tommy Atkins' field ration. Yes: jam for soldiers in time of war. So many ounces of it, substituted, mind you, for so many ounces of the porky, porky, porky, that has ne'er a streak of lean. So, a little currant jelly with your duck or venison is worth breaking all rules for. Such conserves can be repacked by the buyer in pry-up cans that have been sterilized as recommended under the heading *Butter*.

"*Fresh Vegetables*—The only ones worth taking along

are potatoes and onions. Choose potatoes with small eyes and of uniform medium size, even if you have to buy half a bushel to sort out a peck. They are very heavy and bulky in proportion to their food value; so you cannot afford to be burdened with any but the best. Cereals and beans take the place of potatoes when you go light.

"Fresh onions are almost indispensable for seasoning soups, stews, etc. A few of them can be taken along almost anywhere. I generally carry at least one, even on a walking trip. Onions are good for the suddenly overtaxed system, relieve the inordinate thirst that one experiences the first day or two, and assist excretion. Freezing does not spoil onions if they are kept frozen until used.

"*Beans*—A prime factor in cold weather camping. Take a long time to cook ('soak all day and cook all night' is the rule). Cannot be cooked done at altitudes of 5,000 feet and upward. Large varieties cook quickest, but the small white navy beans are best for baking. Pick them over before packing, as there is much waste.

"*Split Peas*—Used chiefly in making a thick, nourishing soup.

"*Dehydrated Vegetables*—Much of the flavor of fresh vegetables is lost when the juice is expressed or evaporated, but all of their nutriment is retained and enough of the flavor for them to serve as fair substitutes when fresh vegetables cannot be carried. They help out a camp stew and may even be served as side dishes if one has butter and milk to season them. Generally they require soaking (which can be done over night) ; then they are to be boiled slowly until tender, taking about as much time as fresh vegetables. If cooking is hurried they will be woody and tasteless.

"Dehydrated vegetables are very portable, keep in any

climate, and it is well to carry some on trips far from civilization.

"*Canned Vegetables*—In our table of food values it will be noticed that the least nourishing article for its weight and bulk is a can of tomatoes. Yet these 'airtights' are great favorites with outdoors men, especially in the West and South, where frequently they are eaten raw out of the can. It is not so much their flavor as their acid that is grateful to a stomach overtaxed with fat or canned meat and hot bread three times a day. If wanted only as an adjuvant to soups, stews, rice, macaroni, etc., the more concentrated puree will serve very well.

"Canned corn (better still, 'kornlet,' which is concentrated milk of sweet corn) is quite nourishing, and everybody likes it.

"A few cans of baked beans (*without* tomato sauce) will be handy in wet weather. The B. & M. ¾ lb. cans are convenient for a lone camper or for two going light.

"*Nuts*—A handful each of shelled nuts and raisins, with a cake of sweet chocolate, will carry a man far on the trail or when he has lost it. The kernels of butternuts and hickory nuts have the highest fuel value of our native species; peanuts and almonds are very rich in protein; Brazil nuts, filberts and pecans, in fat. Peanut butter is a concentrated food that goes well in sandwiches. One can easily make nut butter of any kind (except almonds or Brazil nuts) for himself by using the nut grinder that comes with a kitchen food chopper, and can add ground dates, ground popcorn, or whatever he likes; but such preparations will soon grow rancid if not sealed airtight. Nut butter is more digestible than kernels unless the latter are thoroughly chewed.

"*Fruits*—All fruits are very deficient in protein and (except olives) in fat, but dried fruit is rich in carbohydrates. Fruit acid (that of prunes, dried apricots, and dehydrated cranberries, when fresh fruit cannot be carried) is a good corrective of a too fatty and starchy or sugary diet, and a preventive of scurvy. Most fruits are laxative, and for that reason, if none other, a good proportion of dried fruit should be included in the ration, no matter how light one travels; otherwise one is likely to suffer from constipation when he changes from 'town grub' to 'trail grub.'

"Among canned fruits those that go farthest are pine-apples and blackberries. Excellent jelly can be made in camp from dried apples.

"There is much nourishment in dates, figs (those dried round are better than layer figs) and raisins. Pitted dates and seedless raisins are best for light outfits. And do not despise the humble prune; buy the best grade in the market (unknown to landladies) and soak over night before stewing; it will be a revelation. Take a variety of dried fruits, and mix them in different combinations, sweet and tart, so as not to have the same sauce twice in succession; then you will learn that dried fruits are by no means a poor substitute for fresh or canned ones.

"In hot weather I carry a few lemons whenever practicable. Limes are more compact and better medicinally, but they do not keep well. Lime juice in bottles is excellent, if you can carry it.

"Citric acid crystals may be used in lieu of lemons when going light, but the flavor is not so good as that of lemonade powder that one can put up for himself. The process is described by A. W. Barnard: 'Squeeze out the lemons and sift into the clear juice four to six spoonfuls of sugar to a lemon; let stand a few days if the weather is dry, or a week if wet, till it is dried up then pulverize and put up into capsules.' Gelatin capsules of any size, from one oz. down, can be procured at a drug store. They are convenient to carry small quantities of spices, flavoring, medicines, etc., on a hike.

"Vinegar and pickles are suitable only for fixed camps or easy cruises.

"*Fritures*—Lard is less wholesome than olive oil, or 'Crisco,' or the other preparations of vegetable fats. Crisco can be heated to a higher temperature than lard without burning, thus ensuring the surprise' which prevents getting a fried article sodden with grease; it does as well as lard for shortening; and it can be used repeatedly without transmitting the flavor of one dish to the next one. Olive oil is superior as a friture, especially for fish, but expensive.

"*Beverages*—Tea is better than coffee. Even if you don't use it at home, take along on your camping trip enough for midday meals. Tea tabloids are not bad, but I advise using the real thing. On a hike, with no tea-ball, I tie up enough for each pint in a bit of washed cheesecloth, loosely, leaving enough string attached whereby to whisk it out after exactly four minutes' steeping.

"Cocoa is not only a drink but a food. It is best for the evening meal because it makes one sleepy, whereas tea and coffee have the opposite effect.

"Get the soluble kind if you want it quickly prepared.

"*Condiments*—Do not leave out a small assortment of condiments wherewith to vary the taste of common articles and serve a new sauce or gravy or pudding now and then.

"Salt is best carried in a wooden box. The amount used in cooking and at table is small.

"White pepper is better than black. Some Cayenne or Chili should also be taken. Red pepper is not only a good stomachic, but also is fine for a chill (made into a tea with hot water and sugar).

"Among condiments I class beef extract, bouillon cubes or capsules, and the like. They are of no use as food except to stimulate a feeble stomach or furnish a spurt of energy, but invaluable for flavoring camp-made soups and stews when you are far away from beef. The powder called Oystero yields an oyster flavor.

"Mustard is useful not only at table but for medicinal purposes; cloves, not only for its more obvious purposes, but to stick in an onion for a stew, and perchance for a toothache.

"Celery and parsley can now be had in dehydrated form. Some sage may be needed for stuffing." Onion and celery salt are real additions to the camp cooking outfit.

"If you aim at cake-making and puddings, ginger and cinnamon may be required. Curry powder is relished by many; its harshness may be tempered with sweet fruits or sugar.

"On short trips, salt and pepper will meet all requirements.

"*Packing Food*—Meat of any kind will quickly mould or spoil if packed in tins from which air is not exhausted.

"Flour should not be carried in the original sacks; they wet through or absorb moisture from the air, snag easily, and burst under the strain of a lashrope. Pack your flour, cereals, vegetables, dried fruits, etc., in the round-bottomed paraffined bags sold by outfitters (various sizes, from 10 lbs. down), which are damp-proof and have the further merit of standing up on their bottoms instead of always falling over. Put a tag on each bag and label it in *ink*. These small bags may then be stowed in 9-inch waterproof canvas provision bags (see outfitters' catalogues), but in that case the thing you want is generally at the bottom. * * *

"Butter, lard, ground coffee, tea, sugar, jam, matches,

go in pry-up tin cans, sold by outfitters (small quantities in mailing tubes), or in common capped tins with tops secured by surgeon's plaster. Get pepper and spices in shaker-top cans, or, if you carry common shakers, cover tops with cloth and snap stout rubber bands around them.

"Often it is well to carry separately enough food to last the party between the jumping-off place and the main camp site, as it saves the bother of breaking bulk en route.

"When transportation is easy it pays to pack the bread, bags of flour, etc., in a tin wash-boiler or two, which are wrapped in burlaps and crated. These make capital grub boxes in camp, securing their contents from wet, insects and rodents. Ants in summer and mice at all times are downright pests of the woods, to say nothing of the wily coon, the predatory mink, the inquisitive skunk, and the fretful porcupine. The boilers are useful, too, on many occasions to catch rain-water, boil clothes, waterproof and dye tents, and so forth.

"*A Last Look Around*—Check off every article in the outfit as it is stowed, and keep the inventory for future reference. Then note what is left over at the end of the trip. This will help in outfitting for the next season."

Camp Cooking

Meat and fish are easy to cook and require few utensils. Steaks or chops require from four to twelve minutes to broil rare over a good bed of live coals, depending on the thickness of the meat. Place either directly on the coals in wire broiler and raise only an inch or two above the fire. Turn after about 1½ minutes, and afterward turn a little oftener to prevent burning.

Chicken or duck of broiling size takes about 20 minutes to broil and requires very particular care in frequent turning to prevent burning. Turn about every ½ minute. As portions of the skin show signs of getting too brown baste them with a few drops of hot water from a large spoon. This also tends to keep them moist. The poultry may be cooked by propping the wire broiler upright six to nine inches from a blazing fire. Often the poultry is started this way and finished over the coals, as this saves considerable time in waiting for the fire to burn down. The chicken or duck may be hung close to the fire by a wire from a slanting pole, revolving frequently. An hour is required to roast poultry.

Stew—Cut meat in small pieces, brown in frying pan (use drippings), remove and place in stew pan in which there is sufficient water to cover stew. Cut vegetables in small pieces, place in frying pan a few minutes—long enough to soften—place in stew pan, season with salt and pepper, cook one-half hour—add flour thickening (water and flour), cover with enough water to prevent stew becoming dry and bury in hot oven for two or three hours.

Broiled Fish—Place in wire broiler, rubbing broiler first with salt pork or lard to prevent sticking, and broil over coals for about 20 minutes. All fish that is broiled should be served with a little butter sauce.

Frying Pan Dishes

Fried Fish—Cut the fish in pieces; that is, serving portions. Roll fish in cornmeal (this is not absolutely necessary). Fry for about 20 minutes (depending upon thickness of fish) over hot fire, in about 2 tablespoons of heated frying oil. Tried-out bacon, salt pork, lard, crisco, or prepared cooking oil may be used.

Fish Balls—Fish balls prepared at home and carried along make good camp food. For group of eight: Ingredients—1 bowl dried codfish soaked several hours in cold water, 1 egg, 2 raw potatoes cut in pieces, 2 ozs. butter, frying oil, 2 tablespoons milk. Boil codfish and potatoes together for about 10 minutes, mash, add 1 beaten egg, butter size of ½ small egg (about 2 ozs.), 2 tablespoons milk and stir thoroughly. This mixture should be about the consistency of stiff oatmeal. Heat small amount of frying oil in pan. Drop batter from large spoon into hot oil. When brown, turn and cook on other side. Each patty should cook about three minutes to the side, about six minutes for the whole.

Fried Ham—Boil in frying pan for about 5 minutes, then pour off water and fry about two minutes on each side.

Fried Bacon—Fry gently until fat is tried out. (Save drippings.) Bacon may also be fried on a hot rock, or cooked on sharp pointed stick with forked ends.

Fried Country Saucage—Fry sausages over moderate fire for about 15 minutes till they are brown.

Corn Beef Hash—Carry with the ingredients already prepared 1 part corned beef, chopped, 2 parts chopped cold boiled potatoes. Melt butter or suet into the frying pan. Fry.

Vegetables

Boiled Potatoes—Clean and scrape potatoes. Do not peel. Have water boiling and salted before putting potatoes in pot and keep water boiling until potatoes are soft. Large ones take about 25 minutes to cook. Plan to serve the meal about 25 minutes after the potatoes are put on the fire, for they are best served hot. When potatoes are cooked, drain water and keep hot until served.

Fried Potatoes—Slice cold boiled potatoes uniformly and fry in hot butter until brown.

Fried Raw Potatoes—Slice raw potatoes uniformly,

boil in frying pan 5 minutes and then fry in butter until brown.

Onions—Boil in salted water 30 minutes until tender. Onions and potatoes go well together and campers should boil them together.

Green Peas—Buy them fresh from a farmer near camp if possible. Reject over-ripe pods. Shell and boil about 20 minutes in salted water, keeping peas barely covered. Drain almost all water when cooked and add one ounce of butter.

Green Corn—Boil corn about five minutes in boiling salted water.

Cocoa

One teaspoonful (level) to each person, ½ cup of water to each person, ½ cup of milk to each person. Cook cocoa in water 5 minutes; add to warm milk and allow it to reach boiling point. *Do not boil.*

Bread

When possible carry along a supply of bread.

Toast—Toast may either be made over coals or by propping wire broiler upright before blazing fire.

"Biscuit Loaf—This is a standard camp bread, because it bakes quickly. It is good so long as it is hot, but it dries out soon and will not keep. For four: 3 pints flour, 3 heaping teaspoonfuls baking powder, 1 heaping teaspoonful salt, 2 heaping tablespoonfuls cold grease, 1 scant pint cold water. Amount of water varies according to quality of flour. Baking powders vary in strength; follow directions on can. Mix thoroughly, with big spoon or wooden paddle, first the baking powder with the flour and then the salt. Rub into this the cold grease (which may be lard, cold pork fat, drippings) until there are no lumps left and no grease adhering to bottom of pan. This is a little tedious, but don't shirk it. Then

stir in the water and work it with spoon until you have
a rather stiff dough. Have the pan greased. Turn the
loaf into it and bake. Test center of loaf with a sliver
when you think it properly done. When no dough ad-
heres remove bread. All hot breads should be broken
with the hand, never cut.

"To freshen any that is left over and dried out, sprinkle
a little water over it and heat through. This can be done
but once."

Washing Dishes

Every part of the camp work should be a pleasure,
and there is no reason whatever that dish washing should
be an exception. If the following directions for dish
washing are followed the work may be so quickly and
perfectly done as to be part of the fun.

1. Each girl should throw scraps from her plate into
a trench or receptacle. Do not throw food scraps on
the camp fire, as they make a disagreeable smoke.

2. Wipe each plate and other utensils as clean as possible with paper napkin, and throw napkin in the fire.

3. Scrape out all cooking pots. If any material has
burned on them, boil them out with one ounce of washing soda to one quart of water.

4. Pile all dishes thus prepared beside the two dish-
pans. Partly fill the dish-pans with boiling water, putting
a heaping teaspoonful of powdered soap in one.

5. Wash dishes with dish mop, and rinse in other pan
of hot water.

If the water is kept hot one girl can keep two busy
drying, and the whole operation for a party of four
should not take over ten minutes. If unskillfully done,
without sufficient hot water or preparation, it is a disagreeable task. Try to make it a pleasant one.

The coffee pot should be frequently boiled out with
washing soda.

The wire broilers may be cleaned by rubbing them with ashes from the camp fire.

In nesting a blackened cooking pail, wrap it in paper to prevent soiling the inside of the pail into which it fits.

Use the fewest dishes possible in cooking and you will lighten your labor.

Use the same plates for different courses, rinsing them with hot water.

Be sure to carry in your dish washing outfit, washing soda, powdered soap and dish mops.

"Dutch Cleanser" is very useful in cleaning dishes, pots and pans.

After washing up for the night, put utensils and provision box together and cover with rubber cloth to protect them from the weather.

Cleaning Up

This is important! If you leave your camping place littered with tin cans, paper, etc., you will be spoiling that place for future campers.

Burn all waste paper and string.

Bury tin cans and empty bottles.

Bury food scraps and refuse.

Be absolutely certain that you have extinguished your fire.

You should take pride in leaving your camp site so clean that not one evidence of your camping remains except the ashes of the fire.

PHOTOGRAPH BY G. CYLDE FISHER.

Climb the mountains and get their good tidings. Nature's peace will flow into you as sunshine flows into trees. The winds will blow their own freshness into you and the storms their energy, while cares will drop off like autumn leaves.

—John Muir.

MOUNTAIN CLIMBING

BY ELOISE ROORBACH, GARDEN EDITOR OF "TOUCHSTONE."

Mountain climbing is the final test of a Girl Scout's perseverance in following a trail, in endurance, courage and woodcraftmanship. Nature reserves her choicest beauties and secrets for those who know how to conquer all difficulties. No Girl Scout's education is complete until she has seen mountain peaks like waves of the sea flashing with white snow foam, piercing the blue sky as far as the eye can reach; clouds forming below her feet; breathed rare air found only in high places; drunk from the pure source of rivers, and heard the mighty roar of waterfalls. A climb to a high mountain top is an experience that will enrich and influence the entire after life of whoever has had the hardihood and wisdom to accomplish it.

Before attempting this last test of scouting the girl must be in perfect physical trim, be able to sleep on the ground, have learned to live simply. Girls should train for this experience by taking graduated hikes. On these hikes the girls can practice using the condensed foods that must be depended upon in mountain climbing. The rations for those who wish to climb to high places must necessarily be condensed, for each Scout must carry her own rations for two weeks.

The foundation of a mountain climber's bill of fare is rice, bacon, cheese, chocolate, raisins, dates, dried fruits, powdered soups, whole wheat crackers, and tea. *Tea should be used instead of coffee*. The eating chocolate is sometimes made into a refreshing drink. Only a small amount of sugar and salt can be carried. This fare is augmented by mushrooms, wild fruit and berries and fish. Watercress is a refreshing addition and a good Scout knows where to find it. Some hardened climbers add a little "jerky" (dried meats) to this bill of fare.

No definite rule of distance to be covered in a day can be laid down. In the high mountains ten or twelve miles a day should be considered a maximum, for part of the benefit to be gained from such a trip is the enjoyment of the trip itself. It is better to go a few miles slowly, observing keenly all the time, stopping for frequent rests to examine a flower, to drink at a clear spring, to feast upon the view, than to cover more ground in a hurried way.

The following is a suggestion for the management of a day in high mountain altitudes. Arise with the sun or a little before breakfast. Breakfast consists of rice, dried fruit (put to soak the night before), bacon, and shredded wheat biscuit. Before packing, make a small package of cheese, chocolate, raisins, and biscuit for the noon lunch that can be reached without having to unpack equipment. There should be a rest of at least an hour at noon, eating slowly, throwing off the pack, and if possible relaxing flat on the back for a while. Then another hike of three or four miles, making camp early in the evening, about 5 o'clock. This divides the day into three periods of hikes with a rest in between. The dinner is like the breakfast, with the addition of soup. Soup can be prepared and eaten while the rice is cooking. Mountain trout can be fried with bacon.

The equipment must be of the lightest. Clothing should consist of one pair of stout, high, waterproof, hob-nailed boots; one pair of light moccasins, to rest the feet in camp; short skirt; middy; riding breeches or bloomers (for in crossing difficult passes skirts must be discarded); hat; gauntlet gloves; one change of underclothes; three pairs of wool stockings; one sweater; one comb (no brush); one small pocket mirror; ivory soap or soap leaves; one tube of cold cream; compass; fishing rod, lines and hooks; rope; leather thongs; stout

GIANT ALASKAN MOOSE

The largest member of the deer tribe. The antlers which are worn
only by the male are shed once a year. Range: This and related
forms found in northern United States, Canada, and Alaska. Courtesy
of American Museum of Natural History.

string; notebook and map; small hatchet; matches (in
waterproof case).

No guns, books or cameras can be carried on a high
hike, for their weight is prohibitive. A sleeping bag
made of eiderdown, lined with canton flannel and covered with oiled silk or duck's back can be rolled and carried across the shoulders. A knife, fork and spoon in
addition to the big sheath knife worn at the belt, one frying pan, tin plate and cup (aluminum should be used in
preference as tin rusts easily), a rice and a soup kettle
are all the cooking utensils needed. If a company of

Girl Scouts attempts a high mountain climb, additional covers of clothing and food can be carried on a pack mule, but this chapter is for those who wish to climb unencumbered with pack animals. It is by far the finest way to see the high mountains, though it must be admitted few have the hardihood or courage to try it. The new Roosevelt National Park, one of the most magnificent playgrounds in the world, can be visited in the way just described.

The writer of this chapter has walked all through this park carrying the clothing, food and equipment just described. Every day of the journey found her in better physical trim, vigor, strength, and with keenness of vision and joy of life increased daily.

BUSY BEAVERS AT WORK

The largest gnawing animal in this country, noted for damming streams with trees (which they cut down by gnawing), mud, and stones. Range: This or related races formerly found practically all over this country, and northward into Canada. Detail from Habitat Group in American Museum of Natural History.

THE RED GODS

Now the Four-way Lodge is opened: Now the hunting
      winds are loose,
   Now the Smokes of Spring go up to clear the brain;
Now the young men's hearts are troubled for the whisper
      of the trues,
   Now the Red Gods make their medicine again!

Who hath seen the beaver busied? Who hath watched
      the black-tail mating?
   Who hath lain alone to hear the wild goose cry?
Who hath worked the chosen waters where the ouana-
      niche is waiting?
   Or the sea-trout's jumping crazy for the fly?

Who hath smelled wood-smoke at twilight? Who
      hath smelled the birch log burning?
   Who is quick to read the noises of the night?

Let him follow with the others, for the young men's feet
      are turning
   To the camps of proved desire and known delight!

Do you know the blackened timber? Do you know that
      racing stream
   With the raw, right-angled log-jam at the end?
And the bar of sun-warmed shingle where a man may
      bask and dream
   To the click of shod canoe-poles round the bend?

It is there that we are going with our rods and reels and
      traces
   To a silent, smoky Indian that we know,
To a couch of new-pulled hemlock with the starlight on
      our faces,
   For the Red Gods call us out and we must go!

He must go—go—go away from here!
  On the other side the world he's overdue.
'Send your road is clear before you when the old spring-
    fret comes o'er you
  And the Red Gods call for you!
                              —Rudyard Kipling.

LOON WITH NEST.
From Group in American Museum of Natural History.

SECTION XV

Nature Study for Girl Scouts

FOREWORD

The following section was specially prepared for the Girl Scouts by Mr. George H. Sherwood, Curator, and Dr. G. Clyde Fisher, Associate Curator, of the Department of Public Education of the American Museum of Natural History. All the illustrations used were supplied by the Museum, and the tests in the various subjects were devised by the same authors.

The American Museum of Natural History in New York conducts special courses of lectures in all of the branches of Natural History, and extends a cordial invitation to all Girl Scouts to visit the Department of Education if wishing help in preparation for their Nature Study tests.

Contents

1. Introduction to Nature Study.
2. Plants: Flowers and Ferns and Trees.
3. Animals: Mammals
   Birds
   Reptiles
   Amphibians
   Fishes
   Invertebrates
4. Geology.

AN EGRET "ROOKERY" IN SOUTH CAROLINA.

The demand for the nuptial plumes of this bird in the millinery trade brought it to the verge of extermination. Range: Temperate and tropical America. Habitat Group in The American Museum of Natural History.

1. Introduction to Nature Study

To the solid ground
Of Nature trusts the mind which builds for aye.
—Wordsworth.

To understand nature is to gain one of the greatest
resources of life.
—John Burroughs.

Nature Study means getting acquainted with the multitude of creatures, great and small, which inhabit the land, the water, and the air, and with the objects which surround them. Mother Nature has many, many secrets which she will reveal to sharp eyes and alert minds. It is, of course, impossible for any one to learn all these secrets, but the mastering of a few makes it easier to learn others, until finally it becomes clear that all life is related and that the humblest creature may be of the greatest importance to the welfare if the highest.

It is for these reasons that the *Girl Scout* should learn as much as possible of the Wonders of Nature. This study may begin wherever you are, but rapid progress will be made by rambles afield and by visits to the great Natural History Museums. For example, a visit to the exhibition halls of the American Museum of Natural History in New York will answer many of your questions about animals you have seen and will enable you to answer many others for yourself, when you go out into the country.

Nature Study in its broadest application includes all of the natural sciences, such as zoology, botany, geology, meteorology, and astronomy. So, there are many fascinating fields for study and enjoyment, and it does not matter much where we begin, whether it be Wild Flowers, Trees, Birds, Butterflies, or Stars.

Of the more practical subjects especially suited to the

THE BULLFROG IN ITS NATURAL SURROUNDINGS

See Snake, Turtle and Dragonfly and notice the tongue of the frog. Habitat Group in Museum of Natural History.

activities of the Girl Scout are those civic problems which can only be solved by team-play; that is, by working together. Among these may be mentioned: The preservation of birds, wild flowers, and forests; control of mosquitoes, house-flies, rats, weeds, diseases of plants and animals, including man.

The civic nature of these problems is appreciated when we realize that it would do little good, for example, for one person to destroy the breeding places of mosquitoes on his premises, if his neighbors did not do likewise about their homes; or for one orchardist to cut out the blight from his pear-trees or the black-knot from his plum-trees, if his neighbors did not co-operate with him by ridding their orchards of these diseases.

These practical questions are so well presented, together with plans for their solution, in *Civic Biology*, by Clifton F. Hodge and Jean Dawson (Ginn & Co.), that instead of going into details here, both the *Girl Scouts* and their Leaders are referred to this most useful work.

All objects of Nature are either living (organic) or non-living (inorganic). The non-living bodies include the minerals and rocks. The living bodies are either plants or animals. Plants may be divided into two great groups, the flowerless plants and flowering plants. In general the flowerless plants reproduce by means of spores, like the mushroom and the ferns, while the flowering plants reproduce by means of seeds.

Animals may be separated into two great groups, those without backbones (invertebrates) like an oyster, a cricket, or an earthworm, and those with backbones, e.g., a dog, a man. In this brief study we shall not go into much detail about invertebrates, but with the backboned animals or vertebrates we shall go a little further. These may be divided into five general groups: (1) Fishes; (2) Amphibians, which include frogs, toads, and

ROCKY MOUNTAIN GOAT

This animal is really not a goat, but is more really related to the antelopes. Range: The higher mountains from Alaska south to California. Group in American Museum of Natural History.

salamanders; (3) Reptiles, which include alligators, crocodiles, turtles, lizards, and snakes; (4) Birds; (5) Mammals.

This simple analysis may be clearly shown by the following diagram:

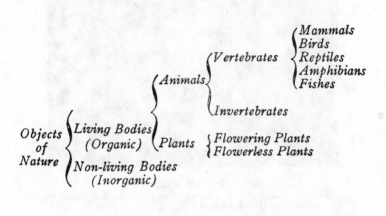

This classification could be carried further at every point, but this will be far enough for present purposes. It should be remembered in any classification that there are no hard and fast lines in Nature. For example, some creatures are on the border-land between plants and animals, and again some animals are between the backboned animals and those without backbones.

GREAT-LEAVED MAGNOLIA.
A forest tree with large solitary white flowers. **Range:** Southern and Southeastern United States.

2. Plants

Wild Flowers and Ferns

Flower in the crannied wall,
I pluck you out of the crannies;
Hold you here, root and all, in my hand,
Little flower—but if I could understand
What you are, root and all, and all in all,
I should know what God and man is.

—Tennyson.

Do you know the earliest spring flower in your neighborhood? In the northern United States it is usually found in bloom before all the snow of winter is gone. In some swamp or along some stream where the snow has melted away in patches it is possible to find the Skunk

TRAILING ARBUTUS

One of our earliest spring flowers, usually growing in patches in sandy or rocky woods. Range: Eastern United States westward to Michigan. Photograph by G. Clyde Fisher.

Cabbage in bloom very early in the spring. See how early you can find it. In the southern United States, one of the earliest spring flowers is the yellow Jessamine, which twines over bushes and trees thus displaying its fragrant, golden bells.

As the season advances, other flowers appear, and we find the Spring Beauty, the Trailing Arbutus, the Blood-root, and the Hepatica. What delightful associations each of these names brings to our minds! By the time summer is here we have an entirely different flower-population in the fields and woods—the Cardinal Flower with its intense red color and the Pink Lady's-Slipper with its drooping moccasin-shaped lip are to be found then. In the autumn we have a different group of flowers still—the Goldenrods, the Asters, and the Fringed Gentian, the

PINK MOCCASIN-FLOWER.

A striking native wild orchid growing in sandy or rocky woods. Range: Newfoundland to North Carolina westward to Minnesota. Photograph by G. Clyde Fisher.

season closing with our latest fall flower, the Witch-hazel.

Some flowers and ferns grow best in the shady woods, others in the sunny fields, some on the rocks and others in the marshes. We soon learn where to look for our favorites. In taking tramps along the roads, across the fields, through the woods, and into the swamps, we would notice along the roadside Bouncing-Bet, Common Yarrow, Dandelion, Thistles, and Goldenrod; in the fields and meadows, we would see the Ox-eye Daisy, Black-eyed Susan, Wild Carrot, and the most beautiful fall flower of the northeastern United States, the Fringed Gentian; in the woods, Mountain Laurel, Pink Azalea, a number of wild Orchids, Maidenhair Fern, and Jack-in-the-Pulpit; in the marshes, Pink Rose-mallow, which reminds us of the Hollyhocks of our Grandmother's garden, Pickerel-weed, Water-lily, and Marsh Marigold.

It is natural to want to know the name of any plant that interests us, and this is important. As in the subject of Birds, there are many helpful books on Flowers and Ferns. Beginners will find "The Flower Guide," by Chester A. Reed (Doubleday, Page & Co.) to be useful. After a good start has been made, such books as Gray's *Manual,* or Britton and Brown's *Illustrated Flora* should be used.

Our pursuit, however, should not stop with the name of a plant. That is a mere beginning. Even slight attention will uncover many fascinating things in the lives of plants. Why can not a farmer raise a good crop of clover-seed without the bumble-bees? What devices are there among the Orchids to bring about cross-pollination? (See "Our Native Orchids," by William Hamilton Gibson). Examine the flower of the wild Blue Flag, and see whether you can determine how the bumble-bee cross-pollinates this plant. Do the Hummingbirds cross-pollinate some flowers? In what plants is the pollen scattered by the wind? Do these plants produce nectar?

How do the various plants scatter their seeds? How are the Hickory-nuts and Walnuts scattered? The

GAILLARDIA OR BLANKET-FLOWER.

Daisy family.   Range: Hills and plains of western United States
and Canada.   Photograph by Albert E. Butler.

Dandelion's and Thistle's seeds have flying-hairs or
parachutes and are blown about by the wind. What
other plants can you find whose seeds are scattered in
the same way? Can you discover a plant whose seeds

BLACK-EYED SUSAN.

A beautiful and abundant flower of the fields.
Range: Eastern North America westward to
the Rocky Mountains. Photograph by G.
Clyde Fisher.

are carried by water? The Witch-hazel shoots its seeds.
What other plants can you find that have explosive
fruits? Cherry-seeds are carried by birds. Mention
some other seeds that are carried in this way. It would
take very little observation to learn how Burdock-burs,
Cockle-burs, Stick-tights, Beggar-lice, Spanish-needles,
and such hooked fruits are scattered.

Learn the names of the principal noxious weeds of
the farm and garden, and also learn the best methods
of combating them.

Learn to know the plants in your vicinity which are
used in the making of drugs.

LOCO-WEED.

A poisonous plant which produces loco-disease in cattle, sheep, and horses that eat it. Range: Plains from Montana to Colorado. Photograph by Albert E. Butler.

Learn to know the poisonous plants around your home and summer camp. Are the following to be found there: Poison Ivy, Poison Sumach, Loco-weed, Bitter-

SHOWY PRIMROSE.

Not a true Primrose, but a member of the Evening Primrose Family.
Range: Prairies of western United States and northern Mexico; also
naturalized farther east. Photograph by Mr. and Mrs. Leo E. Miller.

sweet (*Salanum Dulcamara*), Black Nightshade, Jim-
son-weed, Poke-weed, Poison Hemlock?

Trees

He who wanders widest lifts
No more of beauty's jealous veils,
Than he who from his doorway sees
The miracle of flowers and trees.

—*Whittier.*

The trees of the forest are of two classes, deciduous
trees and evergreen trees. To the former belong those
which shed their leaves in the fall, are bare in the winter, and then grow a new crop of leaves in the spring,
e.g., oaks, elms, maples. The evergreen trees shed their
leaves also, but not all at one time. In fact, they always

RHODODENDRON OR GREAT LAUREL.

A tall shrub, or sometimes a tree, growing in woods and along streams. Range: Eastern North America from Nova Scotia to Georgia. Photograph by Albert E. Butler.

have a goodly number of leaves, and are consequently green all the year round, e.g., pines, spruces, firs.

The uses of wood are so many and various that we

CHRISTMAS FERN.

An evergreen fern growing in woods and rocky places. Range:
Eastern United States and Canada. Photograph by Mary C. Dickerson.

can only begin to mention them. In looking about us
we see wood used in building houses, in making furniture, for railroad ties, and for shoring timbers in mines.
In many country districts wood is used for fuel. And
do you realize that only a short time ago the newspaper
which you read this morning and the book which you
now hold in your hand were parts of growing trees in
the forest? Paper is made of wood-pulp, mostly from
Spruce.

Besides the direct uses of wood, we turn to the forest
for many interesting and valuable products, varying in
importance from a balsam-pillow filled with the fragrant leaves or needles of the Balsam Fir, to turpentine
and rosin (naval stores), produced chiefly by the Long-
leaved Pine of the Southeastern States. Spruce gum is
obtained from the Black Spruce and Red Spruce. Canada balsam used in cementing lenses together in micro-

IN A TURPENTINE GROVE.

The Long-leaved Pine furnishes most of the turpentine and rosin of commerce. Range: Virginia to Florida and Texas. Photograph by G. Clyde Fisher.

scopes, telescopes, and the like, comes from the Balsam Fir. Bark for tanning comes from Oak and Hemlock. The Indians of the Eastern Woodlands or Great Lakes area made canoes and many other useful articles of the bark of the Canoe or Paper Birch. Baskets are made from Willow twigs. Maple sugar comes chiefly from the Sugar Maple.

The turpentine industry is the chief one in parts of the South where the Long-leaved Pine thrives. The United States produces more turpentine and rosin than any other country in the world. The turpentine is used in paints and in various arts. The rosin is used in varnish, laundry soap, etc. These two products come from the sap or "gum" of the pine tree. The sap is secured by tapping or "boxing" the tree, and then keeping the cut ducts of the sap-wood open by "chipping" or "pull-

BLACK SUGAR MAPLE.

The sap of this tree, as well as the more common Sugar Maple, is the source of maple sugar. Range: Eastern United States and southeastern Canada.

ing," that is, by putting a new "streak" on the tree. This has to be done once a week from March 1 to November 1. The sap used to be collected in a "box" or deep notch cut in the base of the tree, but the modern method is to have it run into cups made of zinc or of burned clay similar to flower-pots. The sap is taken to a turpentine-

COMMON FALL MUSHROOM.

An excellent article of food growing commonly in old pasture fields.
Range: Temperate and tropical regions all over the world. Photograph by G. Clyde Fisher.

still where it is heated over a furnace. This drives off
the turpentine or "spirits" as steam or vapor, which is
condensed to liquid again by passing through the worm
of the still surrounded by cold water. The rosin or
resin is left behind.

The Sugar Maple grows from Florida and Texas
northward to Manitoba and Quebec, but it is only in the
northern part of its range that the maple sugar industry
thrives. This delicious food is one of the many that
we learned to utilize from the Indians. The sap is obtained by tapping the tree in the spring before the leaves
come out, the best weather for the flow of sap being
that when it freezes at night and thaws in the daytime.
The sap is boiled down; that is, the water is driven off
and the sugar remains. It takes about three gallons, or
a little more, of sap to make a pound of maple sugar.

Three to four pounds of sugar is an average yield for one tree in a season. Much of the sap, however, is not boiled down into sugar, but the boiling is stopped while it is in the form of syrup. If you have ever eaten buckwheat cakes with real maple syrup you will always esteem the Sugar Maple tree.

The forests perform extremely valuable services for mankind entirely apart from the products they yield.

First, they prevent erosion, or the washing away of soil by the water that falls as rain. After the trees have been cut away, very often, especially upon hillsides, the most productive soil is washed away, usually clear off of the original owner's farm, and deposited in the flood-plains or bottoms of creeks and rivers or in river deltas —in places where it cannot be utilized to any great extent. Thus erosion causes a tremendous loss to farmers, and it is chiefly due to the thoughtlessness of the American people in destroying the forests.

Second, and chiefly related to this, is the fact that the floods upon our rivers, which every year take such heavy toll in property and in human life, are due to the cutting away of the forests. This allows the water from rain and melting snow to reach the streams at times faster than it can be carried off, and so we have a flood. The forest floor, with its undergrowth and humus, in those localities where the forests still exist about the headwaters of our rivers, acts like a huge layer of blotting paper which holds the water back and allows it to escape to the streams slowly, and so floods are avoided.

Third, and related to the above, is the fact that the water supply of our cities would be more constant if the forests had not been cut away. In these cases the summer droughts make much greater the danger from water-borne diseases.

It is only in recent years that the American people

WESTERN YELLOW PINE.

A magnificent tree which furnishes valuable timber. Range: Hills and mountains of western United States. Photograph by Albert E. Butler.

ROADS THROUGH THE ASPENS.

Range: Northern United States and Canada, south in the Rocky Mountains to Mexico. Photograph by Albert E. Butler.

have begun to realize the necessity of the conservation of our forests, and in many sections much has been done to redeem the criminal thoughtlessness in destroying our forests and to restore those devastated by forest fires. Reforestation operations have accomplished a great deal, and the organization to prevent forest fires emphasizes

BALD CYPRESS DRAPED WITH SPANISH "MOSS."

This tree is almost entirely hidden by this "moss," which is really a flowering plant of the Pineapple family. Range: In swamps and along rivers from Delaware to Florida, west to Texas, north to Missouri and southern Indiana. Photograph by G. Clyde Fisher.

the old adage that "an ounce of prevention is worth a pound of cure." Also the people are being taught correct forestry practices, such as cutting only ripe trees and allowing the rest to grow, instead of clearing the land entirely, as was formerly done so universally.

The life history of every tree is interesting; how it breathes by means of its leaves, just as the animals do by means of gills or lungs; how it manufactures starch by means of the green matter in the leaves; how the starch is changed to sugar and other substances which are carried to other parts of the tree in the sap; how the sap flows upward in the vessels in the sap-wood and downward in the vessels of the inner bark; how the entire heart-wood of a tree is dead and the only living part is the sap-wood and the innermost bark.

One of the first things we shall want to know when we get out into the woods is the name of the tree that interests us. For this purpose the books given as references under "Trees" will be useful.

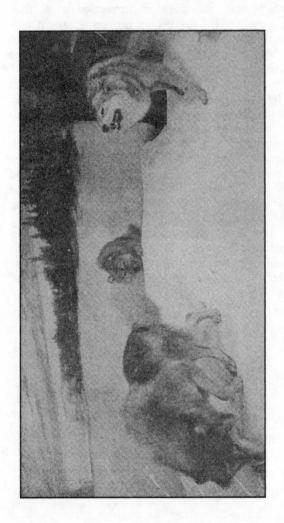

TIMBER WOLVES ON THE TRAIL

Closely related to foxes and dogs. Range: Formerly over most of North America. Habitat Group in American Museum of Natural History.

BABY OPOSSUMS RIDING ON THEIR MOTHER'S BACK.

For the first few weeks after they are born the mother carries her babies in her pocket; later they ride on her back holding on by clinging to her fur with their paws and by wrapping their tails about that of their mother. Range: Middle and Southern States. From Group in American Museum of Natural History.

3. ANIMALS

Mammals

Mammals differ from birds in that they have hair instead of feathers, and that they are first fed upon milk produced by the mother. Unfortunately the mammals are usually called simply *animals,* but the latter is obviously too inclusive a term and should not be used in this way. There is no reason why the name *mammal* should not be commonly used, just as *birds, reptiles, amphibians,* and *fishes* are used for the other groups of backboned animals.

In the United States the lowest or most primitive mammal is the Opossum. The baby Opossums—from six to a dozen of them—are born when very small and

NEW YORK WEASEL IN SUMMER PELAGE

OTTER WITH ITS FAVORITE FOOD

The Otter belongs to the Weasel family, and feeds almost entirely upon fish. Range: This and related varieties over Northern and Eastern North America. From Group in American Museum of Natural History.

NEW YORK WEASEL IN WINTER.

A blood-thirsty cousin of the Otter and the Mink. Range: This and related species found all over United States and Canada. Habitat Group in American Museum of Natural History.

undeveloped and are immediately placed by the mother in an external pouch, where they continue to grow until they are too large to get into their mother's pocket; then they frequently ride upon their mother's back, clinging to her fur with their finger-like toes and wrapping their tails about their mother's tail. The Opossum is the only animal in this country the young of which are carried around in the mother's pocket, and the only one which has a prehensile tail; that is, one used for coiling around and clinging to branches, and the like. Its food is various, consisting of both animal and plant material—insects, young birds, pawpaws, persimmons, etc. In the

RACCOON AT ENTRANCE TO ITS DEN IN A HOLLOW TREE
A near relative of the bears. Note the black face-mark and the ringed tail. Range: This or a related variety occurs in all parts of United States. Photograph from American Museum of Natural History.

food devoured the Opossum probably does more good than harm.

In their food habits many mammals are decidedly injurious. Rats, Weasels, Minks, and Foxes destroy poultry; Wolves and Pumas kill domestic and game animals; Woodchucks or Groundhogs eat clover and various garden plants; Moles damage the lawns; Rats, Mice, and Gophers spoil and devour grain; Mice and Rabbits girdle fruit trees, thus killing them.

On the other hand, many mammals furnish food; e. g., Rabbits, Elk, and Deer. This was more important in pioneer times than at present. Many furnish furs used as articles of clothing; e. g., Raccoon, Fox, Muskrat, Mink, Otter, Marten, Mole, New York Weasel and other northern weasels in their winter coats.

POLAR BEAR
An expert swimmer. Feeds upon seals, fish, ar.d other animal food.
Range: Arctic regions of the world. Habitat Group in American
Museum of Natural History.

Many furs are usually sold under trade names that
are entirely different from the true name of the animal. A list of a few fur-bearing mammals of the
United States having trade names differing from the
true names follows:

The True Fur	*The Trade Name*
Dark blended Muskrat	Russian Otter
Mink blended Muskrat	River Mink
Natural Muskrat*	Natural River Mink
Natural Jersey Muskrat	River Sable
Plucked and Seal-dyed Muskrat	Hudson Seal
Plucked and Seal-dyed Muskrat	Aleutian Seal
Skunk	Black Marten
Striped Skunk	Civet Cat
N. Y. Weasel in winter pelage	Ermine

*Muskrat fur is now also sold under its true name.

SKUNKS—MOTHER AND YOUNG HUNTING FOR GRASSHOPPERS AND CRICKETS

Noted for its ability to emit a most unpleasant odor when disturbed.   Range: Eastern North America.
Portion of Group in American Museum of Natural History.

MINK

A cousin of the Weasel and Otter, the Mink feeds upon frogs, cray-fish, mice, bird's eggs, etc. Range: This and closely related forms over most of United States, Canada, and Alaska. From Group in American Museum of Natural History.

A few suggestions for observation or study:

1. What peculiar instinct or habit has the Opossum developed?
2. How does the flight of a Bat differ from that of a Flying Squirrel?
3. Can you notice any peculiarity in the Rabbit's track?
4. Mention three mammals that hibernate.
5. Describe the methods of defense in the following mammals: Armadillo, Porcupine, Skunk.
6. Why do the front teeth of the Squirrel and the Beaver continue to grow?

The best way to find the answers to these questions is by actual observation of the animals, but when this is impossible, the references given under "Mammals" will be found useful.

RED FOX RETURNING TO ITS YOUNG FROM SOME FARM-ER'S HEN-ROOST

The Cross Fox, the Silver Fox, and the Black Fox are color phases of the Red Fox, and not different species. Range: Northern North America south to Georgia. Habitat Group in American Museum of Natural History.

BALD EAGLE
The American Eagle, the Emblem of our country
Range: United States

Birds

*He who takes the first step in ornithology is
ticketed for the whole trip.—John Burroughs.*

The love of the beautiful seems to be innate; that is,
born in us. And the birds appeal to this in at least two
ways: First, on account of the beauty of their songs,

A GREBE COLONY IN SASKATCHEWAN

Showing the Western Grebe and the smaller Eared Grebe. Note the young Grebe riding on its mother's back. Another parent is covering its eggs preparatory to leaving the nest. Range of both these species: Western North America. Habitat Group in the American Museum of Natural History.

SCREECH OWL
The Screech Owl feeds largely upon mice and other destructive rodents
Range: Eastern North America

and second, on account of the beauty of their plumage.

Among the birds that have especially beautiful songs are the Thrushes, which include the Robin and the Bluebird, the finest singer in this family probably being the Hermit Thrush. In the Southern States there is no more popular singer among the birds than the Mockingbird. But it should be remembered that a bird's song cannot be separated from the associations which it calls up in one's memory. So that the performance of an ordinary

SANDHILL CRANES IN FLORIDA

Unlike the Herons, these birds fly with neck fully extended. Their loud, resonant trumpeting is as characteristic as the hawking of Wild Geese. Range: North America. Habitat Group in The American Museum of Natural History.

GREAT HORNED OWL

Rabbits constitute a favorite food when available.
Poultry and other birds are also destroyed by
this owl. Range: Eastern North America.

songster may be more pleasing to one than that of some
finer one because of youthful associations.

It seems to be a general law of nature that the finest
songsters have the plainest coats.

Among the birds that we enjoy on account of their
beautiful plumage are the Egrets, every feather of their

BROWN PELICANS IN FLORIDA

The Pelicans nest in colonies, and the young feed from the parents' throats.   Range: Gulf coast of U. S. and southward.   Habitat Group in The American Museum of Natural History.

EGRETS: PARENT BIRDS

coats being as white as snow, and the plumes of these birds are so beautiful, and human beings have been so thoughtless that the Egrets have been almost exterminated in order to supply the millinery trade. These plumes, known as aigrettes, grow on the backs between the shoulders of both the male and female birds, and are worn only during the nesting season. The only time during the nesting season that the plume hunter finds it profitable to hunt these birds is when the young are in the nest. At any other time the birds would be so wild that the plume hunter could not easily shoot them. When the young are in the nest the parental love is so strong that the adult birds cannot resist the instinct to return to feed the nestlings when they are begging for food. In this way both the father bird and the mother bird become an easy prey

GOLDEN PLOVER

The Golden Plover makes the longest single flight known to be made by any bird in migration,—that is, 2,500 miles from Nova Scotia across the open ocean to South America. Range: North and South America.

for the ambushed plume hunter, and there is but one thing that can happen to the baby Egrets in the nest after both of their parents have been killed—they starve to death. This is one of the most cruel phases of the plume trade, and there is no other way to secure the aigrette plumes of the Egrets than by killing the adult birds. Fortunately, in the United States it is against the law to shoot these birds, and it is against the law to import the plumes. Until recently it has not been illegal to wear these plumes, and the fact that there are still a few women who adorn their hats with them has encouraged the illegal and cruel killing of these birds in our country, or the smuggling in of the plumes from some other country. In the latter part of 1919 the federal regulations have been interpreted to make it

BOBOLINK
During the autumn migration this bird is the Reedbird or Ricebird
Range: North and South America

illegal to possess aigrette plumes, and henceforth the law will be so enforced. This is the successful culmination of a long fight by the Audubon Society.

A few other birds of striking plumage are the Bluejay, the Bluebird, the Baltimore Oriole, the Scarlet Tanager, the Cedar Waxwing, and the Red-winged Blackbird.

Turning from the esthetic value of birds, which depends, among other things, upon the beauty of their songs and the beauty of their plumage, we may consider the value of birds in dollars and cents.

Every farmer and gardener must cultivate his crops

WILD TURKEY IN WEST VIRGINIA

Our most magnificent game-bird. Note how much the young resembles the dead leaves. Range: Eastern United States west to Nebraska and Texas. Habitat Group in The American Museum of Natural History.

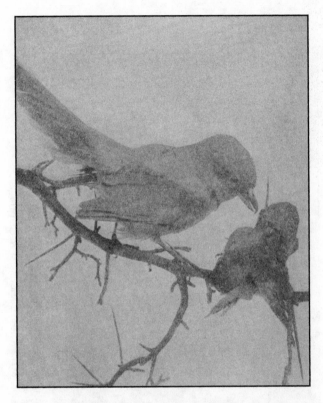

NORTHERN SHRIKE IMPALING A HOUSE SPARROW UPON
A THORN
The habit illustrated here has given the Shrike the name of Butcher-
bird. It is surprising to find a song-bird with the habits of a bird of
prey. Range: Northern North America.

and fight the weeds which are always crowding out the
plants he is trying to raise, and in this fight he is helped
by a great many birds of various kinds. Among these
are the Mourning Dove, the Bob-White, and members
of the Sparrow family, such as the Goldfinch, the Junco,

DUCK HAWKS ON THE PALISADES OF THE HUDSON
The "Noble Peregrine" of falconry carrying a pigeon to its young. Range: North and South America. Habitat Group in The American Museum of Natural History.

A KILLDEER FAMILY

This plover is common in meadows, cultivated fields, and about ponds and lakes. It gets its name from its note. Range: North and South America.

and the Song Sparrow. In this country, in the aggregate, these seed-eating birds destroy every year tons of seeds of noxious weeds, and are therefore valuable friends of the gardener and farmer. For more definite data see bulletins published by the U. S. Department of Agriculture, or "Useful Birds and Their Protection," by Edward Howe Forbush (Massachusetts Board of Agriculture).

Thousands of bushels of grain are eaten or spoiled by small mammals, such as mice, rats, and spermophiles or gophers. To the relief of the farmer, many birds feed upon these destructive little rodents. The Crow occasionally captures a mouse, while the Shrikes or Butcher-birds catch a great many. The Screech Owl feeds largely upon mice. The Red-tailed Hawk is called the Hen-hawk or Chicken-hawk by most farmers,

STARLING

Introduced 1890 into New York City; since spread over northestern states. Range: Western and central Europe, New England and Middle Atlantic States.

but this is very unfair to the bird, for its principal food is mice. In fact, most of the Hawks and Owls of the United States are really valuable friends of the farmer because of the injurious rodents which they devour. (See *"Hawks and Owls of the United States,"* by A. K. Fisher.)

To be fair, it must be admitted that there are a few exceptions; that is, that there are a few Hawks and Owls which do more harm than good. The Sharp-shinned Hawk kills many harmless songbirds and occasionally young game birds and young chickens. The Cooper's Hawk, which nests throughout the United States, is a real chicken hawk, and the worst one in the country. The Duck Hawk, the "Noble Peregrine" of falconry, in this country feeds largely upon domestic pigeons, but no bird student would wish to see it exterminated on account of this habit.

There are a number of birds which are valuable friends to all the people because they are scavengers. The Herring Gull, which is the commonest gull of the harbors of the United States, and which is also found on inland lakes and rivers, by feeding upon all kinds of refuse animal and plant materials makes the waters about our cities more healthful. This is especially true of the coast cities which dump their garbage into the waters not far distant. The Turkey Vulture, the Black Vulture or Carrion-Crow, and the California Condor make the fields and woods of the country more healthful by devouring the carcasses of animals, and the first two species eat the offal from slaughter houses and even scraps of meat from the markets in some of our Southern cities.

The most valuable group of birds from the standpoint of the farmers, the orchardists, and the gardeners

COMMON TERN
A close relative of the gulls
Range: Northern Hemisphere, northern South America, and Africa

GREAT BLUE HERON
Frequently miscalled Blue "Crane." The long legs indicate that this is a wading bird. Range: Western Hemisphere.

is the insect-eating birds. Among these are the Wood Pewee, the Phoebe, the Kingbird, and all of the Flycatchers; the Purple Martin and all of the Swallows; the Nighthawk and Whip-poor-will. The Yellow-billed and Black-billed Cuckoos and the Baltimore Oriole feed largely upon tent caterpillars and other caterpillars which defoliate the fruit and shade trees. The Sparrow Hawk has been wrongly named, for it eats a thousand times as many grasshoppers as it does sparrows. The Chickadees, Brown Creepers, and many of the Warblers feed largely upon insects and insect eggs which they glean chiefly from the trees. The Rose-breasted Grosbeak and the Bob-White eat the Colorado potato-beetle. In the West the Franklin's Gull follows the farmer in the fields and picks up great numbers of destructive insects.

In learning the value of our feathered friends it is necessary to learn to know the birds, and in this quest great help can be obtained from books. Beginners will find the following useful:

"Land Birds East of the Rockies," by Chester A. Reed.

"Water and Game Birds," by Chester A. Reed.

"Western Bird Guide," by Chester A. Reed. (All published by Doubleday, Page & Co.)

For more advanced students the following are recommended:

"Handbook of Birds of Eastern North America," by Frank M. Chapman (D. Appleton & Co.).

"Handbook of Birds of Western United States," by Florence Merriam Bailey (Houghton, Mifflin & Co.)

Our study of birds should not stop with the name, because we shall find many things of interest in the home life of birds, many things that seem to reflect our own lives. (See "Home Life of Wild Birds," by F. H. Herrick. G. P. Putnam's Sons.)

If we like to hear birds sing, if we enjoy the beauty of their coats, and if they are valuable neighbors from the standpoint of dollars and cents, then it is worth while to consider how we may have more of them about our homes. Every girl can do a great deal to attract birds.

First, by putting up nesting boxes. Since the people of our country have destroyed so much of our native forests and undergrowth, have drained so many of our swamps, and have cultivated so much of the grassy prairie, many birds have difficulty in finding suitable places to nest. This can be remedied in the case of birds that nest in cavities, such as the House Wren, Tree Swallow, Purple Martin, Screech Owl, Chicka-dee, and Bluebird, by putting up nesting boxes. For those that nest in shrubbery, like the Catbird and the Brown Thrasher, shrubs and vines may be planted so that the desirable tangle may be had.

Second, by putting out bird baths. In this improved country of ours, there are doubtless large areas in which

A MOTHER MALLARD AND HER FAMILY
The Wild Mallard is the original of many of the domesticated ducks
Range: Northern Hemisphere

wild birds have difficulty in finding suitable places to bathe. Artificial bird baths are more attractive to birds in the summer time than during cold weather, but they will be used even in winter if kept free from ice. Do not place a bird bath so close to a shrub, tree, or building that a house cat may stalk the birds from behind it. The house cat is probably the worst enemy of our native songbirds.

Third, by establishing feeding stations, especially in winter when snow covers the natural food of so many birds. When birds have enough to eat they rarely suffer severely from the cold.

Fourth, by cooperating with the authorities in seeing that the laws protecting the birds are enforced.

The Audubon Society has done much effective work along these lines, and a Girl Scout should join this society, whose headquarters are 1974 Broadway, New York City.

Amphibians

All nature is so full that that district produces the greatest variety which is most examined.
—Gilbert White, Natural History of Selborne.

The group of back-boned animals next above the fishes is the Amphibians, which includes the frogs, toads, salamanders,* and their relatives. The name "amphibian" refers to two modes of life as shown by most of the frogs and toads. A good example is the Common Toad, whose eggs are laid in the water. These eggs hatch out not into toads, but into tadpoles, which have no legs and which breathe by means of gills, as the fishes do. They grow rapidly, develop a pair of hind legs and then a pair

---

*Unfortunately in the Southern States there is an entirely different animal commonly called a "Salamander" which is in reality a pocket-gopher of the group of mammals.

TOAD

A valuable animal in the garden because of the insects which it eats. Range: Eastern United States. Photograph by Herbert Lang.

of front legs, while the tail and gills are absorbed, all within a little more than a month from the time the eggs are laid. During this change a pair of lungs is developed, so that the toads breathe air like human beings do. The eggs of toads and frogs may be collected in the spring in ponds, and this remarkable change from the egg through the tadpole stage to the adult form may be observed in a simple home aquarium. Toads' eggs may be distinguished from those of frogs by the fact that toads' eggs are laid in strings, while frogs' eggs are laid in masses.

Every Girl Scout should know the song of the toad. William Hamilton Gibson says it is "the sweetest sound in nature." (*Sharp Eyes,* p. 54.) If you do not know it, take a lantern or electric flash-lamp after dark some evening in the spring at egg-laying time, and go to the edge of some pond and see the toad sing. Notice how the throat is puffed out while the note is being produced.

BULLFROG

The largest of our frogs, remarkable for its sonorous bass notes. Range: Eastern United States westward to Kansas. Photograph by Herbert Lang.

The belief that warts are caused by handling toads has no foundation in fact.

The toad is a valuable friend of the gardener, for it feeds upon a great variety of destructive insects.

The life of our Salamanders is very similar to that of the frogs and toads. The eggs hatch out into tadpoles, then legs are developed, but the tail is not absorbed. Unlike the frogs and toads, the Salamander keeps its tail throughout life, and in some kinds of Salamanders which spend all of their time in the water, the gills are used throughout life. Salamanders have various common names, some being called newts, others water-dogs or mud-puppies. The mud-eel and the Congo "snake" of the Southern States, and the "hell-bender" of the Ohio valley and south are all Salamanders. The

SPRING PEEPER
The note of this piping hyla is a welcome
sound about the ponds and swamps in early
spring.   Range: Eastern   United   States.
Photograph by Herbert Lang.

belief that any of the Salamanders is poisonous is a
myth and has no basis in fact.

Reptiles

Reptiles include Alligators, Crocodiles, Turtles, Lizards and Snakes. It is commonly said that reptiles are cold-blooded. This means that the temperature of their blood varies and is the same as the surrounding medium. The temperature of an Alligator that has been floating with its nose out of the water is the same as the surrounding water. The temperature of a turtle in the

GILA MONSTER
So called from the Gila River in Arizona. The only member of the
lizard family known to be venomous except the very similar
crust-lizard found in Mexico.

winter time is the same as the mud in which it is buried,
while in the summer time it is much higher. What is
true of the reptiles in respect to temperature is also true
of Amphibians and Fishes. However, this is not true
of Birds and Mammals, for these have a uniform temperature so high that they are called warm-blooded.

In the United States there is but one species of Alligator and but one species of Crocodile, both limited to
the Southeastern States.

There are about fifty kinds of Turtles and Tortoises
in North America, some of which live on the land and
feed largely upon plants, *e. g.*, the Common Box Turtle,
found from the New England States to South Carolina and westward to Kansas, and the Gopher Tortoise
of the Southern States. Others are aquatic, like the
Painted Turtles, which are found in one form or another practically all over the United States.

Many of these reptiles are highly prized as food, *e. g.*,
Diamond-backed Terrapin, Soft-shelled Turtle, Snapping Turtle and Gopher Tortoise.

COMMON BOX TORTOISE
Range: Eastern United States

There are about one hundred species of Lizards in North America, the greatest number being found in the drier parts of the continent. Of this whole number only two species are poisonous, and only one of these, the Gila Monster, is found within the United States, being confined in its range to desert regions of Southern Arizona and New Mexico.

The Blue-tailed Lizard or Skink, which occurs from Massachusetts to Florida and westward to Central Texas, is commonly believed to be poisonous in the Southern States, where it is called the Red-headed "Scorpion," but this is one of the popular myths still too common among intelligent people.

The Glass "Snake" of the Central and Southern States is a peculiar lizard in that it has no legs. That it is able, after being broken to pieces, to collect itself together again and continue to live is another old myth.

DIAMOND-BACKED TERRAPIN

About a dozen kinds of Horned "Toads" are found in the western portions of the United States. Although toad-like in the shape of their bodies and in some of their habits, they are really lizards.

The American Chameleon or "Green" Lizard, which ranges in this country in the coastal regions from North Carolina to the Rio Grande River, has a remarkable power of changing the color of its skin through shades of brown, gray, and green. In fact, it is said to rival or possibly excel the true chameleons of the Old World.

For treatment of the Snakes see Woodcraft section.

FISHES

"It is not all of fishing to fish."

The fishes are the lowest of the true vertebrates or animals with backbones, and all live in the water. They do not have lungs, but breath through gills on the sides of the head. They are cold blooded animals; i. e., the temperature of the blood is the same as that of the water

PADDLE-FISH

So-called from the paddle-like or sponge-shaped snout. Eggs used for caviar. Range: The Mississippi River and its tributaries.

COMMON CATFISH
The barbels which suggest the whiskers of a cat are responsible
for the name. This fish has no scales. Range: Eastern and Central
United States.

in which they are living. Fishes are found in both fresh
and salt water all over the world and have adopted themselves to many conditions; for example, certain fishes
have lived in caves so long that they are blind; some live
in the coldest water, while others can revel in the heat
of the hot springs.

Many fishes are valuable as food and the fisheries are
extensive industries, in which large sums of money are
invested.

There are four great groups of fishes:

1. The sharks and rays, with cartilaginous skeletons.
2. The ganoids of which the sturgeon and garpike are
   examples, with heavy plates or scales.
3. The bony fishes—salmon, pickerel, mackerel, cod,
   halibut, etc.
4. The lung fishes, that live partly in air.

There are many species of sharks. Among the more
common ones in Atlantic waters are the Smooth Dogfish
which has pavement-like teeth; the Sand Shark with cat-
like teeth; the Hammerhead Shark with its eyes on
stalks. The near relatives of the sharks are the Skates,

SHOVEL-NOSED STURGEON

This fish is covered with bony plates instead of scales. The roe is made into caviar
Range: Upper and middle Mississippi Valley

the Sting-Rays and the Torpedo. The Sturgeon is the most common example of the ganoid fish. They are all heavily clad with a bony armor. Most of the fishes that we find, however, belong to the third group, i. e., bony fishes. Among the salt-water species, the cod, the halibut, the mackerel, and the bluefish are especially valuable as food. Of the salt-water fishes that go up the rivers into fresh water to breed, the salmon and the shad are widely known. Of the strictly fresh-water fish, the sunfish and catfish are very common. Among the game-fish are the trout, bass, pickerel, and salmon.

For those who live in cities, a convenient place to begin the study of fishes is in the fish-market. Here we may learn to know the common food-fishes by name, and to know many interesting things about them. If there is a Public Aquarium or a Natural History Museum in your city, you can use it in connection with the fish-market. Especially valuable in Museums are the habitat groups of fishes, that is, those in which the fishes are shown in their natural surroundings. But, best of all, the place to study fishes, as is true of all other animals, is out-of-doors in their native haunts. With your dip-net or hook and line, catch the fish, and then by the aid of one of the books listed below find out what its name is. Then, by observation of the fish see what is interesting in its life-history. Find out where the mother-fish lays her eggs. Does either parent guard them? Has the fish any natural weapons of defense? If so, what are they? Does either parent care for the young after they are hatched? What does the fish feed upon? In what way is the fish protectively colored. In the study of fishes, an interesting means is the home aquarium. Any Girl Scout can easily learn how to install and maintain a balanced aquarium, that is, one in which the water does not have to be changed and in fact should not be changed. In such an aquarium, one may keep and study a great variety of fishes. Some of our local fishes, such as young catfish and suckers, will prove fully as interesting as the goldfish, and many other animals besides fishes will thrive in a small aquarium, such as tadpoles of frogs, toads, and salamanders, adult water-newts, soft-shelled turtles, snails, water-beetles, and nymphs of dragon-flies.

HAMMERHEAD SHARK

The eyes are on the ends of blunt stalks, or extensions of the sides of the head, which suggest the name. Range: All warm seas, north to Cape Cod.

A GARDEN UNDER WATER
Starfishes, Crabs and Sea-anemones

SQUID
Member of same family as Octupus, and is related to the Oyster. Has ink bag for protection.

Animals Without Backbones

In general the Invertebrates are animals without a
backbone; that is, they do not have an internal supporting skeleton of bone, as does the dog or cat. Compared
with mammals or birds, they are all small, and some
are so very tiny that they can be seen only with a very
powerful microscope. Most of them live in the water
or in mud or sand under the water. Hence the best
place to get acquainted with them is along the seashore
or near some lake or stream.

There are several different groups of Invertebrates
and between these groups there are greater differences

SNAILS AND THEIR TRACKS ON THE SEA-BEACH

of structure than there is between a horse and a hummingbird. The principal groups are:

1. The Protozoa, or one-celled animals (nearly all microscopic).
2. The Sponges.
3. The Jellyfishes, Sea-anemones, and Corals.
4. Worms of several groups.
5. Starfishes, Sea-urchins, and Sea-cucumbers.
6. Segmented Worms.
7. Crabs, Lobsters, etc.
8. Oysters, Snails, and Octopi.
9. Insects and Spiders.

Seashore Life

Because of their connection with our industries or our food supply, some of the Invertebrates are familiar

JELLY FISH

to all; for instance, sponges, corals, starfishes, crabs, shrimps, lobsters, clams, and oysters. Others are seldom seen unless one takes pains to look for them.

All life comes from pre-existing life. So every animal living to-day has come from some other living animal and every plant living to-day has come from some other previously living plant. It is believed that the first forms of life came from the water. At any rate, the oldest and lowest forms of life to-day, the Protozoa, are found in the water. As these are nearly all very minute and can be studied only with a microscope, they are omitted from the suggested field work.

All who have access to the seashore have a wonderful opportunity to study the Invertebrates. The long stretches

ANIMALS OF THE WHARF-PILES
Habitat Group in the American Museum of Natural History

of sandy beach, the sections of shore covered with water-rolled pebbles and stones, even the steep, jagged cliffs, are all peopled with these animals of the sea. Twice every twenty-four hours the sea water creeps slowly up the beach until high water is reached, and twice every twenty-four hours it recedes again toward the ocean. It is therefore about twelve hours from one low water to the next. On a gently sloping beach, the distances between the high water mark and the low water mark may be many hundreds of feet, while on a steep beach or a straight cliff this area may be only a few feet in width. It is this area between the high and low water marks that is the haunt of many Invertebrates. These are animals that can live if they are not continually covered with water. Here are the rock barnacles, the soft clams, crabs of many kinds, beach fleas, numerous sea worms in their special houses, snails, and hermit crabs. Others will be found in the pools between the rocks or in the crevasses of the cliffs, which as the tide falls become great natural aquaria. Here will be found hydroids, sea-anemones, starfishes, sea-urchins, phores, hydroids, eggs of fish, tiny copepods, the larvae or young of sea-urchins, starfishes, or oysters. If an old wharf is near by, examine the posts supporting it. The pilings seem to be coated with a shaggy moss of seaweed. Scrape some of this off and put in a dish of water. Sea-spiders, starfishes, hydroids that look like moss, sea-anemones, many varieties of worms, mussels, and crabs are all living here.

Begin your study of these seashore animals with a stroll along the beach. Examine the windrows of sea-wrack or seaweed. Whole troops of sandhoppers rise ahead of you. Oftentimes animals from distant shores or deep water will be found. The empty shells have many a story to tell. The papery egg-cases of the peri-

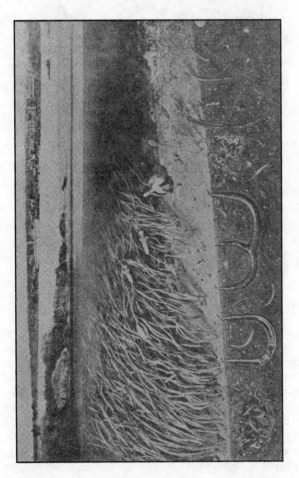

UNDER THE SEA BED
Marine Worms, Whelk, Pecten or Scallop and Periwinkle

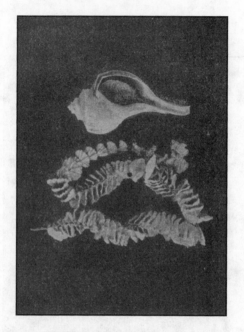

PERIWINKLE AND EGG-CASES

winkle remind one of a beautiful necklace. The air
bubbles rising from the sand or mud as the wave recedes mark the entrance to the burrows of worms.
Stamp hard on the sand. A little fountain of water
announces the abode of the soft clam. Watch the sand
at the edge of the rippling water. The mole-crab may
be seen scuttling to cover. In the little hollows between
rocks a rock-crab or a green-crab may be found on
guard.

For collecting in the pools and shallow water a fine-
meshed net is desirable. Many of the animals can be
caught and placed in glass dishes of sea water for close
observation.

Group showing a starfish attacking an oyster; soft shelled clams; hermit crabs; fiddler crabs, etc.

A few animals that may be found at the seashore

Rocky Shores—Hydroids on the rock-weed, rock-barnacles, snails, amphipods, lobsters, and oysters.

Sandy Shores—Worms in tube houses, mole-crab, sand-hopper, egg-cases, whelks, shrimps.

Muddy Shores—Snails, clams, worms of many varieties, mud-crabs, hermit-crabs, blue crabs, scallops.

Wharves and Bridges (on the piling)—Sponges, hydroids, sea-anemones, ascidians, starfishes, sea-urchins, worms.

On the shores of lakes, ponds, and streams will also be found many invertebrates.

Insects and Spiders

HUMMINGBIRD MOTH

Range: Eastern North America. The larvae or caterpillars of this moth feed upon virburnum, snowberry and hawthorn.

Insects play an important part in Nature's activities. From the point of view of man some are beneficial and some are destructive. In the former group may be mentioned the Dragonflies which feed upon mosquitoes, the Cochineal insects of Mexico, which furnish a dye-

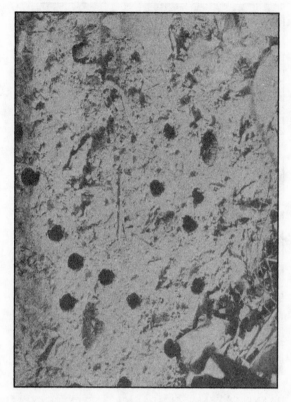

SEVENTEEN-YEAR CICADA OR SEVENTEEN-YEAR "LOCUST"

Range: Eastern United States. Pupae emerging from the ground. Detail from group in the American Museum of Natural History.

stuff, the Lady-bird beetles, which in the larval stage feed upon plant lice; the scale insects of India, which furnish shellac; the Bumblebees, which cross-pollinate the clover, and the Wasps, which fertilize the figs. Dr. Lutz says that the manna which fed the Children of Israel

SEVENTEEN-YEAR   CICADA   OR   SEVENTEEN-YEAR
"LOCUST"
Range: Eastern United States. The pupa climbing tree trunk.
Then it bursts its horny outer skin and crawls out an adult.

was honeydew secreted by a scale insect, and that it is
still eaten.

The Silkworm and the Honey-bee have been domesticated since prehistoric times, the former supplying a
valuable fiber for clothing and the latter an important
article of food.

Among the injurious insects a few may be mentioned: the House Fly or Filth Fly, which may carry disease germs on its feet to the food that we eat; the mosquitoes, which transmit yellow fever and malaria, the rat flea, which carries bubonic plague; the weevils, which destroy rice, beans, chestnuts, etc., and the plant lice, or aphids, which, by sucking the juices from ornamental and food plants, are among the most destructive of all insects.

There are so many insects in the world that we cannot hope to learn them all, even if we wanted to do so, but most of us wish to know the names of those that attract our attention, and to know what they do that is important or interesting. There are approximately 400,000 species or kinds of insects known in the world; that is, about three times as many as there are species or kinds of all the rest of the animals in the world put together. This fact should not hinder us from making a start and becoming familiar with the interesting habits of a few of the insects about us.

The eggs of the Monarch Butterfly may be collected upon the milkweed and brought in, so that the whole life history or metamorphosis of this beautiful insect, from the egg through the larva or caterpillar stage and the pupa or chrysalis stage to the adult butterfly, may be watched. The larvae or caterpillar must be supplied daily with fresh milkweed leaves. Other butterflies and moths and many other insects may be reared in the same way by supplying the larvae with suitable food. If we should find a caterpillar feeding upon the leaves of a maple tree we should continue to feed it maple leaves if we wish to rear it. Silkworms will eat the leaves of Osage-orange, but they seem to prefer mulberry leaves.

Cocoons of moths may be easily collected in winter after the leaves have fallen, and brought in and kept in a cool place until spring when the coming out of the adult moths will be an occurrence of absorbing interest.

The Spiders, although not insects, are interesting little animals. See how many types of webs you can find. Mention a few insects which you know to be preyed

"A GATHERING OF MONARCHS"

Monarch Butterflies resting during migration. The Monarch ranges all over North and South America and it migrates like the birds. Photograph of group in American Museum of Natural History.

upon by spiders. Mention one insect that catches spiders and stores them away as food for its young.

TRACKS OF THE GLACIER

North America at the time of the maximum stage of the Great Ice Age, showing area covered by ice. (After Chamberlin and Salisbury.)

THE KING OF THE NORTHLANDS

GEOLOGY

Finds tongues in trees, books in the running brooks,
Sermons in stones, and good in everything.
—Shakespeare, As You Like It.

The Structure and History of the Earth

There is nothing eternal about the earth except eternal change, some one has said. It requires only a little looking about us to see that this is true. The earth is not as it was in the past. Every shower of rain changes or modifies its surface. And many other and some very great changes have occurred during the past few millions of years. During one age, the coal was formed of plants that grew luxuriantly on the earth's surface. At one period in the development of the earth there were many kinds of invertebrate animals, but no animals with backbones. Later, the vertebrates appeared. At one time the whole Mississippi Valley was under the water of the sea. ("The Story of Our Continent," by N. S. Shaler. Ginn & Co.). These statements suggest just a few of the things that have been going on in the history of the earth. By the study of Geology we can learn much more about it, and we should supplement our study of books with the more important actual observation of conditions out-of-doors. To those living in that part of North America, which is shaded in the accompanying map, the easiest and most natural approach to the subject of the structure and history of the earth is by studying the effects of the continental glacier which formerly moved down over this region.

Tracks of the Glacier

When we see the foot-prints of an animal in the mud or in the snow, we are sure that an animal has passed that way at some previous time. Those who live in Canada or northern United States (See map above) can be just as sure that a great glacier or ice-sheet formerly moved down over northern North America, by the tracks it has left. Although it is estimated by geologists that between 10,000 and 40,000 years have elapsed since the Great Ice Age, these tracks or evidences can still be seen by any one who lives in this region or who can visit it. The principal ones are: (1) Boulders or Lost Rocks which were brought down by this glacier; (2) The Glacial Drift or Boulder Clay which covers nearly all of the glaciated region; (3) Scratches on the bed-rock which show the direction the glacier moved.

Notice in the field the size and shape of the glacial

boulders, where they are found, evidence of the place where the glacier melted off (terminal moraine). Do these boulders increase or decrease in size as we go south over the glaciated area? Can you discover any place where they can be traced back to their native ledge? Present-day glaciers, like the Muir Glacier in Alaska, can be seen transporting boulders and drift just as this great prehistoric ice-sheet must have done.

The drift which consists of clay mixed with pebbles, cobblestones, and boulders, varies greatly in depth. In some places there is none, while at St. Paris, Ohio, it is 550 feet deep. It probably averages 100 feet thick or less.

In your locality note the depth of the drift in cuts made naturally by creeks and rivers or those made artificially for railroads. Oil-wells furnish evidence on this point. Collect a few good examples of scratched or glaciated pebbles or cobblestones which are abundant in the drift. These were scratched while frozen in the bottom of the glacier and pushed along on the bed-rock under the weight of the ice above.

Collect ten different kinds of rocks from the glacial boulders and drift,—there are more than one hundred kinds to be found,—and with the aid of some such book as "Rocks and Rock Minerals," by Louis V. Pirsson (John Wiley & Sons) or "Common Minerals and Rocks," by Wm. O. Crosby (D. C. Heath & Co.) try to identify them.

All soil is composed of disintegrated or decayed rock. And it has been observed that the soil of northern North America is foreign to the bed-rock. Therefore it must have been transported from some other place. The glacier did this huge piece of work. The soil of southern United States contains no boulders or cobblestones and has been formed by the disintegration and decay of rocks in place.

Observe glacial scratches and grooves on the bed-rock, those on Kelley's Island in Lake Erie are famous.

Agassiz was the first to realize that it was a glacier that did this stupendous piece of work, and this conception or discovery greatly added to his fame. It is now easy for us to find the evidences and to enjoy their interpretation.

In fact, the Greenland ice-sheet is a remnant of this prehistoric continental glacier.

ERRATA IN SECTION XV

Page 375. Last line—first Para. For *if* read *of*.
" 378. For *Really* read *Nearly* before the word related.
" 410. For *Hawking* read *Honking*.
" 429. Range of Gila Monster. Desert regions of southern Arizona and New Mexico.
" 430. For *Tortoise* read *Turtle*.
" 431. Range of Diamond Back Terrapin: Salt marshes of the Atlantic Coast and Gulf of Mexico from Massachusetts to Texas.
" 432. For *sponge* read *spoon*, and for *far* read *for*.
" 433. In second line for *adopted* read *adapted*.
" 435. The first two lines should read as follows: The most common example of the ganoid fish is the sturgeon which is heavily clad with a bony armor.
" 438. For *Octupus* read *Octopus*.
" 439. Photograph by Mary C. Dickerson.
" 442. For *crevasses* read *crevices*. After the 21st line the following should have been inserted: "barnacles, mussels. In the shallow water, crabs and shrimps are crawling along the sandy bottom or are lying concealed in the mud, while schools of little fishes scoot across the pool. If a fine silk net is drawn through the water and then emptied into a glass dish a whole new world of creatures will be revealed—jellyfishes, ctenophores, etc."
     For *moss* after shaggy read *mass*.
" 451. Photograph used by Courtesy of Henry Holt & Co.

SECTION XVI
THE GIRL SCOUT'S OWN GARDEN

BY DAVID M. HUNTER

A Garden is a lovesome thing, God wot!
  Rose plot
 Fringed pool,
  Fern'd grot—
 The veriest school
 Of peace; and yet the fool
Contends that God is not—
  Not God! in gardens! when the eve is cool?
 Nay, but I have a sign;
 'Tis very sure God walks in mine.
        —Thomas Edward Brown.

A very old story tells us that when man was created he was put by the Creator into a garden to dress it and to keep it. He could not have been put into a better place nor could a more honorable and necessary occupation have been given to him. No doubt the woman who lived in the garden with him aided him in this work. Not having a house to care for or dressmaking and sewing to do, or cooking to take her attention, there was nothing to prevent her from helping in the dressing and keeping of the lovely garden. At any rate, that is what Milton thought, for he makes Adam speak to Eve of "our delightful task to prune these growing plants and tend these flowers."

Two persons would not need a very large garden, and I will commend this early example to the beginner in gardening and urge a very small garden to start with. For it is well to undertake only what can be easily handled or what can be done thoroughly. There is joy in the contemplation of a perfect work, even though it be on a small scale, that never comes from a more ambitious undertaking imperfectly carried out. Better six square feet of well tilled, weedless, thrifty garden than an acre poorly cultivated and full of weeds.

A Girl Scout who proposes to make a garden will naturally ask herself certain questions. If she has the ground, if she knows already where her garden is to be placed, the next thing, perhaps, that she will wish to know is, what tools will be needed. Then follows the way to treat the soil in order to prepare it for planting the seeds. After that comes the question of seeds and the way to plant them. Then the cultivation of the crops until they are ready to be gathered.

Here, then, we have material for short sections on (1) tools, (2) preparation of the soil, (3) selection of seeds, (4) planting, and (5) cultivation.

(1) Tools

Not many tools will be needed, but some seem to be indispensable. I would suggest: 1. A spading fork. Some like a long-handled fork, others prefer a short-handled one. 2. A hoe. 3. A garden or iron-toothed rake. 4. A hand weeder of some kind. 5. A shovel. In addition to these tools every gardener will find it necessary to have a line for making straight rows. This should be at least the length of the longest dimension of the garden and white that it may be easily seen. There should be two pegs to stick it in with. I should add a board about ten inches wide with straight edges and as long as the bed is wide, and a pointed stick.

(2) The Preparation of the Seed Bed

The first thing to do, after having determined the location of your garden, is to measure your bed. If you have a single bed, one twelve feet long by six feet wide is enough to start with. I should prefer, however, to have two beds, each three feet wide by twelve feet long with a narrow path between, say, twelve inches. The reason for thus laying out the ground in two beds is that it will be easier to reach the whole bed from either side without stepping or kneeling on the cultivated soil. All cultivation can be done from the paths.

The soil for flower beds needs most careful preparation. The bed should be dug out to a depth of two feet, and if the soil is clay, two feet six inches. In the latter case, put broken stones, cinders or gravel on the bottom for drainage. The soil should be a mixture of one-half good sandy loam, one-fourth leaf mould or muck that has been left out all winter. Mix these thoroughly together before filling the beds, sprinkle wood ashes over the beds and rake them in before planting. This is to sweeten the soil. Lime may be used for the same purpose, but in either case get advice as to the amount needed for the soil in question.

Manure. Next in order will come the enriching of this plot of ground by spreading upon it a good coating of well rotted cow manure. In case barnyard manure is not available, a good mixture of commercial fertilizer consists of four parts ground bone to one of muriate of potash applied at the rate of four pounds to the square rod. This done, proceed to fork the whole piece over, thrusting the spading fork into the ground its full length each time, and turning the forkful of earth so that the manure will be covered and not lie on top of the ground.

When the spading has been done, then use your rake and spare it not. Rake until the earth in the beds is finely pulverized and until the whole bed is as level as you can make it.

Now construct your central or dividing path, throwing the soil moved on the beds on either side. To do this you will need a shovel.

Next define or limit your beds, making the sides and ends as straight as possible. You ought now to have two rectangular beds, each three feet by twelve feet, with a narrow path separating them all ready to put in the seeds. It would be a good thing to have your beds raised a little, two or three inches above the general level of the surrounding earth. This will make them more distinct and will obviate the settling of water on your beds; in other words, will drain them.

Seeds

The principal counsel to be given here is to use great care in the selection of seeds because it is a bitter disappointment and a discouraging experience to find that after all your labor your seeds are worthless. It would be well to test a sample of your seeds to determine their germinating power. If you have a reliable friend from whom you can secure your seeds, you are fortunate, but if you must purchase at the dealer by all means patronize one of established reputation.

For the first garden I should plant lettuce, radishes, beets and beans in one of the beds. The other bed may be devoted to flowers.

Planting

Your beds are now supposed to be all ready for the seeds. That is to say, they are shaped and graded and raked fine. The next thing to do is to lay your board across the bed, with one edge six inches from the edge of the bed. Then stand on the board and with a pointed stick make a shallow furrow on each side of the board close to the board. Here I should put the lettuce. It is desirable to have the seeds evenly and not too thickly distributed in the shallow furrows. One way of accomplishing this is by mixing your seeds with some very fine wood ashes in a bowl and spreading the mixed ashes and seeds along the furrows. A better way, I think, in the case of a small quantity of seeds would be to place each seed at a proper distance from the others. This distance will vary according to the size of the full grown heads of lettuce. The smaller varieties might stand six inches apart, while the largest ones would need to be twice that distance or more.

Having planted your lettuce seeds, turn your board over carefully twice. That will bring it into position for two more rows of vegetables. Stand on the board again and proceed as before, making two shallow furrows with a pointed stick. Here I should put the radish seeds. These may be sown more thickly, for the reason that as soon as the radishes become large enough to eat they may be pulled out, leaving room for the rest of the radishes to develop.

Having planted your radish seeds, repeat the preceding operations, making two furrows again, this time for beet seeds. These may also be sown thickly. The plants may be thinned out afterward. The small plants that are pulled out will make excellent greens. When the thinning is completed the remaining plants should stand from four to six inches apart, according to variety; some beets are much larger than others.

The rest of the bed devote to string or butter beans. You will have left for these a space of eighty-eight inches, or a little more than seven feet. The rows of beans must be farther apart than the other vegetables you have planted. Two feet between the rows is not too much. You will have space enough for three rows. Measure from your last row of beets one foot six inches at each side of your bed. Now stretch your line across your bed at this distance from the beets, then with a hoe make a furrow close to the line. This furrow should be two inches deep at least. Much deeper, you see, than the shallow furrows for the smaller seeds. Having made this furrow, measure two feet from it on each side of the bed and place your line at this point and make a furrow as before. Repeat the process for a third furrow. You should now have left a space of eighteen inches between your last furrow and the end of the bed. Into these three furrows place the beans, spacing them.

Your seeds are now all in. At this juncture take your rake and cover the seeds, leaving the whole bed level and smooth.

There is nothing more to be done just at present except to leave these seeds to the forces of nature, to the darkness and the moisture and the warmth of their earthy bed. They are put to bed not that they may sleep, but in order to wake them up. Soon the delicate shoots will begin to appear above the ground, and with them will also appear the shoots of many weeds whose seeds were in the soil. These weeds constitute a call to your next operation which is

Cultivation

Declare war on the weeds. Use your hand weeder between the rows of smaller vegetables and let not a weed escape. If they are in the rows so near to the seedlings that you cannot us the weeder without danger to the delicate little plants that you are attending, then employ your fingers.

For a time you may use the hoe or rake between the rows of beans, but even here near the paths themselves the weeder or hands should be preferred.

There is one caution that old gardeners give which

is not to work among beans when they are wet with dew or rain for fear of "rust." Wait till the sun has dried the foliage.

Frequent and thorough cultivation not only destroys the weeds, thus giving your vegetables a better chance and giving your garden a tidy, well-kept appearance, but it keeps the soil loose and forms a sort of mulch whereby the moisture is conserved. The dryer the season the greater the need of cultivation.

It may seem to you that you are obliged to wait long and spend a good deal of labor without results, but when you have for the breakfast table some cool, crisp radishes and for dinner a head of fresh lettuce, and later a dish of sweet, luscious beets or mess of string beans, you will feel well repaid.

Let us now turn our attention to the other bed, in which you are to grow flowers. This may be treated as a sort of background for the vegetable bed. To do this let the rows of plants run the other way. That is to say, lengthwise of the bed instead of across. It is assumed that the ground has been treated as in the case of the vegetable bed.

When you have accomplished this work of preparation set your line six inches from the side of the bed nearest your vegetables, or the patch between the two beds. Make a shallow furrow the full length of the bed with your pointed stick. In this furrow sow your flower seeds of some low-growing plant such as *sweet alyssum*. Then move your line back toward the other side of the bed one foot. Here you should place some taller plants, such as *asters*. The aster plants should have been raised in the house, or purchased from some grower. Again move your line one foot nearer the rear margin of your bed and in this row plant your tallest plants. *Dahlias* or *cosmos* would be very effective.

You must get the roots for the dahlias somewhere.
Cosmos is planted from seeds. In planting the dahlias
it would be well to dig a hole for each plant so deep
that when the root is set it will be two or three inches
below the surface of the ground. Good results will be
obtained if before putting in the roots you put a handful or two of good manure in the hole and sprinkle a
little soil over it.

I have mentioned these particular plants simply as
specimens. Other choices may be made and a suggested
list is given at the end of this section. But whatever
the selection, two things should be kept in mind. First,
that the rows should contain plants that vary in height,
the lowest being placed in the front row, the tallest at
the back; and second, that plants should be chosen that
will be in bloom at the same time, for at least a part
of the season.

If your work has been well done you ought to have
a small bed of vegetables, thrifty, in straight rows, well
cultivated, clean, and back of that, looking from the
side, another bed if flowering plants that should be a
delight to the eye, especially the eye of the possessor
and maker. Of course, the beds will not present this
perfect appearance for a long time because as the vegetables are used the beds will show where the vegetables
have been removed. It should be mentioned, however,
that it is possible to have more than one planting of
radishes in a season; also of lettuce, and these may be
replaced after the first planting has been used.

There are many satisfactions in gardening. The in-
timacy with nature furnishes one of them. To be with
growing things through all the stages of their growth,
in all weathers and all hours of the day gives a quiet
pleasure that is a healing and soothing influence. To
produce something so valuable, so necessary as food

by one's own exertion and care confers true dignity upon one and a sense of worth. To eat what one has raised oneself adds a flavor to it.

From the garden as a center paths lead out in every direction, paths for thought and study.

My wish for every Girl Scout who undertakes a garden is that she may have all these satisfactions, and may follow all these delightful paths that lead to knowledge, and through knowledge to joy.

Suggested Flowers for Border

Biennials such as Canterbury Bells, Foxgloves and Sweet William should be seeded early in the spring in a reserve bed to be ready for the season's bloom. In order to secure a succession of bloom they should be taken out after flowering and replaced with annuals.

Annuals—Of these some of the most satisfactory are Asters, Calendula, Lupin, Petunias, Rosy Morn, Snapdragon, Stock and Rose Zinnias.

Take out any plants that are not the right colors. Brown earth is better than purple annual Larkspur, magenta Petunias, orange Calendulas or red Zinnias. Keep the color scheme ranging from true blues through rose and salmon pinks, lavenders and deep blue purples and white yellows. If you want brilliant reds or magentas have them in a bed apart.

Bulbs—Tulips, such as Murillo, or *early varieties* (La Reine, Pink Beauty, President Lincoln, Proserpine, Queen of the Netherlands and Rose Luisante), or *late varieties* (La Merveille, La Reve, Moonlight, The Fawn) and Mertensiav Virginica can be planted along the borders of the flower bed.

Darwin Tulips, such as Clara Butt, Dream, Gretchen, La Tristesse, La Tulipe Noire, Mrs. Potter Palmer, Philippe de Commines, Psyche, Rev. Ewbank, Suzon, should be planted in more shaded places.

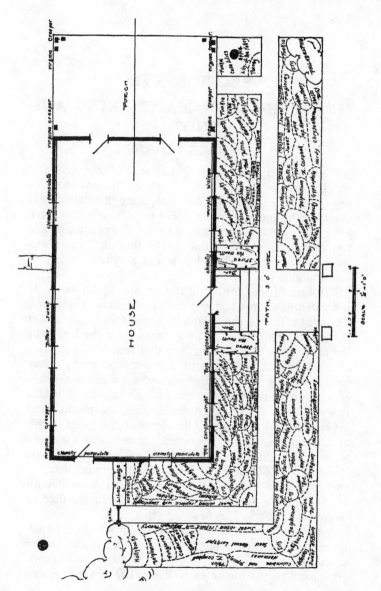

Plan for a border of Perennials

SECTION XVII

MEASUREMENTS, MAP MAKING AND KNOTS

1. MEASUREMENTS

Every country has national standards of measures and weights which are made and kept by the governments as patterns, for measuring and comparing the instruments made for business purposes. The units of measure have been fixed by law, for it is most important that people and countries in dealing with each other shall know exactly what is meant by such words as yard, foot, pint and pound.

The unit of length used in this country is the yard. It is divided into three feet and each foot into twelve inches. The foot refers to the length of a man's foot. It is said that the length of the yard was based upon the length of the arm of an English king, but that sounds like a fairy tale. Many of our units of distance and weight have been borrowed from the English and are more complicated than those used by the French, whose unit of length is the meter. In 1799, or thereabouts, an international convention met at Paris to decide what the exact length of a meter should be, for several countries at that time were using what was known as the Metric System of Weights and Measures. It was finally agreed that the length of a meter should be equal to one ten-millionth of the distance on the earth's surface, from the pole to the equator, or 39.37 inches.

At the same convention a unit of weight was determined. Because water is so important and familiar it was chosen as the basis for this unit. A cube of water at 40 centigrade, and measuring on each edge 1/100 of a meter, was taken and called a gram, which is about equal to 15 of our grains.

All peoples find it necessary in the house, out in the open and in nearly all forms of occupation to measure and weigh in order to accomplish their work.

It is part of a Scout's preparedness to know how to measure and weigh, and how to judge measurements and numbers without using measures and weights.

There are rules for determining length and weight, and it is important to understand them. Measuring a distance means to find out the length of the straight line from one point to another. To get a sraight line in the open when walking fix the eyes upon two objects directly in front, one nearer and smaller than the other. With eyes high walk toward these objects keeping them always in line. When approaching the first one choose another to take its place in line with it and the second. Always have two objects in direct line with the eyes.

This method can be used in marching, rowing, swimming, and when staking out the points of triangles for measuring distance and height, as it will give the shortest distance between two points.

There are three general methods of measuring distance accurately. (1) chaining or taping; (2) telemetry, and (3) triangulation. Less accurate means of measuring are by sound, pacing and timing.

(1) Chaining and Taping. The regulation chain or tape used by surveyors is 100 feet long. A Scout may use a shorter line but must follow the same rules.

Three things must be kept in mind when using a line. a. The straight distance between two points is to be obtained. b. The point where the end of the line comes each time must be marked. e. The line must be stretched tight.

This method can be used in measuring off the distance

for pacing to obtain the average length of one's pace, as suggested in a later paragraph under Useful Personal Measurements.

(2) Telemetry. The second method is used in determining long distances for artillery practice and in surveying. It is called telemetry and the use of an instrument is necessary.

(3) Triangulation. This is a long word but one a Scout can learn to know and use. It means that the length of the distance can be computed by means of triangles staked out on the grounds, when to measure with a line would be impossible or not satisfactory. It is not necessary to make the sides of the triangles, only the points need to be indicated as it is the relative position of the points which make a triangle and not the lines. These can be marked in the country with poles, stakes or stones; in the city Scouts could stand in position at the necessary points.

When using triangles where shall a Scout place the points?

If the width of a stream, road or field is wanted choose a place where its sides are on about the same level and if possible fairly straight. Then proceed as shown in the accompanying diagram a. Select a conspicuous object on the farther bank of the stream, such as a tree, bush or stone and call it X. Stand opposite it at the near edge of the stream or on the bank, and place a stake A in front of you keeping X and A in direct line, walk backward a few feet and plant a stake B in direct line with them. Right or left face—(for a right angle is necessary at this point). Pace a straight line for say 20 feet and plant a stake C, one high enough to be plainly seen; continue the straight line for say 10 feet more and plant a stake D. Turn inland, (another right angle is here necessary) and pace to the point where the ob-

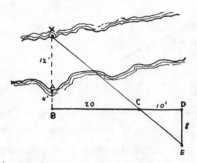

Diagram A. To Measure Width of Stream or Road

ject X on the far side of the stream can be seen in direct
line with the stake C. At this point place stake E.
Measure the distance from E to D. With paper and
pencil mark down the example—for such it is—in this
way:

$$DC : CB :: DE : BX$$

or

as the length from D to C is to the length of C to B

so

is the length from D to E to the length from B to X

or as in this example,

as 10 is to 20 so 8 is to the distance from B to X, which
would be 16. Having discovered the distance between A
and B in the case given, 4 feet from the distance between
B and X and the result will give the width of the stream,
which is 12 feet.

It may not be always necessary to use the line A—B
but if the edge of the stream or road is crooked it is
necessary in order to make B—D a straight line at right
angles to A—X.

In calculating a height, as that of a tree, house or
tower, the triangles can again be used, as shown in
diagram b. Choose a level strip of ground; pace the
distance in a straight line, from the base of the tree A, or

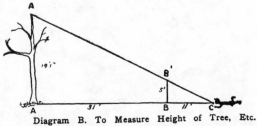

Diagram B. To Measure Height of Tree, Etc.

tower, to a point some distance from the tree, and plant a pole or stake say 5 feet high B; continue pacing the straight line to the point where, lying down with eyes level with the tree base, the top of the tree can be seen on a line with the top of the pole; plant here stake C. The height of the tree AA' wil be to the length of the distance from C to A as the height of the pole, BB' is to the distance between B and C. A Scout can stand in the place of the stake B.

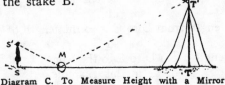

Diagram C. To Measure Height with a Mirror

There are other ways of determining height. As shown in diagram c, place a mirror (M) horizontally on the ground reflector side up, some distance from the base of the object to be measured, in this case a tent. Walk backward from the mirror in a straight line until the top of the tent pole can be seen in it. The problem will read in this way: the distance from the mirror to your heels (MS) is to the distance from your heels to your eyes (GS) as the distance from the mirror to the base of the object (MT) is to the height of the object TT'). Water in a dark pan or tray or a pool on a still day will answer for a mirror.

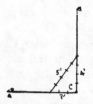

Diagram D. To Test a Right Angle

A right angle can be tested by measuring off 3 feet on one side of the corner and 4 feet on the other side, as shown in diagram d. If the distance between the two points is 5 feet the angle is true; if not 5 feet move one point as much as is necessary to make 5 feet.

South American natives estimate height fairly correctly by turning the back to the object, walking straight away from it to the point where the top of the object can be seen by bending over and looking between the legs. Plant a peg at this point and the distance from the peg to the base of the object is roughly equal to the height.

Sound travels at the rate of 365 yards every second, as many yards as there are days in the year. By counting the seconds between seeing the flash from a gun, or the steam puff from a locomotive and hearing the sound of the explosion or whistle it is possible to figure the length of the distance between yourself and the gun or locomotive.

It is said that the number of seconds between a flash of lightning and the thunder will give the distance between you and the place where the lightning struck.

We use weighing machines or scales in buying food, so that we may compare the actual amount of food we buy with a standard weight, otherwise there would be much confusion and business could not be carried on between peoples. For this reason we use pint, quart, peck and bushel measures, all of which are regulated by law as to the amount they hold.

There are some people who have a true feeling or sense for weight and can tell almost to an ounce the weight of a parcel by lifting it. Others have a good memory and can tell the weight of a quantity by looking at it. Others know distance and can estimate it correctly without use of rule or measure, and likewise judge numbers.

Very few people have this ability naturally, but many have acquired it by practice and patience and a Scout can do so: she will find many times that this particular form of knowledge whether in or out of doors is of benefit.

How often a housekeeper wishes she could tell about how much material to buy for this or that purpose without getting the yard stick and measuring. The seamstress and dressmaker must judge length and width and even height, and the cook constantly has need of a sense of quantity and size. The photographer, the pioneer, the camper, all must know measurements. This matter of judging is something we are called upon to do much more than we have realized. The point is how can we learn the trick? We should start with something we know and compare to it something whose size we do not know. This is where knowing your personal measurements will be of value. Always prove when practicing your idea, otherwise you will not improve your ability. That is, make your estimate, then see how near right it is by measuring. Learn to know how an inch, a foot, a yard look. hen work with longer lengths out of doors with several feet, and several yards. Fences, roads, streets, dooryards, houses, all can be judged as to length.

Height is less easy to estimate for we are not so accustomed to looking up and down as we are to looking forward or back and forth, but the same rules hold good. Learn to know the height of a chair seat, a table, your own height, a room, a house, trees: by measuring and looking, and looking and measuring, you will accomplish much.

To learn to judge weight begin by holding in your hand something that weighs a pound; after holding it a few moments put it down and then take it up again always trying to sense the weight. Do not use your eyes, only your hand. Try a two pound weight, and so on. Then take up something else the weight of which you do not know and see if you can tell its weight. Practice, patience and memory are necessary in this work.

There is another way of judging weight, one in which our eyes help us. Knowing how a pound of butter looks as to size we can judge the weight of a mass of butter by looking at it and comparing it mentally with what we know. We can follow this method in judging the weight of different goods, but as each kind when put in pound quantities looks more or less different from every other kind, experience, and knowledge of the character of the goods is necessary. A pound of butter and a pound of feathers do not make the same size bundle so the weight of each could not be judged by the same eye standard.

By practice a Girl Scout should be able to do the following things in the way of judging height, weight and distance:

(1) Be able to judge within 25 per cent the following: Height of a tree, house, pole, etc., not exceeding 50 feet. Material, 1, 3, 15, 18, 27, 30, 36, 42 and 56 inches. Diameter of the trunk of a tree, a pole, water pipe or similar object. Distance of 6, 10, 15, 25 and 100 feet. (This is useful in camera work.)

(2) Pick out from a miscellaneous assortment bottles

of 2, 4, 6 and 8 ounces. Bottles of 1 pint, 1 quart, 1 gallon. Pails, 1 pint, 1 quart, 2 quarts, 1 gallon.

(3) Be able without scales to weigh out specified amounts of sugar, flour or other household materials, for example, 1, 5 or 10 pounds.

(4) Be able to pick out from an assortment packages of rice, tea, cornmeal, etc., weighing ½, 1, 2, 5 and 10 pounds.

(5) Be able to give in the usual measures, either avoirdupois or metric, capacity of the standard teaspoon, tablespoon, teacup.

(6) Be able to tell when you have walked a mile in open country. This may be done by using Scout's Pace for 12 minutes, on a fifty walk, fifty run rhythm, or by knowing one's own walking step length.

(7) Be able to judge of spaces between distant objects such as the distance between two trees, the width of a road, or a brook, by the triangulation method.

USEFUL PERSONAL MEASURES

It is sometimes a great convenience to measure a length of ribbon, lace or other goods without the use of a rule or tape measure; but what shall we use in their place? Look at your thumb—how long is it from the end to the first joint and the middle finger, from the end to the knuckle on the back of the hand? Isn't it nearly four and one-half inches or one-eighth of a yard? That is what the average grown person's finger measures. To get the correct length of your own finger, hold the end of a tape line to the end of the finger with the thumb of the same hand, draw the tape measure tight over the bent finger to the knuckle. This is a very useful measure for short lengths.

Another measure for longer lengths is the distance

from the end of your nose, when your head is turned sharply to one side, to the end of your thumb when your arm is stretched straight out from the shoulder in the opposite direction. Measure and find out this distance for yourself by holding the very end of a ribbon, tape or rope with the left hand to the end of the nose, head turned to the left, and with the right hand run the fingers along the edge of the ribbon until it is stretched to arm's length. Marking the ribbon with a pin where the right thumb and forefinger have held it, measure the distance with a yard measure or rule from the end of the ribbon to the pin. This length will be about the same as the standard unit of length used in this country. When measuring a long length of goods, use the point held by the right hand as the starting point to be held by left hand.

If you know the distance between the end of your little finger and the end of your thumb when they are stretched apart, the palm of the hand being held flat, you can measure a distance such as the length of a table, shelf, pole, etc. When judging the height of a person, remember that the distance from the top of the head to the chin is about one-ninth of the height of the body. The distance between the middle fingers when the arms are stretched straight out from the shoulders is about equal to the height of the body.

Another personal measure that is of value is the length of one's average pace or stride; that is, the distance from the toe of one boot to the toe of the other when walking a natural gait. It is also useful to know the average number of paces taken in walking a given distance, such as a mile, and the time required to make them. All of this information can be obtained in a very simple way. Measure off as accurately as possible 220 yards, which is one-eighth of a mile, or take a known distance, and pace it back and forth at least eight times, but not all in one

day. Each time keep a record of the number of paces taken and the time required to pace the distance. Divide the sum of the paces by the number of times paced and the result will be the average number of paces for the distance by the number of times paced, and get the average number of paces and get the average length of your pace. Divide the sum of the minutes spent in pacing the distance by the numer of times paced, and get the average length of time required to walk the distance. When the average length of pace is known, the distance between two points can be quite accurately estimated by pacing, if the ground is open, level and solid. If up or down grade, if the ground is muddy or heavy, or there are other causes which retard the gait, a reduction must be made.

None of the above methods for measuring are scientific, therefore are not accurate, but they are useful ways of measuring *approximately* lengths and distances by means of a guide always at hand.

2. MAP MAKING FOR GIRL SCOUTS

The word map calls to our mind a picture of lines, angles, dots and circles which tell us something about a position of the surface of the earth. It gives us an idea of distance and direction, indicates heights and sometimes tells of interesting land conditions. What we see are but symbols representing a more or less true picture. This method of telling a story is very old; as long ago as 1370 B. C. it was used to show the location of the then famous Nubian Gold Mines. This ancient map is now preserved in the Museum of Turin.

Later, in 611 B. C. the first map of the world was made—the world as men knew it then. They thought it was like a hollow cylinder and surrounded by a river. By 276 B. C. maps were used and understood quite generally.

They were named originally after the material upon

which they were painted or drawn. Map from Mappa, meaning cloth, and chart from charta, meaning parchment. Even today maps are made on cloth when for use in the open by cyclists, military men, and so forth, and charts are those maps filling the needs of seamen. Savage tribes used maps made of horn, bone and wood.

In the 15th century the first printed maps were made and now many processes are used in reproducing these valuable and necessary graphic pictures, every line and dot of which have been made out of someone's experience. The explorer, the pioneer, the navigator, all contributing to the store of knowledge of the earth's surface, and many times having thrilling adventures, surviving terrible conditions that the earth may be known as it really appears.

Although maps are made to scale and every distance computed most accurately by the use of very fine instruments, Scouts can accomplish the real purpose of maps in a small and simple way, for they are after all, but guides to those who follow.

Knowing a delightful road or trail, one can by a map guide others to it, or by making a map of a city, or country district help a stranger to find his way about. Our maps must contain as the all important features: Direction, Distance, Points of Identification, and the explanation on the margin of the map of all symbols or conventional signs used. For hiking purposes a starting point and a goal are necessary, all cross-roads must be indicated —streams, bridges, trails, springs, points of interest, vantage points for extended views, and so forth.

A city map should note beside streets, the car lines or bus lines, public buildings, library, churches, hotels, stores, police station, public telephone booths, a doctor's office, fire alarm box and post box.

A village map should show in addition the way to the

nearest large town or city, give the railroad station, and so forth.

Direction is shown by symbol, an arrow or a line with an N pointing to the North, which should be at the top of the map, and all lines and signs should be made in relation to it.

Distance is shown by what is known as scale. It would be impossible and unnecessary in making a map to use the exact measurements of distances existing in any given portion of country, but we can indicate those distances by drawing our map even though very small so that lines, angles, circles and dots will bear the same relation to each other as the points they represent bear to each other. This is done by using a small measure to represent a large measure. If 1 inch was used to represent a mile, a map showing 80 square miles of ground, measuring 8x10 miles could be drawn on a comparatively small piece of paper. Whatever scale is used must be noted on the map, however.

The true distances are found by pacing or by triangulation. The interesting, helpful and necessary points are learned by observation. These are the real guides when using a map and these should be placed most correctly. Some of the symbols most generally used in map making are shown in the accompanying cut.

To be able to read a map is quite as important as making one. Signs must be understood, distances read, and directions known. It will help in ascertaining the latter point to hold the map so its position will be true to the points of the compass—the East to the East. This is called orienting a map.

A sketch map, not made to scale or true as to direction or distance, but giving enough accurate information to serve in guiding a stranger truly, can be made very quickly and easily if the district sketched has been ob-

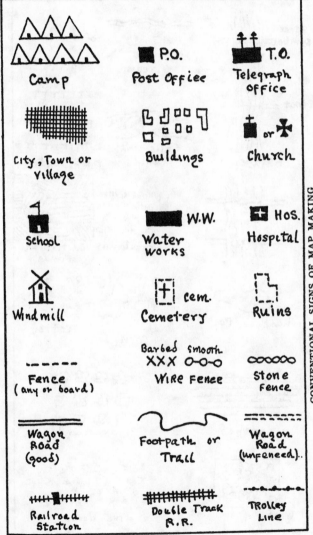

CONVENTIONAL SIGNS OF MAP MAKING

Camp

P.O. Post Office

T.O. Telegraph Office

City, Town or Village

Buildings

☩ or ✝ Church

School

W.W. Water Works

HOS. Hospital

Windmill

cem. Cemetery

Ruins

Fence (any or board)

Barbed smooth
XXX O-O-O
Wire Fence

Stone Fence

Wagon Road (good)

Footpath or Trail

Wagon Road (unfenced)..

Railroad Station

Double Track R.R.

Trolley Line

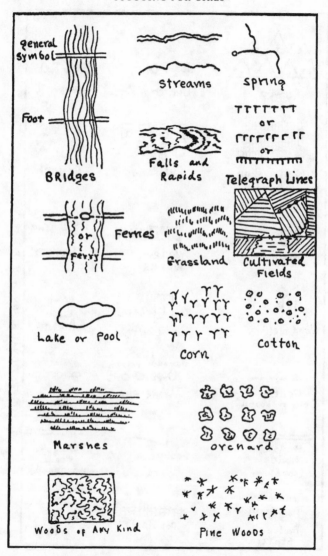

Chester Valley R.R.
P.O.
Cedar Hollow sta.
Map of Girl Scout Camp and Vicinity
N
W
E
S
2½" = ¼ mile
Trenton Cut-Off
Main Line R.R.
Philadelphia →

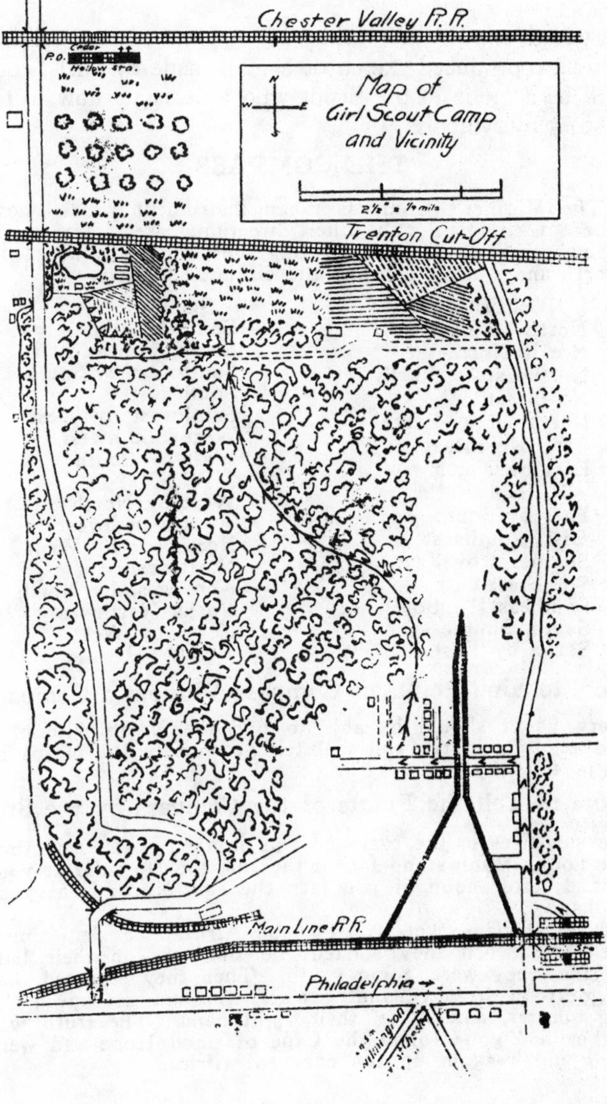

MAP OF GIRL SCOUT CAMP MADE BY SCOUT

served closely. Observation is at the root of map making.

The reproduced sketch of a map made by Girl Scout, will be a guide to the Scout who is learning how to tell a story by symbols.

THE COMPASS

The Mariner's Compass is an instrument which shows where the North, and other directions, are. Boxing the Compass consists in enumerating the points beginning with North and working around the circle as follows:

NORTH
North by East
North, Northeast
Northeast by North
Northeast
Northeast by East
East, Northeast
East by North
EAST
East by South
East, Southeast
Southeast by East
Southeast
Southeast by South
South, Southeast
South by East

SOUTH
South by West
South, Southwest
Southwest by South
Southwest
Southwest by West
West, Southwest
West by South
WEST
West by North
West, Northwest
Northwest by West
Northwest
Northwest by North
North, Northwest
North by West
NORTH

How to Find Points of Compass Without a Compass

Every Scout should be able to find the North without a compass. By day the sun will tell you where the North is, and the stars by night.

How to Tell the Points of the Compass by the Sun

The sun rises in the east and sets in the West. Any time before noon, if you stand facing the sun, the North is at your left hand; after noon, if you face the sun, North is at your right hand.

The Phoenicians, who sailed round Africa in ancient times, noticed that when they started the sun rose on their left-hand side—they were going south. Then they reported that they got to a strange country where the sun got up in the wrong quarter, namely on their right hand. The truth was that they had gone round the Cape of Good Hope and were steering north again up the coast of Africa.

Probably the most accurate way to find North, if you have no compass, is to use an open-faced watch. Holding the watch flat, turn it so that the small or hour hand points directly toward the sun. The South will then be half way between the hour hand and the figure XII on the dial. Before noon the halfway point is between the hourhand and XII clockwise, and after noon it is between the hour hand and XII counter-clockwise.

How to Find North by the Stars

All stars appear to rise in the east and set in the west, which is really due to our earth turning around under them. But one star never moves in relation to us, and that is Polaris, the North Star, which stands still over the north pole to show us where North is.

3. KNOTS AND THEIR USES FOR GIRL SCOUTS

It 'doubtless seems very strange to you that a Girl Scout should have to know how to handle a rope and tie knots according to rules. Most people have never dreamed that there are rules for these things; they have made knots, when necessary, in a way peculiar to themselves and have been quite surprised that the knots come out when they are expected to hold fast and hold fast when they are expected to come out.

Ropes and knots have been in use by all peoples for many years. The rules concerning them have been developed and perfected as time has passed, until now there is no question as to the usefulness of these things and the way to handle them correctly.

As the sailors and the engineers have worked with ropes and knots more than others, it is to them that we go for our information. We need all we can get, for to-day in nearly all forms of occupation twine, cord and rope are used and knots are tied. As the Girl Scout who wants to be a Golden Eaglet takes up many of these occupations, she needs to know how to tie knots quickly, in the dark if necessary, and correctly, for then they will hold fast yet can be readily untied. These are essential requirements to be remembered, but just as important is the fact that the purposes and uses of knots differ greatly.

Every Scout should have five feet of one-quarter inch Manila rope, whipped at both ends. With this small piece, which only represents the much larger rope needed in many cases for practical purposes, all of the required knots can be made and nearly all of their uses demonstrated.

Have you ever made a blanket roll, put it across your shoulder, hiked through the woods or over the hills for a sleep in the open? Where would all your necessary articles have been if you had not tied them snugly in the roll? Without them you would have been far from happy.

Or have you pulled a sled up a long hill over and over again for the sake of the slide down? How about the little knots that held the rope in place—did you ever think of them? There are many things we do for the sake of a good time where knots and rope are indispensable.

An interesting story is told by a Girl Scout who watched two men trying to hang a very large and heavy curtain which was to be used as part of the stage setting for an entertainment. The men tried to tie two ropes together, one of which was considerably larger than the other. Every knot they tied was pulled out by the weight of the curtains. Finally the men were quite ready to say "It cannot be done." It was then that the Girl Scout offered her services. The men looked at her doubtfully, but said, "Go ahead." Of course, she tied a knot that held fast, then she had to teach it to the men. You see, she could be helpful, for she knew the kind of knot that would hold two ropes of unequal thickness together and knew how to make it.

Did you ever notice how few people know how to tie bundles and packages securely and neatly? Yet this is a most helpful thing to do. Parcels that go through the post or by express are handled roughly and unless tied with special care they are not delivered in good condition.

Sometimes we find ourselves in the midst of unusual surroundings where we can be of service if we know what to do and how to do it. A Scout is sometimes called upon to give First Aid, possibly to tie on splints, a bandage, or a sling; or use a life-line.

Once a boat was swept over one of the lesser falls

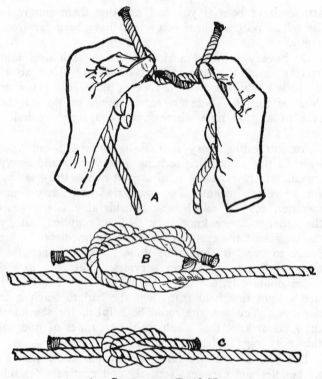

1. Square or Reef Knot

at Niagara. In it were three people—a father, mother and their son. A group of men and women standing on the bridge saw the accident; one of them ran for a rope and threw the end over the side of the bridge calling to those in the water to catch it. One succeeded, but the rope slipped through his hands almost immediately because there was neither a loop nor a knot to hold on to.

These stories, which are true, make us realize the

importance of knowing something of ropes and knots, that we may Be Prepared when our services are needed.

Parts of a Rope

The three parts of a rope are:

1. The End, the part used in leading;
2. The Bight, a loop made by bending the rope back on itself and holding it in place;
3. The Standing Part, the long portion of the rope not used when tying a knot.

1. Square or Reef Knot

The name of the knot the purpose of which is to tie together two ends of equal thickness, either to make them fast or to lengthen a rope, is the Square or Reef knot. It is made so that the ends come out alongside of the standing part and the knot will not jam. It is used when tying bundles, such as the blanket-roll, and packages; for tying on splints, fastening the ends of a sling or mending broken strings, ropes or cords, as shoestrings, clotheslines, etc. It is the knot used more commonly than any other.

To make the Square Knot:

Take an end in each hand;

Cross the end in the right hand over the end in the left hand;

Bend it around the rope in the left hand;

Cross the end in the left hand over the end in the right hand;

Bend it around the rope in the right hand;

Pull tight.

2. Sheet-bend

Another knot that is used for tying two ends together, generally those of unequal thickness, or for fastening an end to a permanent loop, is the Sheet-bend.

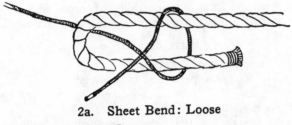

2a.   **Sheet Bend: Loose**

2b.   **Sheet Bend: Drawn Tight**

To make a Sheet-bend:

Make in the end of the larger rope a small bight or use the permanent loop in its place;

Pass the end of the smaller rope up through the bight;

Under the bight;

Over the bight;

Under its own part;

Pull the loops tight.

This is the way the Girl Scout tied the rope together for the stage hands.

3.   Bowline-Knot

If the people on the bridge at Niagara Falls had made a Bowline-knot in the end of the rope before throwing it as a life-line they might have saved one if not three lives. A Bowline is used chiefly for hoisting and lowering; it can be used for a halter or with the Sheet-bend in making a guard-line or fence. It is a knot holding fast a loop which can be made of any size and which will not jam or give.

To make a Bowline-knot:

Take the end in the right hand;

Draw the rope toward you over the palm of the left hand, measuring off as much as is needed to make the required size loop;

Drop the end;

Make a small bight in the palm of the left hand by turning the rope toward the ends of the fingers;

Take the end in the right hand;

Pass it up through the bight;

Back of and around the standing part;

Down through the bight;

Pull the end and the rope forming the loop against the standing part.

When the Bowline is used for hoisting or lowering a person, as in case of fire, the loop should be large enough to be used as a seat; it should be passed over the head and shoulders, the standing part in front of the body, to be held on to with both hands.

When using a rope for a life-line:

Fasten securely one end to something that will not give.

Make a Bowline at the other end of the line large enough to go over the head and shoulders;

Hold the knot in the right hand, the end toward you;

Take the standing part in the left hand, measure off about three feet of rope;

Draw the rope toward you, pass it over the palm of the right hand and hold fast.

Again measure off the same amount, draw the rope toward you, pass it over the palm of the right hand, and hold fast;

Continue this process until enough rope is coiled to more than cover the distance to the person in the water.

Grasp the coil firmly in the right hand;

Hold the standing part in the left hand;

Draw the right arm back from the shoulder;

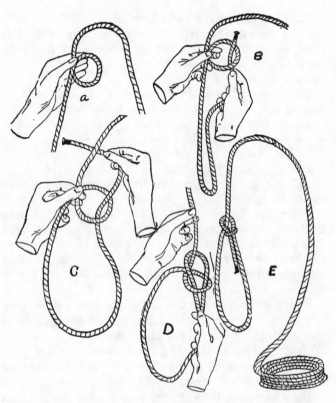

3. Bowline

Swing the arm forward and throw the coil out over the water to the person in distress;

Make sure that the person in the water gets a firm grasp on the rope;

Quickly take the standing part in both hands;

Pull on the rope with a hand over hand motion, keep the line taut and pull the person to safety.

Do not make the mistake of throwing the coil "up"; throw it *out* over the water.

The important points to remember when using a rope for rescue work are to fasten the free end so the rope will not slip out of reach; to coil the rope properly so it will not kink or knot when let out; and to make a Bowline large enough to go around the body.

When a group of Scouts make a guard line, each girl makes a Bowline in the end of her rope, large enough to put her hand through, fastens her right-hand neighbor's rope to it by means of a Sheet-bend and holds her portion of the line in place by using the Bowline in her rope for a handle.

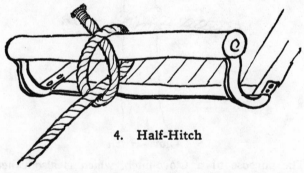

4. Half-Hitch

The purpose of the Half-hitch is to make fast an end of rope to a pole, post, etc. It is a knot that can be easily undone. It is used for hauling, fastening awning ropes, flag ropes, etc.

To make a Half-hitch:

Take the end in the right hand;

Pass the end under and around the pole;

Around the standing part;

Under itself, forming a bight out of which the standing part comes.

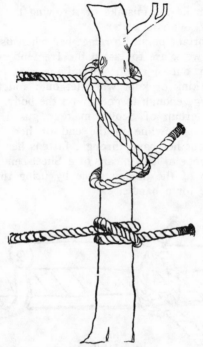

5. Clove-Hitch

The purpose of a Clove-hitch, which is also called the Builders' Knot, is to make fast an end of rope, generally to a post or tree. This knot holds securely and does not slip laterally. It is of value when tethering an animal or tying a boat. It can be used for fastening an awning rope, tent ropes, for tying on splints or fastening the end of a bandage when it is used to confine a delirious person.

A fence or guard-line can be made where trees or posts are available by tying the end of the rope by means of a Half-hitch to the first tree, and then using a Clove-

hitch on the other trees or posts.
To tie the Clove-hitch:
Take the end in the right hand;
Pass it around the post;
Over the standing part;
Continue around the post;
Under the standing part;
Slip the end up through the lower loop;
Pull tight.

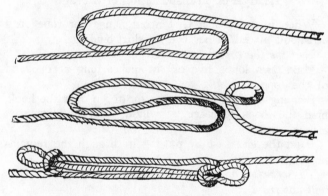

6. Sheep-Shank

The purpose of a Sheep-shank is to take up slack or shorten a rope temporarily. It is used on tent ropes, tow lines.

To make the Sheep-shank:
Cross the hands and take hold of the rope;
Take up the slack by drawing the hands past each other;
Hold the two long loops firmly in one hand;
Make a bight in the rope between the loop and the end;
Pass the loop through the bight;
Do the same thing at the other end.

The knot will stay in place so long as the rope is taut.

If it is necessary to shorten a rope when neither end is held fast, make the Sheep-shank and pass each end through the bight nearest to it.

Ready For Transportation or Storage

When in uniform a Girl Scout hangs her rope on a belt-hook placed in her belt or skirt-binding.

To have the rope in a convenient form:

Make two loops five or six inches long at one end of the rope;

Leaving a small bight at the top to go over the hook, bind the loops together by winding the standing part around them;

Hold the end fast by putting it through the remaining bight.

To serve or whip the ends of a Scout rope so they will not fray:

Take a piece of soft twine twelve or fourteen inches long;

Make a loop two inches long at one end;

Lay the loop on the rope, the end of the twine extending beyond the rope end an inch;

Bind the rope and loop together by winding the standing part tightly and closely around them;

Slip the end down through the loop, which must not be entirely covered by the binding;

Pull the other end of the twine and draw the loop under the binding.

As the twine will be held fast, the ends can be cut off close to the rope.

A "knot board," showing the various knots tied perfectly and names attached, ends of rope whipped, bights, loops and coils, is an interesting bit of work for a Troop of Girl Scouts to do. The board hung in the Troop room would be a help to new Scouts, and it could be loaned to Troops that are not registered, but are learning the Tenderfoot test, which includes knot-tying.

Glossary

Belt-hook—A double hook in the form of the letter S. Sometimes called S-hook.

Bight—A loop made by bending a rope back on itself and holding it in place.

Coil—A series of rings, one on top of another, into which a rope is wound.

Cord—A string or small rope composed of several strands of thread or vegetable fiber twisted and woven together.

End—One of the terminal points of that which has more length than breadth. The part of a rope used in leading.

Hemp—An annual herbaceous plant. The fiber, obtained from the skin or rind by rotting the stalks of the plant under moisture, is prepared in various ways for twisting into ropes, cables, and weaving coarse fabrics.

Knot—An interlacement of twine, cord, rope or other flexible material formed by twisting the ends about each other and then drawing tight the loop thus made.

Life-line—A rope used in rescuing; it should have a Bowline in one end and the other end should be secured to something that will not give.

Loop—An opening through which something can be passed.

Manila rope—A rope made from Manila hemp, a fibrous material which is obtained from the leaves of plants which grow in the Philippine Islands.

Rope—A cord of considerable thickness, technically over one inch in circumference. Ropes are made of hemp, manila, flax, cotton or other vegetable fiber or of iron, steel or other metallic wire. A rope is sometimes called a line. They are composed of threads which are spun or twisted into strands and the finished ropes have special names, according to the number of the strands, and the various sizes are indicated by the circumference in inches.

Standing part—The long portion of a rope not used when tying a knot.

String—A slender cord, a thick thread.

Twine—A double thread; a thread made of two strands twisted.

SECTION XVIII

GIRL SCOUT PROFICIENCY TESTS AND SPECIAL MEDALS

CONTENTS

I. Introduction to Proficiency Tests.

II. Proficiency Tests:

***Subjects marked thus are specially recommended for First Class Scouts or girls at least sixteen years old.

****Subjects marked thus are for Scouts eighteen years and over.

Artist	Economist	Milliner
Athlete***	Electrician	Motorist****
Bee-Keeper	Farmer	Musician
Bird Hunter	First Aide***	Needlewoman
Bugler	Flower Finder	Pathfinder
Business Woman***	Gardener	Photographer
Canner	Handy Woman	Pioneer***
Child Nurse	Health Guardian***	Rock Tapper
Citizen***	Health Winner	Sailor***
Cook	Home Maker	Scribe
Craftsman	Home Nurse	Signaller
Cyclist	Horsewoman	Star Gazer
Dairy Maid	Hostess	Swimmer
Dancer	Interpreter	Telegrapher
Dressmaker	Journalist****	Zoologist
Drummer	Laundress	

III. Group Badges.

IV. Golden Eaglet.

V. Special Medals:

Attendance Stars
Life Saving Medals
   Bronze Cross
   Silver Cross
Medal of Merit
Thanks Badge

Proficiency Tests and Merit Badges

1. INTRODUCTION

A girl must be a Second Class Scout before receiving a **Merit Badge** in any subject. However, this does not mean that she cannot begin to study her subject and plan for passing the test at any time.

Proficiency in these tests is to be determined by the Local Council, or by persons competent (in the opinion of the Council) to judge it. If no Local Council exists, certificates should be secured from persons competent to judge each subject, such as teachers of music, dancing or drawing, riding masters, motorists, electricians, milliners, dressmakers, artists, craftsmen, scientists and so forth... These certificates should be sent to National Headquarters or to the nearest District Headquarters for inspection. Headquarters will either pass on these, or indicate the nearest local body competent to deal with them.

The tests as given are topical outlines of what a Scout should know about the subject rather than formal questions... Captains and others giving the tests will adapt the wording to the needs of the particular case.

With many subjects a list of standard references is given. It is desirable that a girl should read at least one of these books, not in order to pass an examination but that she may be familiar with the general field and the great names and principles associated with it. Where a whole troop is working on a subject, portions of the books may be read at troop meeting, or several Scouts can read together and discuss their impressions.

It is important that every Girl Scout should understand that the winning of any one of the following Merit Badges does not mean that she is a finished expert in the subject.

What does it mean then? It means three things:

1. She has an intelligent interest in the subject
2. She has a reasonable knowledge of its broad principles
3. She is able to present some practical proofs of her knowledge, so that a competent examiner can see that she has not simply "crammed it up" from a book. Doing, not talking or writing is the principle of the Girl Scouts

One of the great things about these Merit Badges is that they require a definite amount of perseverance. This is a quality in which women are sometimes said to be lacking; if this is a fair criticism, the Merit Badges will certainly test it.

Nobody compels any Scout to earn these Badges; she deliberately chooses to do so. Therefore, to fail in a task she has voluntarily set herself, comes straight back to her and shows her what stuff she is made of. For a while it is of no particular importance how many things you start in this life, it is of great importance how many things you finish! Out of goodness of heart, or quick interest, or sudden resolution, a girl will start out to master a subject, earn a certain sum of money, make something for herself or someone else, form some good habit or break some bad one: and after her first enthusiasm has died out, where is she? So that a great many people laugh at a girl's plans—and with reason.

Now while this may be merely amusing, so long as it affects only the girl herself, it becomes very annoying when other people's affairs are involved, and may be positively dangerous if carried too far. If your life depended on a Girl Scout's efforts to resuscitate you from drowning, you would be very glad if she stuck to it. But if she happened to be a girl who had started to win five different Merit Badges, and had given them all up, half way through, what sort of chance do you think you would have?

Girl Scouts are slower to begin than other girls, perhaps, but they stick to it till they've made good. "She carried that through like a Girl Scout" out to become a common saying.

2. PROFICIENCY TESTS

ARTIST

SYMBOL—A PALETTE

Submit a drawing, a painting, or a model of sculpture which in the judgment of a competent professional represents a sufficiently high order of ability to merit recognition.

This badge is offered with the object of encouraging a talent already existing, and it is not suggested that Girl Scouts should select this badge unless they are possessed of sufficient natural talent to warrant presenting their work to a good judge. The standard required for winning the badge is left to the judgment of the professional as it is impossible for the organization to lay down strict requirements in these subjects.

REFERENCES:
"Childrens Book of Art," A. E. Conway, Adam and Charles Black.
"Knights of Art," Amy Steedman, George W. Jacobs and Company.
"Gabriel and the Hour Book," Evaleen Stein.
"Apollo," by S. Reinach, from the French by Florence Simmonds, Scribners.

ATHLETE***

SYMBOL—BASKETBALL

To qualify for this a Girl Scout must be at least fourteen, and must hold the badge for personal health, the "Health Winner."

1. State briefly the value and effect of exercise.
2. Demonstrate habitual good posture, sitting and standing.
3. Demonstrate a) marching steps, quick and double time, and Scout's Pace.
   b) Setting-up exercises, (as shown in Handbook).
4. Present statement from troop Captain, of a hike of at least 5 miles.
5. Demonstrate with basket ball 5 goals out of 7 trials standing at least 5 feet from basket, OR demonstrate with basket ball distance throw of 40 feet.
6. Demonstrate with indoor base ball accurate pitching for distance of forty feet.
7. Write brief description of rules for five popular games.
8. Play well and be able to coach in any three of the following games: Basket Ball, Battle Ball, Bowling, Captain Ball, Dodge Ball, Long Ball, Punch Ball, Indoor Baseball, Hockey—field or ice, Prisoners' Base, Soccer, Tennis, Golf, Volley Ball.

9. Hold swimming badge or bring statement of ability to demonstrate three strokes, swim 100 yards, float and dive.

10. Demonstrate three folk dances, using any nationality, OR be a qualified member of a school or society athletic team, playing one summer and one winter sport, OR be able to qualify for entry in a regular competition in some sport such as Tennis, Skating, Skiing, Running, Pitching Quoits, etc.

REFERENCES:

"Summer in the Girls' Camp," A. W. Coale, Century.
"Book of Athletics," Paul Withington, Lothrop.
"Outdoor Sports and Games," C. H. Miller, Doubleday Page.

BEE KEEPING

SYMBOL—HIVE

1. What constitutes a swarm of bees? How do they live? Tell how honey is gathered and stored and honey comb is built, and what part the queen, drones and workers play in the life of the colony.

2. Be able to recognize and describe each of the following: queen, drones, workers, eggs, larvae, pupae, honey, bee food, wax, pollen, propolis, brood-nest, comb, different queen cells.

3. Have a practical knowledge of bee keeping and assist in hiving a swarm, examining a colony, removing the combs, finding the queen, putting foundation in sections, filling and removing supers, and preparing honey in comb and strained for market, and present a certificate to this effect.

4. Know which flowers afford the best food for bees, and how honey varies according to the flowers in color and flavor.

REFERENCES:

"Productive Bee Keeping," Pellett.
"Bureau of Animal Industry," U. S. Department of Agriculture Bulletin.
"Life of the Bee," Maurice Maeterlinck, Dodd.
"Queen Bee," Carl Ewald, Thomas Nelson and Sons.
"How to Keep Bees," A. B. Comstock, Doubleday Page.

BIRD HUNTER

SYMBOL—BLUE BIRD

To qualify for this badge a Girl Scout must belong to the Audubon Society and be able to answer the following:

1. Give list of twenty wild birds personally observed and identified

in the open and show field notes including at least the date seen, field marks, food habits, nesting habits if known, and migration if any.

2. State game-bird laws of her State.

3. Name five birds that destroy rats and mice.

4. Give list of ten birds of value to farmers and fruit growers in the destruction of insect pests on crops and trees.

5. (a) Tell what the Audubon Society is and how it endeavors to protect the birds.

    (b) Give name and location of two large bird refuges; explain the reason for their establishment and give names of the birds they protect.

6. (a) Know what an aigret is how obtained and from what bird.

    (b) Tell methods to attract birds winter and summer.

1. GENERAL REFERENCES: (At least one must read to qualify for badge).

"Methods of Attracting Wild Birds," Gilbert H. Trafton; Houghton. Mifflin Co.

"Bird Study Book," T. Gilbert Pearson, Doubleday Page Co.

"Wild Bird Guests," Ernest Harold Baynes, E. P. Dutton Co.

2 HANDBOOKS AND SPECIAL BIRD BOOKS:

"Hawks and Owls of the United States," A. K. Fisher.

"Useful Birds and Their Protection," Edward H. Forbush, Massachusetts Board of Agriculture.

"Home Life of Wild Birds," F. H. Herrick, G. F. Putnam Co.

"Land Birds East of the Rockies," Chester A. Reed, Doubleday Page Co.

"Water and Game Birds," Chester A. Reed, Doubleday Page Co.

"Western Birds," Chester A. Reed, Doubleday Page Co.

"Handbook of Birds of Eastern North America, Frank M. Chapman, D. Appleton and Co.

"Bird Life," Frank M. Chapman, D. Appleton and Co.

"Handbook of Birds of Western United States," Florence Merriam Bailey, Houghton, Mifflin and Co.

"Children's Book of Birds," O. T. Miller, Houghton, Mifflin Co.

"Burgess Bird Book for Children," W. T. Burgess, Little Brown Co.

BUGLER

SYMBOL—BUGLE

Play correctly as to notes and time the following calls and marches and play at sight any calls selected:

1, First Call; 2, Reveille; 3, Assembly; 4, Mess; 5, Recall; 6, Fire; 7, Drill; 8, Officers; 9, Retreat; 10, To Colors; 11, To Quarters; 12, Taps.

Reference: Cadet Manual, E. L. Steever, Lippincott.

BUSINESS WOMAN***

SYMBOL—PEN AND NOTE-BOOK

1. Must have a legible and neat handwriting and show a knowledge of spelling and punctuation by writing from dictation a paragraph necessitating use of commas, periods, quotation marks, apostrophe.
2. Must typewrite 50 words a minute, or as an alternative write in shorthand from dictation 40 words a minute as a minimum, and transcribe them.
3. Must show a knowledge of simple bookkeeping and arithmetic.
4. Must show how to make out, and know how and when to use receipts, notes and drafts, and money orders.
5. Must know how to write a simple business letter, such as asking for employment, or a letter recommending a person for employment.
6. Must show how to keep a check book, make out checks and deposit slips, endorse checks, and balance checking account.
7. Must keep a simple cash account to show receipts and expenditures of personal funds for three months, OR the household accounts of the family for three months. (This account may be fictitious).
8. Must be able to write a letter from memory on facts given five minutes previously.

REFERENCES:

"Thrift by Household Accounting," American Economics Association, Baltimore.

"Household Accounts and Economics," Shaeffer, MacMillan.

"What Every Business Woman Should Know," Lillian C. Kearney, Stokes.

"Bookkeeping and Accounting," J. J. Klein, Appleton.

"Essential Elements of Business Character," H. G. Stockwell, Revell.

CANNER

SYMBOL—JAR AND FRUIT

1. Submit the following specimens of canning work: a) six pint jars of two kinds of vegetables showing the cold pack method; b) six jars of preserved fruit, at least two kinds; c) six glasses of jelly, jam or marmalade.
2. What are the essential things to be considered when selecting vegetables to be canned, fruit to be preserved or made into jelly, jam or marmalade?
3. Give general rules for preparing fruits and vegetables for preserving in any way.

4. What kind of jars are considered best for preserving? What other materials are used for making holders besides glass? How should all utensils and jars, glasses, rubbers, be prepared before using?
5. What is essential regarding the heat?
6. What are the general rules for preserving fruit? Give proportions by measure or weight, time of cooking, amount of sugar, water or any other ingredient for the fruits that you have preserved, and for at least two others.
7. Give same rules for jams, marmalades and jellies.
8. Give directions for filling and sealing jars. How can jars be tested within twenty-four hours after filling? If not air tight what should be done?
9. What should be done to all jars, tumblers, etc., before storing? How are canned goods best stored?

REFERENCES:
Government Bulletins... Canning, Preserving and Jelly Making. J. McK. Hill, Little.

CHILD NURSE

SYMBOL—A MALTESE CROSS

1. During a period of three months care for a little child, under two years, for a time equivalent to two hours daily for four weeks. During this period all of the necessary work for routine care of a child must be demonstrated, including feeding, bathing, dressing, preparing for bed, arranging bed and windows, amusing, giving the air, and exercise, and so forth, according to directions in Handbook.
2. What are the most necessary things to be considered when caring for a child under three years of age? Elaborate on these points.
3. What are some of the results of neglecting to do these things? What is the importance of regularity in care, to child, to mother or nurse?
4. Should a child be picked up or fed every time he cries? What is the result of so doing?
5. What are the important things to remember in lifting and handling children?
6. What things are important in connection with their sleeping, either in or out of doors? Up to what age should a child have two naps a day? One nap? What time should a child be put to bed?
7. How can a baby be encouraged to move itself and take exercise?
8. What should be done when preparing a baby's bath? How should the bath be given to a little baby? To an older child?
9. How is a child prepared for bed? How are the bed and room prepared?
10. What is the best food for a child up to nine months? If he cannot have this food, what can take its place, and how should it be given? What are the principal things to remember concerning the ingredients and preparation of this food, and the care of utensils?
11. At what age may a child be given solid food with safety? What foods are best and how should they be prepared?
12. When feeding a child either from a bottle or a spoon, what

precautions should be taken? How often should a child under one year be fed? from one to two years?

13. When suffering from a cold what precautions should be taken? If it is necessary to continue to care for a child in spite of your cold? What is the wisest thing to do first if a child is ill?

REFERENCES:

Wheeler, M... The Baby, His Care and Training... Harper, Kinne and Cooley... The Home and Family... Macmillan Holt, L. Emmet. ..Care and Feeding of Children. Appleton.

THE CITIZEN***

SYMBOL—EIGHT-POINTED STAR

1. Name five things on which the comfort and welfare of your home depends, which are controlled by your government.
2. What can you do to improve the government of your community?
3. What are the principal qualifications of a voter in your state?
4. What is meant by a secret ballot? When you vote how can anyone tell for whom you voted?
5. Who is a citizen? Are all voters citizens? How can a person not born in the United States become a citizen?
6. Tell the duties of the principal officers in your native village or city; also of your country, such as mayor, sheriff, etc.
7. What officer in your community would you go to for help in case of a helpless man without money or friends, a person with scarlet fever, a child who is not in school, a break in the water main in the street?
8. What are the duties of the governor of your state?
9. Who makes the laws in your state? How would you go to work to get a new law passed?
10. What are the duties of the President and of each of his cabinet?
11. Describe how Congress is composed... How are your representatives in Congress chosen?
12. How do laws made by Congress differ from laws made by your state?
13. What political party would you choose to belong to and why would you choose it?

REFERENCES:

"The Woman Movement in America," McClurg and Co., Chicago.

"The Woman Voter's Manual," Forman and Shuler, Century Co., 1918.

"Democracy in Reconstruction," Houghton Mifflin, 1919. Cleveland and Schafer.

"History of Politics," Edward Jenks, Macmillan Co.

"The Subjection of Women," John Stuart Mill, Frederick Stokes.

"Your Vote and How to Use It," Mrs. Raymond Brown, Harper Bros.

"The Story of a Pioneer," Anna Howard Shaw.

"American Commonwealth," James Bryce.

"Promised Land," Mary Antin, Houghton Mifflin.

"Land of Fair Play," Geoffrey Parsons, Scribner.

"Making of an American," J. A. Riis, Macmillan.

"Peace and Patriotism," E. S. Smith, Lothrop, Lee and Shepard.

COOK

SYMBOL—GRIDIRON

This test is based on a thorough knowledge of the article on "Cooking" in the Handbook. It may be taken in sections. A certificate may be presented from a Domestic Science teacher, or from the mother if the Captain knows her and can testify to her competency to judge.

1. Build and regulate the fire in a coal or wood stove, or if a gas range is used, know how to regulate the heat in the oven, broiler and top.
2. What does it mean to boil a food? To broil? To bake? Why is it not advisable to fry food?
3. How many cupfuls make a quart? How many tablespoonfuls to a cup? Teaspoonfuls to a tablespoon?
4. Be able to cook two kinds of cereal.
5. Be able to make tea, coffee and cocoa properly.
6. Be able to cook a dried and a fresh fruit.
7. Be able to cook three common vegetables in two ways.
8. Be able to prepare two kinds of salad. How are salads kept crisp?
9. Know the difference in food value between whole milk and skimmed milk.
10. Be able to boil or coddle or poach eggs properly.
11. Be able to select meat and prepare the cuts for broiling, roasting and stewing OR be able to clean, dress and cook a fowl.
12. Be able to make two kinds of quick bread, such as biscuits or muffins.
13. Be able to plan menus for one day, choosing at least three dishes in which left-overs may be utilized.

REFERENCES:
"Fun of Cooking," C. F. Benton, Century.
"Boston Cooking School Cook Book," Little.
"Hot Weather Dishes," S. T. Rorer, Arnold and Co.
"Food and Health," Helen Kinne and Anna M. Cooley, Macmillan.

CRAFTSMAN

SYMBOL—

PRIMITIVE DECORATIVE

DESIGN

To earn this badge a Girl Scout must qualify in at least one of the following and must read at least one general reference:

1. Tie-dying: Make a tie-dyed scarf using two kinds of tieing.
   Reference: "Dyes and Dyeing," Charles E. Pellew, McBride.
   "Industrial and Applied Art Books, Book 6," Bush.
2. Block Printing: Make an original design for a block print unit

using a flower or bird motif. Apply to a bag or collar in one color using oil paint or dyes.

Reference: "Industrial and Applied Art Books, Book 6," Bush.

3. Stencilling: Make an original stencil design for a border, use flower, bird, boat or tree motif. Apply in two colors to a bag, collar or scarf using oil paint or dyes.

Reference: "Industrial and Applied Art Books, Book 6," Bush.

4. Crochet, Cross-stitch, Darning: Make an original border design on square paper using any two geometric units, or a conventional flower or animal form. Apply the design to a towel in crochet, cross-stitch or darning.

Reference: "Cross-stitch Patterns," Dorothy Bradford, "Industrial Art Text Books, Book 6," "Modern Priscilla," Snow.

5. Weaving, Baskets: Design a basket shape with its widest dimension but less than six inches, and make the basket of raffia over a reed or cord foundation. Use eight stitch or lazy squaw.

Reference: "How To Make Baskets," White... "Practical Basketry," McKay. "Inexpensive Basketry," Marten. "Raffia and Reed Weaving," Knapp.

Weaving, Wool: Weave a girdle, a hat band, or a dress ornament use a simple striped or geometric design, in three or more colors.

Reference: "Hand Weaving," Dorothy Bradford. "Hand-loom Weaving," Todd.

Weaving, Beads: Design and weave a bead chain or a bead band for trimming; use two or more colors.

Reference: "How To Do Beadwork," Mary White, Doubleday Page.

6. Appliqué: Design an appliqué unit in a 7-inch square that might be applied to a pin cushion top, a bag or a square for a patchwork quilt. Use geometric units or conventional flower or bird forms suggested by cretonnes. Work out in cotton materials using two tones of one color or closely related colors, as brown and orange; grey and violet.

7. Pottery: Design an original shape for a bowl, vase or paper weight, and model shape in clay.

Reference: "The Potter's Craft," Binns... "Pottery," Cox. "Industrial Work for the Middle Grades," E. Z. Worst.

8. Posters: Design a Girl Scout poster that will illustrate some law or activity. Poster to be at least 9x12 inches and to consist of a simple illustration and not less than three words of lettering. Finish in crayon, water color, pen and ink, or tempera.

Reference: "School Arts Magazine," Jan. 1920. "Poster Magazine."

9. China Painting: Make a conventional design for a border that can be used on a plate, bowl, or cup and saucer. Work out on the object in one color in a tinted background.

References: Keramic Studio—any number.

10. Decoration: Make an original design for a box top or a tray center adapting units found in cretonnes. Apply to the object using enamel paints and in a color scheme suggested by the same or another cretonne.

Reference: "Industrial Art Text Book No. 8," Snow.

GENERAL REFERENCE BOOKS:

Read regularly: School Arts Magazine, Davis Press. Art Crafts for Beginners, Frank G. Sanford; Century; Handicraft for Girls, McGloughlin... See also: "Wood-Carving," P. Hasbruck, McKay.

CYCLIST

SYMBOL—WHEEL

1. Own a bicycle, and care for it, cleaning, oiling and making minor repairs, readjusting chain, bars and seat.
2. Be able to mend a tire.
3. Demonstrate the use of a road map.
4. Demonstrate leading another bicycle while riding.
5. Know the laws of the road right of way, lighting and so forth.
6. Make satisfactory report to Captain of a bicycle Scouting expedition as to the condition of a road with camping site for an over-night hike.
7. Pledge the bicycle to the government in time of need.

REFERENCES:
"American Girl's Handbook," L. Beard, Scribner.
"For Playground, Field and Forest," D. C. Beard, Scribner.

DAIRY MAID

SYMBOL—MILKING STOOL

1. Take entire care of a cow and the milk of one cow for one month, keeping a record of quantity of each milking.
2. Make butter at four different times, and submit statement of amount made and of the process followed in making.
3. Make pot cheese; give method.
4. Name four breeds of cows. How can they be distinguished? Which breed gives the most milk? Which breed gives the richest milk?
5. What are the rules for feeding, watering and pasturing cows? What feed is best for cows. What care should be given cows to keep them in perfect condition? What diseases must be guarded against in cows? Why is it so imperative to have a cow barn, all implements, workers and cows scrupulously clean?
6. Of what is milk composed? How is cream separated from milk? Name two processes and explain each. How and why should milk be strained and cooled before being bottled or canned?

REFERENCES:
"Stories of Industry," Vol. 2, A. Chase, Educational Pub. Co.
"How the World is Fed," F. G. Carpenter, American Book Co.
"Foods and Their Uses," F. G. Carpenter, Scribner.

DANCER

SYMBOL—FOOT IN SLIPPER

1. Demonstrate three modern social dances.
2. Demonstrate one folk dance.
3. Demonstrate one fancy dance.

REFERENCES:

"Dances of the People," Elizabeth Burchenal, Schirmer.
"Folk Dances and Singing Games," Elizabeth Burchenal, Schirmer.
"Social Games and Group Dances," J. C. Elsom, Lippincott.
"Country Dance Book," C. J. Sharp, Novello.

DRESSMAKER

SYMBOL—SCISSORS

1. Must hold Needlewoman's Badge.
2. Must know the bias, selvage, and straight width of goods.
3. Must cut and make a garment from a pattern following all rules and directions given. It is suggested that two girls work together on this.
4. Be able to clean, oil and use a sewing machine.
5. Demonstrate on other person the way to measure for length of skirt, length of sleeve, length from neck to waist line. Sew on hooks and eyes so they will not show. Hang a skirt, make a placket, put skirt on belt. Skirt must be hemmed evenly and hang evenly.
6. Know what to do if a waist is too long from the neck to the waist line and does not fit well.

REFERENCES:

"Complete Dressmaker," C. E. Laughlin, Appleton.
"The Dress You Wear and How to Make It," M. J. Rhoe, Putnam.
"The Dressmaker," Butterick Publishing Co.
"Clothing and Health," Helen Kinne and Anna M. Cooley, Macmillan.

DRUMMER
SYMBOL—DRUM AND STICKS

Be prepared to play all of the following taps and steps and in order further to show proficiency on the drum, perform any feat selected.

1, "Roll off"; 2, Flam (right and left hand); 3, Five-stroke roll; 4, Seven-stroke roll; 5, "Taps" step; 6, Six-eight step; 7, Two-four step; 8, Four-four step.

REFERENCES:

"Recollections of a Drummer Boy," H. M. Kieffer, Houghton Mifflin.

ECONOMIST
SYMBOL—BEE

A Girl Scout must qualify for 1, and 2, 3, or 4.

1. Offer record of ten per cent savings from earnings or allowance for three months.
   Show card for Postal Savings, or a book of Thrift Stamps.
2. Show record from parent or guardian that she has:
   a. Darned stockings.
   b. Keep shoes shined and repaired.
   c. Not used safety pins or other makeshift for buttons, hooks, hems of skirts, belts, etc.
   d. Kept clothes mended and cleansed from small spots.
3. For girls who have the spending of their money, either in allowance or earnings, show by character of shoes, stockings and gloves, hair-ribbons, handkerchiefs and other accessories that they know how to select them for wearing qualities and how to keep them in repair.
4. For girls who have marketing to do for family, show record of one week's buying and menus in which plans were carried out for using food economically, such as left-overs, cheap but nourishing cuts of meat, butter substitutes, thrifty use of milk such as sour, skimmed or powdered milk, and so forth.

REFERENCES:

"Scout Law in Practice," A. A. Carey, Little.
"Thrift and Conservation," A. H. Chamberlain, Lippincott.

ELECTRICIAN

SYMBOL—LIGHTNING

1. Explain the use of magnets for attraction and repulsion.
2. Describe the use of electricity for forming electro-magnets and their use in: Electric bell; Telegraph; Telephone.
3. What is meant by low and high voltage of an electric current? Describe the use of current in: Dry cell; Storage battery; Dynamo.
4. a. Describe how current is sent through resistance wire resulting in heat and light, in case of Electric lights, Electric stoves, toasters, flat irons, etc., and
   b. How it is converted into working energy in Motors.
5. Describe fuses and their use, and how to replace a burnt-out fuse.
6. Connect two batteries in series with a bell and push button.
7. Demonstrate methods of rescuing a person in contact with live wires, and of resuscitating a person insensible from shock.
8. Know how electricity is used as motive power for street cars, trains, and automobiles.
9. Know the proper way to connect electrical appliances such as flat irons, toasters, etc.

REFERENCES:

"Electricity in Every Day Uses," J. F. Woodfull, Doubleday Page.
"How to Understand Electrical Work," W. H. Onken, Harper.
"Harper's Electricity Book for Boys," J. H. Adams, Harper.
"Electricity for Young People," Tudor Jenks, Stokes.
"Heroes of Progress in America," Charles Morris, Lippincott.

FARMER

SYMBOL—SICKLE

This badge is given for proficiency in general farming. A Scout farmer may have her chief interest in rearing animals but she should know something about the main business of the farmer which is tilling the soil. Therefore, the Scout must fulfill four requirements: either A or B under I, and II, III, and IV.

I. A. Animal Care
    A Scout must have reared successfully one of the following:
    a) A brood of at least 12 chickens under hen or with incubator.
    b) A flock of at least 12 pigeons, 12 ducks, 12 geese or 12 guinea-fowl.

c) A family of rabbits or guinea pigs.

d) A calf, a colt, or a pig.

A certificate as to the condition of the animals must be presented, made by some competent judge who has seen them. Wherever possible a chart should be made by the Scout, showing the schedule of care followed, including feeding, and notes on the development of the animals.

AND she must also have planted and cultivated a small vegetable garden like the one described in the Handbook, in the Section "The Girl Scout's Own Garden" OR

B. Vegetable Raising

A Scout may make her main interest the raising of some sort of vegetable or fruit and may do one of the following:

1. Plant, cultivate and gather the crop from

a) A small truck garden, with at least six vegetables, two berries, and two salads or greens, OR

b) Where the soil is not suitable for a variety of plants she may raise a single vegetable, like corn or tomatoes, or tubers.

2. Tend and gather a fruit crop such as apples, peaches, pears, cherries, oranges or any other tree fruit, OR

Cultivate and tend a small vineyard or grape arbor, and gather the grapes, OR

Plant and cultivate and gather the berries from strawberry, raspberry, blackberry, currant or gooseberry plants.

Whatever the vegetable or fruit chosen a chart should be made and presented, showing the schedule of digging, planting, sowing and tending, with notes on the time of appearance of the first shoots, the size and condition of the crop and so forth. Any obstacles met and overcome, such as insect pests, drouths or storms should be mentioned.

No special size is mentioned for the garden, as the conditions vary so greatly in different parts of the country. The quality of the work, and the knowledge gained is the important thing.

II. Identify and collect ten common weeds and tell how to get rid of each.

III. Identify ten common insect pests, tell what plant or animal each attacks, and how to get rid of each.

IV. Describe four different kinds of soil and tell what is best planted in each. Tell what sort of fertilizer should be used in each soil. Explain the value of stable manure.

STANDARD REFERENCES:

Farmers Bulletins published by the Department of Agriculture, Washington, D. C. Write for catalogue and select the titles bearing on your special interest. The bulletins are free.

The Beginner's Garden Book by Allen French, Macmillan Co.

Manual of Gardening, L. H. Bailey, Macmillan.

Principles of Agriculture, L. H. Bailey, Macmillan.

Essentials of Agriculture, H. J. Waters, Ginn.

FIRST AIDE*

SYMBOL—

RED CROSS IN BLACK CIRCLE

A Girl Scout should know:
1. What to do first in case of emergency.
2. Symptoms and treatment of shock.
3. How and when to apply stimulants.
4. How to put on a sling.
5. How to bandage the head, arm, hand, finger, leg, ankle, eye, jaw.
6. What to do for: a. bruises, strains, sprains, dislocations, fractures; b. wounds; c. burns, frost bite, freezing, sunstroke, heat exhaustion; d. drowning, electric shock, gas accidents; e. apoplexy, convulsions; f. snake bite; g. common emergencies such as: 1. cinder in the eye; 2. splinter under the nail; 3. wound from rusty nail; 4. oak and ivy poisoning; 5. insect in the ear.

A Girl Scout should demonstrate:
7. Applying a sterile dressing.
8. Stopping bleeding.
9. Putting on a splint.
10. Making a stretcher from uniform blanket or Scout neckerchiefs and poles.
11. The Schaefer method of artificial respiration.

REFERENCES:
  Section on First Aid in this Handbook.
  American Red Cross Abridged Text Books on First Aid, Blakiston.

FLOWER FINDER

SYMBOL—FLOWER

1. To pass this test a Scout must be able to tell the difference between plants and animals and the difference between the two general types of plants.
2. A scout must also pass either the test for Flowers and Ferns or Trees given below.

A. FLOWERS AND FERNS

1. Make a collection of fifty kinds of wild flowers and ferns and correctly name them or make twenty-five photographs or colored drawings of wild flowers and ferns.
2. Why were the following ferns so named: Christmas Fern, Sensitive Fern, Walkingleaf Fern, Cinnamon Fern, Flowering Fern?
3. Name and describe twenty cultivated plants in your locality.
4. Be able to recognize ten weeds.

5. How can you distinguish Poison Ivy from Virginia Creeper? What part of Pokeweed is poisonous? What part of Jimsonweed is poisonous? Be able to recognize at least one poisonous mushroom.

B. TREES

1. Give examples of the two great groups of trees and distinguish between them.
2. Why is forest conservation important? What are the laws of your state concerning forest conservation?
3. Mention at east three other uses of trees.
4. Collect, identify and preserve leaves from twenty-five different species of trees.
5. Mention three trees that have opposite branching and three that have alternate.
6. How do the flower-buds of Flowering Dogwood differ from the leaf-buds? When are the flower-buds formed?
7. The buds of what tree are protected by a natural varnish?
8. Mention one whose outer bud-scales are covered by fine hairs. Can you find a tree that has naked buds?
9. From a Sassafras-tree or from a Tulip-tree collect and preserve leaves of as many shapes as possible.
10. Name five trees in this country which produce edible nuts.

REFERENCES:

A. FLOWERS AND FERNS

"New Manual of Botany," Asa Gray, American Book Co.

"Illustrated Flora of the Northern States and Canada," (three volumes), N. L. Britton and Brown, Addison, Scribners.

"Flower Guide," Chester A. Reed, Doubleday Page.

"Flora of the Southeastern States," John K. Small, published by the author, New York Botanical Garden.

"Flora of the Rocky Mountain Region," P. A. Rydberg, published by the author, New York Botanical Garden.

"State Floras.".. There are some excellent State Floras, and in order to keep this list from being too long, it is suggested that the Scout leader write to the Professor of Botany in her State University and ask for the name, author and publisher of the best Flora of her State. Especially is this advised for those living in sections of the country not covered by the above references.

"Our Native Orchids," William Hamilton Gibson.

"Wild Flower Book for Young People," A. Lounsberry, Stokes.

"Field Book of American Wild Flowers," F. S. Matthews, Putnam.

"Emerald Story Book," A. M. Skinner, Duffield.

"Mushrooms," George F. Atkinson, Henry Holt Co., (See Handbook, "Scouting For Girls," Section on Woodcraft.)

B. TREES

REFERENCES:

"Field Book of American Trees and Shrubs," F. S. Matthews, Putnam.

"Trees of the Northern United States," Austin C. Apgar, American Book Co.

"Manual of Trees of North America," Charles S. Sargent, Houghton Mifflin Co.

"Handbook of the Trees of United States and Canada," Romeyn B. Hough, Published by the author, Lowville, N. Y.

"Trees in Winter," A. F. Blakeslee, and C. D. Jarvis, Macmillan Co.

"The Book of Forestry," F. F. Moon, Appleton.

GARDENER

SYMBOL—TROWEL

This test is open to Scouts already members of the Girls' Garden and Canning Clubs throughout the country and a duplicate of their reports, sent in for their season's work, to the state agricultural agents, or agricultural colleges, in cooperation with the Department of Agriculture of the United States, may be submitted as their test material for this badge.

The test may well be worked for by a patrol or even a troop who can share expenses for tools, and cultivate together a larger plot of ground than would be possible for any one girl. Arrangements can frequently be made through the school garden authorities.

1. What are the necessary things to be considered before starting a garden? List them in the correct order.

2. What exposure is best for a garden? Why? At what season of the year is it best to prepare the soil? What care should be given garden tools?

3. Why is it necessary to fertilize the soil for a garden? What kind of fertilizer will you use in your garden, and why?

4. Do all seeds germinte? What precautions must be taken when purchasing seed? During what month should be sown in the ground in your locality? What are the rules for sowing seed as regards depth?

5. What does it mean to thin out and to transplant? When and why are both done?

6. What does it mean to cultivate? Why is it very important? How is it best done? What should be done with pulled weeds?

7. When is the proper time of day to water a garden? Is moistening the surface of the ground sufficient? If not, why not?

8. Name five garden pests common in your locality and tell how to eradicate them. Name three garden friends and tell what they do.

9. At what time of day is it best to pick flowers and vegetables? Mention two things to be considered in both cases.

10. What are tender and hardy plants? Herbaceous plants, annuals, perennials and biennials? Bulbs and tubers?

11. Select a garden site, or if space is lacking use boxes, barrels, window boxes, tubs and so forth: prepare the soil, choose the seed of not less than six annual flowers, and vegetables that will grow well in the soil and climate in which they are planted; take entire care of the garden and bring to blossom and fruit at least 75 per cent. of the seed planted. Keep and submit a record of the garden, including size, time and money spent, dates of planting, blooming and gathering of vegetables, or color of flowers, and so forth.

REFERENCES:

"Harper's Book for Young Gardeners," A. H. Verrill, Harper.
"Beginner's Garden Book," Allen French, Macmillan.
"Home Vegetable Gardening from A to Z," Adolph Krulm, Doubleday.
"Suburban Gardens," Grace Tabor, Outing Publishing Co.
"The Vegetable Garden," R. L. Watts, Outing Publishing Co.

HANDY-WOMAN

SYMBOL—HAMMER

1. Know how to mend, temporarily with soap, a small leak in a water or gas pipe.

2. Know how to turn off the water or gas supply for the house and who to notify in case of accident, OR
Know what to do to thaw out frozen water pipes, OR
Be able to put on a washer on a faucet, OR
Cover a hot water boiler neatly and securely to conserve the heat, using newspaper and string.

3. Know the use of and how to use a wrench and pliers.

4. Demonstrate the way to use a hammer, screw-driver, awl, saw, can-opener, cork screw.

5. Locate by sounding, an upright in a plastered wall, and know why and when this is necessary to be done.

6. Put up a shelf using brackets, strips of wood or both and know under what conditions to use either.

7. Be able to put up hooks for clothes or other articles and properly space them.

8. Be able to measure for and put up a rod in a clothes closet, OR
Be able to repair the spring in a window shade and tack the shade on the roller, OR
Know how to keep clean and care for window and door screens.

9. Must wrap, tie securely and neatly, and label a parcel for delivery by express or parcel post.

10. Be able to sharpen knives using either a grindstone, whetstone, the edge of an iron stove, or another knife.

11. Clean, trim and fill an oil lamp, or put on a gas mantle, OR
Clean, oil and know how to repair the belt of a sewing machine, OR
Lay a fire in a fireplace and tell what to do with the ashes.

12. Choose a wall space for a picture, measure for the wire, fasten the wire to the picture frame and give the rule concerning height for hanging pictures.

13. State how brooms, dry mops, dustpans and brushes should be placed when not in use, and be able to wash brushes and place them properly for drying.

REFERENCES:

"What a Girl Can Make and Do," Lina Beard, Scribner.
"Harper's Handy Book for Girls," A. P. Paret, Harper.
"Handicraft for Handy Girls," A. N. Hall, Lothrop.
"In the Days of the Guild," L. Lamprey, Stokes.

HEALTH GUARDIAN*

SYMBOL—THE CADUCEUS

I. **Recreation and Health.** What is offered to the public in the town you live in, or in that part of the city in which you live, in the way of Play Grounds, Gymnasiums, Baths, Skating Rinks, Tennis Courts, Golf Links, Water Sports?

If there is a public park in or near the town; what privileges does it offer, especially for young people? Is it well taken care of? Well patronized?

Discuss briefly why you think the Government should provide these things and what results may be expected when it does not supply them. How does the lack of them affect the grown people of a town, in the end?

II. **Special Health Facilities in your Locality.**

1. What is the rule as to registering births? What is the advantage of this?

   Of what diseases should the local authorities be notified? What diseases must be quarantined? Isolated? Posted? Reported?

2. **Food Supplies.** What are milk stations? Does your community control the marketing of milk to any degree? Why is the milk question so important?

   Are there any laws for your bakeries?

   What are the regulations as to the storage and protection of meat in local markets?

3. **Housing.** If three families are willing to live in three rooms in your town, may they do so?

   Is there anything to prevent your erecting a building of any size and material you wish in any place?

4. **Medical Institutions.** Is there a public hospital in your town? Who has a right to use it? Who pays for it?

   Is there a public clinic? Why should there be?

   Is there a public laboratory? How would it benefit your community if there were?

   Is there a district nurse? How could Girl Scouts assist such a nurse?

5. **Schools.** Is there any medical inspection in your schools? How did it ever affect you?

   Is its work followed up in the home? How are Girl Scouts particularly fitted to help in this?

   Is there a school nurse? Why does it pay the community to employ one?

   Are luncheons served in your school free, or at low cost? Mention at least two advantages in this and one disadvantage. Are there school clinics for eyes and teeth? Why are some cities providing such clinics?

6. **Baby Hygiene.** Is there any place in your town where young or ignorant mothers can ask advice and instruction in the care of infants? State briefly why you think such help would benefit the community in the end.

III. **Public Services and Sanitation.**

1. Who is responsible for the cleaning of the streets? Dry or wet method used?

2. What are the laws concerning the public collection and disposal of garbage? How much responsibility in this line has your family? Can you do what you please? Is there any practical use for garbage?

3. What is the source of your local water supply? What measures are taken to make and keep it pure?.. State some of the results of lack of care in this matter.

4. Why should there be regulations about spitting in public places? Why are common towels and drinking cups forbidden? What are the general rules for prevention and treatment of tuberculosis?

5. Trace the life history of the house fly or filth fly and tell why it is a menace. How may the fly be exterminated? How are mosquitoes dangerous? How may they be eliminated?

REFERENCES:

"Democracy in Reconstruction," Frederick A. Cleveland and Joseph Schafer, Houghton Mifflin.

"A Manual For Health Officers," J. Scott MacNutt, John Wiley and Sons.

"House of the Good Neighbor," Esther Lovejoy.

"Community Civics," J. Field, Macmillan.

"Town and City," F. G. Jewett, Ginn and Co.

"Good Citizenship," J. Richman, American Book Co.

"Healthy Living," Charles E. Winslow, Merrill Co.

HEALTH WINNER

SYMBOL—THE CADUCEUS IN TREFOIL

I. To earn this badge a Girl Scout must for three months pay attention to those conditions upon which health depends. She should keep a Health Record like that shown in the Handbook, which must cover at least the following points:

1. Position of body: Show improvement in posture.

2. Exercise. (a) Do setting-up exercises as given in Handbook every day. At least twenty minutes should be spent on these, either at one time, or ten minutes night and morning.
(b) Walk a mile briskly or walk steadily and vigorously for fifteen minutes, or take some other active and vigorous outdoor exercise for at least fifteen minutes. To make this point will require a record of compliance for at least seventy-five days in three months.

3. Rest. (a) Go to bed early. Be in bed by at least 9:30 and sleep from eight to ten hours. Do not go to parties, the theatre, movies or any other late entertainment on nights before school or work.

4. Supply needs for Air, Water and Food in the right way:
(a) Sleep with window open.
(b) Drink at least six glasses of water during the day, between meals; taking one before breakfast, two between breakfast and lunch, two between lunch and dinner, and one before going to bed.
(c) Eat no sweets, candy, cake or ice cream except as dessert after meals.

5. Keep Clean:

(a) Have a bowel movement at least once every day, preferably immediately after breakfast or the last thing at night.

(b) Wash hands after going to the toilet, and before eating.

(c) Take a daily tub, shower or sponge bath, or rub down with a rough towel every day; and take a full bath of some sort at least twice a week.

(d) Brush teeth twice a day: after breakfast and just before bed.

(e) Wash hair at least once a month, and brush well every day.

II. In addition to doing the things that make for health, the Girl Scout must know the answers to the following questions:

1. What is the best way to care for your teeth.
2. Why is care for the eyes especially necessary? How are the eyes rested? What are the points to remember about light for work?
3. What is the difference in effect between a hot and cold bath?
4. How can you care for your feet on a hike so that they will not become blistered or over-tired?

III. Read at least one of the following books, or some other standard book passed on by your physician or Captain:

REFERENCES:

"Good Health," F. G. Jewett, Ginn and Co.

"How to Get Strong and How to Stay So." William Blaikie, Harper.

"Keeping Physically Fit," Wm. J. Cromie, Macmillan.

"Exercise and Health," Woods Hutcheson, Outing Pub. Co.

"Handbook of Health and Nursing," American School of Home Economics, Chicago.

"Food and Health," Helen Kinne and Anna M. Cooley, Macmillan.

"Healthy Living," Chas. E. Winslow, Chas. E. Merrill Co.

HOMEMAKER

SYMBOL—CROSSED KEYES

1. In planning a house and choosing a site for it what things should be considered?
2. Draw the floor plan of an imaginary house or apartment to be built in your locality for a family of four, and list the furnishings for each room.
3. Choose a system for heating and state reasons for choice.
4. How will water be furnished? What precautions should always be taken about the water supply and why?
5. How will the house be lighted? How will it be ventilated?
6. State how the walls and floors will be finished and why?
7. Describe the cook stove and ice box; tell why they were selected and the best way to keep them clean.
8. List the utensils used in keeping a house clean.
9. State why it is particularly necessary to keep the cellar, closets, cupboards, wash basins, toilets, sinks, clean. Give ways of cleaning each.
10. State the proper way to prepare dishes for washing and the order in which silver, glass, table and kitchen dishes should be washed.
11. How should rugs, mattresses, pillows, upholstered furniture, papered walls, and windows be cleaned?
12. How should winter clothes and blankets be stored during the

summer? What should be done with soiled laundry prior to washing?

13. What is the most economical way to buy flour, sugar, cereals, butter and vegetables? How should they be kept in the house?

14. What is the law in your community concerning the disposition of trash, ashes and garbage? How will you care for these things in the house? If there is no law what will you do with them and why?

15. Under what conditions do germs thrive and vermin infest? How can both be kept away?

16. Plan the work in your house for one week giving the daily schedule and covering all necessary points.

17. Tell how to make and use a fireless cooker. Explain what it is good for.

18. Take care of your own bedroom for one month. Report just what you do and how long it takes.

REFERENCES:

"Housewifery," L. Ray Balderston, Lippincott.

"The Home and the Family," Helen Kinne and Anna Cooley, The Macmillan Co.

"Foods and Household Management," Helen Kinne and Anna Cooley, Macmillan.

"Shelter and Clothing," Helen Kinne and Anna Cooley, Macmillan.

"Feeding the Family," M. S. Rose, Macmillan.

"Handbook of Food and Diet," American School of Home Economics, Chicago.

MAGAZINES:

"The House Beautiful," "Ladies Home Journal," "Delineator," "Good Housekeeping."

HOME NURSE***

SYMBOL—GREEN CROSS

1. Describe care of the room under following points:
   (a) Ventilation heat and sun; (b) Character and amount of furniture; (c) Cleanliness and order; (d) Daily routine; (e) General "atmosphere."

2. Demonstrate bed making with patient in bed... Bed must be made in seven minutes.

3. (a) Show how to help a patient in the use of the bedpan and urinal. (b) Care of utensils, dishes, linen and their disinfection.

4. Bodily care of patient. Know all the following and be able to demonstrate any two points asked for:
   (a) Bathing; (b) Rubbing; (c) Changing of body linen; (d) Combing hair; (e) Lifting and changing position; (f) Arranging of supports; (g) Temperature, pulse and respiration; (h) Feeding when helpless.

5. Local applications, hot and cold, (fomentations, compresses, etc.) (Demonstrate at least one point.)

6. Common household remedies and their use: castor oil, soda, olive oil, epsom salts, aromatic spirits of ammonia.

7. First treatment of some common household emergencies, cramps, earache, headache, colds, chills, choking, nosebleed and fainting.

8. How to give an enema.

9. Proper food for invalids and serving it. Be able to prepare and serve five of the following. Two foods must be shown to ex-

aminer and three may be certified to by mother or other responsible person.

1. Cereal, as oatmeal, gruel; cereal water, as barley water.
2. Toast, toast water, milk toast, cream toast.
3. Plain albumen, albuminized water, albuminized milk.
4. Eggnog, soft cooked egg, poached egg.
5. Pasteurized milk, junket, custard.
6. Beef, mutton, chicken, clam or oyster broth.
7. Fruit beverage, stewed dried fruit, baked apple.
8. Gelatin jellies, chicken jelly.
9. Tea, coffee, cocoa.

REFERENCES:
"Home Nurses Handbook of Practical Nursing," C. A. Aitkens, Saunders.
"Home Nursing," L. McDonald, Macmillan.
"Red Cross Text Book," C. Lynch, Blakiston.

HORSEWOMAN

SYMBOL—STIRRUP

1. Demonstrate saddling and bridling a saddle horse.
2. Demonstrate riding at a walk, trot and gallop.
3. Demonstrate harnessing correctly in single harness.
4. Demonstrate driving in single harness.
5. What are the rules of the road as to turning out?
6. What are the rules for feeding and watering a horse, and how do these vary according to conditions?
7. What implements are needed for grooming a horse? Show how they should be used.
8. Hitch a horse, using the best knot for that purpose.
9. Know principal causes of and how to detect and how to remedy lameness and sore back.
10. Know how to detect and remove a stone from the foot.
11. Know the principal points of a horse, and the different parts of the harness.

REFERENCES:
"Riding and Driving for Women," B. Beach, Scribner.
"Horsemanship," C. C. Fraser.

HOSTESS

SYMBOL—CUP AND SAUCER

1. Demonstrate receiving, introducing and bidding guests goodbye.
2. Write notes of invitation for a luncheon, dinner party, and write a letter inviting a friend to make a visit.
3. Give an out of door party or picnic planning entertainment, and

prepare and serve refreshments, OR

Demonstrate ability to plan for an indoor party, arranging the rooms, a place for wraps, entertainment of guests, serving of refreshments.

4. Set a table and entertain guests for lunch or dinner or afternoon tea and demonstrate the duties of a hostess who has no maid, or one who has a maid, to serve.

5. What are the duties of a hostess when entertaining a house guest for a few days or more?

GUESTS:

6. When entertained as a house guest what are some of the necessary things to be remembered?

7. What is a "bread and butter" letter? Write one.

8. When invited to a party, luncheon, dinner, or to make a visit, how should the invitations be acknowledged? Write at least two letters to cover the question.

9. What are the duties of a caller, dinner or party guest as concerns time of arrival, length of stay and leaving?"

REFERENCES:

"Manners and Social Usage," Sherwood ($1.25).

"Dame Curtsey's Book of Novel Entertainments," E. H. Glover, McClurg.

"Hostess of Today," L. H. Larned, Scribner.

"Bright Ideas for Entertaining," H. B. Linscott, Jacobs.

INTERPRETER

SYMBOL—

UNITED STATES ARMY EMBLEM

1. Show ability to converse in a language other than English.

2. Translate quickly and accurately a conversation in a foreign language into English, and English into a foreign language.

3. Be able to write a simple letter in a language other than one's own, subject to be given by examiner.

4. Read a passage from a book or newspaper written in a language other than one's own.

5. Write a clear intelligible letter in a foreign language.

JOURNALIST****

SYMBOL—BOTTLE AND PEN

1. Know how a newspaper is made, its different departments, functions of its staff, how the local news is gathered, how the news of the world is gathered and disseminated... Inquire at newspaper office.

2. What is a news item?

3. What is an editorial?

4. Describe evolutions of typesetting from hand composition to

machine composition. Look this up in encyclopedia.
5. Write two articles, not to exceed five hundred words each, on events that come within the observation of the Scouts. For instance give the school athletic events or describe an entertainment for Scouts in church or school or rally.
6. Write some special story about Scoutcraft such as a hike or camping experience.

REFERENCES:
"Newspaper," G. B. Dibble, Holt.
"Handbook of Journalism," N. C. Fowler, Sully.

LAUNDRESS

SYMBOL—FLAT IRON

1. What elements are needed to clean soiled clothes?
2. Show a blouse that you have starched and folded, OR Show a skirt and coat you have pressed.
3. How is starch made? How is it prepared for use?
4. What is soap? How is it made? What is soap powder?
5. How can you soften hard water? How are a wringer and a mangle used?
6. Name steps to take in washing colored garments.
7. Should table linen be starched? Why?
8. Why do we run clothes through blueing water? What is blueing? How made?
9. Know the different kinds of irons and how to take care of irons.
10. How to remove stains; ink, fruit, rust, grass, cocoa and grease. Why must stains be removed before laundering?
11. What clothes should be boiled to make them clean? How are flannels washed? What should be done to clothes after drying before they are ironed?

REFERENCES:
"Saturday Mornings," C. B. Burrell, Dana Estes.
"First Aid to the Young Housekeeper," C. T. Herrick, Scribner.
"Guide to Laundry Work," M. D. Chambers, Boston Cooking School.
"Approved Methods for Home Laundry," Mary Beals Vail, B.S., Proctor Gamble Co.

MILLINER

SYMBOL—BONNET

1. Renovate a hat by removing, cleaning and pressing all trimmings and the lining, turn or clean the hat and replace trimmings and lining.
2. Trim a felt hat and make and sew in the lining.

3. Make a gingham, cretonne or straw hat using a wire frame.
4. What is felt and how is it made into hats?
5. What is straw and how is it prepared for millinery purposes?
6. How is straw braid for hats sold?
7. What is meant by "a hand-made hat?"
8. Can the shape of a felt or straw hat be materially changed? If so by what process?
9. What kind of thread is best for sewing trimming on to a hat?
10. How is the head measured for ascertaining the head size for a hat?

REFERENCES:
"Art of Millinery," Anna Ben Yusef, Millinery Trade Pub. Co.

MOTORIST****

SYMBOL—A WINGED WHEEL

To qualify for this badge a Scout must be at least eighteen, and must pass the examination which is required for the Motor Corps of the National League for Women's Service.

This includes:
1. A certificate of health from a physician.
2. Possessing the First Aide Badge.
3. A Diploma from a certified training school for motorists, with a mark of at least 85 per cent.
4. A driver's license from her state, signed by the Secretary of State.
5. Taking the oath of allegiance.

REFERENCE:
Putnam's Automobile Handbook, H. C. Brokaw, Putnam.

MUSICIAN

SYMBOL—HARP

For pianist, violinist, cellist or singer.
1. Play or sing a scale and know its composition.
2. Write a scale in both the treble and base clef.
3. Know a half-tone, whole tone, a third, fifth and octave.
4. Be able to distinguish a march from a waltz, and give the time of each.
5. What is a quarter, half and whole note, draw symbols.
6. Name five great composers and one composition of each, including an opera, a piano composition, a song. Two of the foregoing must be American.
7. Play or sing from memory three verses of the Star Spangled Banner. The Battle Hymn of the Republic and America.
8. Play or sing correctly from memory one piece of good music.
9. For instrumentalist: Be able to play at sight a moderately

difficult piece and explain all signs and terms in it.

For Singer: Show with baton how to lead a group in singing compositions written in 3/4 and 4/4 time.

10. What is an orchestra? Name at least five instruments in an orchestra.

REFERENCES:

"Art of the Singer," W. T. Henderson, Scribner.

"How to Listen to Music," H. E. Krehbiel, Scribner.

"Orchestral Instruments and What They Do," D. G. Mason, Novello.

NEEDLEWOMAN

SYMBOL—

SPOOL, THREAD AND NEEDLE

1. Know how to run a seam, overcast, roll and whip, hem, tuck, gather, bind, make a French seam, make button hole, sew on buttons, hooks and eyes, darn and patch. Submit samples of each.
2. Show the difference between "straight" and "on the bias," and how to make both.
3. Know the difference between linen, cotton and woolen, and pick out samples of each.
4. Know how thread, silk and needles are numbered and what the numbers indicate.
5. Show how to measure and plan fullness for edging or lace.
6. Know how to lay a pattern on cloth, cut out a simple article of of wearing apparel and make same. Use this article to demonstrate as much of question 1 as possible.
7. Knit either a muffler, sweater or baby's jacket and cap and crochet one yard of lace or make a yard of tatting.
8. Hemstitch or scallop a towel or bureau scarf and work an initial on it in cross stitch.

REFERENCES:

"Complete Dressmaker," C. E. Laughlin, Appleton.

"Art in Needlework," S. F. Day, Scribner.

PATHFINDER

SYMBOL—A HAND POINTING

1. Describe the general plan of the city, town or village in which you live, locate the principal shopping, business and residence districts and know how to reach them from any quarter of the city, town or village. Be able to direct a person to the nearest place of worship to which they desire to go, OR
   Describe in a general way the township or county in which you live giving the principal roads, naming two of the nearest and largest cities or towns, giving their distance from your residence and telling how to reach them.
2. Know the routes of the principal surface car and subway lines, or

The name of the nearest railroad division to your residence and four of the principal cities or towns through which it passes within a distance of one hundred miles.

3. Know at least three historic points of interest within the limits of your city, town or village, how to get to them and why they are historic, OR
Tell of three things of interest concerning the history of your own community.

4. Know the name and location of the Post Office, Telegraph and Telephone Stations, Public Library, City or Town Hall, one Hospital of good standing, one hotel or inn, three churches, one Protestant, one Catholic, one Synagogue, and the nearest railroad, OR
Know the name, location and distance from your home or village, of the nearest Library, Hospital, Church, Post Office, Telegraph and Telephone and Railroad Stations.

5. Know the name and location of three buildings or places in your city, town or village, of interest from a point of beauty either of architecture, decoration or surroundings, OR
Know and locate three places of interest within ten miles of your home, because of beautiful views or surroundings, OR give directions for taking a walk through beautiful woods, lanes or roads.

6. Draw a map of the district around your home covering an area of one quarter square mile, noting streets, schools and other public buildings, fire alarm boxes, at least one public telephone booth, one doctor's office, one drug store, one provision store, and four ɔints of the compass. Draw to scale, OR
Draw a map covering a half square mile of country around your home noting schools and any other public buildings, roads, lanes, points of interest, historic or otherwise, streams, lakes and four cardinal points of the compass. Map must be drawn to scale.

7. Know how to use the fire alarm, how to consult telephone directory, how to call for assistance in case of water leak, accident, burglary, forest fire and how to call the police for any other emergency.

8. Find any of the four cardinal points of the compass by sun or stars, by use of a watch and a cane or stick.

REFERENCES:
Sections in Handbook on "Woodcraft," and "Measurements and Mapmaking," and publications of local Historical Societies, Guides and Directories.

PHOTOGRAPHER

SYMBOL—

CAMERA ON STANDARD

1. Submit six good photographs, interior and out of door, taken, developed and printed by self, OR twelve good photographs taken by self including portraits, animals, out of door and indoor subjects.

2. What constitutes a good picture?

3. Give three rules to be followed in taking interiors, portraits and out of door pictures.

4. Name and describe briefly the processes used in photography.

5. Tell what a camera is and name and describe the principal parts of a camera.

6. What is a film? What is a negative?

7. What position in relation to the sun should a photographer take when exposing a film?
8. Should a shutter be operated slowly? If so, why?
9. What causes buildings in a picture to look as if they were falling?
10. What precautions should be taken when reloading a camera and taking out an exposed film?
11. What is an enlargement? How is it made?
12. What are the results of under exposure and over exposure?
13. What are the results of failing to take the proper camera distance, having improper light and allowing the camera to move?
14. If there is more than one method of exposing a film what determines the method to be used?

REFERENCES:
"How to Make Good Pictures," Eastman Kodak Company.
"The Photo Miniature," such numbers as appear to be needed.
"Nature and the Camera," A. R. Dugmore, Doubleday.
"Photography for Young People," T. Jenks, Stokes.
"Why My Photographs Are Bad," C. M. Taylor, Jacobs.

PIONEER***

SYMBOL—AXES

1. Tell four things that must be considered when choosing a camp site.
2. Know how to use a saw, an axe, a hatchet.
3. Know how to select and fell a tree for building or fuel purposes. Know a fork and sapling and their uses.
4. Build or help three others to build a shack suitable for four occupants.
5. Make a latrine, an incinerator, a cache.
6. Make a fire place for heating and cooking purposes and cook a simple meal over it.
7. Know how to tell the directions of the wind.
8. Know how to mark a trail.
9. Tell what to do to make water safe for drinking if there is any question as to its purity.

REFERENCES:
"Camping and Woodcraft," Horace Kephart, Macmillan.
"On The Trail," L. Beard, Scribner.
"Vacation Camps For Girls," Jeannette Marks, D. Appleton.
The Girl Scout's Camp, Pub. by Nat. Hdqrs. Girl Scouts.

ROCK TAPPER

SYMBOL—

PICK AND SHOVEL

1. Collect and correctly identify ten rocks found among the glacial boulders.

2. Make photograph or make sketch of glacial boulders.
3. Collect two or three scratched or glaciated pebbles or cobble-stones in the drift.
4. Make a sketch or photograph of an exposed section of glaciated or scratched bed-rock and note as accurately as you can the direction of the scratches or grooves.

REFERENCES:
"The Story of Our Continent," N. S. Shaler, Ginn and Co.
"The Great Ice Age and Its Relation to the Antiquity of Man," D. Appleton and Co.
"A Text Book of Geology," portion of Chapter XXV entitled "The Glacial Epoch in North America.".. D. Appleton & Co.
"Physiography for High School," Chapter V entitled, "The Work of Snow and Ice," Henry Holt and Co.
"An Introduction To Physical Geography," Chapter VI entitled, "Glaciers," D. Appleton, or any other good text book of geology or physical geography.
"Travels in Alaska," John Muir.

SAILOR*

SYMBOL—ANCHOR

Qualify for questions under A, one to eleven, and one other test on rowboat, sailboat, canoe or motor boat.

A. GENERAL.
1. Swim twenty-five yards with clothes and shoes on, or hold the swimming merit badge.
2. Know sixteen points of the compass.
3. Find any one of the four cardinal points of the compass by sun or stars.
4. Know the rules for right of way.
5. Know how to counteract the effect of current, tide and wind.
6. Demonstrate making a landing, coming along side, making fast, pushing off.
7. What is a calm? What is a squall? What are the sky and water conditions that denote the approach of the latter?
8. Why are squalls dangerous?
9. What are the dangers of moving about or standing in a boat?
10. Tie four knots for use in handling a boat. Prepare, tie and throw a life line a distance of 25 feet.
11. Which is the "port" and which the "starboard" side of the boat, and what color lights represent each?

B. ROWBOAT.
1. Demonstrate hoisting a sail, taking in a reef, letting out a reef, oars, feather the oars, turn around, row backward, back water, keep a straight course.
2. Name two types of row boats.
3. Demonstrate rowing alone on a straight course for a period of one-half hour. Keep stroke with another person for the same length of time.
4. Demonstrate sculling or poling.
5. Bail and clean a boat.
6. What does it mean to "trim ship?"

C. SAILBOAT.
1. Demonstrate hoisting a sail, taking in a reef, letting out a reef,

steering, sailing close to the wind, before the wind, coming about, coming up into the wind.

2. What is meant by tacking?
3. What is the difference between a keel and centerboard type of boat? Tell the advantage of each.
4. Coil the ropes on a sailboat.
5. Name three different types of sailboats.

D. CANOE.
1. Where and how should a canoe be placed when not in use?
2. Demonstrate putting a canoe into the water, stepping into it, taking it out, and the technique of bow and stern paddling.
3. Overturn, right and get back into a canoe.
4. Name two standard makes of canoes.
5. What does it mean to make a portage?

E. MOTORBOAT.
1. Know how to oil the engine and the best kind of oil with which to oil it.
2. Demonstrate cleaning the engine; cranking the engine.
3. Know how to measure gas in tank, how much gas the tank holds, and how long the engine will run when the tank is full. Know how to judge good gasoline.
4. Why should a motor boat never be left without turning off the gas? State reasons.
5. Be able to rectify trouble with the carburetor.
6. Know proper weight of anchor for boat; how to lower and hoist anchor; how to ground anchor so boat will not drag; know the knot to fasten rope to anchor and rope to boat, and how to throw out anchor.
7. Demonstrate how to coil rope so it will not kink when anchor is thrown out.
8. Know channels and right of way by buoys and lights.

REFERENCES:
Harper's Boating Book for Boys," C. J. Davis, Harper.
"Boat Sailing," A. J. Kenealy, Outing.

SCRIBE

SYMBOL—OPEN BOOK

1. Submit an original short story, an essay or play or poem.
2. Know three authors of prose and their compositions.
3. Mention the names and some works of three novelists, two essayists, three poets, two dramatists of the present century, at least three of them American.

SIGNALLER

SYMBOL—CROSSED FLAGS

SEMAPHORE
1. Give alphabet correctly in 30 seconds, or less.

2. Give the following abbreviations correctly:
   AFFIRMATIVE, ACKNOWLEDGE, ATTENTION, ERROR, NEGATIVE, PREPARATORY, ANNULLING, SIGN OF NUMERALS.
3. Send message not previously read, of twenty words, containing three numerals and sent at the rate of 50 letters per minute. Only one error to be allowed. Technique to be considered and judged.
4. Receive unknown message of twenty words, containing three numerals at the same rate. Two errors to be allowed. Scouts may have someone take message down in writing as they read it, and five minutes in which to rewrite it afterwards.

WIGWAG

1. Give alphabet correctly in two and a half minutes or less.
2. Give numerals up to ten correctly.
3. Send message not previously read, of twenty words, containing three numerals, at the rate of ten letters per minute. Only one error allowed; technique and regularity to be considered and judged.
4. Receive unknown message of twenty words, containing three numerals, to be given at the rate of 10 letters per minute... Two errors to be allowed. Conditions for receiving, the same as in Semaphore.

BUZZER

GENERAL SERVICE CODE

1. Send message of twenty words, not previously read, at the rate of ten letters per minute. Two errors allowed.
2. Receive unknown message of twenty words to be given at the same rate. Two errors allowed. Scouts to be allowed five minutes in which to rewrite message, afterwards.

REFERENCES:
   "How to Signal by Many Methods," J. Gibson, Gale.
   "Cadet Manual, " E. Z. Steever, Lippincott.
   "Boys' Camp Manual," C. K. Taylor, Century.
   "Outdoor Signalling," Elbert Wells, Outing Pub. Co.

STAR GAZER

SYMBOL—STAR GROUP

1. Explain briefly the Solar System.
2. Make a diagram showing the relative positions and movements of the earth, sun and moon. What governs the tide? What causes an eclipse? What is a comet, a shooting star, a sun spot?
3. Name the planets in their order from the sun. Which planet is nearest the earth and give its distance?
4. How fast does light travel?
5. What is the difference between planets and fixed stars and name three of the latter.
6. What is a constellation? Name and be able to point out six. Name two constellations which are visible throughout the year.
7. Draw a chart of the Big Dipper and Cassiopeia and the North Star at intervals of three hours through the night using a fixed

frame and drawing from the same spot.
8. Observe a sunrise and a sunset.
9. What is the Milky-Way? Give its course through the heavens.
10. What is a morning star? What is an evening star?
11. Explain zenith and nadir.
12. What is the Aurora Borealis? Have you seen it?

REFERENCES:

"Field Book of Stars." W. T. Olcott, Putnam.
"The Book of Stars," R. F. Collins, D. Appleton.
"Around The Year With The Stars," Garrett P. Serviss, Harper.

SWIMMER

SYMBOL—LIFE BUOY

1. Swim 50 yards.
2. Demonstrate the Breast Stroke and 3 strokes in addition from the following: Back Stroke, Side Stroke (English underarm), Side Stroke (Australian overarm), Trudgeon, Crawl, Treading Water.
3. Swim 25 feet under water.
4. Demonstrate floating.
5. Demonstrate three ways of diving.
6. Retrieve an object from a depth of 8 feet.
7. Prepare and throw a life line to a person in the water 25 feet away and pull him to safety.
8. Rescue a supposed drowning person.
9. Demonstrate the Schaefer method of resuscitation.
10. Swim 25 yards in clothes, skirt and boots included, and undress in water over one's head.
11. Know how to row a boat and how to dive from it.

REFERENCES:

"Modern Swimming," J. H. P. Brown, Small.
"How to Swim," Dalton, D., Putnam.
"On the Trail," L. Beard, Scribner.

TELEGRAPHER

SYMBOL—TELEGRAPH POLE

1. Send 22 words per minute using a sounder and American Morse Code.
2. Receive 25 words per minute and write out the message in long hand or on a typewriter directly from sound.
   No mistakes allowed.

REFERENCE:

"Harper's Beginning Electricity," D. C. Shafer, Harper.

ZOOLOGIST

SYMBOL—SEAHORSE

I. To pass this test a Scout must be able to tell in a general way the differences between plants and animals, the different kinds of animals, Invertebrates and Vertebrates, and among the Vertebrates to distinguish between Fishes, Amphibia, Reptiles, Birds and Mammals.

II. She must also pass the test on Mammals and the test on at least one other group: either Invertebrates, Fishes, Amphibia, Reptiles or Birds, (For this see special test under Bird Hunter.)

A. MAMMALS

1. Give a list of ten wild mammals personally observed and identified in the open.
2. Name two mammals that kill fruit trees by girdling them.
3. Mention three mammals that destroy the farmer's grain.
4. State game laws of her State which apply to mammals.
5. Name and locate one great game preserve in the United States and mention five game mammals protected there.
6. Mention three furs that are sold by their true names, and three that are sold under trade names that differ from the true ones, giving both names.

B. REPTILES

1. Mention some uses of the leather made from Alligator skins.
2. Give names of three Turtles that you have identified in the open.
3. What is the only poisonous Lizard in the United States?
4. Name and describe the poisonous Snakes of your State.

C. AMPHIBIANS

1. Describe the life history of the frog or the toad.
2. Describe the wonderful power of changing color shown by the common Tree-frog.
3. What is the difference in the external appearance of a salamander and a lizard?
4. Give a list of five Amphibians that you have identified in the open.

D. FISHES

1. Describe the habits of feeding and egg-laying in one of our native fishes.
2. Mention a common fish that has no scales, one that has very small scales, and one that has comparatively large scales.
3. Name five much-used food fishes of the sea, and five fresh-water food-fishes.
4. What are some necessary characteristics of a game-fish? Mention a well-known salt-water game fish, and two fresh-water ones.
5. Describe the nest of some local fish, giving location, size, etc.

E. INVERTEBRATES

(Either of the following)

a. Insects and Spiders

1. How may mosquitoes be exterminated?
2. Collect, preserve and identify ten butterflies, five moths, ten other insects, and three spiders.
3. Describe the habit that certain ants have of caring for plant-lice or aphids which secrete honey-dew.
4. Describe the life-history of one of our solitary wasps. (See "Wasps Social and Solitary," by George W. and Elizabeth G. Peckham; Houghton Mifflin Co.)
5. Describe the life of a hive or colony of honey-bees. (See "The Life of the Bee," by Maurice Maeterlinck, Dodd Mead Co.)

b. Sea Shore Life

1. Name five invertebrates used as food and state where they are found.
2. What is the food of the starfish? How are starfish destroyed?
3. Name twenty invertebrates which you have seen and give the locality where they were found.
4. Name five invertebrates that live in the water only and five that burrow in the mud or sand.
5. What invertebrate was eaten by the Indians and its shell used in making wampum? Where have you seen this animal?

GENERAL REFERENCES

A. MAMMALS

"Life-Histories of Northern Animals," 2 vols., Ernest Thompson Seton, Scribner.

"American Animals," Stone, Witmer, and Wm. E. Cram, Doubleday Page.

"American Natural History, Vol. 1, Mammals," Wm. T. Hornaday, Scribner.

"Squirrels and Other Fur-Bearers," John Burroughs, Houghton Mifflin.

"Kindred of the Wild," C. G. D. Roberts, Doubleday Page.

"Animals, Their Relation and Use To Man," C. D. Wood, Ginn and Co.

"Popular Natural History," J. G. Wood, Winston.

B. REPTILES

"Reptile Book," Raymond L. Ditmars, Doubleday Page.

"The Poisonous Snakes of North America," Leonhard Stejneger, Report U. S. National Museum, 1893.

C. AMPHIBIANS

"The Frog Book," Mary Cynthia Dickerson, Doubleday Page.

"Manual of Vertebrates of the Northern United States," David Starr Jordan, A. C. McClurg Pub. Co.

"Nature Study and Life," Clifton F. Hodge, Ginn and Co.

D. FISHES

"American Food and Game Fishes," David Starr Jordan and Barton W. Evermann, Doubleday Page.

"The Care of Home Aquaria," Raymond C. Osburn, New York Zoological Society.

"The Story of the Fishes," James Newton Baskett, D. Appleton and Co.

E. INVERTEBRATES

a. Insects and Spiders

"Butterfly Guide," W. J. Holland, Doubleday Page... (For beginners).

"Our Common Butterflies," Frank E. Lutz, (Guide Leaflet No. 38, American Museum of Natural History).

"How to Collect and Preserve Insects," Frank E. Lutz, (Guide Leaflet No. 39, American Museum of Natural History.)

"The Moth Book," W. J. Holland, Doubleday Page.

"The Butterfly Book," W. J. Holland, Doubleday Page.

"The Spider Book," J. H. Comstock, Doubleday Page.

"Moths and Butterflies," Mary C. Dickerson, Ginn and Co.

"Manual for the Study of Insects," J. H. and A. B. Comstock, Comstock Publishing Co.

"The Wonders of Instinct," Jean Henri Fabre, Century Co.

"Field Book of Insects," Frank E. Lutz, Putnam.

b. Sea Shore Life

"The Sea-Beach at Ebb Tide," A. F. Arnold, The Century Co.

"Sea-Shore Life," A. G. Mayer, (New York Zoological Society, 1906).

"Introduction to Zoology," C. B. and G. C. Davenport, Macmillan Co., 1900.

III. GROUP BADGES

The Scout who follows one line of interest sufficiently long to qualify in several related subjects may take a Group Badge signifying proficiency in the general field. All Group Badges must be passed on by National Headquarters.

1. Community Scout (any four)
   Citizen***
   Health Guardian***
   Economist
   Business Woman***
   Telegrapher
   Interpreter
   Motorist****
   Canner

In Preparation.

2. Scout Entertainer (any two)
   Musician
   Dancer
   Leader of Games (test in preparation)
   Recitationist or Dramatic Reader (test in preparation)
   Story Teller (test in preparation)
   Hostess

3. Scout Aide
   Child Nurse***
   Cook
   First Aide***
   Home Nurse***
   Homemaker
   Health Winner
   Health Guardian

4. Woodcraft Scout (any three)
   Athlete***
   Motorist****
   Horsewoman
   Sailor
   Swimmer
   Pioneer
   Pathfinder

5. Scout Naturalist

To earn this badge a Scout must have passed three of the tests of Bird Hunter, Flower Finder, Rock Tapper, Star Gazer or Zoologist. She must also pass the following brief test:

1. What sorts of things are included in Nature Study?
2. What are the other names for living and non-living objects?
3. Read one of the following general books on Nature Study.

GENERAL NATURE STUDY REFERENCES:

"Handbook of Nature Study," Anna Botsford Comstock, Comstock Publishing Co. (Manual for Leaders).
"Nature Study and Life," Clifton F. Hodge, Ginn and Co.
"The Story Book of Science," J. Henri Fabre, Century Co.
"Leaf and Tendril," John Burroughs, Houghton Mifflin.
"Wake Robin," John Burroughs, Houghton Mifflin.
"Natural History of Selbourne," Gilbert White.
"Travels in Alaska," John Muir.
"My First Summer in the Sierras," John Muir.

6. Land Scout
   Gardener
   Farmer
   Dairy Maid
   Bee Keeper

IV. GOLDEN EAGLET

SYMBOL—A GOLD EAGLET PIN OR PENDANT

Qualifications: Only First Class Scouts are eligible for this, the highest award offered to Girl Scouts. To obtain this a girl must have won twenty-one Merit Badges, of which fifteen must be:

Athlete	First Aide***
Bird Hunter or Flower Finder or Zoologist	Health Guardian***
	Health Winner
Child Nurse***	Homemaker
Citizen***	Home Nurse***
Cook	Hostess
Dressmaker	Laundress
Economist	Pioneer

V. SPECIAL MEDALS

ATTENDANCE STAR

To earn this a Scout must attend every troop meeting held by her troop. A year is counted as one meeting a week for eight months, or two meetings a week for four months.

1. The gold star is given for attendance at all regular troop meetings held during a period of one year... Punctuality is required and no excuses are allowed.
2. The silver start is given for attendance at 90 per cent of all regular troop meetings.
3. The attendance badge may be given only to a girl who has belonged to the organization for one year; the badges therefore denote how many years a girl has been a Scout.

LIFE SAVING MEDALS

1. The Bronze Cross is awarded as the highest possible award for gallantry, and may be won only when the claimant has shown special heroism or has faced extraordinary risk of life.
2. The Silver Cross is awarded for saving life with considerable risk to oneself.
3. These two medals are worn over the right pocket.
4. Applications must be made by the girl's Captain, who should send to National Headquarters, through the Local Council, if there is one, a full account with written evidence from two witnesses of the deed.

MEDAL OF MERIT

1. The Medal of Merit is designed for the Scout who does her duty exceptionally well, though without grave risk to herself, or for specially good work in recruiting on behalf of the Girl Scout movement, or for specially good record at school for one year in attendance and lessons.
2. This medal is worn over the right pocket.
3. Only registered Scouts are entitled to this medal.
4. Application for this medal should be made by the girl's Captain, who should send to National Headquarters, through the Local Council, if there is one, a full account of the circumstances upon which the claim is based. If the claim is based upon a school record, the girl's report card or a copy of it signed by her teachers, should accompany the Captain's letter. Cards will be returned promptly.

THANKS BADGE

1. The Thanks Badge may be given to anyone to whom a Scout owes gratitude for assistance in promoting Scouting. Every Girl Scout anywhere in the whole world when she sees the Thanks Badge, recognizes that the person who wears it is a friend and it is her duty to salute and ask if she can be of service to the wearer of the badge.
2. The Thanks Badge may be worn on a chain or ribbon.
3. The approval of National Headquarters must be obtained before the Thanks Badge is presented to anyone. Applications may be sent to National Headquarters by any registered Scout (whether Captain, Lieutenant, or Girl Scout) giving the name of the person to whom the badge is to be given and the circumstances which justify the award. Unless the badge is to be presented to the Captain herself, her recommendation is required.

VI. GIRL SCOUT OFFICERS AND CLASS INSIGNIA

CAPTAIN'S PIN

LIEUTENANT'S PIN

TENDERFOOT PIN

SECOND-CLASS BADGE

FIRST CLASS BADGE

CORPORAL

PATROL LEADER

EX-PATROL LEADER

VII. FLOWER CRESTS FOR TROOPS

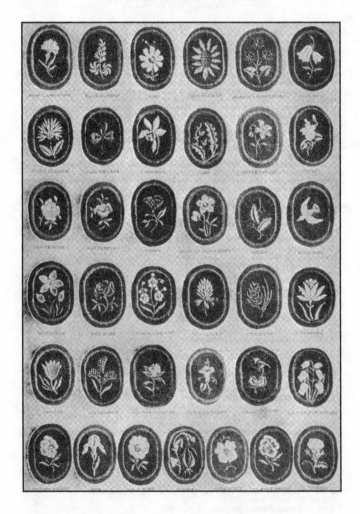

SECTION XIX

REFERENCE READING FOR GIRL SCOUTS

The following books have been selected for Girl Scouts with two ideas in mind: first, to list some of the best books of the world, with which all persons should be familiar, and second, to give books that should be easily available in all parts of the country. In some cities the Public Libraries have "Girl Scout Shelves." Has your library one? In some places the Libraries have Reading Clubs for young people, conducted by the boys and girls themselves under the guidance of specially trained librarians who know just how to help bring the right book to hand, on any subject a Scout would be interested in. In Manhattan there are no less than thirty such clubs in connection with the various district libraries. Why not have one of these in your town?

The American Library Association, whose headquarters are in Washington, will help to bring books to rural districts and places without regular public libraries. Write to them for help if you need it.

The Congressional Library may be called upon at any time for bibliography on any special topic.

The books in this section are in addition to the special references for Proficiency Tests in Section XVIII.

HANDBOOKS OF ALLIED ORGANIZATIONS

Boy Scouts of America, Handbook for Boys, Doubleday and Page, 1914.

Boy Scout Camp Book, Edward Cave, Doubleday and Page.

The Camp Fire Girls, (Handbook of Camp Fire Girls), 31 East 17th Street, N. Y. C.

Girl Guiding, Sir Robert Baden-Powell, C. Arthur Pearson Ltd., London.

Scouting for Boys, Sir Robert Baden-Powell, C. Arthur Pearson, Ltd., London.

Woodcraft Manual for Boys and Woodcraft Manual for Girls by Ernest Thompson Seton, Doubleday and Page.

ADVENTURE

Robinson Crusoe, Daniel DeFoe.

Jim Davis, John Masefield.

A Woman Tenderfoot; Two Little Savages; Ernest Seton Thompson and Grace Gallatin.

David Balfour, Kidnapped, Treasure Island, Robert Louis Stevenson.

Round the World in Eighty Days, Twenty Thousand Leagues Under the Sea, The Mysterious Island, Jules Verne.

Swiss Family Robinson, Wyss.

ANIMAL STORIES

Jungle Books, First and Second; Just So Stories; Rudyard Kipling.

The Call of the Wild, Jack London.

Bob, Son of Battle, Ollivant.

Wild Animals I Have Known, Ernest Seton Thompson.

Black Beauty, Sewell.

Lad, a Dog; Albert Payson Terhune.

FAIRY AND FOLK TALES

Fairy Tales, Hans Christian Anderson... Mrs. Edgar Lucas' Edition.
Arabian Nights.
Peter Pan in Kensington Gardens, James M. Barrie.
Granny's Wonderful Chair, F. Browne.
Davy and the Goblin, Guy Wetmore Carryl.
Celtic Fairy Tales, J. Jacobs.
Norse Fairy Tales, Sir George Dasent.
Folk Tales of Flanders, Jean De Bosschere.
Fairy Tales, Grimm Bros., Mrs. Lucas editor.
Uncle Remus, His Songs and Sayings, Joel Chandler Harris.
Mopse the Fairy, Jean Ingelow.
Water Babies, Charles Kingsley.
Wonderful Adventures of Nils, Selma Lagerlöf.
Blue, Red, Green and Brown Fairy Books, Andrew Lang.
Pinocchio, C. Lorenzini.
Back of the North Wind; Double Story; The Princess and Curdle;
The Princess and the Goblin; George MacDonald.
Czecho-Slovak Fairy Tales, Parker Fillmore.
Ting a Ling Tales; The Queen's Museum and Other Fanciful Tales,
Frank Stockton.

HISTORY AND PERIOD NOVELS

The Story of France, Mary MacGregor.
The Little Book of the War, Eva March Tappan.
Story of the World, Elizabeth O'Neill.
Story of the War for Young People, F. A. Kummer, Century, 1919.
Story of the Great War, Roland Usher.
Story of a Pioneer, Anna Howard Shaw.
Old Timers in the Colonies, Charles C. Coffin.
The Boys of '76, Charles C. Coffin.
Drum-Beat of the Nation, Charles C. Coffin.
Redeeming the Republic, Charles C. Coffin.
Lafayette, We Come! Rupert S. Holland.
Historic Events of Colonial Days, Rupert S. Holland.
History of England, Rudyard Kipling.
Hero Tales from American History, Lodge and Roosevelt.
Famous Scouts, Charles H. Johnston.
Famous Frontiersmen and Heroes of the Border, Charles H.
Johnston.
Boys' Life of Theodore Roosevelt, Herman Hagedorn.
Boys' Life of Abraham Lincoln, Helen Nicolay.
American Hero Stories, Eva March Tappan.
A Gentleman of France, Weyman.
A Tale of Two Cities, Charles Dickens.
Cardigan, Robert Chambers.
Deerslayer, Fenimore Cooper.
Fortunes of Nigel, Walter Scott.
Henry Esmond, William Makepeace Thackery.
Hugh Wynne, Weir Mitchell.
Ivanhoe, Walter Scott.
Janice Meredith, Paul Leicester Ford.
Joan of Arc, Laura E. Richards.
Last of the Mohicans, Fenimore Cooper.
Maid at Arms, Robert Chambers.
Man Without a Country, Edward Everett Hale.
Master Simon's Garden, Caroline Meigs.
Pool of Stars, Caroline Meigs.
Master Skylark, Bennett.
Merry Lips, Beulah Marie Dix.
Otto of Silver Hand, Howard Pyle.
Quentin Durward, Walter Scott.

Romona, Helen Hunt Jackson.
Rewards and Fairies, Rudyard Kipling.
Richard Carvel, Winston Churchill.
Soldier Rigdale, Beulah Marie Dix.
The Crisis, Winston Churchill.
The Perfect Tribute, M. S. Andrews.
The Prince and the Pauper, Mark Twain.
The Refugees, Conan Doyle.
The Scarlet Pimpernel, Baroness Onczy.
The Spartan, Caroline Snediker.
The Three Musketeers, Alexandre Dumas.
The White Company, Conan Doyle.
Two Little Confederates, Thomas Nelson Page.
Via Crucis, Marion Crawford.
Westward Ho, Charles Kingsley.
A Yankee at King Arthur's Court, Mark Twain.

MYTH AND LEGEND

Story of Roland, James Baldwin.
The Sampo (Finnish), James Baldwin.
The Story of Siegfried, James Baldwin.
Children of the Dawn, (Greek), Elsie Buckley.
Pilgrim's Progress, John Bunyan.
The Stories of Norse Heroes, Wilmot Buxton.
Don Quixote, Cervantes.
Stories of Charlemagne and the Twelve Peers of France, A. J. Church.
Greek Tragedies, Church.
Adventures of Odysseus and The Tale of Troy, Padraic Colum.
Sintram and His Companions, De la Motte Fouqué.
Undine, De la Motte Fouqué.
Tanglewood Tales, Nathaniel Hawthorne.
The Wonderbook, Nathaniel Hawthorne.
Rip Van Winkle, Washington Irving.
Heroes, Charles Kingsley.
Robin Hood, Howard Pyle.
The Story of the Champions of the Round Table, Howard Pyle.
The Story of the Grail and the Passing of Arthur, Howard Pyle.
The Story of King Arthur and His Knights, Howard Pyle.
The Story of Sir Launcelot and His Companions, Howard Pyle.

NONSENSE

Goops, Gillett Burgess.
Inklings for Thinklings, Susan Hale.
Child's Primer of Natural History, Oliver Herford.
The Nonsense Book, Edward Lear.
Alice's Adventures in Wonderland, Lewis Carroll.
Through the Looking Glass, Lewis Carroll.
The Hunting of the Snark, Lewis Carroll.
Nonsense Anthology, Carolyn Wells.
Parody Anthology, Carolyn Wells.

NOVELS AND STORIES

Aldrich, Thomas Bailey; Marjorie Daw.
Austen, Jane; Pride and Prejudice.
Bacon, Josephine Daskam; Ten to Seventeen, Madness of Philip.
Barrie, James M.; Little Minister, Little White Bird, Sentimental Tommy.
Bjornson, Bjernsterne; A Happy Boy, Arne, A Fisher Lassie, Synove Solbaken.
Blackmore, R. W.; Lorna Doone.

Bronte, Charlotte; Jane Eyre.
Bunner, H. C.; Short Sixes.
Chesterton, Gilbert K.; The Club of Queer Trades, The Innocence of Father Brown
Collins, Wilkie; The Moonstone.
Craik, D. M.; (Miss Mulock) John Halifax, Gentleman.
Crawford, Marion; Marietta, Mr. Isaacs, the Roman Singer.
Daskam, Josephine; Smith College Stories, Sister's Vocation, other stories.
Davis, Richard Harding; Soldiers of Fortune, Van Bibber and
Deland, Margaret; Tales of Old Chester.
Dickens, Charles; David Copperfield, The Christmas Carol.
Eliot, George; Mill on the Floss.
Farnol, Jeffrey; The Broad Highway.
Fox, John; Little Shepherd of Kingdom Come, Trail of the Lonesome Pine.
Green, Anna Katherine; The Leavenworth Case, The Filigree Ball.
Haggard, Rider; King Solomon's Mines.
Holmes, Sherlock; Hound of the Baskervilles.
Hope, Anthony; Rupert of Hentzau, The Prisoner of Zenda.
Jacobs, W. W.; Light Freights, Many Cargoes.
Johnson, Owen; The Varmint.
Hornung; Adventures of Raffles, the Gentleman Burglar.
Kipling, Rudyard; Captains Courageous, Soldiers Three, Wee Willie Winkle, Kim, The Nalaukha, The Light That Failed.
Lincoln, Joseph; Captain Erle.
McCarthy, Justin; If I Were King.
Merriman, Henry Seton; Dust, With Edged Tools.
Meredith, Nicholson; In the Bishop's Carriage.
Poe, Edgar Allen; Tales, The Gold Bug.
Reade, Charles; The Cloister and the Hearth, Foul Play.
Rinehart, Mary Roberts; The Amazing Interlude.
Smith, F. Hopkinson; Fortunes of Oliver Horne, Colonel Carter of Cartersville.
Stowe, Harriet Beecher; Little Pussy Willow, Uncle Tom's Cabin.
Stockton, Frank; Rudder Grange, The Lady or the Tiger, Casting Away of Mrs. Leeks and Mrs. Aleshine.
Tarkington, Booth; Monsieur Beaucaire, Gentleman from Indiana, Seventeen, Penrod, Penrod and Sam.
Wells, Carolyn; The Clue, The Gold Bag, A Chain of Evidence, The Maxwell Mystery.
White, Edward Steward; The Blazed Trail.
Wister, Owen; The Virginian.
Woolson, Constance F.; Anne.
Alcott, Louisa M.; Eight Cousins, Little Women, Little Men, Rose in Bloom, etc.
Burnett, Frances Hodgson; Little Lord Fauntleroy, Sarah Crewe.
Coolidge, Susan; Clover, In the High Valley, What Katy Did and other Katy books.
Craik, Mrs.; (Miss Mulock); The Little Lame Prince.
Cummins, Maria Susanna; The Lamplighter.
Dodge, Mary Mapes; Donald and Dorothy, Hans Brinker and the Silver Skates.
Ewing, Juliana; Jackanapes, Six to Sixteen.
Hale, C. P.; Peterkin Papers.
Hughes, Thomas; Tom Brown's School Days.
Jackson, Helen Hunt; Nelly's Silver Mine.
Jordan, Elizabeth; May Iverson, Her Book.
Nesbit, E.; The Wouldbegoods, The Phoenix and the Carpet.
Ouida (de la Ramée); Bimbi Stories.
Richards, Laura E.; Hildegarde Series, Margaret Montford Series.
Shaw, F. E.; Castle Blair.
Spyri, J.; Heidi.
Twain, Mark; Huckleberry Finn, Tom Sawyer.
Warner, Susan; The Wide Wide World.

Wiggin, Kate Douglas; The Birds' Christmas Carol, Polly Oliver's Problems, Rebecca of Sunnybrook Farm.

GIRL SCOUT STORIES

Abbott, Jane; Keineth, Larkspur.
Blanchard, Amy E.; A Girl Scout of Red Rose Troop.
Widdemer, Margaret; Winona's Way and other Winona Books.

POETRY

Verse for Patriots, Jean Broadhurst and Clara Lawton Rhodes.
Golden Staircase, (An Anthology), L. Chisholm.
Lyra Heroica, William Ernest Henley.
Blue Book of Poetry, Andrew Lang.
Story Telling Poems, F. J. Olcott.
Book of Famous Verse, Agnes Repplier.
Home Book of Verse for Young Folks, Burton Egbert Stevenson.
Child's Garden of Verse, Robert Louis Stevenson.
Children's Book of Ballads, Mary W. Tileston.
Golden Numbers, Kate Douglas Wiggin.

WONDERS OF SCIENCE

Magic of Science, Collins.
The Story Book of Science, Jean Henri Fabre, Century.
Field, Forest and Farm, Jean Henri Fabre, Century.
In the Once Upon a Time, Lillian Gask.
Book of the Ocean, Ingersoll.
Careers of Danger and Daring, Cleveland Moffett.
Science at Home, Russell.
Wonders of Science, Eva March Tappan.
The Book of Wonders.
Magazines: Popular Science, Popular Mechanics, Scientific American.

FOR CAPTAINS, LIEUTENANTS, COMMISSIONERS AND OTHER GIRL SCOUT OFFICERS

After a thorough study of Scouting for Girls, the authorized American Handbook, Scout Captains and Lieutenants are urged to read the following list of allied Handbooks for Leaders as containing many practical hints for workers with young people, and emphasizing the essential unity of these manuals.

A study of these manuals will bring out very clearly the fact that though our methods of approach and phraseology may differ in certain instances, our ultimate aim and our broad general principles are precisely the same.

The books in the following list which have been starred are recommended as particularly practical for all students and friends of young people. They represent the latest thought of the greatest authorities on the subjects most closely allied with the sympathetic study of adolescence. It is impossible to isolate a study of the girlhood of America from the kindred topics of women in industry and politics, the growth of the community spirit, the present theories of education, and in general a brief survey of economics, sociology and psychology.

Many of these titles appear technical and dry, but the books have been carefully selected with a view to their readable and stimulating qualities, and no one need be a profound student or a highly educated person in order to understand and appreciate them.

It is especially advisable that Leaders in the Girl Scout organization should be reasonably well informed as to the principal social movements of the day so as to relate the effective organization of the young people of the country with corresponding progress along other lines. The more broadly cultivated our Captains and Councillors be-

come, the more vital and enduring will be the work of the Girl
Scouts, and this breadth of view cannot be obtained from the knowledge and practice of what might be called the "technique of Scouting"
alone.

LEADERS' HANDBOOKS OF ALLIED ORGANIZATIONS

The Boy Scout Movement Applied by the Church.. Richardson-
Loomis, Scribners.

The Camp Fire Guides. National Headquarters of Girl Guides, 76
Victoria Street, London, S. W. 1. Handbook for a special group of
older Guides with a combination program of Girl Guides and Camp
Fire Girls.

Girls Clubs, Helen Ferris. E. P. Dutton and Co., 1919. Suggestions
for programs, community cooperation, practical methods and helps
in organization. Bibliography.

The Girl Guides. Rules, Policy and Organization, 1918.

Senior Guides, Rules, Policy and Organization, 1918. Both official
manuals for Guiders. Nat. Hdqrs. Girl Guides, 76 Victoria Street,
London, S. W. 1.

Handbook for Scoutmasters. Nat. Council of the Boy Scouts, 200
Fifth Avenue, New York City.

Model Treasurer's Book for Girls' Clubs. National League of
Women Workers, 25 cents.

The Pine Tree Patrol, James Austin Wilder. Boy Scouts of
America.

PRACTICAL AND GENERAL READING

Abbott, Edith; Women in Industry. Appleton, $2.00.

Addams, Jane; Twenty Years at Hull House, Spirit of Youth in
the City Streets, A New Conscience and an Ancient Evil, Macmillan.

*Angell, Emmett D.; Play.

*Bancroft, Jessie H.; Games for the Playground, Home, School and
Gymnasium. Macmillan, $1.50.

*Burchenal, Elizabeth; Dances of the People... Shirmer.

*Byington, Margaret; What Social Workers Should Know About
Their Own Communities. Russell Sage Foundation, N. Y.

Cleveland, Frederick and Schaefer, Joseph; Democracy in Reconstruction, Houghton Mifflin, $2.50. Discussion by recognized leaders
of the great social movements of to-day. Recommended as a background for placing the Girl Scout movement.

Daggett, Mabel Potter; Women Wanted. George H. Doran. A book
about women in all walks of life, as affected by the war.

*Dewey, John; Schools of Tomorrow, School and Society. Showing
the growth of the "Scout Idea" in our modern educational methods.
Practical and stimulating.

*Douglass, H. Paul; The Little Town, Macmillan. The latest and
best treatment of rural social conditions. Especially recommended
for Scout leaders in localities outside the great cities.

*Hoerle, Helen, and Salzberg, Florence B., The Girl and the Job,
Henry Holt, $1.50.

Gilman, Charlotte Perkins; Women in Economics, In This Our
World, A Man Made World, Concerning Children... All: Small and
Maynard. The most brilliant American writer on the woman move-
ment. Sound economics and good psychology cleverly presented.

James, William; Principles of Psychology, 2 vols. The psychologist
who wrote like a novelist. Chapters of special interest: Habit,
Instinct, Will, Emotions and The Stream of Consciousness. Talks
to Teachers on Psychology, and to Students on Some of Life's Ideals.
Memories and Studies, especially essay on the Moral Equivalents of
War... All: Henry Holt and Co.

Key, Ellen; The Century of the Child.

*Lovejoy, Esther; The House of the Good Neighbor, Macmillan, 1919.
Social and Medical work in France during the war by the President
of the Women's International Medical Association.

*MacDougall, William; Social Psychology, Luce and Co. Study of how people act and feel in a group.

Mill, John Stuart; The Subjection of Women, Frederick Stokes.

*Norsworthy, Naomi and Whitley; The Psychology of Childhood, Macmillan, 1919. Best and latest general child psychology.

Parsons, Elsie Clews; Social Control, Social Freedom, The Old Fashioned Woman, The Family. All: Putnam.

*Patrick, G. T. W.; Psychology of Relaxation. Houghton Mifflin. The necessity for and guidance of the play instinct.

*Perry, Clarence A., Community Center Activities. Russell Sage Foundation, New York City, 30 cents.

Pillsbury, W. B.; Essentials of Psychology, Macmillan. Good, brief treatment of general psychology for popular reading.

*Playground and Recreation Association of America Publications: What the Playground Can Do for Girls, Games Every Child Should Know, Folk and National Dances, The Home Playground. Headquarters 1 Madison Avenue, New York City.

*Puffer, J. Adams; The Boy and His Gang. Houghton Mifflin.

Putnam, Emily; The Lady.

Schreiner, Olive; Woman and Labour.

Sharp, Cecil J.; One Hundred English Folksongs. Charles H. Gitson & Co.

*Slattery, Margaret; The Girl in Her Teens, The Girl and Her Religion, The American Girl and Her Community, The Woman's Press.

*Thorndike, Edward L.; Individuality, Riverside Educational Monographs, Houghton Mifflin. What constitutes the "average person." The danger of "sizing up" people too rapidly.

*Terman, Lewis; The Hygiene of the Child, Houghton Mifflin.

*Woods, Robert A.; Young Working Girls, Houghton Mifflin.

Trotter, W.; The Herd Instinct in Peace and War, Macmillan. How "public opinion" exerts its influence on conduct.

Wallas, Graham; Human Nature in Politics, and The Great Society, Macmillan.

Ward, Lester F.; Psychic Factors of Civilization and Applied Sociology... Ginn and Co. Psychological interpretation of civilization.

CAMPING AND HIKING

A special Manual on Camping for Girl Scouts in preparation will contain a full and annotated bibliography. The following is a select list for temporary use.

The Boy Camp Manual, Charles Keen Taylor.

Camping and Outing Activities, Cheley-Baker. Games, Songs, Pageants, Plays, Water Sports, etc.

Camp Cookery, Horace Kephart, Macmillan Co.

The Camp Fire Girls' Vacation Book, Camp Fire Girls, New York City.

Camping and Woodcraft (2 vols.), Horace Kephart, Macmillan.

Camp Kits and Camp Life, Charles Stedman Hanks.

Camping Out, Warren Miller, Geo. Doran Co.

Caravaning and Camping-out, J. Harris Stone... Herbert Jenkins, Ltd., 12 Arundel Place, London.

Harper's Camping and Scouting, Joseph Adams, Harper Bros.

Shelters, Shacks and Shanties, D. C. Beard, Scribners. Illustrated.

Summer in a Girls' Camp, Anna Worthington Coale, Century.

Swimming and Watermanship, L. de B. Handley, Macmillan Co.

Touring Afoot, Dr. C. P. Fordyce, N. Y. Outing Publishing Co.

Wilderness Homes, Oliver Kamp, Outing Publishing Co.

GOVERNMENT BULLETINS AND HOW TO GET THEM

1. The publications of all departments of the United States Government are in the custody of the Superintendent of Documents, Washington D. C. Price lists of various subjects are sent free.

The following list of subjects will be found especially useful in preparing for many of the proficiency tests. The numbers given are the official ones by which the catalogs of prices and special titles may be ordered:

(11) Foods and Cookery. (16) Farmers' Bulletins. (31) Education. (38) Animal Industry. (39) Birds and Wild Animals. (41) Insects (including household and farm pests, and bees.) (43) Forestry. (44) Plants. (50) American History and Biography. (51) Health. (53) Maps. (54) Political Science. (55) National Museums and National Academy of Science. (67) Immigration. (68) Farm Management.

2. The United States Interdepartmental Commission on Social Hygiene publishes pamphlets and specially prepared lecture outlines and reading courses on sex education and hygiene. Apply also to state and local societies for social hygiene, for literature, lectures and suggestions.

3. The Children's Bureau of the U. S. Dept. of Labor has a special list of articles on Child and Infant Care and Health. Write direct to the Bureau for these.

4. For State publications on Health, Education, etc., apply to Secretary of State if special officer in charge is unknown.

6. Apply to town hall or special departments for city documents on health, child care, education, etc.

7. The following organizations publish bulletins and cheap authoritative books and pamphlets for general consumption on health, first aid, child care and other topics of interest to Girl Scouts.

The Red Cross, National Headquarters, Washington, D. C.

The Metropolitan Insurance Company, 1 Madison Avenue, N. Y. C.

Child Health Organization, 156 Fifth Avenue, Miss Sally Lucas Jean, Director.

The Posture Standards Company, 1 Madison Avenue, N. Y. C.

The Inter-Church World Movement, 45 West 18th St., N. Y. C.

INDEX

Accidents, First Aid for 164 ff
  Water 191 ff
Act to establish flag 69
Adam 456
Adventure, books of 540
Africa 27
Agassiz 455
Alaska 454
Alcott, Louisa 23
Allied Organizations, Handbooks of 540
Alignments 92
Alligator 429
"America" 74, 75
"America the Beautiful" 66
American Museum of Natural History 373 ff
Amphibians 425
"Anacreon in Heaven" 74
Animal Stories 540
Aphids 449
Apoplexy, care of 186 ff
Aquarium 435
Arnold, Sarah Louise 106
Artist test 499
Aspen 395
Asphyxiation, prevention of 197 ff
Asters 381
At ease 87
Athlete test 499
Attendance stars 536
Attention 85
Audubon Society 425
Australia 27
Axe, use of 326 ff
Azalea 383

Background 40
Back step 89
Baden-Powell 1 ff
Balsam fir 390
Bandages, making of 204 ff
Barnacles 442
Bathroom, care of 119
"Battle Hymn of the Republic" 77
Beach fleas 442
Beaver 370
Bedroom, care of 119
Beekeeper test 500
Birds 407 ff
Bird baths 424
Birds, economic value of 415 ff
Bird Hunter test 500

Bird Woman 21
Biscuit loaf 363
Bites, care of 190 ff
Black Eyed Susan 383, 385
Blood root 381
Blue Bird 409
Blue Flag 383
Blue tailed lizzard 430
Bobolink 415
Bog potatoe, 288
Border, flowers for 464 ff
Boulders 453
Bouncing Bet 383
Bowline, knot 488 ff
Box turtle 430
Brandywine, battle of 469
Bread 363
Breakfast 133 ff
Broiled fish 361
Brown, Thomas Edward 456
Bubonic Plague 449
Bugler's test 501
Bull frog 376, 427
Burroughs, John 375, 407
Business Woman test 502
Butterfly 449
Business meeting 457
Butler, Albert E. 384, 388, 394
Bumble bees 447

Cambridge flag 68
Camp cooking 360 ff
  recipes 362 ff
  utensils 340, 344, 361
Camping and the Guide Law 36
Camping for Girl Scouts 313 ff
  hiking 314 ff
  site 319 ff
  fires 327 ff
  provisions 345 ff
Camp sanitation 323
Canada 27
Canner 502
Captain 14
Captain's pin 538
Cardinal flower 381
Cassiopeia 302
Cat fish 433
Cellar 107
Ceremonies, Forms for Girl Scouts 44 ff
  Alternate Forms 48ff
Chaining 467 ff

Chairman 57
Chameleon 431
Change step 90
Chevrons 538
Chief Scout 35
Child, care of 157 ff
Child Health Organization 547
Child Nurse, 157 ff, test 503
Child, routine of 162 ff
Christmas fern 389
Cicada 447
Citizen's test 504
Civic biology 377
Clams 442
Class tests 60 ff
Cleaning 126
Clermont 69
Closing exercises 57
Clothing for hiking 317
Clove hitch 492 ff
Cochineal 446
Cocoa 363
Cod 433
Colds, care of 247 ff
Color guard 46
"Common minerals and rocks" 454
Community Scout, group badge 533
Compass 482 ff
Congressional Library 540
Conservation of forests 393 ff
Continental Code 97, 99
Conventional signs for maps 479
Convulsions, care of 186 ff
Cooking devices 340
Cooking in camp 360
Cook test 505
Copepods 442
Coral 439
Corned beef hash 362
Corporal 13, 538
Council 14
Court of Honor 45
Crabs 437, 439
Craftsman test 505
Crinkle root 289
Crocodile 429
Crosby, William O. 454
Cultivation 461
Cyclist test 507
Cypress, bald 396

Dancer test 518
Dandelion 383
Dairy Maid test 507
Dash, General Service Code 98
Daughter of New France 20
Dawson, Jean 377
Deciduous 387
Declaration of Independence 68
Diamond Back Terrapin 431
Dickerson, Mary C. 389
Diminish front 96
Dinner 139 ff
Director, National 15

Dish washing 117
Dishes, washing in camp 364
Dislocations, care of 177 ff
Distance, to take in drill 92
Direction 478
Dot, in General Service Code 98
Double time 88
Doughty, Arthur G. 20
Dow, Ula M. 133
Dragon flies 446
Dressmaker 508
Dress, right or left 85
Drill, Girl Scout 84 ff
    Tenderfoot 84
    Second Class 90
    First Class 95
Drummer test 509
Duck hawks 418
Dutch Cleanser 365

Eagle 407
Eclaireuses de France 31
Economist test 509
Eel 456
Egrets 374, 411 ff
Electrician test 510
Emergencies, aid for 164 ff
Erosion 393
Evergreen 387
Exercises 275 ff
Explorer 21
Eyes, Health of 259 ff
Eyesight, tested by stars 303
Eyes right or left 80

Facings 86
Fall in 84
    out 87
Falkland Islands 27
Fairy Tales 541
Farmer test 510
Feet, care of 315
Fellowship 2
Fire, control of 199 ff
Fireless Cooker 111 ff
Fishes 432 ff
Fishes, groups of 433
Fishballs 361
Fisher, G. Clyde, 366, 373 ff
First Aide, 164 ff test 512
First Class Badge 538
    Conferring of 50
    Test 64 ff
First Girl Scout 20
Flag 67 ff
    Colors 67
    History 67 ff
    How to make 77
    Respect due 70 ff
    Regulations for flying 71 ff
Flashlight signalling 100
Floods, cause of 393
Floor, kitchen 108

Flower crests 539
Flower Finder test 512
Flower garden 462 ff
Fly, House, fighting of 121
Folk Tales 541
Food for Camps, 362 ff
Food for the Sick 249 ff
Food furnishing animals 402
Food habits 402
Food, storage of 123 ff
Foot 466
Forbush, Edward Howe 419
Forests, uses of 393 ff
    fires 395
Formation for G. S. Ceremony, military 48
    non-military 55
Forward 86
Fox 406
Fractures, care of 177 ff
France 31
Freezing 40
    care of 188 ff
Fried bacon 362
Fried fish 361
Fried ham 362
Fried country sausage 362
Fried potatoes 362
Fringed gentian 381, 383
Frying pan, 361 ff
Fulton, Robert 59
Fungi 289
Furnishing, 107

Gaillardia 384
Gamefish 435
Ganoid 433
Garden, Girl Scout's Own 456 ff
Gardener test 514
Gas stove 110
General service code 97
Geology 452 ff
Germs, fighting of 121
Gibson, William Hamilton 383, 426
Gila Monster 429
Gills 431
Girl Guides 1, 18 ff
Girl Scout Stories 544
Glacial Drift 453
Glacier 451 ff
Glass snake 430
Golden Eaglet 45, 52, 535
Golden Plover 414
Goldenrod 381
Government Bulletins 456
Grand Union Flag 68
Great Blue Heron 422
Great horned owl 411
Great Ice Age 453
Grebe 408
Grey, Lord 20
Group Badges, 533 ff
Guide, the Flower 383
Guides, War Service 27

Half-hitch 491 ff
Halibut 433
Half step 89
Halt 89
Hammerhead shark 436
Handbooks of Allied Organizations 540
"Handbook of Birds in Eastern North America" 423
"Handbook of Birds of Western United States" 423
Hand Signalling 103
Handywoman test 515
Hawks 420
"Hawks and Owls of the U. S." 420
Health Guardian test 516
Health Winner 257, test, 517
Heating house 124
Heights, to estimate 459 ff
Hemlock 390
Hepatica 381
Hermit crab 442
Hickory nut 383
Hiking 314 ff
History novels 541
History of the American Girl Scouts 1
Hog peanuts 289
Hodge, Clifton 377
"Home Life of Wild Birds" 423
Hollyhocks 383
Homemaker, the, 23, 106, test 518
Home Nurse, the, 217 ff; test 519
Honeybee 448
Honeydew 448
Horsewoman test 520
Hostess test 520
House fly 449
House planning 106
Howe, Julia Ward 77
Hummingbird 383
Hummingbird moth 446
Hunter, David M., 456
Hydroids 441
Hyla 428

Ice Chest 114 ff
"Illustrated Flora" 383
Illnesses, common, 245 ff
India 27
Indian cucumber 288
Indian turnip 289
Injuries, major 177 ff
    minor 169 ff
Inorganic 377
Insects 439, 446 ff
Insect eating birds 421 ff
Insignia, Scouts and officers 538
Inspection 56
Interchurch World Movement 547
Interpreter test 521
Interval, Gen. Serv. Code 98
    Semaphore 101
Invertebrate 377. 438 ff

Jack In the Pulpit 383
Jean, Sally Lucas 547
Jelly fish 439
Jessamine 381
Jones, John Paul 68
Journalist test 521
Judging weights and measures 467 ff

Kelley's Island 455
Kephart, Horace, 313 ff
Key, Francis Scott 73
Kildeer 419
Kindling 334 ff
Kipling, Rudyard 376
Kitchen 108
Knots 484 ff, glossary 495

Labor saving 124 ff
Lady Slipper 281
Lafayette 69
"Land Birds East of the Rockies" 423
Land Scout, Group Badge 535
Lang, Herbert 426
Lantern, signalling 100
Latrine in camp 323
Laundress test 522
Laws of Girl Scouts 4 ff
Leader's Handbooks of Allied Organizations 545
Legends 542
Lewis and Clark Expedition 21
Lobsters 439
Loco Weed 383
Lone Scout 13
Loon 372
Low, Mrs. Juliette, founded G. S. 1
Lunch 148 ff
Lung fishes 433
Lutz, Dr. 447
Life Saving Medals 536
"Little Women" 23
Living room 118
Library, American Association 540
Lieutenants 14

Mackerel 433
Magdelaine de Verchères 20
Magnolia 380
Maiden Hair Fern 383
Malaria 449
Mallard Duck 424
Mammals 399 ff
Manna 447
Manners, good 129 ff

Manual by Grey 383
Manure 458
Map of camp 481
Maple, black sugar 391
Mappa 477
Maps, history, uses, how to make 476 ff
Marine worms 443
Mark time 88
Marsh Marigold 383
Measurements 268 ff, 466 ff
Medal of Merit 536
Medals, special 536
Medicines 241 ff
Meeting, Girl Scout 55 ff
Menus 133 ff
Metre 466
Metric System 466
Metropolitan Life Insurance Company 547
Merit Badges, conferring 51
Miller, Mr. and Mrs. Leo 387
Milliner test 522
Milton 456
Mink 415
Minutes 58
Mississippi Valley 453
Moccasin Flower 382
Mocking bird 409
Mole crab 444
Monarch butterfly 449, 450
Moon 303
Moose 369
Morris, Robert 68
Morse Code
    American 97
    International 97 ff
Mosquito 449, fighting of 121
Motorist test 523
Motto of Girl Scouts 3
Mountain Climbing 367 ff
Mountain Laurel 383
Mud eel 427
Mud puppy 427
Musician test 523
Muscular strain, avoiding 261 ff
Mushrooms 289 ff, 392
Mussels 442
Muir Glacier 454
Muir, John 366
Myths 542

National Convention 1
National Director 15
National Headquarters 1
National Organization 15

Nature, classification 379
Nature in city 39
Nature Study 36, 43
Nature Study for Girl Scouts 373 ff
Naturalist, Scout, group badge 534
Needlewoman's test 524
Nesting boxes 424
Newts 427
New York 1
Noble Peregrine 418, 420
Nonsense 542
North America 451
North Pole 69
Novels 542
Nubian Gold Mines 476
Nurse, the Child 157 ff, home 217 ff

Oak 390
Oblique March 93
Observation 39
Octopus 439
Oil stove 110
One celled animals 431
Onions 363
Opossum 399, 401
Orchids 383
Organic 377
Organization 13 ff
Orion's Sword 304
Otter 400
"Our Native Orchids" 383
Out of Door Scout 35 ff
Ox Eye Daisy 383
Oyster 439, 445

Pace, Scout's 314
Pacing 475, 478
Paddle fish 432
Parade 87
Parade formation 80 ff
Pathfinder's test 524
Patients, amusing of 251, feeding 251, routine 252
Patriotic songs 72
Patrol 13
Patrol Leader 13
Patrol system 324 ff
Peary, Robert 69
Pecten 443
Peeper, spring 428
Pelicans 412
Periwinkle 442, 443, 444
Personal measures 474
Photographer test 525
Pickerel 453
Pickerel weed 385

Pickersgill, Mrs. Mary 74
Pine, long leaved 389
Pine tree patrol system 325
Pine rose mallow 383
Pioneer 24, test 526
Pirsson, Louis V. 454
Pivot, moving 93, fixed 94
Planting 459
Plants 380 ff
Plants, edible, wild 285 ff
Plants poisonous 386 ff
Pledge 3
Pleiades 302
Poetry 544
Poison, antidotes for 202 ff
Polar bear, 402, 452
Policy 16
Posture Standards Company 547
Position, right 373 ff
Poultry, destroyed 402
Preparation of seed bed 457
Presentation of badges, 21, 45 ff
Princess Pat 21
Principles of Girl Scouts 3 ff
Proficiency tests 497 ff
Promise 4
Protozoa 439
Proverbs, out-door 284
Provisions for camping 345 ff
Public Health 355 ff

Quick time 87
Quebec 20

Raccoon 402
Rat flea 449
Rally 45
Rays 433
Recipes, camp 362 ff, home 133 ff
Red Cross, National 214 ff, 547
"Red Gods," 371
Reed, Chester A. 383, 423
Reef knot 487 ff
Reference reading, Captains' 544, Scouts' 540 ff
Refrigerator, iceless 115 ff
Remedies 241 ff
Reptiles 428 ff
Rests 86 ff
Rhododendrons or Great Laurel 383
Right angle, to test 471
Robin 409
Rock crab 444
"Rocks and Rock Minerals" 454
Rocky Mountain Goat 378
Rock Tapper test 526
Roorbach, Eloise 367

Ropes, parts of 487
Ross, Betsy 67, Colonel 68
Roumanian Scout 29
Russian Revolution 29

Sacajawea 21
Sailor test 527
St. Paris, Ohio, 454
St. Paul 70
Salamander 425
Salmon 433
Sandhill cranes 410
Sand hoppers 442
Sanitation in camp 323
Scale insect 447, maps made to 478
Scallop 443
Scavengers, bird 421
Science, wonders of 544
Scout Aide 105 ff, Group Badge 534
Scout Cook, the 133 ff
Scout Entertainer Group Badge 533
Scout Naturalist Group Badge 534
Scout's pace 314
Scratches glacial 453
Screech owl 409
Scribe test 528
Sea anemone 439
    cucumber 439
    spiders 442
Seashore animals 439 ff
Second class badges 49
    drill 90
    test 61 ff
Secretary 57
Seeds 459
Segmented worms 439
Semaphore signalling 101 ff
    code 102
Setting-up Exercises for Girl Scouts
    373 ff
Seventeen Year Locusts 447 ff
Shakespeare 452
Shaler, N. S. 453
Shaw, Anna Howard 25
Sheep shank 493 ff
Sheet bend 487 ff
Sherwood, Geo. H. 373 ff
Shocks, care of 186 ff
Shoes, for hiking 315
Shovel nosed sturgeon 434
Sharks 433
Showy primrose 387
Shrike 417
Sick bed 221 ff
Sick, care of 217 ff

Sick room 218 ff
Side step 89
Signalling 97 ff
Signal flag, Gen'l Service 97, Sema-
    phore 101
Signaller test 528
Signs and blazes 305
Silk worm 448
Simmons College 106, 133
Sink 116 ff
Skink 430
Skunk 404
Skunk cabbage 380
Slogan 3
Smith, Samuel F. 55
Smoke signals 308
Snail 439
Snake bite 297
Snakes 294 ff
Social forms 129 ff
Soft shelled crab 445
Soil 458
Solomon's Seal 389
Song birds 409
Sounds, measuring distance by 471
Spanish Moss 396
Spiders 439, 450, 446 ff
Sponges 439
Spring Beauty 381
Spruce, black, red 389
Square knot 487 ff
Squid 438
Stains 127 ff
Stalking 39
Steps and marchings 87
Stew 361
Stars 78 ff, 298 ff
Starfish 437, 445
Star Gazer test 529
Starling 409
Star Spangled Banner 73 ff
"Story of Our Continent" 453
Stove 109
Supper 148 ff
Sun stroke, care of 188 ff
Swimmer's test 530

Table manners, 130 ff, setting 131
Tadpoles 425
Taping 467 ff
Tenderfoot enrollment 44, 48
    pin 538
    test 60 ff
Tennyson 380
Tents 322 ff
Telegrapher test 530
Telemetry 467, 468

Teodorroiu, Ecaterina 29
Timber wolves 398
Thanks badge 537
Thistle 383
Thrushes 409
Toad 425 ff
Toadstools 289 ff
Toast 363
Tools 457
Totem 309
Tracking 40
Trade name and true name of furs, 403
Trailing arbutus 381
Trans-Atlantic flight 69
Treasurer, report of 57 ff
Trees 387 ff
Triangulation 467 ff, 478
Troop 14
Troop crests 539
Turin 476
Turpentine 389 ff
Turtles 429 ff

Uniform, one piece 83, two piece 92
Union, the 70
Union Jack 68
Units of measure 466
"Useful Birds and Their Protection" 419

Vega 304
Vegetable garden 459 ff
Vertebrates 377

Walnuts 383
Wapato 288
War service 226 ff
Water dog 427

Water and game birds 423
Water lily 383
Water, selection, 320; supply 125 ff
Wasp 447
Waste 122
Weasel 400 ff
Weather wisdom 282 ff
Weeds 461
Weevils 449
Weights and measures 135 ff, judging 467 ff
West Indies 27
"Western Bird Guide" 423
Wharf pile animals 441
Whelk 443
Who Are the Scouts 17 ff
Whistle 100, 103
White, Gilbert 425
Whitman, Walt 313
Whittier 387
Width, to estimate 468 ff
Wig Wag 97
Wild carrot 383
Wild flowers and ferns 380 ff
Wild turkey 416
Witch hazel 382
Woodcraft 280 ff
Woodcraft Scout Group Badge 534
Woods, twelve secrets of the 280 ff
Woolen things 122 ff, clothes, 317 ff
Wood, uses of 388 ff
Wordsworth 375
Wounds, care of 181 ff
Wright, Wilbur 69

Yard 466
Yarrow 383
Yellow fever 449
Yellow pine 394

Zoologist test 531

GIRL SCOUTS
INCORPORATED

National Headquarters
189 LEXINGTON AVENUE, NEW YORK CITY

The Girl Scouts a National Organization, is open to any girl who expresses her desire to join and voluntarily accepts the Promise and the Laws. The object of the Girl Scouts is to bring to all girls the opportunity for group experience, outdoor life, and to learn through work, but more through play, to serve their community.

Officers 1920

Founder
MRS. JULIETTE LOW

Honorary President
MRS. WOODROW WILSON

President
MRS. ARTHUR O. CHOATE

First Vice-President
MRS. JAMES J. STORROW

Second Vice-President
MRS. HERBERT HOOVER

Treasurer
MRS. NICHOLAS E. BRADY

Chairman, Executive Board
MRS. V. EVERIT MACY

Counsel
DOUGLAS CAMPBELL

Director
MRS. JANE DEETER RIPPIN

Executive Board

MRS. SELDEN BACON	MRS. ROBERT G. MEAD
MRS. NICHOLAS F. BRADY	MISS LLEWELLYN PARSONS
MISS ELLEN M. CASSATT	MRS. HAROLD IRVING PRATT
MRS. ARTHUR O. CHOATE	MRS. THEODORE H. PRICE
FRANCIS P. DODGE	MRS. W. N. ROTHSCHILD
MISS EMMA R. HALL	MRS. GEORGE W. STEVENS
MRS. JULIETTE LOW	MRS. JAMES J. STORROW
MRS. V. EVERIT MACY	MRS. CHARLES WELCH
MRS. WM. G. McADOO	MRS. PERCY WILLIAMS

Permanent Committees

Education,   Chairman, MISS SARAH LOUISE ARNOLD
          Secretary, DR. LOUISE STEVENS BRYANT

Publications, Chairman, MRS. JOSEPHINE DASKAM BACON
          Secretary, DR. LOUISE STEVENS BRYANT

Field,   Chairman, MRS. ROBERT G. MEAD
          Secretary, MISS MARY C. CLENDENIN

Standards,   Chairman, MISS LLEWELLYN PARSONS
          Secretary, MISS MARY C. CLENDENIN

Business,   Chairman, MRS. PERCY WILLIAMS
          Secretary, MR. SIDNEY M. MacDOWELL

Finance,   Chairman, MRS. NICHOLAS F. BRADY

Advisory Committee on Business and Finance
          Chairman, MR. CHARLES FRED ALLEN

GIRL SCOUT PUBLICATIONS

Scouting for Girls. Official Handbook of the Girl Scouts. 572 pages. Profuse illustrations. Bibliography. Khaki cloth cover, flexible, $.75; Officers' Edition, board, $1.00.

Campward Ho! Manual for Girl Scout Camps. 125 pages. Illustrations. Bibliography, cuts and diagrams. Paper Edition, $.75; Cloth, $1.00.

The Blue Book of Rules for Girl Scout Captains. 32 pages. All official regulations, constitution, etc., $.25.

A Training Course for Girl Scout Captains. Outline approved by National Headquarters. Lectures and practical lessons, $.15.

The Girl Scout's Health Record. A convenient form for recording the points needed to cover for badge of "Health Winner", $.10.

Girl Scouts: Their History and Practice. Pamphlet, 2 cents.

Girl Scouts: Their Works, Ways and Plays. Pamphlet, 2 cents.

Your Girl and Mine, by Josephine Daskam Bacon. 2 cents.

Why I Believe in Scouting for Girls, by Mary Roberts Rinehart. 2 cents.

The Girl Scouts. A Training School for Womanhood, by Kate Douglas Wiggin. 2 cents.

The Constitution and By-Laws of the Girl Scouts, Incorporated. 5 cents.

THE AMERICAN GIRL formerly the Rally). A Scouting Magazine for girls. Monthly. 10 cents the copy, one dollar the year.

IN PREPARATION

Girl Scout Officers' Manual. For Captains, Lieutenants, Commissioners and Councillors.

Brief Training Course for Girl Scout Captains. 10 lessons.

Girl Scout Officers' Field Book. A notebook with all necessary material for troop work, including much manual information in loose leaf form.

Senior Scout Program.

Brownie or Junior Program.

Girl Scout Awards. Requirements for Proficiency and Class Badges, and all special medals.

Outlines of Lectures on Sex Hygiene, in collaboration with the United States Bureau of the Public Health Service.

Studies in Applied Psychology and Anthropology, in collaboration with the American Museum of Natural History.

A Girl Scout Book Shelf, in collaboration with the New York Public Library.

"It is thanks to Mrs. Juliette Low, of Savannah, that the [Girl Guides] movement was successfully started in America, and though the name Girl Scouts has there been used, it is all part of the same sisterhood, working to the same ends and living up to the same laws and Promise."
— Lord Baden-Powell, founder of the Scouting movement